LIBRARY OF HEBREW BIBLE/
OLD TESTAMENT STUDIES

609

Formerly Journal for the Study of the Old Testament Supplement Series

Editors
Claudia V. Camp, Texas Christian University
Andrew Mein, Westcott House, Cambridge

Founding Editors
David J. A. Clines, Philip R. Davies and David M. Gunn

Editorial Board
Alan Cooper, John Goldingay, Robert P. Gordon,
Norman K. Gottwald, James E. Harding, John Jarick, Carol Meyers,
Carolyn J. Sharp, Daniel L. Smith-Christopher, Francesca Stavrakopoulou,
James W. Watts

GOING UP AND GOING DOWN

A Key to Interpreting Jacob's Dream (Genesis 28:10–22)

Yitzhak (Itzik) Peleg

Translated by Betty Rozen

LONDON • NEW YORK • OXFORD • NEW DELHI • SYDNEY

T&T CLARK
Bloomsbury Publishing Plc
50 Bedford Square, London, WC1B 3DP, UK
1385 Broadway, New York, NY 10018, USA

BLOOMSBURY, T&T CLARK and the T&T Clark logo are
trademarks of Bloomsbury Publishing Plc

First published in Great Britain 2015
Paperback edition first published 2018

Copyright © Yitzhak Peleg, 2015

Yitzhak Peleg has asserted his right under the Copyright,
Designs and Patents Act, 1988, to be identified as Author of this work.

All rights reserved. No part of this publication may be reproduced or
transmitted in any form or by any means, electronic or mechanical,
including photocopying, recording, or any information storage or
retrieval system, without prior permission in writing from the publishers.

Bloomsbury Publishing Plc does not have any control over, or responsibility for,
any third-party websites referred to or in this book. All internet addresses given
in this book were correct at the time of going to press. The author and publisher
regret any inconvenience caused if addresses have changed or sites have
ceased to exist, but can accept no responsibility for any such changes.

A catalogue record for this book is available from the British Library.

ISBN: HB: 978-0-56766-025-1
PB: 978-0-56767-244-5
ePDF: 978-0-56766-026-8

Peleg, Itzik.
Going up and going down : a key to interpreting Jacob's dream (Gen. 28:10-22) / by
Yitzhak (Itzik) Peleg ; translated by Betty Rozen.
pages cm. – (Library of New Testament studies; 609)
ISBN 978-0-567-66025-1 – ISBN 978-0-567-66026-8 (epdf) 1. Bible. Genesis, XXVIII,
10-12–Criticism, interpretation, etc. 2. Jacob's ladder (Biblical dream) I. Title.
BS1235.52.P45 2015
222'.1106–dc23
2014044602

Typeset by Forthcoming Publications Ltd

To find out more about our authors and books visit
www.bloomsbury.com and sign up for our newsletters.

Contents

Preface	xiii
Acknowledgments	xv
Abbreviations	xvii

Chapter 1
PREFACE TO THE STORY OF JACOB'S DREAM:
JACOB'S DREAM AS A *MISE EN ABYME* 1
  1. Dream Descriptions in the Bible and in the Ancient Near East 4
    1.1. Introduction: The Dream as Phenomenon or as Story 4
    1.2. Typological Classification: Dream Theophany
        and Symbolic Dreams 7
        1.2.1. Two methodological cautions 8
        1.2.2. Characteristics of the symbolic dream 11
        1.2.3. Characteristics of the dream theophany 12
        1.2.4. Is Jacob's Dream a theophany
             or a symbolic dream—"both…and,"
             not "either…or"? 14
    1.3. Dream Incubation 14
        1.3.1. Defining the term 14
        1.3.2. Does incubation occur in the Hebrew Bible? 15
    1.4. "The Biblical Perception" of the Dream: A Problem 16
        1.4.1. Distribution of the biblical dream—
             problems of identification 16
        1.4.2. The "problem" of "biblical perception":
             contrary statements about dreams 17
        1.4.3. Explaining such contradictions—if possible 17
        1.4.4. Can such contradictory expressions
             be explained—and if so, how? 20
        1.4.5. The importance of dreams in the Jacob
             story cycle 22

2. Research Methods and Methodology 23
   2.1. The Aims Method or the Source Criticism Method 23
   2.2. Links Between Form and Content, Structure
        and Significance 25
   2.3. Inner-Biblical Interpretation—the Polemic Approach 26
   2.4. The Hypothetical "Editor" in the Bible—the Narrator 27
   2.5. The Reading with Multiple Meanings,
        or the Two Meanings, in the Biblical Story 28
        2.5.1. Two readings—a definition 28
        2.5.2. Two readings in art 28
        2.5.3. How do the two readings relate to one another? 30
        2.5.4. Interrelationships between the two readings:
               Are they necessarily the result of biblical editing? 31
        2.5.5. Two readings are no accident
               and no misunderstanding 34
        2.5.6. Two readings of the David and Bathsheba
               story (2 Samuel 11): An ironic look at the king 36
        2.5.7. Examples of two readings in the biblical story 40
   2.6. Broadening Circles of Commentary 41
   2.7. The Research Process 42
3. A Survey of the Research on Jacob' Dream:
   The Bible Story in General and the Story of Jacob's Dream
   in Particular 43

Appendix:
The Jacob's Dream Story (Genesis 28:10–22)
According to Its "Sources" 48

Chapter 2
THE STORY OF JACOB'S DREAM AT BETHEL: GENESIS 28:10–22 49
1. Structure and Significance of the Jacob's Dream Story 49
   1.1. Introduction: Two Readings of the Story
        of Jacob's Dream at Bethel 49
   1.2. The Text of the Dream 50
   1.3. Stating the Problems 51
   1.4. Rejecting the Division of the Story According
        to Classic Source Theory 52
   1.5. Structure and Boundaries of the Work 54
        1.5.1. Two readings of *maqom* ("place") as a keyword
               in the story 55
        1.5.2. Comparing v. 11 and vv. 18–19a 56

		Contents		vii

1.6. Setting the Boundaries of the Dream (vv. 12–15)   59
     1.6.1. The dream boundaries:
between "and he dreamed" (v. 12)
and "and Jacob awaked" (v. 16)   60
     1.6.2. "Place" (*maqom*) as a keyword helping
to mark the dream boundaries   60
1.7. Conclusion   61

2. The Dream Vision as *Mise en Abyme*
of the Jacob's Dream Story   62
   2.1. How Does the Vision Connect to the Verbal Message?   64
     2.1.1. "And behold" (*vahinneh*) as a literary signal
in the story of Jacob's Dream   66
     2.1.2. Are there two possible readings for
"And the Lord stood above it" (v. 13)?   67
     2.1.3. A close reading of the verbal message
(vv. 13–14): God's promise   70
   2.2. The Dream Vision (vv. 12–13a) and Jacob's Verbal
Response (vv. 16–17)   77
     2.2.1. The vision and its (concrete) meaning
within a concentric framework   77
     2.2.2. "Behold" and "this" as literary markers
identifying the dream and its meaning   81
     2.2.3. A proposed second reading:
the concentric structure   81
     2.2.4. Two readings: the concentric and chiastic
vantage points   82
     2.2.5. "Surely the Lord is in this place" (v. 16)   83

3. The Vision in the Dream (Realistic and Symbolic Readings)   88
   3.1. The First Element: The Ladder (*sullam*):
Its Nature and Purpose   88
     3.1.1. The etymology of *sullam*   89
     3.1.2. The biblical *sullam* as an analogy
to the Babylonian ziggurat   90
     3.1.3. Literal and symbolic readings of *sullam*   95
     3.1.4. Summary: The collected data supporting
the second, symbolic reading   97
     3.1.5. Conclusion   99
   3.2. The Second Element in the Dream Vision:
"The Angels of God"—What Are They,
and What Is Their Role?   101
     3.2.1. Why, according to the Sages,
do the angels first ascend then descend?   105

	3.2.2.	What is the symbolic meaning of the dream?	107
	3.2.3.	Why do God's angels first ascend and then descend?	109
3.3.		The Third Component in the Dream Vision: The Verbs *'alah* (Ascend) and *yarad* (Descend) as a Key to Interpretation	111
	3.3.1.	Understanding *'alah* and *yarad* (in Genesis 28:12) metaphorically	111
	3.3.2.	The verbs *'alah* and *yarad* in the story of Judah and Tamar (Genesis 38)	112
	3.3.3.	The verbs *'alah* and *yarad* in the Golden Calf story (Exodus 32)	114
	3.3.4.	The verbs *'alah* and *yarad* in the Samson Story (Judges 13–15)	115
	3.3.5.	The verbs *'alah* and *yarad* in the story of Elijah's ascent to heaven (2 Kings 2:1–2)	115
	3.3.6.	The verbs *'alah* and *yarad* in the book of Jonah: "had gone down… and fell asleep (*vayeradem*)" (Jonah 1:5)	116
	3.3.7.	How the metaphorical meaning of *'alah* and *yarad* originated	117
3.4.		Is Jacob's Dream a *Dream Theophany* or a *Symbolic Dream*?	118
	3.4.1.	Jacob's dream as a *dream theophany*	119
	3.4.2.	Jacob's Dream as a *symbolic dream*	120
	3.4.3.	A note on methodology in favor of two readings for the dream and its meaning	123
	3.4.4.	Gudea's dream as a theophany dream and symbolic dream	124
	3.4.5.	Conclusion: "It takes three trees to make a row"	125
3.5.		Is There Incubation in Jacob's Dream	127
	3.5.1.	Are the four conditions for incubation present in Jacob's Dream?	128
	3.5.2.	Two readings of *yfga' bamaqom* in v. 11	129
	3.5.3.	Is this *unintended incubation*?	133
4. Two Readings of Jacob's Dream—A Tentative Conclusion			134
4.1. Verse 10			136
4.2. Verse 11			137
4.3. Verses 12–13a			138
4.4. Verses 13b–15			139
4.5. Verses 16–17			139
4.6. Verses 18–19: One Reading or Two?			140
4.7. Conclusion			141

5. The Vow as a Contribution to Understanding and
   Interpreting Jacob's Dream 141
   5.1. Introduction 142
   5.2. "So that I come again to my father's house in peace"
        (v. 21a) 145
        5.2.1. The structure of the vow:
               its condition (protasis)
               and its promise (apodosis) 146
        5.2.2. Where does the promise (apodosis) begin? 148
   5.3. The Link of the Vow to God's Promise (v. 15) 151
        5.3.1. A table of comparison 151
        5.3.2. Two readings of the unique phrase
               "into this land" ("to this soil"—Fox; v. 15)"
               (*adama*) 153
        5.3.3. Two readings of "in peace" (*beshalom*) (v. 21a) ... 155
   5.4. Return to the Homeland: A Comparison
        with Absalom's Vow (2 Samuel 15:7–8) 155
        5.4.1. One of three formulations of the vow's content ... 155
        5.4.2. Returning from exile—Absalom's vow 156
   5.5. Returning in Peace: A Comparison
        with Jephthah's Vow (Judges 11:31) 157
   5.6. Conclusion: Two Readings of the Vow 159

Chapter 3
THE JACOB'S DREAM STORY AS *MISE EN ABYME* OF THE JACOB STORY CYCLE 161

1. Subject and Boundaries 161
2. Defining "Jacob Story Cycle" Boundaries and Place
   in the Discussion 162
3. *Mise en Abyme* in the Bible and in Ancient Near Eastern
   Literature 166
   3.1. What Is the *Mise en Abyme*'s Place
        in "the Story Within a Story"? 166
   3.2. The *Mise en Abyme* Role in the Story 168
   3.3. Jacob's Dream as Anticipation and Retrospection 170
   3.4. The Dream of Utanapishtim as *Mise en Abyme*
        of the Gilgamesh Epic 172
   3.5. Utanpishtim's and Jacob's Dreams:
        Their Literary Function as *Mise en Abyme* 172
   3.6. Biblical Examples of the *Mise en Abyme* 174

4. The Dream Vision as *Mise en Abyme* of Entering
and Leaving the Land in the Jacob Story Cycle ... 175
   4.1. The Two-directional Path of Entering
and Leaving the Land ... 175
   4.2. The Journey to Haran: Three Readings of Reasons
for Jacob's First Departure ... 177
      4.2.1. Jacob is fleeing from his brother (27:43) ... 177
      4.2.2. Jacob goes to take a wife (28:1) ... 177
      4.2.3. The third reading: Jacob goes to Haran
with God's approval (28:15) ... 178
   4.3. Jacob's Return Journey from Haran: Three Readings ... 179
      4.3.1. The first reading: Jacob returns
on his own initiative (ch. 30) ... 180
      4.3.2. The second reading: Jacob returns
on God's initiative (ch. 31) ... 181
      4.3.3. Third reading: Jacob flees from Laban
to his father's house (31:17–21) ... 182
   4.4. Returning to Canaan: "And Jacob went on his way" ... 183
      4.4.1. The angels of God in Jacob's Dream (28:12)
and angels of God at Mahanaim (32:2) ... 184
      4.4.2. Jacob's return to the homeland:
"Jacob arrived safely (*shalem*)
in the city of Shechem, which is
in the land of Canaan" (33:18) ... 192
      4.4.3. Jacob's return to Bethel in 35:1–8
(attributed to the E source) ... 194
   4.5. Jacob's Second Departure from the Homeland:
The Descent into Egypt Story (46:2–5)
and Its Link to 28:12 ... 196
5. Jacob's Dream as *Mise en Abyme*
for the Patriarchal Narrative ... 202
   5.1. Abraham the Patriarch, the First Immigrant
(*'oleh*): Two Readings or Two Sources? ... 203
      5.1.1. Four readings as to why Terah left Ur
of the Chaldees ... 204
      5.1.2. Why Terah only reached Haran
and did not continue to Canaan: two readings ... 210
      5.1.3. Comparing Terah's departure with Abraham's ... 213
      5.1.4. A fourth, retrospective, reading:
God is the One who brought Abraham
out of Ur of the Chaldees by means of Terah ... 216

	5.2.	"Abram Went Down to Egypt" (12:10)	222
		5.2.1. Abraham the first emigrant (*yored*): two readings of Genesis 12:10	222
		5.2.2. Two readings of the story of Sarah in Pharaoh's house	233
	5.3.	"From Egypt Abram Went Up" (Genesis 13:1)	242
		5.3.1. Why did Abraham return to the Promised Land?	242
		5.3.2. Going up (*'alah*) to the land, not only from Egypt	243
6.	The Departures and Returns of the Patriarch According to the W-Shaped Model		245
7.	Conclusion: The Vision in Jacob's Dream as *Mise en Abyme* of the M-Shaped Model		247

Chapter 4
CONCLUSION AND DEPARTURE POINT:
"THE GATE OF HEAVEN" JOURNEYS FROM BABYLON
TO BETHEL AND TO JERUSALEM CYCLE   248

1.	Two Readings of Jacob's Dream Summed Up: Concentrated Data on "Going Up and Going Down—A Key to Interpreting Jacob's Dream" (Genesis 28:10–22)		248
2.	The *Mise en Abyme* as a Miniature Reflection		249
3.	Jacob's Dream Is a Theophany and a Symbolic Dream		249
4.	Support for the Symbolic View of Jacob's Dream		250
	4.1.	What the Ladder (*sullam*) Symbolizes	250
		4.1.1. The etymology of *sullam*: its link to the Babylonian ziggurat	251
		4.1.2. *Sullam* in summary	252
	4.2.	The Role of the Angels of God (*mal'akkei 'elohim*) in Jacob's Dream	252
	4.3.	The Metaphorical Significance of *'alah* and *yarad* ("Ascend" and "Descend")	253
	4.4.	On the Combination: "Angels of God" in Genesis 28:12 and 32:2	253
	4.5.	The Verbal Message Supports the Symbolic Vision	254
5.	The Jacob's Dream Story as *Mise en Abyme* of Patriarchal Journeys		255
	5.1.	The M-Shaped Model of the Patriarchal Journeys	256

6. The Tower of Babel (Genesis 11:1–9) and Jacob's *Sullam* 256
   6.1. Comparing the Two 256
      6.1.1. Structure and meaning of the Tower of Babel story 256
      6.1.2. The Tower of Babel story and the story of building the E-sag-ila 258
      6.1.3. Similarities between the Tower of Babel and *sullam* of Jacob stories 259
      6.1.4. Linking the Tower and the *sullam* with the Babylonian ziggurat 260
      6.1.5. Points of difference between the Tower of Babel and Jacob's *sullam* 261
   6.2. The Differences Between the Two Stories Help to Interpret Jacob's Dream 262
   6.3. Establishing the Gate of Heaven at Bethel, Not Babylon 263
7. In Conclusion: The Gate of Heaven in Jerusalem— A Departure Point for Further Research 264

Bibliography 269
Index of References 283
Index of Authors 292

Preface

Close study of Jacob's dream enables, from a literary perspective, two simultaneous readings and therefore two interpretations. The first reading/interpretation is that Jacob's dream is a "dream theophany," one which describes and means to explain how Bethel became a sacred place—a story whose core is the *maqom* ("place"). The second reading/interpretation is that Jacob's dream is a "symbolic dream," which tells about Jacob leaving Canaan (his home land) in order to return in the future; a story whose core is the *derek* ("way").

The image of angels going up and down between earth and heaven has been understood variously and has only occasionally been taken as a symbol of something. The description of the *sullam*, and especially that of the movement of the angels, is not embellishment, supplementation or scenic background, of God's message, but "the vision" symbolizes the way, the path, taken by the patriarchs to and from the Promised Land. That is to say, the *sullam* symbolizes "the way" to and from the Promised Land, and the symbolic message of the "Angels of God" in the dream is reflected in their actual movements.

The vision in the dream (vv. 12–13a), functions as a *mise en abyme*. One can view the story of Jacob's dream, and in particular the vision in the dream, as a miniature tale embedded in the Patriarchal Narratives according to the literary model of "a tale within a tale." In a compact and symbolic manner, the vision in the dream reflects the attitude towards the patriarch's entering and leaving the Promised Land in the framework of the wider narrative. Furthermore the "narrative context" and the "visual description" in the dream in which "Angels of God were going up and down it" appears when Jacob is on his way to Harran, that is to say, when he is about to leave Israel. At that point God addresses Jacob: "Remember, I am with you: I will protect you wherever you go *and will bring you back to this land*" (28.15). We have an analogy between going up the ladder and between return (*aliya*) from Exile to the Promised Land. Both instances of "going" (*aliya*) earn a positive evaluation, since the pilgrim goes towards the Deity, *literally as well as metaphorically.*

In conclusion, in light of the interpretation of the entire story (Gen 28:10–22), one can sum up by saying, that only a reading that approaches both readings/hypotheses simultaneously and that takes their interplay into account, qualifies as a valid reading.

This book is based on my thesis that was written under the supervision of Professor Edward L. Greenstein. The title of my thesis reflects its message: "Going Up and Going Down: A Key to Interpreting Jacob's Dream." The ladder, *sullam*, in Jacob's dream is both horizontal and vertical: vertically, between sky and earth; and horizontally, between the Promised Land and the Diaspora. The vertical movement of God's angels on the ladder symbolizes the travels of the Patriarchs and their descendants to and from "the land."

Acknowledgments

Following the completion of my doctorate, throughout my work, and in every intersection during my academic life, Professor Ed Greenstein has accompanied me with patient listening and with warm wisdom and advice. I wish to thank Professor Greenstein for being my mentor and a model. I thank Betty Rozen for her translation, Michal Cristal for providing the registration for the publisher, Professor Athalya Brenner and Professor Yairah Amit for the support and wise advice; the editor Professor Claudia V. Camp and Dr. Dominic Mattos the publisher for their assistance in editing the final book.

My sincere thanks to Beit Berl College and Gordon College for their assistance and donation towards the publication of this book.

Portions of the book were completed during a short sabbatical in 2012 at the University of Sidney in Australia. I wish to thank Professor Ian Young and Dr. Ari Lobal for their warm hospitality.

Many, many thanks to my Kibbutz, Ein Hashofet, for the support and understanding during this long journey.

To my wife, Naomi, who has accompanied me from my first steps, commented wisely and encouraged me to believe in myself. To my dear daughters, Sharon, Orit and Hadar, my love and belief:

> That a future generation might know—
> children yet to be born—
> that in turn tell their children. (Ps. 78:6)

* * *

Section 5 of Chapter 4 was published previously as Chapter 19 of Bethsaida in *Archaeology, History and Ancient Culture: A Festschrift in Honor of John T. Green* (Cambridge Scholars Press, 2014). It is reproduced here, in slightly modified form, with the copyright holder's kind permission.

The author and publishers are grateful for permission to reproduce the following copyright material:

Material on p.141 of this book was originally published as "Was the Ancestress of Israel in Danger? Did Pharaoh Touch Sarai?" Beit Mikra Quarterly, 2003, pp. 54–64. Reproduction here is with kind permission of Beit Mikra Quarterly.

A version of the same material was also published as "Was the Ancestress of Israel in Danger? Did Pharaoh touch Sarai?" in ZAW (2006). pp. 197–208. Reproduction here is with kind permission of the ZAW.

Some material in this book also appeared first in Hebrew as 'Lekh lekha: mas´e ha-avot be-sipure ha-Miḳra', [Go you forth : The Journeys of the Patriarchs in the Biblical Narrative], Resling, 2013, Tel Aviv © Resling Publication, Tel-Aviv, Israel.

ABBREVIATIONS

AB	Anchor Bible
ANET	*Ancient Near Eastern Texts Relating to the Old Testament*. Edited by J. B. Pritchard. 3d ed. Princeton, 1969
AnOr	Analecta Orientalia
AOAT	Alter Orient und Altes Testament
BDB	Brown, F., S. R. Driver, and C. A. Briggs. *A Hebrew and English Lexicon of the Old Testament*. Oxford, 1907
BEL	The Biblical Encyclopaedia Library
BHH	*Biblisch-historisches Handwörterbuch: Landeskunde, Geschichte, Religion, Kultur*. Edited by B. Reicke and L. Rost. 4 vols. Göttingen, 1962–66
BHK	*Biblia Hebraica*. Edited by R. Kittel. Stuttgart, 1937
BJS	Brown Judaic Studies
BLS	Bible and Literature series
BZ	*Biblische Zeitschrift*
BZAW	Beihefte zur Zeitschrift für die alttestamentliche Wissenschaft
CAD	*The Assyrian Dictionary of the Oriental Institute of the University of Chicago*. Chicago, 1956–
CBQ	*Catholic Biblical Quarterly*
DFWH	*Dictionary of Foreign Words in Hebrew*. Edited by D. Pines. Tel Aviv, 1959
EB	*Encyclopaedia Biblica*. Edited by M. D. Cassuto et al. 8 vols. Jerusalem, 1950–82
EH	*Encyclopaedia Hebraica*. Edited by J. Klausner et el. 32 vols. Jerusalem, 1948–80
ER	*Encyclopedia of Religion*. Edited by M. Eliade. 16 vols. New York, 1987
ExpTim	*Expository Times*
FOTL	The Forms of the Old Testament Literature
Fox	E. Fox, *The Five Books of Moses: A New Translation with Introductions, Commentary, and Notes*. New York, 1995
HAR	*Hebrew Annual Review*
HBI	The Heritage of Biblical Israel
HSM	Harvard Semitic Monographs
HUCA	*Hebrew Union College Annual*
HUCM	Monographs of the Hebrew Union College
ICC	International Critical Commentary
IDB	*The Interpreter's Dictionary of the Bible*. Edited by G. A. Buttrick. 4 vols. Nashville, 1962
JANES	*Journal of the Ancient Near Eastern Society*
JAOS	*Journal of the American Oriental Society*

JBL	*Journal of Biblical Literature*
JJS	*Journal of Jewish Studies*
JQR	*Jewish Quarterly Review*
JSOTSup	Journal for the study of the Old Testament supplement series
KAT	Kommentar zum Alten Testament
KBL	Koehler, L., and W. Baumgartner, *Lexicon in Veteris Testamenti libros*. 2d ed. Leiden, 1958
OEANE	The Oxford Encyclopedia of Archaeology in the Near East. Edited by E. M. Meyers. New York, 1997
OTL	Old Testament Library
OtSt	*Oudtestamentische Studiën*
RPJSI	Research Projects of the Jewish Studies Institute
RSP	*Ras Shamra Parallels*
SBE	Studies in Bible and Exegesis
SBLAIL	Society of Biblical Literature Ancient Israel and Its Literature
SBLDS	Society of Biblical Literature Dissertation Series
SBT	Studies in Biblical Theology
SJOT	*Scandinavian Journal of the Old Testament*
SSN	Studia semitica neerlandica
TAPS	Transactions of the American Philosophical Society
TBC	Torch Bible Commentaries
TDOT	*Theological Dictionary of the Old Testament*. Edited by G. J. Botterweck and H. Ringgren. Translated by J. T. Willis, G. W. Bromiley, and D. E. Green. 8 vols. Grand Rapids, 1974–
THL	Theory and History of Literature
UF	*Ugarit-Forschungen*
VTC	*Veteris Testamenti Concordantiae*. S. Mandelkern. 6th ed. Jerusalem, 1965
VTSup	Supplements to Vetus Testamentum
WBC	World Biblical Commentary
WMANT	Wissenschaftliche Monographien zum Alten und Neuen Testament
ZAW	*Zeitschrift für die alttestamentliche Wissenschaft*

Chapter 1

PREFACE TO THE STORY OF JACOB'S DREAM:
JACOB'S DREAM AS A *MISE EN ABYME*

This book proposes that the story of Jacob's Dream at Bethel (Gen 28:10–22), and in particular the vision scene (vv. 12–13a), is to be understood as the symbolic and structural centerpiece of the Jacob story cycle, and that, furthermore, it reflects, in condensed form, the story of the Patriarchs, the central theme of which is ascent to and descent from the Promised Land.

In what follows, I seek to show that the (biblical and modern) Hebrew verb designating emigration from the Land of Israel, *yarad* ("to descend"), seemingly carries a negative connotation. Furthermore, and by contrast, the verb *'alah* ("to ascend") will be shown to designate immigration into the Land of Israel, a movement that clearly possesses positive connotations.

In order to achieve my objectives, I shall argue that the reader of Jacob's Dream should approach the story as a cohesive whole, as a unified narrative set within the stories of the Patriarchs in Genesis. Central to this is a reading of Genesis *in its final form*.

My reading of the story of Jacob's Dream is founded on the observation that Jacob is about to leave the Land of Israel, and that God, identifying Himself as the God of Abraham and Isaac (28:13), promised to return him there (28:15). The vision of the ascending and descending angels on the ladder leads me, *as a reader of the final form of Genesis*, to consider how that sight relates to the stories of the Patriarchs. Crucially, reading the story of Jacob's Dream within the wider context of Genesis leads to the observation that the Patriarchs ascend (*'alah*) to and descend (*yarad*) from the Land. This observation compels me to suggest that the story of Jacob's Dream be regarded as reflecting the journey of the Patriarchs.

Furthermore, it is my contention that the story of Jacob's Dream should be seen as *a story within a story*. Accepting André Gide's meaning of the term, the story of Jacob's Dream can be understood as a *mise en abyme* of the Patriarchal narratives. Indeed, it is to be most deeply and most profitably understood as such.

The concept of *mise en abyme*, which was first used in critical theory in the 1940s, gradually took a foothold in the guild of Biblical Studies. Progress was not swift, however. Indeed, as recently as 2004, J. A. Berman wrote that "no full length treatment of the *mise en abyme* has been conducted within biblical studies."[1] D. A. Bosworth's 2008 study, *The Story Within a Story in Biblical Hebrew Narrative*, sought to "fill this gap," arguing that "biblical Hebrew narrative includes three instances of *mise en abyme*, specifically Genesis 38, 1 Samuel 25, and 1 Kings 13." Bosworth was not, however, "convinced that there are any additional examples."[2]

The aim of the present work is to challenge Bosworth's assertion, and to offer the story of Jacob's Dream as a further instance of *mise en abyme*, specifically of the stories of the Patriarchs as they come into (*'olim*) or depart from (*yordim*) the Promised Land. Moreover, it will be argued that understanding the story of Jacob's Dream as a *mise en abyme* will help to decode Jacob's vision (Gen 28:12–13a). While my interpretation is not obligatory, I hope it will be seen as an acceptable one.

Mise en abyme, a term taken from heraldry and later the visual arts, has been adopted into literary theory, including research on biblical literature. A *mise en abyme* is "a figure, trope, or structure that somehow reflects in compact form, in miniature, the larger structure in which it appears."[3] Originally used in relation to the coats of arms of the nobility, which often contained a smaller shield in the center of a larger one—a symbolic representation of the nobleman's dynasty[4]—Claude Matisse

---

1. J. A. Berman, *Narrative Analogy in the Hebrew Bible: Battle Stories and Their Equivalent Non-battle Narratives* (VTSup 103; Leiden: Brill, 2004), 25.

2. D. A. Bosworth, *The Story Within a Story in Biblical Hebrew Narrative* (CBQ Monograph Series 45; Washington, D.C.: Catholic Biblical Association of America, 2008), 1.

3. E. L. Greenstein, "The Retelling of the Flood Story in the Gilgamesh Epic," in *Hesed Ve-Emet: Studies in Honor of Ernest S. Fredrichs* (ed. J. Magnes and S. Gitin; Atlanta, Ga.: Scholars Press, 1998), 197–204; L. Dallenbach, *The Text in the Mirror* (trans. J. Whiteley and E. Hughes; Chicago: University of Chicago Press, 1989), 1.

4. M. Bal, *Lethal Love: Feminist Literary Reading of Biblical Love Stories* (Bloomington: Indiana University Press, 1987), 146. Bal emphasizes that the transfer of *mise en abyme* from the graphic to the literary medium marred it, so she prefers

used the technique extensively in his paintings. According to Rimmon-Kenan, *mise en abyme* is "a type of analogy in some degree parallel to Matisse's painting of a room reflected on one wall as a miniature of itself."[5]

As a literary device, *mise en abyme* appears through the generations and across cultures. Hence a separate chapter in the present work will be devoted to its appearance in the Gilgamesh Epic in Ancient Near Eastern (ANE) literature and in the Bible. (Chapter 4 will discuss the dream of Utanapishtim as *mise en abyme* of the Gilgamesh Epic.)

The classic *A Thousand and One Nights*, in which Scheherazade tells amazing stories night after night to save herself from her husband's death threat, exemplifies the framework story.[6] More significantly, one particular story, "The Merchant and the Demon,"[7] is an unambiguous *mise en abyme*. The tale tells of three old men satisfying the demon by telling him stories so he will not kill the merchant—an analogy to the framework story, whose theme is identical: stories can save from death.

My aim here is once again to apply the concept of *mise en abyme* to the biblical literature, and to show its relevance for interpreting the Bible. It will be demonstrated that the story of Jacob's Dream in Gen 28:10–22, particularly the vision in vv. 12–13a, functions as a *mise en abyme* that unlocks the wider Patriarchal narratives. It shows the angels of God ascending and descending in a symbolic vision, which offers a compact representation of the Patriarchs entering and leaving the Promised Land. Additionally, Jacob dreams his dream just as he is about to leave the Land. The dream contains a promise that God will bring him back to the Land (Gen 28:15). The present chapter will attempt to decipher the significance of the vision in Jacob's Dream at Bethel in the light of the above insights. I begin with a question: Is the dream a human phenomenon or a story?

---

the term "mirror text"; Dallenbach, *Mirror* (in French "*le récit speculaire*"); S. Rimmon-Kenan, *The Poetics of Contemporary Fiction* (Tel Aviv: Sifriyat Poalim, 1984), 91. See also G. Rouiller, "Parabole et Mise En Abyme," in *Mélanges Dominique Barthelémy* (ed. P. Casetti, O. Keel and A. Schenker; Göttingen: Vandenhoeck & Ruprecht, 1981), 321. Rouiller too describes the source of *mise en abyme* as the coats of arms of the nobility, with its pictorial representation of the dynastic symbol.

5. Rimmon-Kenan, *Poetics*, 91, prefers "miniature reflection."
6. Bal, *Lethal Love*, 143.
7. N. Diengott, *The Poetics of Fiction* (Tel Aviv: Open University, 1986), 119.

1. *Dream Descriptions in the Bible and in the Ancient Near East*[8]

1.1. *Introduction: The Dream as Phenomenon or as Story*

The human dream is a visual and/or verbal experience a person has while asleep. The phenomenon has been studied extensively in various fields, including anthropology,[9] sociology,[10] and modern psychoanalysis.[11] Dreams have also featured in the study of religions, both modern and ancient.[12] Yet it concerned me deeply that, after so many interpretations of Jacob's Dream, I was seeking to attempt to unravel Jacob's vision. Was there, I wondered, anything to be gained from proposing another and different interpretation of his vision? Even an awareness that dreaming is a natural human activity (we all dream) did not help, since that relates not to *dream interpretation*, but to dreaming itself.

As if that were not enough, the dream literature from Mesopotamia[13] and Egypt shows that interpretation of dreams[14] lay exclusively in the hands of experts. In the Bible too there is difficulty in expounding dreams. Pharaoh, for instance, dreamed and then consulted "all the magicians of Egypt and all its wise men, but none could interpret them" (Gen 41:8). My uncertainty grew when I considered Joseph's answer to Pharaoh's cup bearer and his baker when asked to explain their dreams: "Surely God can interpret!" (Gen 40:8).

In my mind, then, I imagined Jacob's Dream marshalling additional dreams to accuse me: "Who made you chief and ruler over us [Exod 2:14],

---

8. A. L. Oppenheim, *The Interpretation of Dreams in the Ancient Near East: With a Translation of an Assyrian Dream-Book* (TAPS; Philadelphia: American Philosophical Society, 1956), 186–217; S. A. L. Butler, *Mesopotamian Conceptions of Dreams and Dream Rituals* (Münster: Ugarit-Verlag, 1998).

9. J. G. Frazer, *Folklore in the Old Testament: Studies in Comparative Religion, Legend and Law* (abr. ed.; London: Macmillan, 1923).

10. R. K. Gnuse, *The Dream Theophany of Samuel: Its Structure in Relation to Ancient Near Eastern Dreams and Its Theological Significance* (Lanham, Md.: University Press of America, 1984), 4.

11. S. Freud, *The Interpretation of Dreams* (trans. M. Brachiahu; Tel Aviv: Yavneh, 1959); K. G. Jung, *On Dreams* (trans. H. Shoham and I. Toren; Jerusalem: Dvir, 1982); Y. Levin, *Psychology of the Dream* (Tel Aviv: Dekel, 1980).

12. M. Eliade, *Myths, Dreams and Mysteries: The Encounter Between Contemporary Faiths and Archaic Realities* (trans. P. Mairet; New York: Harper & Row, 1960), 13–20. Oppenheim, *Interpretation*, 185, sounds a cautionary note: "Dreams recorded in ancient Near Eastern Literatures cannot be expected to reflect the psychological status of the dreamer."

13. Ibid.

14. Gnuse, *Samuel*, 15.

so that you dare interpret the dream of the ladder?" With this in mind, I proceed with extreme caution. My incomplete studies in modern psychology and its approach to the meaning of dreams do not qualify me in that field. Moreover, on the literary level, the biblical text as it stands does not explicitly state the meaning of Jacob's vision.

It was with a sense of relief however, that I read M. Sternberg's discussion of dreams in the Joseph story.[15] His remarks, presented later, appear to endorse the benefits of engaging with Jacob's vision, offering encouragement to bring the issue into the open; they also respond to judgments passed on my proposal. Sternberg's article aptly expresses the sense of obligation I feel, as a reader who has studied this dream in depth, to present my theory.

First of all, Sternberg notes the difference between perception of dreams in the ANE as an "external sign" (a clear sign from a god),[16] rather than as internal signals (the modern psychological explanation). As Zakovitch maintains, "The biblical dream is one of the channels of communication…one means of transmitting a message from heaven to earth."[17] As Joseph himself explained, "Pharaoh's dreams are one and the same: God has told Pharaoh what He intends to do" (Gen 41:25).

Having accepted this claim, one can deal with the dream as a literary text, a story to be analyzed using literary, not psychological, methods. Indeed, there is significant scholarly debate as to whether the fields in which the dream is studied today, especially modern psychological

---

15. M. Sternberg, "The Repetition Structure in the Bible Story: Superfluous Information Strategies," *Hasifrut* 25 (1977): 125.

16. On the difference between the two approaches, see Levin, *Psychology*, 26; Gnuse, *Samuel*, 26. See also F. Polak, *Biblical Narrative: Aspects of Art and Design* (BEL 11; Jerusalem: Mosad Bialik, 1994), 258: "The dream as a message from God"; Oppenheim, *Interpretation*, 205–6; R. Fidler, "The Dream Theophany in the Bible, Its Place in the History of Biblical Literature and Israelite Religion" (Ph.D. diss., The Hebrew University, 1996), since published as *Do Dreams Speak Falsely? Dream Theophanies in the Bible: Their Place in Ancient Israelite Faith and Traditions* (Jerusalem: Magnes, 2005), 2. Butler, *Conceptions*, 2, argues: "Ancient and primitive people believed that dreams were divine communications, while the psychoanalysts claim that our subconscious is trying to express itself while the conscious censor is dormant. Even if one derides the ideas that dreams are applicable to reality, these subjective experiences affect one's mood, and nightmares are impossible to ignore."

17. Y. Zakovitch, "Of the Food Came forth the Eater: On the Dream and Its Interpretation," in *Varied Opinions and Views on Dream in Israelite Culture* (ed. D. Kerem; Varied Opinions and Views in Israelite Culture 5; Rehovot: Kibbutz Education Department, 1995), 35.

dream theory, can advance the understanding of dream stories in the Bible and in the ANE in general,[18] or of Jacob's Dream in particular.

An additional affirmation of the limitations of modern dream research in explicating dreams of those ancient times and places is that before us is a written *literary* text, not the immediate report of last night's dream.[19] This leads to my point of departure: *the concern here is not with the dream as phenomenon, but as story*. I shall attempt, then, to reveal and interpret the dream and its meaning as I would any other biblical text. What is special about this particular text is that it is told as a dream.[20]

Consequently, even anthropological studies that compare the contemporary dreams of so-called primitive societies to those of the ancient world, instructive and impressive as such approaches may be, relate to the dream as a phenomenon. As such, the contribution of such research would be limited, as would the folklore research of E. A. Speiser, which helps the anthropologist, the sociologist and the psychologist to understand the dream as a phenomenon.

The present book, however, as previously stated, is concerned rather with *the dream as a story*, as a biblical text.[21] Hence the reader should follow my literary approach and methods as a point of departure for understanding the story of Jacob's Dream and what it means.

It is worthwhile to look again at Sternberg, who distinguishes between the reader's perception and the perception of the participants themselves. In his opinion,

> In terms of the biblical reality, the dream is a clear sign from God, and in compositional terms, an introspective look on the narrator's part... As to the status of the dream in the narrative structure, it is perceived as a

---

18. On problems of employing psychological research, see Gnuse, *Samuel*, 5; Fidler, *Dream Theophany*, 14, 16; L. Ehrlich, *Der Traum im Alten Testament* (BZAW 73; Berlin: Töpelmann, 1953), v. By contrast, see A. Resch, *Der Traum im Heilsplan Gottes: Deutung und Bedeutung des Traums im Alten Testament* (Freiburg: Herder, 1964), 5, 38. Contradicting Resch is Fidler, *Dream Theophany*, 22–23. See also Butler, *Conceptions*, 13–14.

19. Fidler, *Dream Theophany*, 21.

20. Gnuse, *Samuel*, 8: "Many of the categories of modern study cannot be applied to ancient and biblical dreams, because the disciplines are often concerned with real dreams, whereas the latter are literary creations." See also Fidler, *Dream Theophany*, 21: "*When the subject of the study is not the dream as phenomenon... but how it is presented in literary descriptions*, the need to use different sciences...[though] this is not entirely ruled out..." (emphasis added).

21. With that, great is the temptation to adopt modern dream research ideas, having identified in Jacob's Dream some symbolic elements. Jacob, as we know, is about to leave the country and God promises to return him to the Promised Land.

forecast, though not necessarily one that is easily understood. In this respect, then, the reader's perception is similar to those of the participants themselves...though the parallel or position of equality does not continue, *for in other respects the reader from the outset receives additional hints that give him a viewing position superior to the participants'. That advantage is the direct result of the close connection typical of the biblical story between the broad context of the book and the Joseph stories.*[22]

What Sternberg writes on the dreams of Joseph and of Pharaoh fits in with and hence is applied to our discussion of Jacob's Dream. Understanding the link between the dream and the wider Jacob story, and the Patriarch stories in general (as *mise en abyme*), helps one understand the dream's meaning and role.

To sum up, having decided to discuss the Jacob's Dream not as phenomenon but as story, recourse to the behavioral sciences is not necessary, meaning that we are free to embark on a literary journey. Furthermore, since the discussion will not be phenomenological in nature, literary approaches to the Bible can be used to guide us in interpreting the dream, as in the case of any other literary text.[23] After all, Jacob's Dream is reported in the context of literary work. Methodologically, on the other hand, one can maintain that accounts of dreams are based on actual dreams—just as accounts of battles are based on actual battles. This being the case, it is admissible to explore the contributions that modern psychological analysis can make to our understanding literary texts recording dream events.

Before presenting the basic premises of my literary method in interpreting Jacob's Dream, I offer here some background on dream descriptions and classifications in the ANE literature.

1.2. *Typological Classification: Dream Theophany and Symbolic Dreams*

Studies of dreams in the literature of both the Bible and the ANE classify dreams as "dream theophany" or "symbolic dreams." Both types have their characteristic language and structure. In general, in a dream theophany, the god appears and delivers his message verbally in the dream, while in a symbolic dream the message is delivered in a visual-symbolic

---

22. Sternberg, *Repetition*, 125 (emphasis added).
23. See, as an analogy, A. Shinan, "The Dream in Midrash and the Midrash of the Dream," in Kerem, ed., *Varied Opinions*, 44: "I gave the article this title to focus it on two related matters: the writings of the Sages, particularly the Midrash (commentary) on dreams ('The Dream in the Midrash') and the technique followed there in discussing and clarifying dreams ('Commentary as Dream')."

manner, which therefore requires interpretation. Oppenheim argues that: "Both types follow a fixed pattern that reconstructed from sources ranging from Sumer in the third millennium B.C.E., through Homeric times (ninth century B.C.E.) to Ptolemaic Egypt (first century B.C.E.)."[24]

Hence, identifying and classifying the two types, one may assume, will be simple and speedy, as Fidler remarks:

> There is an accepted method for determining dream types in the Bible and in the ANE, which generally is not seen as a problem.[25] There is the message dream in which the dreamer is given a direct, literal message and the symbolic dream[26] in which the message is in visual symbols, and which therefore usually requires interpretation... With that, the accepted classification system seems problematic when applied in...Gen 31:10–13 and 28:12 ff. (Jacob's Dream).[27]

The following discussion affirms this view.

1.2.1. *Two methodological cautions.*

a) *Analogy with Ancient Near Eastern literature and its hazards.* Extra caution is required when comparing dream descriptions from the Bible with ANE literature. The heading given to the present section, "Dream descriptions in the Bible and the Ancient Near East," suggests an affinity between the two. Indeed, accepted literary research assumes it exists. Yet we must avoid being swept into false analogies. At the beginning of his book, Gnuse deals with the issue at length:

> The comparison of biblical material with ANE material is fraught with danger. An extreme often exhibited is the discovering of parallels between biblical and Near Eastern material no matter how tenuous their relationship. Many so-called parallels have been adduced on the basis of superficial similarity. Certain phrases, expressions, or aspects of literary form may coincide, but the essence of the material may be totally disparate. These do not constitute authentic parallels. Instances where there is a similar use of language for different purposes with different meanings are questionable parallels. The Israelites were Semitic, as were many of their neighbors. Similar concepts and attitudes may have developed out of this common environment, both physical and intellectual, which have no direct relationship with each other. Such examples are not authentic parallels.

---

24. A. L. Oppenheim, "Halom," *EB* 3:144.
25. Gnuse, *Samuel*, 16: "Classification of ancient dreams by modern scholars is somewhat artificial."
26. Oppenheim, *Interpretation*, 206–17, 237–45. See also Gnuse, *Samuel*, 16.
27. Fidler, *Dream Theophany*, 29.

> We must seek to avoid such avid parallel hunting and search for only legitimate ancient Near Eastern influence on Biblical material. The text must show more than coincidental development out of the same Semitic milieu.[28]

Aware of the danger, Gnuse concentrates his research on the proof that the message dream in the ANE and in 1 Sam 3 *belong to the same literary genre* and contain similar elements:

> The comparison between the two will be *on the basis of genre* structure and of the individual parts. For this purpose we shall carefully evaluate ancient Near Eastern dreams to perceive their form, function and content; then we shall analyze the form, function and content of 1 Samuel 3. The commonality between the two is to be found in form and content. The relationship is not one of superficial similarity. This will become evident with the fuller explication of both sets of material. Further biblical material in the other books of the Old Testament will be reviewed to indicate that 1 Samuel 3 is not an isolated instance.[29]

This claim of belonging to the same genre gives rise to the second methodological caution:

b) *Literary genre—helpful or misleading?* Typologically, as previously noted, the common practice is to divide biblical and ANE dreams into the broad categories of "dream theophany" and "symbolic dream." Most scholars classify Jacob's Dream as "dream theophany." Some scholars note the distinctiveness and complexity of Jacob's Dream and suggest that, in addition to its classification as "dream theophany," it contains elements that also justify its classification as a "symbolic dream."[30] However, this distinction has not prompted an exploration of the symbolic meaning of Jacob's Dream.

An attempt to classify Jacob's Dream as one of these genres may help in its understanding—or it may mislead it. Scholars who see the dream as a theophany are unlikely to look for symbolism in the dream vision. By contrast, those who find signs of the symbolic dream could reasonably be asked about the symbolic significance of the "vision" in it. The potential exists for supporters of this view to remain loyal to the accepted concept

---

28. Gnuse, *Samuel*, 2. See also M. Malul, "Studies in Legal Symbolic Acts in Mesopotamian Law" (Ph.D. diss., University of Pennsylvania, 1983); idem, *The Comparative Method in Ancient Near Eastern and Biblical Legal Studies* (AOAT 227; Kevelaer: Butzon & Bercker, 1990), 98–112.
29. Gnuse, *Samuel*, 3.
30. See L. Ehrlich, "Traum," *BHH* 3:20–23; E. Baruch, "The Prophetic Dream and Its Rejection by the Deuteronomic School" (M.A. diss., University of Haifa, 1987), 19; Fidler, *Dream Theophany*, 32, 154, 156 n. 131.

of Jacob's Dream as a theophany, meaning that even finding signs of the symbolic dream does not lead them to seek their significance, as they facilely relegate dreams to being mere ornaments,[31] with no intrinsic meaning. This will be discussed in detail later. For the moment, it suffices to stress the danger of becoming beholden to specific approaches—like disciples of Structuralism, who shut themselves off, as it were, from seeking additional meanings in a text.

This is true for any concept that shuts out any other meaning. We shall see how source-critical analyses of the Jacob's Dream story have mislead rather than helped.[32] So also with the issue of whether Jacob's Dream is a theophany or a symbolic dream. Any attempt to decide one way or the other misleads, limits and closes off the varied layers of the dream's significance.[33]

Speaking of the reader's role in filling in the gaps, Perry and Sternberg write of a process of constructing "the world of literary text." They stress that the process cannot be arbitrary "according to the free inclinations and tastes of the reader."[34] Criteria for filling the gap must take into account, for instance, the genre of the work in question, and the process must "follow the conceptual system that the nature of the genre arouses in the reader." They quote a passage from a nineteenth-century social novel to illustrate this:

> For more than an hour he told Madeleine about his trip. Then suddenly, when he looked at her he saw that her eyes were closed and her face expressionless; she seemed to be asleep.

"No doubt," the authors write,

> the reader is full of compassion for the girl lulled to sleep either by fatigue or by boredom, a hypothesis to be examined as further details of the text come to light. But now we present that same passage, but from a recently published detective story.

---

31. N. M. Sarna, *Understanding Genesis* (HBI 1; New York: Jewish Theological Seminary of America, 1966), 193; J. P. Fokkelman, *Narrative Art in Genesis: Specimens of Stylistic and Structural Analysis* (SSN 17; Assen: Van Gorcum, 1975), 54; A. De Pury, *Promesse Divine et Légende Cultuelle dans le Cycle de Jacob: Genèse 28 et les Traditions Patriarcales* (2 vols.; Paris: Gabalda, 1975), 378; Fidler, *Dream Theophany*, 172.

32. See below for a separate discussion on the structuralist approach and its limitations.

33. For a more comprehensive discussion of a multifaceted approach to a text and its contribution to the understanding of Jacob's Dream, see below.

34. M. Perry and M. Sternberg, "The King Through Ironic Eyes," *Hasifrut* 1 (1968): 264.

There is nothing for the reader to do here except wait for the police to be called in to find the mysterious killer. What is said is identical in both cases, but in each one it is directed to the filling of entirely different gaps suggested by different genres that activate different inferences of meaning, and suggestibility [operating] in a different direction from the very same sentences.[35]

By the same token, deciding whether to classify Jacob's Dream into either one of the categories found in ANE research—theophany or symbolic dream—creates a system of expectations that determines how the reader fills in gaps, as well as hypotheses as to the meaning of the dream. Furthermore, it should be borne in mind that the division of the dreams into two categories is to an extent artificial,[36] a construct of modern scholarship, making it advisable to avoid sweeping and exclusive classification of biblical dreams as one type or the other.

My literary approach, allowing more than one reading for a biblical text, led to the symbolic interpretation of the dream. It contrasts with restrictive "either...or" concepts that may have prevented researchers from reaching a broader "both...and" interpretation. Now we examine the main characteristics of each dream type.

1.2.2. *Characteristics of the symbolic dream.* The symbolic dream is mainly about *a visual message.*

a) *The names given to the "symbolic dream."*[37] What I refer to as "the symbolic dream" has also been called "the enigmatic dream,"[38] "the allegorical dream,"[39] "the visual dream" or "the sealed dream." These names help to distinguish between the two types of dreams. Thus, for example, while *an auditory message dream* stresses the use of the sense of hearing, what is defined as a visual dream stresses the role of sight. The symbolic dream, consisting mainly of visual images, requires and interpretation of the sight that appears as a symbol. The symbolic dream defined as a sealed or an enigmatic dream is contrasted to the revelation or dream theophany characterized as a transparent or simple dream.

---

35. See ibid., 264 n. 5.
36. See Gnuse, *Samuel*, 16: "Classification of ancient dreams by modern scholars is somewhat artificial."
37. Oppenheim, *Interpretation*; Ehrlich, *Der Traum*; Gnuse, *Samuel*; I. Mendelsohn, "Dream," *IDB* 1:868; M. Ottoson, "חלם, חלום," *TDOT* 4:421–32.
38. Y. Kaufmann, *The History of Israelite Belief: from Ancient Times to the End of the Second Temple* (Tel Aviv: Mosad Bialik, 1972), 507.
39. Fidler, *Dream Theophany*, 30 n. 11 writes: "Some researchers, notably the French, call the symbolic dream an allegorical dream."

Among the names and definitions for the symbolic dream, Gnuse's "symbolic message dreams" is, in my opinion, the best.[40] It emphasizes the basic elements of message, expressed as a symbol that is visual rather than verbal. The dream theophany, by contrast, gives an explicit verbal message.

b) *Elements of the symbolic dream model*. W. Richter set forth a model of the symbolic dream, having five components.[41] These are:

1. Announcement of the Dream ("He had a dream," Gen 28:12)
2. Introductory Dream Formula (*vehinneh*,[42] 28:12)
3. Dream corpus: Image or Expression (28:12–13a)
4. Meaning ("abode of God," 28:17; "on this journey," 28:20)
5. Fulfillment (Gen 31:13; 33:18; 35:1)

1.2.3. *Characteristics of the dream theophany*. The main feature of the dream theophany is *the verbal message* from God, revealed in a dream.

a) *The names given to the dream theophany*. The "dream theophany" has been called "a message dream,"[43] "an auditory message dream,"[44] "a theological dream,"[45] "a prophetic dream,"[46] "a simple dream,"[47] and "a transparent dream."[48] The variety of terms testifies to the complexity of defining a dream theophany, and thus of finding the right model for Jacob's Dream. At the same time, the various terms may help by revealing criteria.[49] Distinctions between the theophany and the symbolic dream will be discussed later.

---

40. Gnuse, *Samuel*, 17. I prefer the designation "symbolic message dreams" to A. L. Oppenheim's "symbolic." This is because there is a message, and the message is expressed by *visual* symbols.

41. See W. Richter, "Traum und Traumdeutung im AT: ihre Form und Verwendung," *BZ* 7, no. 2 (1963): 203–9. In his discussion of Joseph, Richter calls the model "the dream with the artistic structure." See also Gnuse, *Samuel*, 79–80. Gnuse places the Midianite's dream (Judg 7:13–14), and those in the book of Daniel in this category. The present research adds Jacob's Dream.

42. See Gen 37:7, 9; 40:9, 16; 41:1–3, 5–6; Judg 7:13. See Baruch, "The Prophetic Dream," 14; Fidler, *Dream Theophany*, 171.

43. Oppenheim, *Interpretation*, 186. I prefer Fidler's formulation (*Dream Theophany*, 16).

44. Gnuse, *Samuel*, 19.

45. Oppenheim, *Interpretation*, 507–9.

46. Kaufmann, *History*, 507–9.

47. Mendelsohn, *Dream*, 868.

48. Fidler, *Dream Theophany*, 35.

49. It is similar to what emerges from the etymology of the word *dream* in other languages. See, e.g., Oppenheim, *Interpretation*, 146, who maintains: "'*shuttu*', meaning dream in Akkadian, and '*shittu*,' sleep, have a common root. Differently,

1. Preface to the Story of Jacob's Dream

One way to define the dream theophany is by contrast with the symbolic dream, and vice versa, although Ottoson,[50] for one, defines the first as a non-symbolic dream, hence his definition of it as *transparent*,[51] in contrast with the *opaque* symbolic dream.

b) *Elements of the dream theophany model.* These follow the model derived from the ANE, as described by Oppenheim:[52]

Framework	1. Circumstances of the dream: time and place, appearance of the god or his messenger
Essence	2. Message of the divine entity who is revealed
Framework	3. The dream's end, awakening of the dreamer and fulfillment of the revelation (if relevant).

In this category researchers generally place the dreams in Gen 20:3–8; 26:4–23; 28:12, 17–18;[53] 31:10–13, 24; 46:1–5; Num 22:3–8, 19–21; 1 Sam 3; 1 Kgs 3:5–15.

To conclude, then, dreams in the Bible and in ANE literature belong to one of two groups determined by two main criteria: whether the dominant sense involved is *sight or hearing*, and by the degree to which the dream and its meaning are transparent to the dreamer and/or those around him. Thus the symbolic dream is visual[54] and opaque and the theophany auditory, verbal and transparent.

---

the noun 'dream' in Egyptian derives from the root 'awake,' suggesting that the sleeping dreamer is in some sense awake." On the etymology of "dream," see "חלום," BDB 321, as well as Gnuse, *Samuel*, 25, 59; Baruch, "The Prophetic Dream," 3; Fidler, *Dream Theophany*, 23, 24 n. 85, 26–27 n. 97. Oppenheim, *Interpretation*, 226, declares: "The words parallel to 'dream' in Ugaritic, Aramaic and Arabic derive from a root connected with visual experience..." See also Fidler, *Dream Theophany*, 226, supported by Oppenheim, *Interpretation*, 190, noting that the word defining "dream" is "open eye" (recalling Song 5:2: "I was asleep, but my heart was wakeful"), leading to the intrinsically important issue of whether dream descriptions attest to the perception of the dreamer and/or the narrator, who sees continuity between dream and reality, and hence perhaps the difficulty of separating dream time from waking, as expressed in the dreamer's wonder when he awakes (see Jacob's reaction in Gen 28:16–17).

50. Ottoson, *TDOT* 4:429–30.
51. Fidler, *Dream Theophany*, 35.
52. Oppenheim, *Interpretation*, 186.
53. I see Jacob's Dream in this text as belonging to both categories.
54. Henceforth Jacob's Dream seems to contain both a vision and an auditory message from God. When Joseph says, "God has told Pharaoh what He is about to do" (Gen 41:25), one infers that the symbolic dream may be expressed in verbal as well as visual terms. See also Fidler, *Dream Theophany*, 51 n. 29.

Fidler, who discusses the classification of dreams in biblical and ANE literature, is keenly aware of its limitations. She writes: "It is better to see them as characteristics (which may be present to one degree or another in different types) and not as criteria."[55]

1.2.4. Is Jacob's Dream a theophany or a symbolic dream—"both... and," not "either...or"? An attempt will be made to convince readers that the form of Jacob's Dream makes it possible to assign the event to both categories, and that, accordingly, its interpretation comes from two directions. The first direction derives from my understanding the dream *as a story*, and my belief that one can deal with the dream as a literary text, a story to be analyzed by literary, not psychological, means. The second understanding is my synchronic literary attitude, which recognizes the possibility of multiple readings.

It seems to me that the literary approach allowing twofold readings of a biblical text is the key to resolving the issue. Hence the two readings will be presented as a background to the discussion of Jacob's Dream and its twofold significance/interpretation. The reason for so doing lies in the fact that the dream contains a verbal message from God (which research recognizes as the sign of a *theophany dream*), as well as a picture (recognized as the mark of *symbolic dream*), encouraging the reader to interpret the dream in both ways, as a theophany dream as well as a symbolic dream.

1.3. *Dream Incubation*

1.3.1. Defining the term. Incubation[56] indicates the dreamer's active anticipation of a dream message, evidenced by spending the night in a sacred place[57] and making ritual preparations in the effort to elicit a message (revelation) from the god through the dream. "The custom is first known from the rites of the Greek health god Escalpius. The sick came to his temples, cleansed themselves, prayed and wept and fell asleep there in fervent hope of a revelation regarding their cure."[58]

---

55. Ibid., 34.
56. From the Latin *incubare*, meaning "to sleep in a particular place." See Fidler, *Dream Theophany*, 17 n. 49; Butler, *Conceptions*, 217–39. Butler (p. 217) quotes the definition of *The Shorter Oxford English Dictionary on Historical Principals* (the G. W. S. Friedrichsen rev. ed., 1987): "The practice of sleeping in a temple or sacred place for oracular purposes."
57. Expectation of a theophany in a sacred place expresses the belief that the deity is present there. This will be discussed further in Chapter 3.
58. Baruch, "The Prophetic Dream," 28, quoted from Ehrlich, *Der Traum*.

1. *Preface to the Story of Jacob's Dream*

Oppenheim defines an incubation dream as "a dream experienced in a temple or sacred place" and sees it as the source and prototype of the "revelation/message dream," assuming that "the dividing line between a dream and a vision, between the appearance of the god to a sleeper in his dream and a true revelation is not absolute and clear in every case."[59]

Several necessary conditions characterize an incubation dream:

1. *Intent/initiative* of the dreamer to attract the god's attention.
2. The dream occurs *during sleep*.
3. It occurs in a *sacred place*.
4. The dream comes *after specific preparations*.[60]

1.3.2. Does incubation occur in the Hebrew Bible? The ANE literature frequently describes the incubation dream. Is such a concept present in biblical dream descriptions generally and in Jacob's Dream specifically? Scholarly opinion ranges from denying any incubation dreams in the Bible[61] to identifying them in all revelations on holy ground.[62] Gnuse, for instance, left the possibility of incubation texts open as regards Gen 15; 28:10–19; 46:1–4; 1 Sam 3 and 1 Kgs 3.[63] Ehrlich, on the other hand, points only to 1 Kgs 3:4–15 as a clear case of incubation,[64] while Gaster points to Gen 46:1–4 and Num 22:8.[65] According to Fidler, "The disagreement may be at least in part imaginary, so that each of the opposing positions may accord with a particular historical stage of the tradition…"[66]

---

59. Oppenheim, *Interpretation*, 190.
60. T. H. McAlpin, *Sleep, Divine and Human in the Old Testament* (JSOTSup 38; Sheffield: Sheffield Academic, 1987), 158–59; Butler, *Conceptions*, 217–39.
61. Resch, *Heilsplan*, 114–15; Fidler, *Dream Theophany*, 18 n. 49.
62. A. Jirku, *Materialen zur Volksreligion Israels* (Leipzig: Deichert, 1914), repr. in *Von Jerusalem nach Ugarit: Gesammelte Schriften* (Graz: Akademische Druck-u. Verlagsanstalt, 1966), 297–313.
63. See Gnuse, *Samuel*, 38: "The Old Testament accounts lack a clear reference to any incubation procedure. If there were such a process, it is hidden in the text. Possible incubation texts include Gen 15; 28:10–19; 46:1–4; 1 Sam 3, and 1 Kgs 3. But none of these texts gives the clear indication of being an incubation dream in the manner of the ancient Near Eastern models…"
64. Ehrlich, *Der Traum*, 19.
65. T. H. Gaster, *Myth, Legend, and Custom in the Old Testament: A Comparative Study with Chapters from Sir James G. Frazer's Folklore in the Old Testament* (New York: Harper & Row, 1969), 331.
66. Fidler, *Dream Theophany*, 18 n. 49.

Our attention will focus on the present form of the stories, and in greater detail regarding Jacob's Dream. Additionally, there will be further discussion of Oppenheim's proposal to recognize what has been called *unintended incubation*, though this is a contradiction in terms, for the dreamer's initiative in eliciting a divine message is essential.

1.4. *"The Biblical Perception" of the Dream: A Problem*[67]
1.4.1. *Distribution of the biblical dream—problems of identification.* The Hebrew root *hlm* appears a total of 85 times in the Hebrew Bible and in Genesis 48 times, of which 39 occurrence are in the Joseph stories. In the historiographic literature words deriving from the root appear just occasionally (Judg 7:15; 1 Sam 28:5–6 and 1 Kgs 3:5, 15). In the Prophets it appears fairly frequently, although not in every instance where the root appears is a dream described. If the biblical descriptions of dreams are divided into the two accepted categories, we find the dream theophany model[68] in Gen 20:3–8; 26:4–23; 28:12, 17–18; 31:10–13, 24; 41:5; Num 22:3–8, 10–21; 1 Sam 3 and 1 Kgs 3:5–15. The symbolic model appears in Gen 37:6–8, 9–10; 40:9–13; 41:1–7; Judg 7:13–15 and Dan 2:31–36; 4:7–14; 7:2–12 and 8:16–26.

God's appearance to Jacob in a dream at Beersheba, before his descent into Egypt (Gen 46:1–5), is also listed among the dream theophanies. While the root *hlm* does not appear, the account is generally accepted as describing a dream.[69] Neither does the dream root appear in the revelation to young Samuel in 1 Sam 3. Is the root *hlm*, then, the sole criterion for identifying a biblical dream? Are God's nocturnal revelations to the prophets considered dreams, even in the absence of that root? Identifying dream descriptions is important mainly for the discussion of Jacob's Dream "in a vision by night" at Beer-Sheba prior to the descent into Egypt.[70]

---

67. Ibid., 36–95, discusses the range of opinions on dreams, illustrating from the Bible. See also J. M. Husser, *Dreams and Dream Narratives in the Biblical World* (Sheffield: Sheffield Academic, 1999), 139–45.

68. Scholars advocating source criticism stress that the God revealed in a dream is in most places in the Bible called "Elohim" and not "Lord" (*Jehovah, YHWH*), and regard this as a means of distinguishing between Elohistic (E) and Yahwistic (J) sources. Thus God revealed in a dream indicates an E source. I discuss this later *vis-à-vis* Jacob's Dream.

69. See the separate discussion of Gen 46:1–5.

70. Fidler, *Dream Theophany*, 23–29. On the identification problem, see the descriptions of the biblical dream.

1.4.2. *The "problem" of "biblical perception": contrary statements about dreams.* I employ the word "problem" here deliberately. As for "biblical perception," can one question whether that such a general thing actually exists. The concept is problematic for any subject, the discussion of dreams included, since the Bible has no single, ordered and systematic central theory. Hence, "Multiple views are the natural state in literature so varied as to the genres, periods and schools of authors that have a part in it."[71]

a) *Positive biblical statements regarding the dream.* Among the positive statements about dreams are, for instance, "And Saul inquired of the Lord, but the Lord did not answer him, either by dreams or by *Urim* or by prophets" (1 Sam 28:6).[72] In addition, there is "and he said, Hear these my words: when a prophet of the Lord arises among you, *I make myself known to him in a vision, I speak to him in dreams*" (Num 12:6).

b) *Negative statements in the Bible regarding the dream.* By contrast, other texts belittle or even gainsay the importance of the dream—as, for instance, in Jer 23:25–32, particularly in vv. 28, 32:

> Let the prophet who has a dream tell his dream, and let him who has received My word report My word faithfully. How can straw be compared to grain? Says the Lord. My word is like fire, declares the Lord, and like a hammer that shatters rock. Assuredly I am going to deal with the prophets who steal my words… I am going to deal with those who prophesy *lying dreams*, declares the Lord, who relates them to lead My people astray…

We should also note, "pay no heed to the dreams they dream" (Jer 29:8); "…dreams come with much brooding, so does foolish utterance with much speech… Much dreaming leads to futility…" (Eccl 5:2, 6); "And *dreamers speak lies* (or falsely) and console with illusions" (Zech 10:2).

1.4.3. *Explaining such contradictions—if possible.* Before resolving the question, its full complexity must be understood. With this end in view, I focus on two examples. One appears to express a positive view of the dream (Num 12:6–8) and the other a negative view (Zech 7:10). We shall

---

71. Ibid., 39.
72. Ibid., 49. Fidler examines the dream's authenticity, i.e. its legitimacy, reliability and efficacy. Regarding this dream, she states: "the legitimacy of dreams, *Urim* or prophets does not depend on efficacy but rather on viewpoint… according to which these methods express the will of God" (48). Fidler cites the Hittite king Morshalish II beseeching his god to let him know the reason for the plague in his land by these same three mantic means: a sign, a prophet or a dream. See *ANET*, 394–96; see also Oppenheim, *Interpretation*, 199; Gnuse, *Samuel*, 27, and 60: "The Old Testament writers viewed dreams as legitimate mode of revelation, and for this reason dreams usually came to be responsible representatives of God."

then see that what appears to be unequivocally positive or negative in the first reading, may be seen differently in the second, indicating how complex and ambiguous the issue is.

a) *Two readings of Num 12:6–8 "plainly and not in riddles."*

Hear these my words
- v. 6:
  - a. When a prophet of the Lord arises among you
  - b. I make myself known to him in a vision
  - c. I speak to him in a dream

- v. 7: Not so with my servant Moses

- v. 8:
  - c′. With him I speak mouth to mouth
  - b′. plainly and not in riddles
  - a′. and he beholds the likeness of God

Content and structure complement one another. The content of the statement "Not so with my servant Moses" presents a contrast between the two, framed within a chiastic structure.[73] Does this describe a preference for direct revelation over revelation in a dream of either type? Is there a hierarchy in which the revelation "directly and plainly" to Moses stands above one "in riddles" to others, between "Mouth to mouth I talk to him" (to Moses, v. 8) and "I speak with him in a dream" (v. 6) as regards other prophets? The contrast is between a direct revelation of God and one in a dream that is merely symbolic. This hints at a hierarchy between the two types of dreams, in favor of the dream theophany, the dream of revelation.

Lichtenstein notes that although various modes are equally recognized as legitimate means for discovering God's will (1 Sam 28:6), a hierarchy may be inferred from Num 12:4–9, that is, there is a qualitative difference between the direct word of God, "mouth to mouth" to Moses, in contrast with the indirect speech, the riddles, that He speaks with others.[74] According to Lichtenstein, "Not so with my servant Moses" contrasts with the dream/vision cited as legitimate forms of divine revelation to a prophet. Hence he concludes that the vision/dream of God's prophet is equal to the "riddles" in v. 8, with all three terms relating to the symbolic/enigmatic dream and not to the dream of revelation." In his opinion, the fact that all existed simultaneously in the time of the J source is evidence of alternative ways of communicating with God, and even the legitimacy of doing so, and any developmental theory regarding the

---

73. J. S. Kselman, "A Note on Numbers XII 6–8," *VT* 26 (1976): 500–504. See also Husser, *Narratives*, 146–47.

74. M. Lichtenstein, "Dream Theophany and the E Document," *JANES* 1, no. 2 (1969): 49.

medium of revelation must take this into account. "This passage testifies to simultaneous existence (at the time of J) of alternate legitimate method of divine communication, and any evolutionary theory of revelatory media must take this into account."[75]

My own approach is to examine the text in its present form, deliberately "ignoring" the connection with J or another source that "locks" the significance and stands in the way of "openness" to additional embedded meanings. Therefore, I do not deal with a "primary unit" as opposed to a "secondary unity," with all due respect to the source theory.

Lichtenstein's conclusion is clear: "Indeed, in many cases, it would seem that in the ancient Near East the distinction between symbolic dreams, dream-theophanies, and corporeal revelation is more a matter of literary preference than of theological necessity."[76]

Lichtenstein's examples[77] that show the two types of dreams in the same text reinforce my thesis that in Jacob's Dream, the dream theophany and symbolic dream appear side by side—an important topic that will be discussed in greater detail below.

Fidler,[78] by contrast with Lichtenstein and Ehrlich,[79] maintains that the term "riddle" does not refer to a type of dream, but rather to the dream and the prophetic vision as one whole (compare v. 6) to be considered as a concealed means of communication, and hence inferior to the direct dialogue between God and His faithful servant.

From the beginning, even as the data are being presented in Num 12:4–9, for example, we have seen no agreement among scholars as to whether to interpret the text as affirming the dream or negating it. Does this refer to a type of dream or to dreaming in general? At times biblical expressions may not be absolutely clear and can be understood in two ways.

b) *Can there be two readings for "and false dreams speak" in Zechariah 10:2?* Zechariah 10:2 reads: "For the *teraphim* spoke delusion. And the augers predicted falsely; and false dreams speak.[80] And console

---

75. Ibid.
76. Ibid., 51.
77. Ibid. See also Gnuse, *Samuel*, 31, 73, who exposes the weakness of the examples.
78. Fidler, *Dream Theophany*, 52.
79. Ehlrich, *Der Traum*, 138–39. He deduces that the term *riddles* refers to a dream requiring interpretation, i.e. a symbolic dream.
80. I reject the translation: "And dreamers speak lies." In the Hebrew Bible the subject of this verse is the dreams, not the dreamers. I prefer "falsely" to "lies." I cannot even accept Fidler's translation "and dreams speak falsely." The Hebrew *halomot hashavas* as it appears in the present text means only false dreams and not dreams in general.

with illusions. That is why My people have strayed like a flock. They suffer for lack of a shepherd." This passage, like Jer 27:9 and 29:8, combines *dreams* with *augers*, *lies* and *false prophecies* of peace, like the texts that bring to mind dreams in Deuteronomy and Jeremiah. Zechariah compares belief in *teraphim* to idolatry.

I think it impossible to read the Masoretic texts "and false dreams speak" in two ways. The only plausible reading is that *lies/false* merely defines one type of dream. That is, (only) "false dreams" speak, not other dreams. Thus the reproach according to this reading is for a certain type of dream and not for dreams in general. The implication is that there are true dreams that should not be disparaged.

Thus the phrase "the false dreams speak" (literally "the lying dreams"), in its present formulation, as Fidler maintains, cannot be read in two ways. It is easier to find two meanings in the construct "lying dreams" (Jer 23:32)—either an ambiguous reading or two readings. It is unclear whether the construct "the false dreams," *halomot hashav*, signifies that all dreams are false, or whether the lie is a modifier limiting dreams, referring to certain dreams as lies, and not the dream phenomenon as deceptive.

1.4.4. *Can such contradictory expressions be explained—and if so, how?* How can one explain the varied views regarding dreams in ANE and biblical literature—through individual preferences of authors and editors, or literary genre, or *Zeitgeist*? Does the negative attitude relate to dreaming as a phenomenon—and if so, does opposition to it arise from refusal to see it as a legitimate means of contact with God? Is the negative attitude towards a type of dream and not to the entire phenomenon? Can one assume an evolving biblical attitude towards the dream?

a) *The negative attitude relates to symbolic dreams only.* A possible explanation for contrary statements was, as previously stated, to attribute the negative attitude to a particular dream type—the symbolic dream, for instance—and not to the dream phenomenon as a whole as a legitimate channel/vehicle[81] for divine messages. In Lichtenstein's opinion, the biblical opposition is directed to enigmatic or ambiguous dreams only. He argues:

---

81. On the validity of the dream in the Bible as determined by legitimacy, credibility and efficacy, see Fidler, *Dream Theophany*, 48.

1. *Preface to the Story of Jacob's Dream* 21

> The ambiguous dream requires an interpreter, and thus naturally falls into the same category as omens, *auspices* and the like. Consequently, the Old Testament speaks derogatorily of the *cholem* "dreamer" (cf. Deut 13:2–6) and links his activities with *ot* or *mophet* or with *qesem* (Jer 27:9; 29:8), *keshef* (Jer 27:9) and *teraphim*…[82]

The dream in the Bible is one means of revelation, of transmitting a message from the heavens to the earth. As Joseph explained to Pharaoh: "God has told Pharaoh what He is about to do" (Gen 41:25). In the ANE, attempts were made to learn the god's will—for example,[83] by examining livers of animals, oil patterns on water, formations within smoke, studying the stars, birds in flight and the weather. Dreams were an additional way.

b) *Prophecy opposed the interpretation of dreams, fearing competition.* In the Bible, a person turned to God through the priest and the prophet. Does the abundant criticism against the interpretation of dreams in the prophetic writings, then, indicate a struggle of prophecy to maintain its place as a channel to God?[84] Did the dream threaten and compete with the prophet? In that case, the negative attitude to the dream can be understood as criticism of its legitimacy as a source of divine messages.

Concluding his study, Gnuse assumes a developmental process in the biblical attitudes to dreams:

> Throughout the developing biblical tradition evidence of changing attitudes exists. Early traditions preserved in the epic literature and historical narratives attest a positive attitude toward dreams as a source of divine revelation. But with the later classical prophets, Isaiah and especially Jeremiah, this attitude changed. Perhaps the conflict with false prophecy caused dreams to be discredited gradually as a valid source of revelation… However, when prophecy began to decline as a living theological movement, dreams began to regain their popularity in apocalyptic literature and post-exilic novel forms like Daniel and the Joseph cycle. Dreams again became an acceptable mode of revelation, but *the emphasis moved from auditory dream theophanies to symbolic* and mantic dreams, which required the dream interpreter.[85]

c) *Three factors for change in the biblical attitude to the dream.* Fidler lists three scholastically accepted factors that explain positive or negative changes regarding the prophetic nature of the dream—the literary source;

---

82. See Lichtenstein, *E Document*, 49.
83. Gnuse, *Samuel*, 15.
84. Ibid., 62.
85. Ibid., 248 (emphasis added).

the chronological developmental dimension (*Zeitgeist*); the literary genre—each of which led her to the same conclusion, that "In most cases scholars needed some link between the factors, having understood that none by itself could provide a comprehensive solution."[86]

Oppenheim, explaining viewpoints regarding the dream in ANE literature, notes the following factors: "individual preference or authors and editors, literary genres, stylistic conventions and *Zeitgeist*."[87]

1.4.5. *The importance of dreams in the Jacob story cycle.* Within the Jacob story cycle[88] the dream is central, as shown in Jacob's three dreams: the first at Bethel as he was leaving the country for Haran (Gen 28:10–22; the second in Laban's home as he was about to return to Canaan (31:10–13); and the third when he was preparing to leave Canaan and descend into Egypt (46:1–5). Fidler notes that the dreams appear at "three biographical-geographical junctures in Jacob's life."[89] From the literary standpoint as well, Jacob's dreams are milestones and serve as links in the story in which they are embedded. Thus the dreams at Bethel and in Laban's home serve as boundaries for the stories about Jacob and Laban in chs. 29–31, and God's word (28:15; 31:13) is a link to stories about Jacob and Esau.[90] Fidler emphasizes:

> In all three depictions Jacob receives divine messages directed toward his next steps, whether through a specific instruction (31:13) or through reinforcing encouragement to continue along the path he has already embarked on (28:15, compare with 28:10; 46:3b–4 and 46:1). Thus the impression is created that God who protects and directs Jacob, contacts him mainly through dreams.[91]

Significantly, in all three instances the motif of returning to the Land is an explicit part of the divine message. For our purpose, disclosure of contradictory biblical utterances regarding the dream, in all its problematic complexity, further reveals the complexity and uniqueness of Jacob's Dream.

Jacob's Dream is presented as a means of conveying a message from God, both in words and in the vision of the ascending and descending angels. I intend to examine in detail its verbal and visual (symbolic)

---

86. Fidler, *Dream Theophany*, 39.
87. Oppenheim, *Interpretation*, 167; cf. 199. See also Fidler, *Dream Theophany*, 41 n. 171.
88. See the discussion of the term "the Jacob story cycle" in Chapter 3
89. Fidler, *Dream Theophany*, 132.
90. Ibid., 132–33 n. 6.
91. Ibid., 133, 203–7.

messages separately, and to show how they combine with and interpret one another.

An attempt will be made to show how Jacob's Dream proves that dreams are central not only in the Jacob story cycle but in the stories of the Patriarchs as a whole. The centrality seems to emerge clearly in approaching the dream as a literary work. As indicated in the introduction to this chapter, interpreting the dream and its message is a task of literary analysis in which the symbolic vision focuses on the *mise en abyme* of the stories of the Patriarchs as they come into (*'olim*) or depart (*yordim*) from the Promised Land.

In addition, if we accept that the biblical dream functions as a communication channel between God and humans, Jacob's Dream makes a unique contribution. Furthermore, the very fact that the narrator chose the dream as a channel of communication between God and Jacob shows his own positive attitude towards dreams and their prophetic value.

2. Research Methods and Methodology

2.1. The Aims Method or the Source Criticism Method[92]

The purpose of this study is to try to understand more fully the biblical story of Jacob's Dream at Bethel in its final form. Specifically, it seeks to examine the narrative's form and its significance. I prefer a synchronic investigation[93] over a diachronic one,[94] and so my study centers on a close reading[95] of the text itself.

92. M. Buber, *The Way of the Bible* (Jerusalem: Mosad Bialik, 1964), 319. Buber writes: "We see before our eyes how purposes criticism is pushing out source criticism."

93. Y. Gitay, "Theories of Literature and the Question of (Hebrew) Biblical Theology: A Prolegomenon," *SJOT* 10 (1996): 68: "The focus is on the text as a whole."

94. On the distinction between the terms diachronic (comes from Greek = *dia* means "way"; *chronos* means "time") and synchronic (*syn* in Greek means "with"), see, e.g., T. Rodin Obersky, *From the Oaks of Mamre to Sodom (Genesis 18–19): Structure and Literary Formulation* (Jerusalem: Simor, 1982), 11; A. Roitman, "The Structure and Significance of a Jewish Book" (Ph.D. diss., The Hebrew University, 1992), 3–35. See also Polak, *Narrative*, 345–57. Polak opens the discussion of the terms *diachronic* and *synchronic* thus: "A study of the literary formulation assumes in advance that the unit under discussion…is of a piece and as such came to the mind of the narrator. Thus the work is examined as a whole, without considering questions of its historical development." With that, Polak (438–39) considers the biblical story as one that developed over generations, and writes: "In this sense it [the Bible story] resembles the great ornamented churches of Europe that were built over the centuries, tier on tier, and since building was the work of generation, it

More attention will be paid to the aims that emerge from the completed text in its present form than to the sources from which the story emerged. I agree with E. L. Greenstein, who wrote:

> It is used to be taken for granted that the way to explain the meaning of a thing would be to trace its history. To borrow an illustration, one would explain a house by recounting the stages in its planning and construction rather than by describing its architecture, the functions and interrelations of its parts, its situation in its environment, and so forth. Similarly, it was assumed in such modern classics of Biblical exegesis as Speiser's *Genesis* and Sarna's *Understanding Genesis* that the best way to expound the meaning of a Biblical text, such as a story, would be to trace its history—the way that the story evolved into its present form. If we could reconstruct its literary or cultural history, it was thought, we could discover its meaning or significance.[96]

In his preface to *Reading the Fractures of Genesis*, D. M. Carr wrote: "This book attempts to build bridges between methods that are often seen as mutually contradictory: *diachronic* study to a text's formation and *synchronic* study of the texts present form."[97]

An attempt will be made, however, to show that classic source criticism applied to the story of Jacob's Dream (Gen 28:10–22) only serves to make it harder to understand. This becomes clearer when we discuss the boundaries of the dream and the division into sources.

---

shows evidence of changes in plan. Nonetheless there is comprehensive artistic unity: even a building that evolved in this way necessarily evidences a general plan that cannot be ignored, a definite stylistic perception and a clearly defined outlook as to the different parts and the architectural nature of the whole. All these elements come together to create the majestic appearance that grows in the course of the generations."

95. I shall take into account such literary features as keywords, designations, multiple verbs and story boundaries. I shall point out the links between parts of the story and be alert to double causation, apposition, and connections between the story and those nearer and farther from it. This is in the spirit of intra-Bible commentary on biblical stories.

96. See E. L. Greenstein, "The Torah as She Is Read," in *Essays on Biblical Method and Translation* (BJS 92; Atlanta, Ga.: Scholars Press, 1989), 29.

97. D. M. Carr, *Reading the Fractures of Genesis: Historical and Literary Approaches* (Louisville, Ky.: Westminster John Knox, 1996), vii. In his 1999 article, Carr challenges the views of Van Seters: "Genesis 28, 10–22 and Transmission-Historical Method: A Reply to John Van Seters," *ZAW* 111 (1999): 399–403. See J. Van Seters, "Divine Encounter at Bethel (Gen 28:10–20) in Recent Literary-Critical Study of Genesis," *ZAW* 110 (1998): 503–13. I see the argument mainly as diachronic, focusing on the emergence of the story; I and am uncertain regarding its contribution to the story's synchronic aspect.

2.2. Links Between Form and Content, Structure and Significance

There is a link between form and content, both of which serve the purpose of a given story. Moreover, the structure of a work is linked to its significance, which can find expression only through its formal design, and only close scrutiny of the form discloses the message within the literary work. M. Weiss is our guide:

> Every idea formulated in language can exist only in that form, in those letters, in this linguistic combination, in this rhythm. All taken together are the essence of the work, not ornaments to it, not a uniform in which the writer dressed his ideas and which he can remove without changing the entire work's essence and quality. The relationship between an idea and its formulation must not be compared to the one between body and its attire.[98]

In the present discussion I shall try to reveal the story as it is, not how it came into existence. As Fish aptly puts it, "A modern scholar facing a complex text that contains contradictions, signs of deletion and the like generally tends to conclude that the text is structured from 'different sources' or 'different traditions' or that it has been through 'different editorial stages.'"[99]

In contrast to the source-critical approach to a biblical text, Fish presents the structuralist approach, an approach that

> it is not interested in "historical aspects" of the text...does not investigate a. the historical background of the events related in the text. Nor does it examine b. "how the text came into being," that is, its division into documents and the dating of each one. The issue of "earlier and later," essential in other systems of investigation, is irrelevant in the method of researchers following the structuralist approach.[100]

The structuralist method dates from the mid-twentieth century. Among its progenitors are F. de Saussure in linguistics, and Claude Lévi-Strauss[101] in anthropology. Researchers in biblical literature also adopted the structuralist approach, a move which has made a significant contribution to their understanding of Bible stories and the linkage between them.

---

98. M. Weiss, *Scripture in Its Own Image* (Jerusalem: Mosad Bialik, 1963), 20. See also M. Weiss, *Scriptures in Their Own Light: Collected Essays* (Jerusalem: Mosad Bialik, 1988), 293. See, further, Y. Zakovitch, *Life of Samson (Judges 13–16): A Literary-Critical Analysis* (Jerusalem: Mosad Bialik, 1992), 13, on the link between form and content.

99. A. H. Fish, "Eldad and Medad Prophesy within the Camp: A Structuralist Study of Numbers 11," *SBE* 5 (1997): 45.

100. Ibid.

101. A. Shapira, "Jacob and Esau: A Reading for Multiple Meanings," *SBE* 4 (1996): 250 n. 9; C. Lévi-Strauss, *Structural Anthropology*, vol. 1 (trans. C. Jacobson and B. Grundfest Schoepf; New York: Basic, 1963).

Gitay maintains—rightly, in my view—that moving from the diachronic to the synchronic approach changes the research purpose as he defines it.[102] The change requires study and acceptance of "the text as given" as an integral whole, not focusing exclusively on the historical intent of the original author. With that, the structuralist approach need not be accepted as the only objective theory, barring us from other interpretations embedded in the text. A few criticisms of the structuralist approach as applied to the Jacob story cycle follow.

2.3. *Inner-Biblical Interpretation—the Polemic Approach*

Biblical interpretation began within the Bible itself. As Zakovitch defines it,

> The beginning of biblical interpretation can be found within the Bible itself.[103] Inner-biblical interpretation is the light one biblical text sheds on another. The interpreting verse is used either to solve a difficulty in the interpreted text, or to adapt the interpreted text to the interpreter's own ideas. The interpreting text may be found far from the interpreted one, close to it, or even incorporated in it.[104]

In *An Introduction to Inner-Biblical Interpretation*, Zakovitch writes:

> By inner-biblical interpretation we mean the light that one text sheds on the other, whether to solve a problem in the immediate or remote context or to adapt the text to the beliefs and opinions of the commentator... Not in every case will one be the comment and the other the commented upon: sometimes commentary is mutual.[105]

The synchronic literary approach encourages dialogue between stories. As Todorov has noted, "There is no utterance without relation to other utterances and that is essential."[106] Recognizing the dialogue/polemic

---

102. Gitay, *Theories*, 63.
103. See M. Fishbane's important book: *Biblical Interpretation in Ancient Israel* (Oxford: Clarendon, 1985).
104. Y. Zakovitch, *"And You Shall Tell Your Son": The Concept of the Exodus in the Bible* (Jerusalem: Magnes, 1991), 15.
105. Y. Zakovitch, *An Introduction to Inner-Biblical Interpretation* (Even Yehuda: Reches, 1992), 9. Zakovitch follows a diachronic approach when stating that one text explicates another. I favor the synchronic intra-textual approach that disregards historical affinity between the texts. The reader brings the two texts together, as Roland Barthes maintains in his famous article, "The Death of the Author."
106. From Gitay, *Theories*, 64, quoting T. Todorov, *Michail Bakhtin: The Dialogical Principle* (trans. W. Godzich; THL 13; Minneapolis: University of Minnesota Press, 1984), 60.

between stories helps to understand them. Any comparison requires an examination of similarities and differences in language and content. Similarities may reveal a connecting link, whereas differences betray the divergent messages that each wanted to stress.

There are two modes, then, in biblical commentary. One is the open type relating specifically to a familiar text, like the reworking of the historiographic literature in the book of Chronicles. The second is concealed commentary to be discerned by the sensitive reader who is aware of this possibility. Here I shall try to reveal the concealed commentary that helps reveal the message in the dream.

2.4. *The Hypothetical "Editor" in the Bible—the Narrator*

With Zakovitch and others I agree that the editor "is not confused, bringing together thoughtlessly and by chance stories that he has come across, but a thinking, creative artist who crafts a mosaic that is no less a work of art than the original tiles that make it up." Zakovitch adds: "The work of explication is creative in the full sense of the word, so that any distinction between authors and editors, compilers and commentators is both difficult to make and artificial. The editor is a commentator, as is the author attempting to explicate a story on the basis of one he has written himself to place it beside the story he is explicating."[107]

In view of the foregoing, let us try to understand Jacob's Dream.

The term "editor" emerges as a problematic one, not only because he/she cannot be identified, but because my interest is in the meaning or meanings within the text in its *present form*.[108] I shall not discuss the hypothetical editor's work unless it produces some advantage in understanding the completed text. Hence, that problematic term is replaced with "narrator." The author is swallowed up, as it were, within the story.[109] The reader must assume he/she is there, relating the story the reader is reading. In discussing the two readings, I shall take up another aspect of the editorial role in the Bible story.

---

107. Y. Zakovitch, review of J. P. Fokkelman, *Narrative Art in Genesis: Specimens of Stylistic and Structural Analysis*, *Shnaton: An Annual for Biblical and Ancient Near Eastern Studies* 14 (1980): 302–8.

108. See E. L. Greenstein, "Theory and Argument in Biblical Criticism," *HAR* 10 (1986): 77–93; see also Gitay, *Theories*, 63, who recognizes the diachronic approach and supports Greenstein.

109. D. M. Gunn and D. N. Fewell, *Narrative in the Hebrew Bible* (Oxford: Oxford University Press, 1933), 53. Gunn and Fewell suggest categorizing the narrator similarly to the characters in the story, noting, however, the difference between them. Gunn and Fewell note, for instance, that the narrator relates the story while the others act in it.

2.5. *The Reading with Multiple Meanings, or the Two Meanings, in the Biblical Story*

2.5.1. *Two readings—a definition.* When referring to "two readings" of a story, I am seeking to imply that at least two understandings of it, and at least two meanings, are possible. The number "two" is not to be understood literally, but rather is an indication that more than one meaning is possible. In literary analysis this has also been called "double significance reading," "multiple significance reading," and the like. My working assumption is that two meanings in a biblical text are reflected within that text itself and do not come from the imagination or wishful thinking of the reader.[110] The two (or more) meanings are not mere possibilities; the narrator, in fact, at times even encourages them. As readers we are asked to reveal this phenomenon and use it to disclose the complexity and richness of the message now revealed in its full greatness. Emphasis is on the writing, not on the reader. The assertion that the number of possible readings is as numerous as the potential number of readers refers *to readerly viewpoints*, and does not bespeak of the multifaceted nature of the work itself.

This definition relates to more than one reading in the order of the broadening concentric circles that make up the text: "the word" with its varied meanings; "the word combinations" in the story; "the sentence" or the verse; the links between verses—are they descriptive or causational, for instance? Two readings, then, derive from the legitimate possibility of more than one reading for each component of the story.

2.5.2. *Two readings in art.* The possibility of two readings has an established place not only in literature but in art. In the famous graphical example presented below—which Menahem Perry has discussed at length[111]—do we see one woman or two? Is she young or old?[112] The answer, of course, is that we see both. The dichotomy in our nature leads us to make "yes" or "no" decisions that often mislead. The young woman's chin becomes the nose of the old woman, and the young woman's neck the mouth of the old woman.

---

110. The reader aware of the possibility of two readings understands also that not everything is obvious, and is open to there being more than one truth in a text. Being aware of multiple readings requires creativity and involves the shedding of old prejudices, going beyond familiar and accepted concepts to examine others' opinions.

111. M. Perry, "The Dynamics of the Literary Text," *Hasifrut* 28 (1979): 14 n. 10: "The original, drawn by the caricaturist V. A. Hill, appeared in *Puck* on November 6, 1915 over the caption 'My wife and my mother-in-law'."

112. Both faces are in profile, making possible the interchange of parts.

The second example of two readings is another famous image, "The Goblet." Do we see two black images in profile or only a white goblet? The answer, again, is both. The facing profiles create the goblet.[113]

113. According to Professor E. L. Greenstein, "Until you showed me I didn't see the old woman at all, meaning that the 'reader' has to be trained… But there aren't many works in which you can find two [fully overlapping] faces!" I fully agree. This view seems to strengthen my contention that not every text allows for two readings. The reader will not find them if they are not there. Hence I find most apt the following statement by A. Oz, *A Tale of Love and Darkness* (Jerusalem: Keter, 2002), 38, who notes that we are discussing "the area between the work and the reader." These aspects are interdependent. Without a trained reader the double significance in the word is not discovered, but if there is no double meaning no one will discover it.

S. Rimmon-Kenan notices the phenomenon of two readings in literature and in art.[114] On the story of Jacob's Dream I will demonstrate the phenomenon called *mise en abyme*, which was explained in the introduction to the present chapter. As noted, *mises en abyme* occur in art as well as in fiction. Multiple readings are also an integral part of biblical creativity. Its purpose is not simply ornament or esthetic variation, and it is found not only in poetry but in prose fiction.[115] It is not an outcome of will, creative invention[116] and arbitrariness on the reader's part. Both readings are reflected in the text itself—from its language (word, sentence/verse, entire story).[117] Indeed, a claim that there are multiple readings for a Bible text cannot be arbitrary: proof must be brought from the text itself.

2.5.3. *How do the two readings relate to one another?* "The two hypotheses together are the legitimate reading of the story."[118]

The point of departure is that the two readings are present within the work itself, and that if readers find them, their understanding of the story will be enriched. The focus, then, is on the area (the space) between the text and the reader, asking as well how the two readings are linked, and how the link contributes to the understanding of the story.

---

114. Rimmon-Kenan, *Poetics*, 91, on the link between illustration and written text. On double meaning in the biblical text, see J. Grossman, "Ambiguity in the Biblical Narrative and Its Contribution to the Literary Formation" (Ph.D. diss., Bar Ilan University, 2006).

115. D. Yellin, "Educational Theory," in *The Writings of David Yellin*, vol. 6 (ed. E. Z. Melamed; Jerusalem: Reuven Mass, 1983), 254: "Words of the language having more than one definition have served poets and orators as means of ornamentation. They may have used them two or three times in a single statement/article, and each time differently, while at other times they may have used a word just once, but in a way that suggested both definitions, so it could be explained either way…in two ways."

116. The Midrashic statement that "The Torah has seventy faces" allows for more than one reading, but within the theological and ideological considerations of the reader. Shapira, "Multiple Meanings," 250 n. 8, relates to this issue: "Clearly motivation for the midrashic reading is theological" (reflecting the view of its author). I, however, maintain that the basis for the double significance lies within the language itself, by its very nature. I accept Shapira's statement.

117. Professor E. L. Greenstein states: "It is interesting how the text gets a double message across without a reader." This, I would contend, does not happen. While I would accept that there is interdependence—i.e. that without a reader to reveal it there is no ambivalence—the reader does not discover ambivalence that is not in the text.

118. Perry and Sternberg, *Ironic Eyes*, 286.

Shapira[119] lists four types of multiple significance readings:

1. A double significance reading ($a + b$, where a differs from b)
2. An ambivalent reading ($a + b$, where a contradicts b)
3. An ambiguous reading (a or b)
4. A dialectic reading (where a positive a arises from a negative b, or vice versa).

I see these four as four possible relationships between the two readings. It is not enough to recognize each one: one should ask how each helps to understand the text. In each story, then, one should seek out the nature of the linkage, to see how it contributes to the understanding of the text.

2.5.4. *Interrelationships between the two readings: Are they necessarily the result of biblical editing?* The two readings are not, in my view, solely the result of biblical editing. In her *Hidden Polemics in Biblical Narrative*, Yairah Amit writes: "An additional premise is that this literature, which developed over centuries, is naturally polyphonic, a literature with many voices. The multiple voices are the outcome of the circumstances and process of its development."[120] The assumption that multiple voices are the outcome of biblical development from different sources is one that I find inadequate.

I agree that one plausible explanation for the multiple voices in the biblical canon before readers today is the way that canon developed. Nonetheless, it is just as plausible that the narrator and/or editor chose,

119. Shapira, "Multiple Meanings," 249.
120. Y. Amit, *Revealed and Hidden in the Bible: Hidden Polemics in Biblical Narrative* (Tel Aviv: Yediot Aharonot, 2003), 15. In her *The Book of Judges: The Art of Editing* (Jerusalem: Mosad Bialik, 1992), 2, Amit writes: "Attention to the variety of narrators and the long process of transcription and editing prevents a return to the original text and moves the center of gravity from narration to editing." On biblical editing, she writes: "Even the reader of biblical literature aware of complex transmission and editing processes must…assume in some sense…a unified composition…to seek out links between the elements linked in the guiding editorial line… The assumption of unity should not become a sole purpose…but acts as a brake on commentary that pursues sources, traditions and primary units, creating artificial problems that help factor the text down into its components" (p. 23). On p. 17, Amit writes about the *hidden editor*: "the summaries of narrator-editors and compilers of the text, who worked toward a central principle of unity, or in spite of their involvement, did deviate from it or divert parts of it away from the editorial guideline, giving an integrated character to all its parts." See also the reference to D. Ravid, *Joab Son of Zeruiah: Controversial Hero* (Tel Aviv: Hakibbutz Hameuhad, 2009), 11 n. 2.

consciously or unconsciously, to tell the story in its full complexity, showing how rich and how complex the story is. Amit's assumption is based on a diachronic approach that deals with the history of the text's development, while in my book, that center/focus moves to the text itself in its final form, or, more specifically, to the space embracing the work and the reader. I see focus on the text itself as the reader's goal, not merely as a means and a restraint.

Amit's book emphasizes the work of the editors and editing in the Bible,[121] giving them full credit for its pluralism,[122] since they did not censor either revealed or concealed polemics. She states:

> The polemics are possible because of the pluralism and the polyphonic character of the biblical editors who did not prefer one voice over the other, but preserved the varied voices. Thus the editing process reflected different positions... Is this pluralism artificial, forced—reflecting different attitudes... Does this pluralism reflect hesitation, want of courage and of ability to decide among the later generations who left opposing positions side by side because they could not choose between them? Or does it perhaps indicate the conscious unwillingness of the editors to decide unequivocally, as they knew the multifaceted nature of the human spirit and hence the importance of presenting different views?... There is room to praise, laud and extol the open mindedness of these editors, by whose grace the Book of Books serves so many and such different [people] as a guidebook for life.[123]

Despite the impressive analysis, I agree but also disagree. Amit has given too much credit to the editors, and not enough to the writers, narrators[124] and authors. I recognize editing as creativity and am grateful to those who preserved and did not censor out beliefs and opinions. But who am I to decide whether they or the author created the two readings in the text? True, the editors have the final word and one assumes their influence over the finished product. Nonetheless, I believe that Amit's praise, with which I concur, is due to both authors and editors. To separate them is both impossible and unnecessary.

Hence I prefer to speak of "varied facets," rather than "multiple voices." Even if not explicitly stated, the latter may conceal numerous

---

121. See, e.g., J. Rosenberg, "Biblical Narrative," in *Back to the Sources: Reading the Classic Jewish Texts* (ed. B. W. Holtz; New York: Simon & Schuster, 1984), 31–82.
122. Amit, *Hidden*, 16.
123. Ibid., 252.
124. The narrator is a figure embedded in the story. I prefer to call the teller of "the story writer," "the author" or "the creative scribe."

authors and compilers that the editor brought together. "Varied facets" is better because it relates to the text as it is (a synchronic approach), while "multiple voices" points to the diachronic development of the text.

My approach rejects[125] the traditional literary view that the commentator must look for the one meaning.[126] Is this one meaning the true one? M. Greenberg dealt with this problem at length.[127] He recognizes that the teaching and studying of the Bible are intended to facilitate "the simple, authentic meaning of the texts... However, how can we the contemporary readers do this if the text is basically composed of elements from different periods?"[128]

Does this detract from the value of the biblical writing? Greenberg thinks not: "The outstanding aspect of the Bible's sacred character throughout the generations is the work of interpreting it, its abundantly varied nature making it a valid guide and a standard of what is worthy and exalted, at all times and everywhere..."[129] More than that, "The power of the Bible stems precisely from the wealth of significances that its readers, scholars, devotees and attackers found in their interpretations of it."[130]

The Bible reader is used to looking for the "correct" literal meaning of the written text. I do not propose to go into the theoretical issue of whether such an interpretation exists. It suffices to say that so often the biblical text invites us to find a double meaning, and the two will be fully or partially explicated in the literary unit. Such as approach explains Ps 62:12: "One thing God has spoken; two things have I heard."[131]

---

125. See H. Barzel, *New Interpretations of Literary Texts: From Theory to Method* (Ramat Gan: Bar Ilan University Press, 1990), 83; Shapira, "Multiple Meanings," 258. See also W. Brogan, "Plato's Pharmakon: Between Two Repetitions," in *Derrida and Deconstruction* (ed. H. J. Silverman; New York: Routledge, 1978), 8.

126. See W. Empson, *Seven Types of Ambiguity* (London: Chatto & Windus, 1930). Empson was outstanding among scholars who disputed the traditional literary assumption that one must look for the author's one precise meaning.

127. See M. Greenberg, *On the Bible and Judaism: A Collection of Writings* (Tel Aviv: Am Oved, 1984), xx. I reject any attempt to reveal "the one, true correct meaning" for the same reason as I reject the structuralist approach regarding a so-called objective element in the text, to be discussed further in connection with the Jacob story cycle.

128. Ibid., 345.

129. Ibid., 348.

130. Ibid., 344.

131. Y. Zakovitch, *"I Will Utter Riddles from Ancient Times": Riddles and Dreams-Riddles in Biblical Narrative* (Tel Aviv: Am Oved, 2005), 88.

2.5.5. *Two readings are no accident and no misunderstanding.* Although I agree with Greenberg as to "the wealth of meanings Bible readers have discovered in their interpretations," I stipulate nonetheless that the interpretations must not be arbitrary.[132] In this sense I am close to the approach advocated by Perry and Sternberg in their ground-breaking work on the issue of two readings in the Bible.[133] According to them, reading for multiple meanings helps reveal the complex world of the story. Shapira lucidly defined his approach to ambiguity: "The ambiguity of a word or an expression is no accident[134] or misunderstanding of the expression, but on the contrary, enriches it. It is the text at its best, a focus of the interpretive process, of which the entire text is composed. Hence every explicator or critic of a text (including the biblical text) must consider this premise as the basis of his reading."[135]

The primary basis of this approach is awareness that the language is ambiguous. We know that in Hebrew the same word may have opposite meanings. *nkr*, for example, is the root of both verbs featuring in the encounter of Joseph with his brothers, when "he recognized (*vayakirem*[136]) them but he acted like a stranger (*vayinaker*) toward them" (Gen 42:7). Another example comes from Job 2:9, where the words of Job's wife to

---

132. Greenberg, *Bible*, 346, aware of this, maintained: "While Rashi understood the Bible in the context of the Sages' world, Radak, who lived after him, did so in the context of the Rashbam's theological philosophy. The main difference between us and them is that we are aware that meaning is relative to its context, and consequently of the relative nature of 'the true meaning.' Thus a door is open for us to investigate layers of biblical meaning."

133. Perry and Sternberg, *Ironic Eyes*, 283.

134. S. A. Geller, "The Struggle of the Jacob: The Uses of Enigma in a Biblical Narrative," *JANES* 14 (1982): 49. He criticizes "the historical approach that sees the internal tension as an accident of history, the result of clumsy assembling on the part of careless editors."

135. Shapira, "Multiple Meanings," 251–52. See also Y. Zakovitch, "'One thing God has spoken; two things have I heard': Ambiguous Expressions in Biblical Literature," in *Memorial Gathering in Memory of Professor Meir Weiss Thirty Days After His Death* (ed. S. Japhet, B. Schwartz and Y. Zakovitch; Jerusalem: The Hebrew University Institute for Jewish Studies, 1999). Zakovitch, however, sounds more cautious, saying: "I have no intention of addressing the…issue of whether there exists a single correct interpretation. Suffice it to say that often the text arouses us to discover a double meaning, and often both meanings will be expressed fully or in part in the literary unit." Concluding with "the Midianite dream" (Judg 7:13) Zakovitch says "The numerous possibilities for interpreting 'a loaf of barley bread was whirling…' *enriches* the reading and gives it depth."

136. See Ruth 2:10: *lehakireni* veanokhi *nokhriya*.

her stricken husband—"Blaspheme (*barekh*) God and die!"—makes use of two meanings of the word *barekh*, which also carries the sense of "bless."[137]

To return to Shapira on reading for multiple significances as an aid to understanding the Bible: "According to Alter, Barth, Geller, Greenstein, Weiss, Miscal, Fokkelman and others, such a reading enriches both reader and text. Since it is open and in constant tension, it allows the reader to delve deeper into the complex reality reflected in the text."[138]

Once again, it does not suffice to identify the two readings: their affinity and interrelationship must also be recognized. Yellin, in reference to two readings for the same word, writes: "With that word the poet relates to its two definitions simultaneously, he surprises the hearer by letting the double meaning stand."[139]

To conclude the discussion, I should state that I do not intend to present a comprehensive literary theory, but rather to acquaint readers with the guidelines of my approach. A key quotation from the introduction to D. Ravid's book[140] on the biblical Joab illustrates my point:

> Significantly, the narrator does not simplify the readers' task, for although trustworthy and omniscient,[141] he does not tell all he knows,[142] and hence does not state his opinion of Joab unequivocally. And so it is left to the

137. E. L. Greenstein, "Job's Wife: Was She Right After All?," *Beit Mikra* 49 (2004): 19–31.
138. Shapira, "Multiple Meanings," 257.
139. Yellin, *Educational Theory*, 254–55. I wish to extend Yellin's definition beyond the poet to every author, and from the poem to the story.
140. Ravid, *Joab*, 13.
141. See Sternberg, *Repetition*, 133: "The biblical narrator is blessed with superhuman abilities: he is omniscient, completely trustworthy and in conscious control of his story material." However, with due respect to the narrator's awareness, the unconscious element in the story cannot be ignored. Sternberg stresses further (p. 136): "the biblical writer's control over his world extends to God himself, as when he penetrates His thoughts or assembles a composition of judgments greater than God's whose name he proposes to exalt." See also Polak, *Narrative*, 313–14; See and Y. Amit, "'The Glory of Israel Will Not Lie Nor Repent; For he Is Not a Man, That he Should Repent': On the Trustworthiness of Narrators and Spokesmen in the Bible Story," in *Or leYa'akov: Research Studies on the Bible and the Dead Sea Scrolls in Memory of Yaakov Shalom Licht* (ed. Y. Hoffman and F. Polak; Jerusalem: Mosad Bialik, 1997), 50.
142. Perry and Sternberg, *Ironic Eyes*, 288–91; idem, "Caution, Literature! On Problems of Interpretation and Poetics in the Bible Story," *Hasifrut* 2 (1970): 629; B. Arpeli, "Caution, Biblical Literature! On the Story of David and Bathsheba and Questions of Poetics in the Biblical Story," *Hasifrut* 2 (1970): 597; Y. Amit, *Reading Biblical Stories* (Jerusalem: Misrad Habitakhon, 2000), 105; R. Alter, *The Art of Biblical Narrative* (New York: Basic, 1981), 178–80.

reader to ferret out the secret of Joab's character, which breathes life into the text.[143] Izhar notes: 'Obviously there is nothing new in the assumption that the reader is a necessary partner for the author, for as there is no literary work without an author, so there would be no literary work without an interested spectator: it would remain a potential, a possibility, waiting for its hour as a field waits for rain.'[144] The reader is to bring to life or to wipe out a work of art...as an individual reader or through a group's collective response. A work of art has no status unless people give it that status.[145]

As the approach that focuses on the writer is unacceptable, neither, in my view, is the one focusing on the reader. The emphasis must be on the work itself—on the Bible story itself as an objective, not as a means to one. With that, understanding requires knowledge of the author, his time, his viewpoint, as far as they are known, and of the reader as well. Authors and readers are, in my view, partners in understanding. The question which deserves more attention is in itself problematic. Amos Oz writes, "Whoever looks for the heart of the story in the space between the work and the author, is making a mistake. The place to look is...in the space between the text and the reader."[146]

As I see it, rather than deciding whether the key point for understanding a literary work lies in the work itself or in the reader, one should focus, as Amos Oz so aptly says, "on the place/space between the text and you."[147] The idea runs like a scarlet thread through the/our entire book: not "either...or" but "both...and."

2.5.6. *Two readings of the David and Bathsheba story (2 Samuel 11): An ironic look at the king.*[148] Since my way of showing the simultaneously

---

143. W. Iser, "Indefiniteness and the Response of the Reader of the Short Story to the Structure of Affinity in the Literary Text," *Hasifrut* 21 (1975): 2.

144. Samekh Izhar, *To Read a Story* (Tel Aviv: Am Oved, 1982), 225.

145. Professor E. L. Greenstein enacted this to me: He opened a Bible, looked at it and asked aloud: "What does it say?" He and I and the work are all silent. "Did you ever see a text speak by itself?," he asked. A literary work says nothing without a reader. The reader determines how the text is understood. Greenstein continued, emphasizing that the text depends on the reader: "It has no meaning save what the reader understands." I would add that the reader depends on the text s/he reacts to. Without the text there is no reader, so that the definition relating to the space between the work and the reader is perfectly congruent here.

146. Oz, *Love*, 38.

147. Ibid., 39.

148. Perry and Sternberg, *Ironic Eyes*, 263–92; Y. I. Peleg, "Two Readings of the Story of David, Bathsheba and Uriah" (paper presented at the International Meeting of the SBL, Tartu, Estonia, July 27, 2009, under the theme: "The Strings of King David's Life").

1. *Preface to the Story of Jacob's Dream*

revealed and the concealed readings of Jacob's Dream is broadly in agreement with that of Perry and Sternberg,[149] I begin by considering the way these two scholars have approached the David and Bathsheba story. Their view is that to understand the world of the text, the reader has to build a network of gaps to fill the void, resolving the questions and connections that are not treated explicitly. The reader does this while reading, through assumptions and hypotheses that link up the details, and link them to the work as a whole. The writer "imposes" the process on the reader by not providing specific answers.

The reader cannot be arbitrary in this task. A significant criterion in accepting or rejecting an hypothesis is its relevance to a maximum number of details in the work itself.[150] The David and Bathsheba story, told in a seemingly neutral manner, creates a gap and a tension with the events themselves. There is no judgmental statement about the king's act, nor do we contemporary readers know, for instance, what Bathsheba and Uriah thought about it, what they knew and what they did not know. The reader has to fill in the blanks. Lacking an insight into the minds of the protagonists who arouse so much suspense and curiosity, readers have to provide one for themselves if they are to understand the story.

Perry and Sternberg see this as a deliberate authorial strategy, taking advantage of the fact that the reader must fill in the gaps to create irony.

One means that allows for an ironic reading is the frequent use of the Hebrew conjunction *waw*, which has the double meaning of "and" and "but," allowing the reader to see either an addition or a contrast. Thus "*and* David remained in Jerusalem" may also be read "*but* David remained in Jerusalem." Translation rules out the possible double sense of the Hebrew original,[151] so that the charm of the hidden irony is lost.

The following shows the two readings of the Hebrew conjunction *waw*:

---

149. The link between my commentary and theirs on Jacob's Dream is my initiative and my sole responsibility.

150. Perry and Sternberg, *Ironic Eyes*, 265. Their examples of non-legitimate hypotheses include some that were put forward by the Sages, coming from their own world and not that of the text. At the same time, the authors note that the Sages' questions are not only legitimate but reveal a lack in the world of the text.

151. In Jacob's vow, the *waw* seems to link two sentences and cannot be used to place the transition between Jacob's conditions to his obligations. If the *waw* had been replaced by *az*, "then," the transition issue would be resolved. By contrast, the English translation does use "then," ruling out the alternative possibility present in the Hebrew original. On the frequent use of the contrasting *waw* in the Jacob story cycle, see A. Shapira, "Jacob and Esau: Two Readings" (Ph.D. diss., The Jewish Theological Seminary, 1988), 54–55.

> *And* it came to pass, after the year was expired, at the time when kings go forth to battle that David sent Joab,
> *And* his servants with him
> *and* all Israel
> *and* they destroyed the children of Ammon
> *and* besieged Rabbah;
> *but* David tarried at Jerusalem. (2 Sam 11:1 KJV)

This opening presents the story background to the reader. The question is whether one is looking at an innocently neutral informative description or whether the description is ironically critical of David's conduct, so different from that of all the others (the kings, Joab, all Israel).

The ironical criticism of David is strengthened when we, the contemporary readers, examine the repeated use of the letter *waw* ("and"), which is not a separate word, but an element prefixed to the following word. After a sequence of verbs beginning with *waw* meaning "and" in v. 1—וַיִּשְׁלַח...וַיַּשְׁחִתוּ...וַיָּצֻרוּ—there is a change in usage when we come to David's remaining in Jerusalem. Here we have וְדָוִד יוֹשֵׁב בִּירוּשָׁלַיִם, "But David tarried at Jerusalem." Is this difference simply a matter of style? Or does it signify that *waw* here is the negative "but," whose purpose is to describe David in contrast to the kings and in contrast to his people?

Indeed, according to the context, two readings of the *waw* are possible.[152] With the "and" meaning we contemporary readers have an informative description of what happened. However, the second option, where David's tarrying at home is prefaced by "but," the description is not neutral—its goal is to present David ironically, in negative contrast not only to the kings, but also to his people. The Hebrew source allows for the ambiguity—and therein lies its beauty—whereas the translation allows for only one meaning, resulting in a loss of power.[153] This distinction has linguistic support, since the connecting *waw* in the sense of "and" is consistently attached to the verb, while at the end of the passage, in the sense of "but," it is attached to the noun ("but David tarried still at Jerusalem").

Another possibility for two readings surrounds the possibility of whether Uriah knew his wife had been unfaithful.[154] The text appears to

---

152. The grammatical changes in the sentence lend additional support to the ironic interpretation. Using *veDavid yoshev*, rather than *veyashev David*, is intended to suggest to the reader that the function of this verb, in contrast to those preceding it, has changed, i.e., that David, in contrast to his people who went to war, remained at home.

153. The New JPS translation (1985) offers a neutral reading that preserves the ambiguity: "David remained in Jerusalem."

154. Perry and Sternberg, *Ironic Eyes*, 271.

take advantage of the impossibility of filling two sets of gaps. It has to maintain both of them, and benefits from the tension between the two. David asks Uriah, "Why did you not go down to your house?" (2 Sam 11:10), and Uriah answers, "The Ark and Israel and Judah are located at Succoth, and my master Joab and your Majesty's men are camped in the open; how can I go home, eat and drink and sleep with my wife?" (v. 11)

The first reading is that Uriah is the ideal soldier, a guileless man loyal to his commander and his comrades. The second reading is that Uriah's answer conceals irony, upbraiding the king: "go [Hebrew: come] home… and sleep with my wife." The Hebrew uses "come," with its sexual connotation seemingly confirmed by "sleep with my wife." Uriah's choice of verb stands in contrast to the David's "go." Another ambiguity follows. "As you live, by your very life, I will not do this!" Does Uriah mean "what you did to my wife," or is he proclaiming his devotion? Perry and Sternberg cite three examples of the two readings from non-biblical literature: H. N. Bialik's "The Dead of the Wilderness,"[155] "The Turn of the Screw" by Henry James[156] and Nikolai Gogol's "The Cloak."[157]

In the story of Jacob's Dream, the relationship between the revealed and the concealed interpretations, the realistic and the symbolic, is different, as I shall try to show. Here the symbolic interpretation does not contradict the realistic one, but rather the two complement[158] and explain one another. In any case, one must look for the connection between the readings and what it teaches us about the text.

---

155. J. Ha'efrati, "The Dead of the Wilderness: A Descriptive Poem," *Hasifrut* 1 (1965): 101–29, writes of a poem "structured from the two simultaneous impressions with no decision made between them… We are in perpetual doubt as to whether the situation is mythic or realistic."

156. Perry and Sternberg, *Ironic Eyes*, propose two schools of interpretation. In one, "the ghosts of the servants seen by the governess are actual ghosts," in which case this is a ghost story. The other school maintains that the governess is hallucinating and imagines them, and that this is a psychological story. Their response sheds light on our issue. It is impossible to decide between the two hypotheses. Perry and Sternberg state: "A full reading obliges one to reject each separately, but to accept them as they appear together."

157. In this story, as in James's, Perry and Sternberg maintain, tension exists between possibilities of a realistic or a fantastic reading. Any legitimate reading must make use of both, and of those tensions (*Ironic Eyes*, 286).

158. M. Sternberg, "A Delicate Balance in the Rape of Dinah," *Hasifrut* 4 (1973): 193–231 (esp. 226), relates to this theoretical possibility. See also Shapira, "Multiple Meanings," on four literary phenomena that allow for reading for multiple meanings.

2.5.7. *Examples of two readings in the biblical story.* The previous discussion defined the concept of two (i.e. multiple) readings in the Bible and exemplified two readings of the David and Bathsheba story. It is appropriate to exemplify the two readings approach with selected biblical stories, in which the stories are not a means to an end but an end in themselves.

Deep love and regard for the Bible as a supremely creative work led me to recognize the two readings approach, so that the Bible story remains the focal point and is used to exemplify the literary phenomenon that makes full, holistic reading possible, while the reading experience is preserved. The examples illustrate and clarify the principle of two readings with stories from elsewhere in the Bible. Five illustrative stories have been selected:

1. Jacob's struggle with the angel (Gen 32:23–33).[159] In the context of Jacob's return to the homeland, there are several possibilities for multiple readings.
2. The sale of Joseph (Gen 37:27–28, 36).[160]
3. Jephthah's daughter (Judg 11:31).[161]
4. The book of Jonah.[162]
5. The End of Days vision (Isa 2:2–4; Mic 4:1–5).[163]

The common element of these stories, as will be shown later, is linked to the theme of my book in which they appear—journeys to and from the Land of Israel.

159. Discussed below in Chapter 3.
160. Discussed below in Chapter 3. See also Y. I. Peleg, "'I am the Lord Who Brought You Out from Ur of the Chaldeans': Who Brought Abraham Out and Whence?," *Moed: Annual for Jewish Studies* 17 (2007): 34–35.
161. Discussed below in Chapter 3. See also Y. I. Peleg, "'And If I Came Back in Peace to my Father's House' (Gen 28:21): The Vow and Its Contribution to Understanding and Interpreting Jacob's Dream," *Beit Mikra* 46 (2001): 335–52.
162. See Y. I. Peleg, "'Yet Forty Days, and Nineveh Shall Be Overthrown' (Jonah 3:4): Two Readings of the Book of Jonah," in *God's Word for Our World: Biblical Studies in Honor of Simon John De Vries* (ed. J. H. Ellens et al.; JSOTSup 388; London: T&T Clark International, 2004), 262–74.
163. Discussed below in Chapter 3. See also Y. I. Peleg, "End Time and Afterlife in Judaism: Two Readings of the Vision of the End of Days," in *Heaven, Hell, and the Afterlife: Eternity in Judaism, Christianity, and Islam.* Vol. 1, *End Time and Afterlife in Judaism* (ed. J. H. Ellens; Santa Barbara, Calif.: Praeger, 2013), 7–33. An earlier version of this article was published in Hebrew: see Y. I. Peleg, "The Peace Vision of the End of Days in Isaiah 2:2–5 and the Peace Vision in Micah 4:1–5," *Shnaton: An Annual for Biblical and Ancient Near Eastern Studies* 20 (2010): 27–50.

2.6. Broadening Circles of Commentary

Just as the term "editor" must be explained and defined, so must the term "commentary." In this book I expose the text rather than offer commentary.[164] Greenstein writes: "In my view it is the proper role of literary study to enable the reader to experience the text thoroughly—not to explain the text but to expose it."[165] Should the commentator, then, be objective or subjective?[166] In my view, the text should be approached in the light of empathy, which does not preclude reading it critically.

Every literary unit, and Jacob's Dream in particular (Gen 28:10–22), is examined in the context of its place in widening circles—as an independent unit, within its immediate environment (i.e. juxtaposition), and in its broader context.[167] Here Fokkelman's conclusion expresses my view.[168] Interpreting the story of Jacob's Dream in the *mise en abyme* framework reinforces its link to the stories of the Patriarchs.

---

164. See Shapira, "Two Readings," 12–13, on the distinction between commentary and revealing.

165. E. L. Greenstein, "An Equivocal Reading of the Sale of Joseph," in *Literary Interpretation of Biblical Narrative*, vol. 2 (ed. K. R. R. Gros Louis et al.; Nashville: Abingdon, 1982), 116.

166. Tamar Ross, "The *Musar* Movement and the Hermeneutic Problem in the Talmud Torah," *Tarbiz* 59 (1980): 192, notes a potential problem from "the idea that every scholar requires some sympathy or personal involvement to understand the text… Do these not interfere with scholarly objectivity? For the sake of understanding, what are the desirable proportions between personal involvement and scholarly objectivity?" A distinction between sympathy and empathy seems in order: sympathy is closer to identification, and empathy to ability to sense and understand, though not necessarily identify with a text. I see empathy in this sense as the desired relationship between the subject (reader) and the object (text). Empathy does not rule out critical reading. See the comprehensive discussion in Z. Levi, *Hermeneutics* (Tel Aviv: Sifriyat Poalim, 1986).

167. See Zakovitch, *Inner-Biblical*, 57: "Even if the reader is sure he has found the beginning and the end of the story, he must decide whether it is an independent literary unit that can be explicated without reference to its literary surroundings, or whether it radiates into a broader system from which it gets its own light…" He compares the independent story to "a tile in a broad literary mosaic… As an isolated gem it appears differently than it does in a jewel composed of many gems!"

168. See Fokkelman, *Genesis*, 241: "Following Jacob so closely can easily involve too narrow a range of vision; in tracing the Story of Jacob we have not yet taken in account the broader perspective requisite to the investigation of the Story of Jacob, together with Gen 26, 34 and 36, into its context, viz. the book of Genesis as inner circle and the Hexateuch as outer circle. At a distance, thus, with wider range of vision, the texts appear to us in perspective; the themes of land and of family-history are functions of even larger perspective that God's plan of salvation means to a chosen people on its way to a promised land."

2.7. The Research Process

In view of the above assumptions, the discussion will proceed by make use of the following strategy:[169]

- A *Text boundaries*—The first stage of analyzing a literary text is to determine its boundaries, which in a biblical text do not always follow those of the chapters. Any such determination is already permeated with commentary.
- B *Text structure*—In the second stage one determines the boundaries between parts of the text. A controversial point in our story is the establishment of boundaries of the dream itself. After analyzing each part, one has to ask how it advanced the plot line and how it helped formulate the message (vv. 12–13a).
- C (1) *Close reading*—The system developed, formulated for general literary research, discusses first of all the story itself, then looks at each word and its links, key words, metaphor, chiasmus, symmetry and the like.

    (2) *"Integrative interpretation"*—Along with close reading, integrative interpretation has been adopted by Bible researchers. Weiss describes it as "understanding all the formal elements that through their activity and their function contribute to the unified image of work."[170]
- D *Circles of commentary*—Including juxtaposition and dialogue.
- E *Support from specific studies*—In commentary on literature, extensive use is made of earlier work in the field: the literature of the Sages, Hebrew commentary of the Middle Ages and of modern times, as well as specific handbooks and studies that refer to the whole or to details of a particular text.
- F *Ancient Near East literature*—Use will also be made of ANE literary material mainly to understand the dream phenomenon, how it is described in fixed literary patterns, and also the extent to which they are reflected in biblical dreams in general and in Jacob's Dream particularly. It will be interesting to study the use of dreams in Mesopotamian works, in the Gilgamesh saga and in Gudea's dream.

---

169. Y. Zakovitch, *"Every High Official Has a Higher One Set Over Him": A Literary Analysis of 2 Kings 5* (Tel Aviv: Am Oved, 1985), 14.

170. Weiss, *Image*, 22.

3. A Survey of the Research on Jacob' Dream: The Bible Story in General and the Story of Jacob's Dream in Particular

Commentary on Jacob's Dream is a classic example of modern biblical interpretation. Source criticism since Wellhausen has dominated biblical research, and hence the questions that it has asked. All other issues related to the final text (the synchronic view) were secondary and were examined on the basis of the insights garnered from source criticism.[171]

Research on Jacob's Dream in particular has taken two approaches. In terms of chronology, the first is the diachronic and the second, from the 1970s, is the synchronic. Hence when the diachronic approach dominated, there were studies on Jacob's Dream by such renowned scholars as Wellhausen, Gunkel, Skinner, Eissfeldt, Speiser and others, all of whom made use of such research tools as text criticism, philological analysis, literary criticism, history of tradition, form criticism and redaction criticism. All accentuated the contradictions and duplications, resolved on the basis of the assumption that this, like other biblical stories, was collated from E and the J sources. S. R. Driver suggested this way of dividing the story:

J: 28:10   28:13–16   28:19
E: 28:11–12   28:17–18   28:20–22[172]

This provides two parallel stories, each with a unified plot line and style. E tells of the dream revelation of the angels of God (*mal'akei 'elohim*) as they ascend and descend the ladder (v. 12), while J tells of another direct revelation from God (v. 13) with its promise to Jacob and his descendants (vv. 14–15). Fidler states:

> The main reason that source criticism fails in this story is because it does not meet its own goals: first, it did not reconstruct two complete stories that could be regarded as versions of the same event; second, the two reconstructed versions are not compatible in their characteristics to E and J according to source criticism theory.[173]

---

171. R. Rendtorff, "Jakob in Bethel," *ZAW* 94 (1982): 511–23.
172. S. R. Driver, *The Book of Genesis* (2d ed.; Westminster Commentaries; London: Methuen, 1904), 264. See the Appendix on p. 55 for a division of the story into its sources. For the limitations of this system, see Z. Weisman, *From Jacob to Israel: The Cycle of Jacob's Stories and Its Incorporation within the History of the Patriarchs* (Jerusalem: Magnes, 1986), 57–63; Fidler, *Dream Theophany*, 157.
173. Fidler, *Dream Theophany*, 157. See also Rendtorff, *Bethel*, 511–23; M. D. Cassuto, *Commentary on the Book of Genesis*, vol. 2 (Jerusalem: Magnes, 1964), 52–54; idem, *The Book of Genesis and Its Structure* (Jerusalem: Magnes, 1990), 167–68. See also Weisman, *Cycle*, 60–61.

Lichtenstein opposes that division.[174] The dream and its angels were perceived by the adherents of the *documentary hypothesis*[175] as an E element designed to "purify" the direct revelation attributed to the J source.[176]

The purpose of dividing the story between two separate sources was, as previously noted, to resolve the contradiction between the divine promise (v. 15) and Jacob's vow (vv. 20–22), and of course to explain the duplications. This was not entirely successful.

Firstly, it did not resolve the issue that interests us most: what was the message of the present text, even if it came from two sources? What editorial purpose was served by the text in its present form?[177]

Secondly, as Weisman explains well, "This cut-and-paste division did not produce two complete stories…with internal coherence."[178] One of his unresolved questions serves to illustrate the point. While in one story from the E source, God reveals Himself in a dream, in the J source story He reveals Himself directly. Weisman points out that the direct revelation is not completely separated from the nighttime dream, for v. 16, attributed to J, states: "Jacob awoke from his sleep." According to source critics, the dream belongs entirely to E. Lichtenstein uses v. 16 to show that Jacob's Dream (vv. 10–22) is a single literary unit. His reasoning is more relevant for us than the conclusion he draws.

Lichtenstein does not accept the basic premise of source criticism. For him, divine revelation in dream theophanies "represents a distinct religio-philosophical stage of development in the history of Israelite religion, viz. a stage more sophisticated than J, and less sophisticated than P."[179]

Based on evidence from Ugaritic literature, the Mari letters and Bible texts including Gen 28:10–22, Lichtenstein concludes: "Symbolic dreams, dream theophanies, corporeal theophanies, and the like, are mutually interchangeable both in a given period and, occasionally, in the same text. Consequently, both the evolutionary theories of biblical revelation

---

174. Lichtenstein, *E Document*, 44.
175. The name given to the source criticism theory reflects appropriate reservations. A theory is no more than a sound educated assumption.
176. H. Gunkel, *Genesis* (Göttingen: Vandenhoeck & Ruprecht, 1964), lxxxvii; E. A. Speiser, *Genesis* (AB 1; Garden City, N.Y.: Doubleday, 1964), xxix–xxx; A. W. Jenks, *The Elohist and North Israelite Traditions* (SBL Monograph Series 22: Missoula, Mont.: Scholars Press, 1977), 135–36. See Fidler, *Dream Theophany*, 239, on the phenomenological aspect.
177. See above, on my decision to adopt the term "narrator" instead of "editor," and to regard the narrator as a creative artist in his own right.
178. Weisman, *Cycle*, 60.
179. Lichtenstein, *E Document*, 45.

1. Preface to the Story of Jacob's Dream

media, as well as the validity of their implications for source divisions in the text of the Pentateuch, must be seriously questioned."[180]

Lichtenstein does not find it typical, then, of a source of the Torah. Instead, he notes: "Indeed, in many cases it would seem that in the ancient Near East the distinction between symbolic dreams, dream theophanies, and corporeal revelation is more a matter of literary preference than of theological necessity."[181]

Is it a literary convention having characteristics similar to ANE literature? We may either accept or reject Lichtenstein's claim that a dream revelation is no criterion for distinguishing between sources J and E. Nonetheless, the combined appearance of direct and symbolic dream revelations in that literature indicates that Jacob's Dream in its present form followed a familiar pattern. There is no point in locating the sources of our story, as "Any attempt to reconstruct the original story would be pure speculation."[182] Attempts to find the story's sources, then, appear not to have brought us closer to understanding Jacob's Dream in its present form, but rather have distanced us from that goal.

In the 1970s, as noted above, the methodology of biblical research, including the study of Jacob's Dream, took a different turn. Parallel with the historical-traditional diachronic methods, synchronic methods began to develop, concentrating on the completed text in its present form. As Buber put it, "With our own eyes we see how criticism based on aims is pushing aside the criticism based on sources."[183] H. Yazun, in "The Formalist School in Research on Folk Literature," and especially in analyzing Propp's method, notes:

> Like all the folklorists, then and now, Propp was trained in the philological-historical approach. This looks at the historical development of a work of folk literature, assuming that in the distant past several stories were composed by anonymous authors, and have since been reworked orally from generation to generation. The stories we can hear today from simple farmers and workmen have degenerated from an ancient source, and so have no inherent literary worth. The purpose of folklore research is to discover the time and place of the story, its original form and its transformations through the generations… Following the formalists, Propp opposed this approach and maintained that "any story told by a talented narrator is a work of art in its own right."[184]

180. Ibid., 54.
181. Ibid., 51.
182. Weisman, *Cycle*, 64.
183. Buber, *The Way*, 319.
184. H. Yazun, "The Formalist School in Research on Folk Literature," *Hasifrut* 3 (1971): 54–55.

Something similar appears to have happened in the history of biblical research, both as regards the assumed original oral source, written down for the first time, and the changes in the 1970s, when attention was focused on the value of the text in its present form. As I see it, the canonical text, even if composed of several earlier sources, is by no means inferior to the earlier unknown version.[185] In fact, the opposite is true: "The final result is the art."[186]

This approach brought greater attention to the form–content[187] as well as structure–significance links, and encouraged close reading of the text. Some scholars, like Fishbane,[188] held that any progress in Bible criticism, particularly as regards Jacob's Dream, could occur only with a transition from a diachronic to a synchronic basis that focused analysis on the story as a structural unit.

Structural analysis examined the story within the Jacob story cycle.[189] Thus Fishbane, Gammie[190] and others saw the cycle as a carefully planned chiastic structure, one that would, once identified, shed light on the text's significance.[191]

The story of Jacob's Dream is comprehensively studied here because of the opportunity it affords to reconstruct its two main foci: the *how* and the *what*:

1. The *how* involves the widespread use of multiple readings (two readings) as a literary phenomenon. Jacob's Dream at Bethel provides a marvelous example of the value of two readings in understanding a Bible text. Individual words may be read in two

---

185. Our conclusion, in both senses of the word, is that there is no originality without an original.
186. Greenstein, *Torah*, 34 n. 20: "Our Torah is not a painting but a collage." See also R. Alter, *The Art of the Biblical Story* (Tel Aviv: Adam, 1988), 152; Zakovitch, *Inner-Biblical*, 11: "The real finished work, a wonder of mosaic art, was no accident, no result of shuffling a deck of cards."
187. Weiss, *Image*, 20.
188. M. Fishbane, "Composition and Structure in the Jacob Cycle (Gen 25:19–35:22)," *JJS* 26 (1975): 15–38.
189. See Chapter 3 on the Jacob story cycle.
190. J. G. Gammie, "Theological Interpretation by Way of Literary and Tradition Analysis: Genesis 25–36," in *Encounter with the Text: Form and History in the Hebrew Bible* (ed. M. J. Buss; SBL Semeia Supplements; Philadelphia, Pa.: Fortress, 1979), 117–34.
191. My great hope is that, just as the presence of a chiastic structure in the text has been accepted in biblical research generally and to discussions of Jacob's Dream in particular, so too will an appreciation of *mise en abyme* reveal the additional significance embedded in it.

1. *Preface to the Story of Jacob's Dream* 47

ways, such as the verbs *vayfga'*, *sullam*, *'alah*, *yarad*. So may word combinations like *meavney hamaqom*, "of the stones of that place"; *vehashivotikha el haadama hazot*, "will bring you back to this land"; *ma nora'*, "how awesome." These words provide linguistic support from Hebrew for two readings of the story.

For the dream as a whole there are also two possibilities: the dream theophany and the symbolic dream with its twofold interpretation. One reading seems to see the "place" as holy, while the second relates to the "way" to and from that place. This double reading leads us to the second focus of the book.

2. The second focus, on *what* is to be studied, is the way to and from the Land of Israel. Jacob dreams his dream sleeping on the ground on the way out of the Land, "Jacob left Beer-Sheba and set out for Haran" (28:10). In his dream (v. 12) he sees a *sullam* (the JPS translation is "stairway") "and angels of God were going up and down on it." Then God promises: "I am with you and I will protect you wherever you go, and bring you back to this land" (v. 15). All the verbs seem to express going and coming, and thus interpret one another.

(Appendix overleaf.)

Appendix: The Jacob's Dream Story (Genesis 28:10–22) According to Its "Sources"

Since the table does not reflect agreement even among source theory adherents regarding sources, it does not encourage support of that approach.

	v. 10 a+b	v. 11 a+b	v. 12	v. 13	v. 14	v. 15	v. 16	v. 17	v. 18	v. 19 a+b	v. 20	v. 21 a+b	v. 22
S. R. Driver 1906	J	E	E	J	J	J	J	E	E	EJ	E	E	E
R. Smend 1912	E	E	E	J2	J2	J2	J2	E	E	E			
O. Eissfeldt 1922	E	E	E	J	J	J	J	E	E	J	E	E	E
O. Procksch 1924	J	J+E	E	J	J	J	J	E	E	JJ	E	JJ	E
J. Skinner 1930	J	E	E	J	J	J	J	E	E	J?R	E	RE	E
M. Noth 1948	J	J+E	E	J	J	J	J	E	E	RJ	E	RE	E
C. A. Simpson 1948	J2+E	E	E	J2	R	J2	J2	E	E	J2	E	E	RE
G. Von Rad 1950	E	E	E	J	J	J	J	E	E	JJ	E	E	E
E. L. Ehrlich 1953	J	E+J	E	J	R	J	J	E	E	RJ	E	E	E
E. A. Speiser 1964	J		E	J	J	J	J	E	E	JJ	E	JE	E
H. Gunkel 1964	J	E	E	J	R								
W. Richter 1967		E	E	J		J	E?	E			E	E	E
R. J. Clifford 1972	E	E	E	J	J	J	J	E	E	J	E	E	E
C. Houtman 1977		E⊐	E	J	J	J	J	E			E		E
R. Fidler 1996		E+J	E	J	R	J	J	E	E	RJ	E	E	E
J. M. Husser 1999	J	E	E	J	J	J	J	E	E		E	E	E

Chapter 2

THE STORY OF JACOB'S DREAM AT BETHEL: GENESIS 28:10–22

1. *Structure and Significance of the Jacob's Dream Story*

1.1. *Introduction: Two Readings of the Story of Jacob's Dream at Bethel*
The story of Jacob's Dream is our focus of interest for two main reasons. Firstly, it is an outstanding example of the literary phenomenon of a text having two readings. In addition, the dream itself may be read as a theophany and a symbolic dream. In the first case, attention focuses on the sacred character of the *place*, and in the second, on the *way* to and from it. That two readings—the one of *place* and the other of the *way* to and from it—leads to the story's second focus on the theme, the journey to and from the Promised Land. I plan to show that as a symbolic dream within the Patriarchal narrative it exemplifies a *mise en abyme*. Fleeing to Haran, Jacob has a dream when he stops for the night: "And Jacob went out from Beersheba and went to Haran." In his dream he sees a ladder (v. 12), on which angels of God are ascending and descending. God promises him: "And, behold, I [am] with thee, and will keep thee in all [places] whither thou goest, and will bring thee again into this land; for I will not leave thee, until I have done [that] which I have spoken to thee of" (v. 15 KJV).

Researchers classify biblical and ANE dreams as either theophanies or symbolic dreams. Jacob's Dream is commonly regarded as a *theophanic dream*, explaining how the place became sacred (*beth-El*, "house of God") in the cultic etiology. A careful, sensitive reader, however, one who is aware of the possibility of two readings, also discerns a symbolic dream that makes use of characteristic language and structure. The message is delivered in a visual-symbolic manner, which therefore requires interpretation.

I plan to show that the action conveyed in the vision—the ascending and descending of the angels of God on the ladder—may represent symbolically the way Abraham and Jacob traveled to and from the Land.

At the same time, I will seek to show that two readings may be possible—the dream as a theophany regarding *maqom* ("place"), and as a symbolic dream of *derekh* ("way"). If this can be shown to be the case, the interaction of these aspects and their combined contribution to our understanding of the dream should be examined.

Jacob's Dream and its interpretation make two simultaneous readings possible from a literary perspective:

Reading A: The story describes and explains how Bethel became a sacred place—a story whose core is the *maqom* ("place").

Reading B: The story tells about Jacob who leaves Israel to return in the future, a story whose core is the *derekh* ("way").

In the present study, these two readings will be shown to enrich rather than to contradict one another.

I argue that support for the two readings may in fact come from the linguistic field, with the very choice of words supporting the argument: the use of *vayifga'* and *sullam*, and the verbal roots *'alah* and *yarad*, as well as such combinations as "of the stones of that place" and "I will bring you back to this soil" (Fox), and "how dreadful."

1.2. *The Text of the Dream*

The KJV's translation of Gen 28:10–22 reads:

v. 10: And Jacob went out from Beer-Sheba, and went toward Haran.

v. 11: And he lighted (JPS: came) upon *maqom* (a certain place), and tarried there all night, because the sun was set; and he took of the stones *of that place* (JPS: one of the stones)
and put [them for] his pillows (JPS: and put it under his head; Fox: and set it at his head), and lay down *in that place* to sleep.

v. 12: And he dreamed, and behold, a ladder set up on the earth, and the top of it reached to heaven: and behold *mal'akei 'elohim* (the angels of God) ascending and descending on it.

v. 13: And, behold, the LORD stood above it, and said, I [am] the LORD God of Abraham thy father, and the God of Isaac: the land whereon thou liest, to thee will I give it, and to thy seed.

v. 14: And thy seed shall be as the dust of the earth, and thou shalt spread abroad to the west, and to the east, and to the north, and to the south: and in thee and in thy seed shall all the families of the earth be blessed.

v. 15: And, behold, I [am] with thee, and will keep thee in all [places] whither thou goest, and will bring thee again into this land (Fox: bring you back to this soil) for I will not leave thee, until I have done [that] which I have spoken to thee of.

v. 16: And Jacob awaked out of his sleep, and he said, Surely the LORD is in *this place* and I knew [it] not.

v. 17: And he was afraid, and said, How dreadful [is] this place! This [is] none other but the house of God, and this [is] the gate of heaven.

v. 18: And Jacob rose up early in the morning, and took the stone that he had put [for] his pillows, and set it up [for] a pillar, and poured oil upon the top of it.

v. 19: And he called the name *of that place* Bethel: but the name of that city [was called] Luz.

v. 20: And Jacob vowed a vow, saying, If God will be with me, and will keep me *in this way* that I go, and will give me bread to eat, and raiment to put on,

v. 21: So that I come again to my father's house in peace; then shall the LORD be my God (Fox: YHWH shall be God to me).

v. 22: And this stone, which I have set [for] a pillar, shall be God's house: and of all that thou shalt give me I will surely give the tenth unto thee.

1.3. *Stating the Problems*

Problems arise from the first reading—i.e. the dream as an explanation of how Bethel became a sacred space—mainly due to contradictions that seemingly exisit between parts of the story. For example, Jacob sets conditions in vv. 20–21 that contradict God's promises in the dream in vv. 13–15. That Jacob should seek to establish conditions sheds some doubt on his righteousness—his faith is seemingly based on anticipated gain.[1]

There are further contradictions in the text. For instance, Jacob appears to fall asleep twice: "And he lighted upon a certain place and tarried there all night" (v. 11a) and he "lay down in that place to sleep" (v. 11b).[2] Furthemore, two revelations are described: the first is in v. 12 ("And he dreamed, and behold a ladder set up on the earth, and the top of it reached to heaven: and behold the angels of God ascending and descending on it"), and the second in v. 13 ("And, behold, the LORD stood above it"). Twice Jacob awakens from the dream: first in v. 16 ("And Jacob awaked out of his sleep") and again in v. 18 ("And Jacob rose up early in the morning"), and twice he has a first response to the revelation ("And Jacob awaked out of his sleep, and he said, Surely the LORD is in this place and I knew [it] not," v. 16; "he was afraid, and said, How dreadful [is] this place!," v. 17). Lastly, Jacob's recognition of

---

1. As Satan said to God in Job 1:9, "Does Job not have a good reason to fear God?" We will return to the connection of the vow to this issue later.

2. Fidler, "Dream Theophany," 157, attributes this to "the overfill of detail at the beginning of the story."

the place in which he dreamt as God's house (v. 17) contradicts his vow regarding a future house of God (v. 22a).

So far, no comprehensive explanation of the text has emerged. With this in mind, I seek to offer one further interpretation.

1.4. *Rejecting the Division of the Story According to Classic Source Theory*[3]

A familiar means of resolving contradictions and duplications in Bible stories in general, and in the story of Jacob's Dream in particular, is to divide the text into parallel accounts that display different styles and content. Thus, for instance, as noted in Chapter 1, S. R. Driver divides our text into material derived from the J and E sources:

J:	28:10	28:13–16	28:19
E:	28:11–12	28:17–18	28:20–22[4]

According to Driver's application of source criticism, two parallel stories within the same narrative are identified: one describing the *mal'akei 'elohim* (angels of God) ascending and descending on a ladder (v. 12), and a second describing the direct revelation of God (v. 13) promising the Land to Jacob and to his seed (vv. 14–15). Furthermore, for Driver, vv. 13–16 describe another direct revelation not made in a dream. The division proposes to resolve the contradiction between the divine promise in the dream (v. 15) and Jacob's vow (vv. 20–22), and also to explain the duplications.

Importantly, however, Driver's reading does not seem to have resolved all the problems. For example, the theological distinction that while in the E source God is revealed in a dream, in the J source He

---

3. On rejection of the proposal to divide the Jacob's Dream story into sources, see Rendtorff, "Bethel"; E. Blum, *Die Komposition der Vätergeschichte* (WMANT 57; Neukirchen–Vluyn: Neukirchener Verlag, 1984), 7–35; Weisman, *From Jacob to Israel*, 60–61; Fidler, "Dream Theophany," 159.

4. Driver, *Genesis*, 264; see also idem, *Introduction to the Literature of the Old Testament* (New York: Meridian, 1957), p. 16. See the Appendix to Chapter 1 for a table showing the research proposals based on applying source theory to the story of Jacob's Dream. The many proposals appear to indicate problems with the system. See J. Skinner, *Genesis* (ICC; Edinburgh: T. & T. Clark, 1930); Speiser, *Genesis*; Gunkel, *Genesis*. Husser, *Narratives*, 129, argues: "The analysis of documentary critics seems to solve the problem by discerning a visual dream in the Elohistic account and a typical message-dream in the Yahwistic version. However, most commentators have felt the need to add a word from the divinity to the original E document, the result of which it to render the dream atypical once more. It is my opinion that the solution to the different questions posed by theory, given that the structure of the account seems to exclude the combination of two parallel sources."

reveals Himself face to face, remains problematic. Such a reading holds that a divine revelation in a dream belongs to and typifies the E source only, while in the J source there is a direct divine revelation. How, then, does one explain that v. 16, attributed to J, which is not supposed to recognize dream theophany, begins with "And Jacob awaked out of his sleep"?

Another approach has been taken by M. Lichtenstein, who uses v. 16 to show that the entire story (vv. 10–22) is a single literary unit.[5] He rejects the assumption, intrinsic to source criticism, that the revelation of God in a dream represents a more advanced theological perception than the anthropomorphic J (Yahwistic) description. Attributing a direct revelation in this way to two different sources (a direct revelation and a dream) is, Lichtenstein maintains, a fundamental error.

On the basis of analyses of Ugaritic literature, the Mari documents and biblical texts (notably, including the present one), Lichtenstein concludes that material and abstract elements appear together when describing the revelation experience. Hence, in his opinion, a dream theophany is not typical of one Torah source or another, but forms a literary combination having qualities common to those of other ANE literary sources.[6]

Regardess of whether or not Lichtenstein's assumption that dream theophanies do not help us distinguish between the E and J sources is accepted,[7] the simultaneous appearance of direct material revelation and more abstract dream theophanies across the ANE and biblical literature clearly shows that Jacob's Dream is a complex narrative, though one following familiar literary patterns.

5. Lichtenstein, "E Document," 44. On Jacob's twofold reaction in vv. 16–17, see G. Savran, *"He Came Upon the Place": Biblical Theophany Narratives* (trans. H. Aschheim; Bene Barak: Hakibbutz Hameukhad, 2010), 108. Savran writes: "Jacob's response to the dream of the *sullam* in two similar verses (28:16–17) may indicate a double source for the text. As I understand it, however, this double response reflects two separate aspects of human response to a theophany. What appears to be repetitive language describes a complex response comprising contrary feelings that exist side by side, or following one another. Verse 16 expresses fascination, not terror... By contrast, in v. 17 Jacob reflects fear and awe of the divine presence" (108). Savran, following Rudolph Otto, defines the double human response to a theophany as *mysterium fascinans et tremendum*. See R. Otto, *The Idea of the Holy* (trans. J. W. Harvey; London: Oxford University Press, 1950).

6. Lichtenstein, "E Document," 54.

7. See Gnuse, *Samuel*, 25, 31, 73, particularly as regards Lichtenstein's ANE examples. I prefer Gnuse's more precise definition, "The Hypothetical Elohist Tradition of the Pentateuch" (71), over Lichtenstein's "E Document." I also prefer his definitions, "a simple oral message (auditory) message dream" and "visual symbolic dream, often enigmatic in content and requiring interpretation" (70).

1.5. *Structure*[8] *and Boundaries of the Work*

Given the connection between structure and significance, "the first stage in analyzing a literary work from the Bible is to determine its boundaries."[9] To be sure, it is my belief that there is a link between form and content, both of which serve the story's purpose. Thus, I begin here by establishing the boundaries of the story of Jacob's Dream, before going on to discuss its details, particularly those related to the description of the dream.

The accepted outer limits of the story of Jacob's Dream at Bethel are vv. 10 and 22. Thus the account culminates in the making of a vow. We have already seen the theological difficulty created by the apparent contradiction between God's promise to Jacob (v. 15) and the conditions Jacob makes in his vow (vv. 20–21). At first glance, it might appear that without the vow we would be dealing with a cohesive story, one complete in both structure and content.[10]

The story starts in v. 11, which states that Jacob "lighted upon *a certain place*, because the sun was set." He then took "of the stones" at his head and went to sleep. The story reaches its conclusion the following morning: "And Jacob rose up early in the morning." Once awake, Jacob took the stone and "set it up [for] a pillar" (v. 18). Most

---

8. Regarding the structure of the story, Husser, *Narratives*, 129, argues: "It appears to have been constructed with great care; it is made up of three concentric frames, each one fitting neatly into the other so ad to form a structure organized around a central axis, the latter dividing the account into two symmetrical parts, ABCC'B'A'. The outer frame (AA': vv. 11a + 19a) defines of the keyword of the passage, *maqom*. The latter appears no fewer than six times between vv. 11 and 19; indeterminate at the beginning, this place finds its meaning and identity as the narration advances, and finally receives its name in v. 19a. The intermediary frame (BB': vv. 11 + 18)… The inner frame (CC': vv. 12–13a + 16–17)."

9. Zakovitch, *Introduction*, 57. He says: "A mistake in setting boundary marks may lead to a misunderstanding of the story" (p. 57). See also idem, *"Every High Official,"* 15.

10. See Rendtorff, "Bethel," 516. Rendtorff regards the vow (vv. 20–22) as independent and separate from vv. 11–19, which deals with "beginning the establishment of a memorial sanctuary at Bethel." He regards the passages as "two formal units, each closed within itself." See Husser, *Narratives*, 130: "Whatever may have been the relationship between this dream account and the cultic tradition at Bethel, it takes on its definitive character on its integration into the epic Jacob cycle, thanks to the addition of Jacob's vow (vv. 20–22). It not only integrates the episode into the general movement of the hero who moves away and comes back again, but also transforms the etiological value of the incident."

importantly for the present purposes, the story opens[11] with "And he lighted upon *a certain place*...and lay down in *that place* to sleep" (v. 11), and ends with the same words: "And he called the name of *that place* Bethel" (v. 19a). In the interval, Jacob has a dream.

1.5.1. *Two readings of* maqom *("place") as a keyword in the story.* Reading the story of Jacob's Dream, we notice that the word *maqom* occurs repeatedly, and at prominent places within the narrative. Is this an accidental repetition, a weakness in the narrator's verbal dexterity, or is it a deliberate stylistic device exemplifying narratorial skill? According to Fokkelman, "The repetition, if useful, makes the word a key word... For *maqom* to be a key word, integrated in the whole, it must refer to, anticipate, the main theme of the story."[12]

Maqom, in my view, represents a central theme of the story. The word "place" appears six times in total: in v. 11 it appears three times, and then again in vv. 16, 17 and 19, serving as the keyword that reveals the boundaries of the story.[13] The meaning of *maqom* seems to undergo a transformation from simply a place where Jacob chanced to spend the night "because the sun was set," becoming a *holy place* due to the divine revelation in the dream. This reading has led many scholars to conclude that the purpose of Jacob's Dream was to offer an explanation of how Bethel came to be a regarded as a sacred location.[14] They saw the story of Jacob's Dream story as cultic etiology, the *hieros logos* of Bethel. The dream interpretation appears clearly in v. 17.

---

11. After v. 10, linking the story to the preceding text that describes Jacob on his way.

12. Fokkelman, *Genesis*, 49. See also Rendtorff, "Bethel," 521. Rendtorff argues that "The multiple uses of *maqom* (place) make it a key word in the story (v. 11 twice, vv. 16, 17, 19), also setting its boundaries." Fidler, "Dream Theophany," 165, supports Fokkelman and Rendtorff in setting the story boundaries at vv. 11–19a.

13. See Buber, *The Way*, 284–99. See also Y. Amit, "The Problem of Multiple Uses of the Term 'Key Word'," *Sadan* 1 (1994): 35–47; Y. I. Peleg, "The Place (*Maqom*) in the Story of Jacob's Dream," *Al Haperek* 18 (2001): 83–91.

14. See I. L. Seeligmann, "Etiological Elements in Biblical Historiography," *Zion* 26 (1961): 141–69; Sarna, *Understanding*, 192. R. Otto, "Jakob in Bet El," *ZAW* 88 (1976): 174, notes that analysis of the story structure shows that its center of gravity is recognizing the sacred nature of the place and its significance in the etiology of the sanctuary at Bethel. See Rendtorff, "Bethel," 516, 520; C. Westermann, *Genesis 12–36: A Commentary* (trans. J. J. Scullion; Minneapolis: Augsburg, 1985), 452, 458; Fidler, "Dream Theophany," 153, 163–64, 188; H. Gunkel, *The Legends of Genesis: The Israelite Literature* (trans. A. Zeron, R. Peled and D. Amara; BEL 16; Jerusalem: Mosad Bialik, 1998), 4, 37–31, especially 34.

1.5.2. *Comparing v. 11 and vv. 18–19a.*

a) *Place* (maqom) *undergoes a change or a reversal.* To show the transformation that occurred at "that place," the two descriptions of the location, in vv. 11 and 18–19a, need to be examined further. The many similarities in form and content make it easy for the reader to identify common threads running through the narratives: the repeated use of the same nouns and verbs, and the mention of places and times in a similar order, all call attention to a deliberate connection between the opening and closing portions of the dream account. A second look, however, reveals differences and contradictions that indicate different messages in vv. 18–19a and in v. 11. While the table below illustrates the similarities, we pay most of our attention to the differences.

Genesis 28:11	*Genesis 28:18–19a*
He came upon a certain place and stopped there for the night, for the sun had set (JPS)	Early in the morning (JPS)
and he took *of the stones* of that place (KJV)	Jacob took *the stone*
and put *them* under his head (JPS)	that he had put under his head and set *it* up as a pillar, and poured oil on the top of *it* (JPS)
and lay down in the place (JPS)	v. 19: And he called the name of that place Bethel (KJV)

The first difference relates to the time of the event. Verse 11 sets the scene at nighttime, "because the sun was set," while in v. 18 Jacob "rose up early in the morning." In both cases his actions were appropriate to the time of day.

b) *"Of the stones of that place" (v. 11)—two readings.* Verse 11 states that Jacob "took of the stones (*meavnei hamaqom*—in the Hebrew *meavnei hamaqom* can be understand to be plural) of that place," while v. 18 relates that he "took the stone (singular)...and set it [= *ha'even* = the stone] up [for] a pillar, and poured oil on the top of it."

The second difference relates to the function/role of the stone(s). This difference requires explanation: in the Hebrew, the combination *meavnei hamaqom*, "of the stones," is ambiguous.

From linguistic point of view, "of the stones" may translated as "one of the stones" or "some of the stones." If the narrator had wished to note that there was only one stone he would have said "one of the stones in the place." As it is, however, the wording as it appears to the reader of the text in its final form permits two possible readings. According to the first reading, one may understand that Jacob took a single stone for a pillow;[15] according to the second, Jacob placed several stones[16] around his head to protect it. That is, the stone(s) were not for comfort,[17] but for protection.[18]

c) *Two readings regarding the role of variations in the word "stone" (v. 18)*. While v. 18 clearly relates to one single stone, not several, possibly the reader at this stage might already have decided in retrospect form the information telling us that "Jacob took *the stone* that he had put under his head and set it up as a pillar" (v. 18), it was one, not several stones.[19] It is no longer a random stone, but a specific one (with the definite article, "the stone"), one possessing with a ritual, a cultic function ("and poured oil on the top of it").

While v. 11 leaves the question unresolved, v. 18 unquestionably tells of a single stone.

The main difference between the two verses, however, lies in the role of the stone(s). While in v. 11 the stone(s) served Jacob alone and seemingly assumed an earthly role—whether as a pillow or as a means of protection—in v. 18 the stone takes on ritual significance. Rendtorff notes that it is not by chance that the story begins in v. 11 with "he took of the stones of that place, and put [them for] his pillows," and concludes with "and took the stone that he had put [for] his pillows, and set it up [for] a pillar, and poured oil upon the top of it."[20] He has no doubt

---

15. On identifying the role of the stone as plow, see Skinner, *Genesis*, 375. See also Sarna, *Understanding*, 191: "his head resting on a stone"; Fokkelman, *Genesis*, 48: "Jacob uses a stone as a head-rest"; Otto, "Bet El," 172; Rendtorff, "Bethel," 512. See also Gnuse, *Samuel*, 67, who notes that some scholars think the incubation dream resulted from sleeping on a sacred stone.

16. Following this reading, "and set it up [for] a pillar" is a metonym for "them," referring to several stones.

17. With difficulty, can one see a stone as a comfortable head-rest.

18. On identifying it as a means of defense, see C. Houtman, "What Did Jacob See in His Dream at Bethel?," *VT* 28 (1977): 342. Houtman mentions the Septuagint translation and the commentator Benno Jacob (1934). In this case one could follow Rashi's understanding: "He put stones around him lest he be injured in his sleep by man or beast."

19. The Sages, according to their custom, expounded the difference by saying that the stones changed into one large stone. See *Genesis Rabbah* on v. 11 and Rashi; see also Houtman, *Dream at Bethel*, 342 n. 22. I believe Houtman was mistaken in saying that v. 11 states that Jacob took several stones before lying down to rest: in v. 11 there is no mention of how many he took. Only in v. 18 do we realize that Jacob took "a stone."

20. See Rendtorff, *Bethel*, 512.

that this is no mere verbal repetition; instead, the stone's function has changed: the stone Jacob placed under his head as a pillow has become a commemorative pillar.[21]

It is my contention that while *similarities* between the two verses serve to highlight linkages that invite the reader to compare them, the *differences* serve to foreground a dramatic alteration in the nature of the stone between vv. 11 and 18. The changes both in language formulation and in the role of the stone reflect[22] the dramatic transformation of *that place* as a whole.[23] The story's structure and the deliberate positioning of vv. 11 and 18 support this contention. The verses function as parallel components, opening and closing the story within the chiastic structure,[24] or, as others emphasize, the "reply or response structure."[25] The two

---

21. See also Fokkelman, *Genesis*, 66: "Apart from the anonymous *maqom* there was one detail which had attracted our attention in the beginning: the peculiar mention of a stone as Jacob's pillow provoked our curiosity. This thread is now also cast off (for the time being). The stone in v. 11 was justified: it was to be a *matseba* (a pillar), a monument, as we now see. To make the connection the narrator takes care to repeat the words wayyiqaḥ 'et h-a'eben…sām mᵉra' 'ªšōtāw."

22. On the stone as a reflection of the place as a whole, see n. 26 below, also regarding the role of the stone in the Jacob story cycle. See also N. Ne'eman, "Bethel and Bet Onn: The Problem of Locating Ancient Ritual Sites in Israel," *Zion* 50 (1985): 21. He mentions *Bet Even* as "the sacred ritual site of *Bethel*". See p. 22: "There is no doubt that the prophets of the Eighth and the Seventh Centuries knew the name of *Bet Even* well, distorting the spelling and calling it *Bet Onn*, referring to *Bethel* and its sanctuary (Hos 4:15; 5:8; Amos 5:5; Jer 4:15)." See also Y. Zakovitch, "Status of the Synonym and the Synonymous Name in Name Explication," *Shnaton: Annual for Biblical and Ancient Near Eastern Studies* 2 (1977): 112–13; idem, "Jabbok, Penuel, Mahanaim, Bethel: Name Midrashim as Reflections of Ideological Struggles," *Ariel* 100–101 (1994): 195–97.

23. See the additional discussion below. Does the definite article with "place" indicate an incubation dream, and a separate discussion of the place as "the abode of God"?

24. See Rendtorff, "Bethel," 516, and also pp. 512–13 regarding "concentric structure." See also Otto, "Bet El," 172–73, who sees vv. 11–19a as a unit whose chiastic structure stands out in vv. 11–12 and 17–19a. Note too Fidler, "Dream Theophany," 152 n. 2.

25. See S. Bar-Efrat, *The Artistic Design of the Biblical Story* (4th ed.; Tel Aviv: Sifriyat Poalim, 1993), 122. See Polak, *Narrative*, 223–24. Polak, like Bar-Efrat, follows Fokkelman, stressing the two-part structure: (1) Jacob's preparation for sleep and the dream in which God promises to protect him on his way (vv. 11–15), and (2) Jacob's response—after he wakes up he dedicates the stone pillar to God and vows to Him (vv. 16–22). See also Fidler, "Dream Theophany," 152 n. 108, and Husser, *Narratives*, 129, who argues that the story "is made up of three concentric frames, each one fitting neatly into the other to form a structure organized around a central axis, the latter dividing the account into two symmetrical parts."

verses, parallel to one another within this framework, show firstly that they are linked, and secondly, the inverted chiastic nature of that link. Thus, structure and content combine to create the message of a randomly chosen place transformed into a holy site, "the house of God."

d) *Conclusion.* Comparison shows that while in v. 11 two readings of the *place* are possible—either as a known place or as a location chanced upon—by vv. 18–19a a singular, known location is in view. Moreover, as a consequence of the divine revelation that took place there in a dream, this location has become the sacred place where God dwells ("And he called the name of that place Bethel [= the house of God, in Hebrew]," v. 19a). As Rendtorff states,

> The story is built with consummate skill, enclosed within a chiastic structure. Through the dream and its interpretation the place and the stone[26] become the place of God's presence and thus a recognized sacred site: hence its name. The anonymous location became Bethel and an ordinary stone became a pillar monument. Thus the end of the story supports the cultic etiology explanation of how Bethel came to be a holy place.[27]

1.6. *Setting the Boundaries of the Dream (vv. 12–15)*

Having examined the boundaries of the chiastic framework,[28] we now look at the links and affinities that form it. My point of departure is the

---

26. On the stone in the Jacob story cycle and perception of it as God's dwelling place, as a *numen*, see A. Rofé, *Belief in Angels in the Bible* (Jerusalem: Makor, 1979), 231: "According to the perception of the narrator in Gen 28:10–22, the stone serves as God's dwelling place." See also Fokkelman, *Genesis*, 67, 78–79. Ne'eman, "Ritual Sites," 15–25, assumes that not by chance is *stone* so frequently mentioned, and that the original name of *Bethel* was *Bet Even*, commemorating the stone (*even*) erected there as a pillar monument (v. 18), showing that *place* sets the boundaries of the story (vv. 11–19a). Shapira, "Two Readings," 129–34, lists five pivotal events in Jacob's life where a stone or stones appear. Fidler, "Dream Theophany," 173–74, assumes that "the presence of God in a commemorative pillar may have evolved from the *numen* that dwells in a stone." See also A. Pagolu, *The Religion of the Patriarchs* (JSOTSup 277; Sheffield: Sheffield Academic, 1998), 145, stating that in the three instances where the pillar is mentioned in the Jacob story cycle (Gen 28:18–22; 35:1–11, 9–15), it signifies place and not a commemorative stone, and no textual evidence indicates that it was an "abode for God." Significantly, the place, not the stone, is called *Bethel*.

27. Rendtorff, "Bethel," 514.

28. The terms "chiastic" and "concentric" as related to research on the structure of Jacob's Dream reflect both a viewpoint and the desired interpretation. For emphasis on the dramatic change at the "place," I prefer "chiastic." To emphasize the centrality of its sacred character as the place where God was revealed and where

observation that in the structure of every literary work—including the story of Jacob's Dream—the links between component parts help disclose its meaning.

1.6.1. *The dream boundaries: between "and he dreamed" (v. 12) and "and Jacob awaked" (v. 16)*. Proponents of source criticism, as noted above, maintain that description of the dream is confined to v. 12.[29] Nonetheless, given the story in its present form, it is quite reasonable to see v. 16 as the actual ending of the dream account, so that the entire narrative within vv. 12–16 takes place in the dream. Further support comes from the verbal formulations: while Jacob is awake, before and after the dream, past tense constructions are attested. By contrast, during the dream all six verbs are cast in the present tense.[30] Fokkelman has also noted that v. 13b begins a new phase that in some way continues the preceding material, the link between them being apparent in the chiastic structure.[31]

1.6.2. *"Place" (*maqom*) as a keyword helping to mark the dream boundaries*. Additional literary support for the dream's boundaries appears through the use of the word *maqom* ("place"), which is deployed no fewer than six times in the text (three times in v. 11 and once each in vv. 16, 17 and 19). Such usage delineates the boundaries of the text itself, and also of the dream. Some scholars[32] note that the word *maqom*

He dwells, "And, behold, the Lord stood above it" (v. 13) and "Surely the Lord is in this place" (v. 16), the structure is preferably called "concentric." While the chiastic structure stresses the inverted relationship between parts of the structure, the concentric highlights the centrality of the theme, the *vertical structure* that provides its more familiar name.

The distinction is most helpful in the two readings of Jacob's Dream and its interpretation, and supports the approach to story structure as a reflection of significance.

29. Westermann, *Genesis*, 456, argues that vv. 16–18 "report Jacob's reaction to his dream (v. 12). There is no sign here of any reference to the promise in vv. 13–15.... Both v. 16 'awaked' and v. 17 'and he was afraid' can follow directly on v. 12. In any case, v. 16 presupposes the assignment of 'and lay down' in v. 11 and v. 16 to two different sources."

30. Rendtorff, "Bethel," 513; Fidler, "Dream Theophany," 171.

31. Fokkelman, *Genesis*, 56.

32. Ibid., 49: "The repetition, if useful, makes the word a key word... For *maqom* to be a key word, integrated in the whole, it must refer to and anticipate, the main theme of the story." See also Rendtorff, "Bethel," 512: "The frequent use of 'place' makes it a key word (twice in v. 11, and in vv. 16, 17, 19), determining the extent and boundaries of the story." See also Fidler, "Dream Theophany," 165, and

sets the story boundaries between vv. 11–19a. In addition, *maqom* helps to set the boundary of the dream. Careful reading shows that the word "place" appears only when Jacob is awake, before and after the dream; during the dream itself, however, "the earth" and "the land"/"this soil" are used instead.[33]

Before the dream—when Jacob is awake (v. 11):
The word "place" (*maqom*), then, marks the dream boundaries as follows:

- A1. And he lighted upon a certain place (*maqom*) and tarried there all night, because the sun was set;
- B1. and he took of the stones (JPS: one of the stones) of that place (*maqom*) and put [them for] his pillows (JPS: and put it under his head; Fox: and set it at his head),
- C1. and lay down in that place (*maqom*), to sleep.

During the dream—when Jacob is asleep (vv. 12–15): see section 1.2

After the dream—when Jacob is awake (vv. 16–19)
- C. Surely the LORD is in this place (*maqom*) (v. 16)
- B. How dreadful [is] this place! (*maqom*) (v. 17)
- A. And he called the name of that place (*maqom*) Bethel (v. 19)

1.7. Conclusion

The preceding discussion has established that *maqom* serves as a literary structural marker in the story of Jacob's Dream in two circles:

1. In the outer circle, beginning with *maqom* (three times) (v. 11) and ending with *maqom* (three times) (v. 19a).[34]
2. In the inner circle, the dream itself, beginning with "and he dreamed" (v. 12) and ending with "and Jacob awaked" (v. 16).

Fokkelman, *Genesis*, 49, 63, who regards "place" as the boundary of the story (vv. 11–19a) and understands it to have a link with the change of the status of the "place" from a nameless site to "the house of God" and "the gate of heaven." Fidler, "Dream Theophany," 165, adds: "If there is still a sense that the language of the text suggests the special quality of the place, it can be explained by the deliberate ambiguity of the narrator who, unlike Jacob, knows it is the house of God."

33. "Earth" and "land"/"soil" are used to indicate a link with the divine promise to Abraham in Gen 13:15–17; 12:3.

34. See Bar-Efrat, *Design*, 122; Polak, *Narrative*, 223–24. Both follow Fokkelman, who stresses the reply or "response structure."

Below, I will discuss the signifying word *hinneh* ("behold"), attempting to prove that the word functions as a further literary device that delimits the boundaries of the dream itself.[35]

v. 12   And he dreamed, and *hinneh* (behold) a ladder set up on the earth, and the top of it reached to heaven: and *hinneh* (behold) the angels of God ascending and descending on it.
v. 13   And, *hinneh* (behold), the LORD stood above it, and said…
v. 15   And, *hinneh* (behold),[36] I [am] with thee, and will keep thee in all [places]…

2. *The Dream Vision as* Mise en Abyme *of the Jacob's Dream Story*

It is my contention that the description in vv. 12–15 functions as a *mise en abyme* of the entire story of Jacob's Dream (vv. 10–22). Therefore we have to examine the links between the parts of the story. I will start with a question: How does the vision (vv. 12–13a) connect to the verbal message (vv 13b–15)? I will then examine the link between the dream vision (vv. 12–13a) and Jacob's verbal response (vv. 16–17), and conclude with the story of the vow (vv. 20–22) and its link to the dream vision (vv. 12–13a).

Jacob's Dream has two consecutive parts: the visual (vv. 12–13a) and the verbal (vv. 13b–15).[37] Significantly, and somewhat surprisingly, these parts are not only adjoining, but also seem to complement and interpret one another. This view runs contrary to the majority of scholars, especially adherents of source criticism, who stress the differences between the narrative segments. Typically, the vision in the dream has been

---

35. As to whether *hinneh* ("behold") introduces a surprise sentence and a new picture, or reflects the dreamer's viewpoint rather than the narrator's, and the gradual comprehension of the vision in the dream, see Richter, "Traum," 20. See also Fidler, "Dream Theophany," 171 n. 212. I accept Fidler's view that "behold" presents the view of the dreamer, supporting the view that "set up above" refers to the ladder (see the separate discussion, below). Significantly, at this stage it is both a literary marker of the narrator, and a boundary of the dream.

36. Fokkelman, *Genesis*, 61, says: "The particle *hinneh* in v. 15 brings about a connection with v. 12f. The vision, narrated with *hinneh*, repeated three times, now ends with and finds its cause in the word 'I am with you.'" See Ps 23:1: "The Lord is my shepherd, I shall not want."

37. On the division, see S. Klein-Braslavi, "The Rambam's Commentaries of the Jacob's Dream Story," *Bar Ilan* 22–23 (1988): 332.

assigned to the E source, and God's verbal message in a direct revelation—not a dream—has been assigned to the J source. Thus, the proposal made here to find common elements that interpret each other may seem boldly innovative.

It is worthwhile here to state my objectives clearly. In what follows I will present evidence that the earthly (horizontal) movement of the patriarchs corresponds to the angels' (vertical) movement on the ladder. Furthermore, focusing on the verbs in the dream we will see that they all denote movement back and forth—the verbs *'alah* ("to ascend") and *yarad* ("to descend") in v. 12 in some sense serve to explain the "go" and "return" of v. 15.

With the help of Meir Weiss I shall also argue that a similar literary structure is discernible within the book of Isaiah, where vision and voice "speak" with each other. Weiss's methodology is particularly noteworthy, in that it foregrounds the links between *sight* and *sound*.

The present discussion will also propose that the story of Jacob's Dream serves to establish links with, and emphasize the cohesion of, the broader Jacob story cycle. As will be shown, the rare combination "angels of God," which appears only twice in the Bible—first in the vision in the dream (28:12) when Jacob is about to leave the Land, and second at Mahanaim (32:2) when Jacob is about to return to the Land—creates a chiastic link between the two stories. This link encourages the sensitive reader to notice that God's angels appear when Jacob is about to *leave* or *enter* the Promised Land.

Moreover, I propose to demonstrate that the order of the angels' actions in the dream (they first *go up* and then *go down*) is a case of *hazara* (הזרה):[38] after all, we would expect of angels that they would first *come down* from heaven and then *go up*. The sensitive reader will pause and ponder: "Why do the angels first go up and then go down?" This sense of strangeness, *hazara*, encourages us to seek an unexpected, symbolic meaning. I suggest an answer to this question by claiming that the angels represent the Patriarchs. Abraham first went *up* to the Land of Canaan from Ur of the Chaldean and then went *down* into Egypt. This strangeness hints at the symbolic meaning that I am suggesting for Jacob's Dream.

A separate discussion will be devoted to understanding Jacob's Dream as a *symbolic dream*. Here, I will bring forward a number of arguments in support of my suggestion that Jacob's symbolic dream is structured according to a conventional format attested elsewhere in the biblical and ANE literature.

38. For more on *hazara* ("Ostranenie" in Russian), see n. 197 below.

Finally, let me state that an overarching objective of the present work is to expose the reader to evidence that will increase the sense of connection between Jacob's vision and its symbolic meaning.

2.1. *How Does the Vision Connect to the Verbal Message?*

In a treatment of the revelation appearing Isa 6, Meir Weiss highlighted the potentially signficant fact that, on occasions, the description of a vision and the adjoining verbal message appear to explain one another. According to Weiss, there exist

> a few visual passages in which the vocal message to the prophet seems to be the chronological sequel of the visual revelation, but has no connection to what was previously revealed. It is as if the vision was merely a scenic backdrop, and when the curtain comes down, the voice follows, as in Isaiah 6 and Ezek 1:3–4; 3:13.[39]

Importantly, while previous scholarship has rightly proposed that Jacob's vision (the *sullam*, commonly translated as "ladder," and the angels) should be understood as a scenic backdrop for the verbal message Jacob received,[40] they have nevertheless maintained that vision ended—when the "curtain" came down, to use Weiss's term—the picture disappeared and the voice followed.[41] Significantly, although Weiss does not identify Jacob's Dream among his examples—I believe I am the first to propose that the vision and the verbal message of the Jacob story function, in a sense, symbiotically[42]—the approach he advocates is of immense importance for the present study:

> I propose to point out the structural rules implemented, the consistency between the seen and the heard, that determine the tectonics of these verses. This has escaped scholars' attention so that they failed to notice the

---

39. M. Weiss, "Interpretation of Isa 6," in *Scriptures in Their Own Light: Collected Essays* (Jerusalem: Bialik Press, 1988), 99.

40. See Sarna, *Understanding*, 193. See also Fokkelman, *Genesis*, 54, who argues that the ladder and the messengers of God (the angels) are "the servants, whose presence at once reminds one of their boss—and indeed, there is the master himself! Consequently, when the ladder and the angels have accomplished their task, they do not occur again, just as Moses' burning bush was also a mere eye-catcher." See too De Pury, *Promesse*, 378, and Fidler, "Dream Theophany," 172, who states that the main point of the dream is "God's appearance and His message," while the ladder and the angels are "an accompaniment or scenic background to that revelation." Note also Van Seters, "Encounter," 508.

41. I do not compare the seraphs' role in Isa 6 to that of the angels in Jacob's Dream, but rather apply the method that links sight and sound.

42. Y. Zakovitch advocates a similar approach to 1 Kgs 19: see his "'A still small voice': Form and Content in 1 Kings 19," *Tarbiz* 51 (1982): 340–42.

depth of the literal texts and came to erroneous conclusions... I intend to show that in these passages too the visual and the auditory elements are not simply consecutive, but mainly and perhaps most importantly, they are one within the other, one for the purpose of the other... More precisely they explain one another and by their contact they establish the purpose of this unit.[43]

Weiss's views are entirely consistent with my own understanding of the vision in Gen 28:12–15, especially the nature of the connection between the vision and the ensuing verbal message. It becomes clear that in both, the verbs of motion move back and forth with respect to one another, whereas the direction of their movement differs. In the visual revelation we see movement along the vertical axis, while in "God's words" it is horizontal, as the table shows:

Vertical movement (vv. 12–13a)	*Horizontal movement (v. 15)*
back and forth between heaven and earth	back and forth between the Land and exile
"and behold the angels of God ascending and descending on it" (v. 12)	"And will keep thee in all [places] whither thou goest and will bring thee again into this land" (v. 15)
"And, behold, the Lord stood above it" (vv. 12–13a)	

The common elements within the narrative, then, invite us to make a comparison between the visual and auditory elements, while the differences indicate how one explains the other.

As in the description of Isaiah's consecration in Isa 6 discussed by Weiss, so in the Jacob's Dream story we see the visual and auditory elements combining with and illuminating one another. I therefore propose that the contribution of the verbal message is to explain the ascent and descent of the *mal'akei 'elohim* ("angels of God")[44] as symbolic reflection of Jacob's entry into and departure from the Promised Land. Similarly, the vision elucidates the verbal message in portraying entry into the Land as ascent and departure as descent.

---

43. Weiss, "Interpretation of Isa 6," 99.
44. Later I discuss why the angels of God first ascend, then descend, enlarging to show the dream vision as *mise en abyme* for the Patriarchal stories, chiefly those about Abraham whose story begins as he enters (ascends to) the Land.

To understand how these verbs *'alah* ("ascend") and *yarad* ("descend") explain the verbs "go" and "return," one must recognize "the Lord stood above it" as an integral part of the vision. Moreover, despite scholarly differences, the pronoun "it" is generally related to the ladder—that is, the Lord stands above of the ladder, in heaven. Ascent, then, means drawing closer to him (literally and metaphorically), while the descent of the angels of God distances them from God. Elsewhere in the Bible too[45] *'alah* ("ascend") may have a positive metaphorical connotation and *yarad* ("descend") may have a negative one, so that to leave the country is to move away from God, while to return is to move closer to Him once more. Therefore, Jacob's journey to Haran may be understood as a going away (*yerida*) from God, as a negative act, while his return may be understood positively, as a return to God.

If this reading is accepted, it, crucially, sits alongside—not in place of—the accepted cult etiology of the dream. It is a new reading on the symbolic plane, one focusing on the way from, and the return to, the Land. We now proceed to a close reading of the vision scene, before moving on to examining its literal message. This, it is hoped, will provde additional and compelling support for the proposal that the two descriptions should be read as mutually explanatory.

2.1.1. *"And behold"* (vahinneh) *as a literary signal in the story of Jacob's Dream.* The word *vahinneh* appears four times, as a literary signal helping to locate the borders of the dream, and supporting the affinity between the dream vision and God's message (v. 15).

a) *"And behold"* (vahinneh) *as a signal and a literary hint as to the borders of the dream.* In contrast to adherents of source criticism, who attribute v. 12 to the E and v. 13 to the J sources,[46] I view the passages as consecutive and cohesive, not only because writing is by nature lineal, but also because of the linguistic, structural, descriptive and content links between them. In discussing the dream's boundaries, I maintained that v. 13 is integral to the vision in the dream: the repetitions of "and behold" further support that view. The phrase appears twice in v. 12 and again in v. 13. What is its function there? To me, "and behold,"[47] appearing again

---

45. See the separate discussion below of the verbs *'alah* and *yarad* in the Bible.
46. Ehrlich, *Der Traum*, 27–28. For more detail, see Fidler, "Dream Theophany," 158 n. 137, who offers a synoptic table of writers who divide the chapter according to source-critical principles. Fidler is here following the survey in De Pury, *Promesse*, 34–35 n. 5.
47. A surprise sentence beginning "And behold" is typical of symbolic dreams: see, e.g., Gen 37:7, 9; 40:9, 16; 41:1–3, 5–6; Judg 7:13. See Baruch, "Deuteronomic," 14, 29. See also Fidler, "Dream Theophany," 156; S. Kogut, "On the

in v. 15, serves as a signal. The narrator seems to have chosen it to inform readers that before them is a single description, starting in v. 12 and continuing through v. 15.[48]

b) *"And behold" as a literary signal of affinity between the vision in the dream and God's words (v. 15)*. The formulaic expression "and behold" appears to function additionally as a literary signal, as a key word, helping the reader to understand that all the statements it introduces are linked. That is, the verbal message (v. 15) is not only an integral part of the dream, but is also designed to explain in words the vision that precedes it. If this supposition is correct, we have additional support for the view that Jacob's departure from the Land (v. 15a) and his return to it (v. 15b) explain the symbolic ascent and descent of God's angels on the ladder, even as Jacob's going and coming is explained by their action, descending and ascending.

2.1.2. *Are there two possible readings for "And the Lord stood above it" (v. 13)?* Despite differing scholarly opinions (see section 1.5.1), the pronoun "it" in v. 13 refers to the ladder. What do Jacob on one hand and the reader on the other think about the Lord standing above "it"? Is this

---

Meaning and Syntactical Status of *hinneh* in Biblical Hebrew," in *Studies in Bible* (ed. S. Japhet; ScrHier 31; Jerusalem: Magnes, 1986), 145. Kogut notes that the verb *halam* ("to dream") may also express seeing when followed by "and behold," as, e.g., in Gen 41:5 and obviously in 28:2. The discussion to follow will deal with the vision of Jacob's viewpoint, and the importance of this distinction in understanding the dream. Moreover, the word is known to express Jacob's surprise at the vision revealed in his dream. A fine example of "behold" to signify total surprise is "behold, twins were in her womb" (Gen 38:27 KJV). It is to be remembered that composition of the biblical narrative preceded prenatal ultrasound imaging by several millennia! See also Y. Zakovitch, "On Recognizing Methods of Hidden Intra-Biblical Commentary," in *Biblical and Talmudic Studies* (ed. S. Japhet; Jerusalem: The Hebrew University, 1987), 56.

48. Kogut, *Hinneh*, 151. In his chiefly linguistic discussion of "and behold," he notes: "Because it begins a clause it is also a boundary. The distinction enhances understanding of the syntactic structure and significance of many Bible verses. For example, 'Wherefore hearest thou men's words, saying Behold, David seeketh thy hurt? Behold, this day thine eyes have seen how that the Lord hath delivered thee today into mine hand' (1 Sam 24:9–10)." See slo Weisman, *Cycle*, 66, who notes the conjunctive force of "and behold." Despite criticizing source criticism regarding Jacob's Dream, he nonetheless uses its terminology. Weisman writes: "The Yahwistic source wanted to stamp his approval on this important story. It was insufficient to include God's promise: he tried to adapt it to the story context to his own ideological purposes by means of *and behold* that links God's appearance to the preceding vision (v. 12)."

good or bad for Jacob? Can Jacob's awakening responses, "Surely the Lord is in this place" (v. 16) and "How dreadful is this place!" (v. 17), help us in this regard?

a) *Positive and negative readings of "stand"* (ntsb). Wherever the root *ntsb* refers to God or His angel,[49] to humans or to Israel in the Bible, it may be read in one of two contrasting ways:

1. As a sentence of doom or an adversary—as in the message of Sodom's destruction (Gen 18:2; Amos 7:7; 9:1; Isa 3:13).
2. As a instruction to enter a covenant—as in "He saw three men standing near him" (Gen 18:2).

Shapira points out that the revelation in Gen 18:2 may be interpreted either as a sentence of doom on Sodom and Gomorrah or as a reference to the making of a covenant with the promise that Sarah is to bear a son: "Nevertheless, Sarah your wife will bear you a son…an everlasting covenant" (Gen 17:19). As Shapira states,

> God's revelation to Jacob as he *nitsav alav* ("was standing beside him," 28:13) would arouse in the biblical reader, as in Jacob, strong anxiety…a covenant and mercy or accusation and doom. There would be two readings: the first obvious one would be optimistic and positive, but the ambiguous force of *nitsav alav* ("was standing") conceals another reading with an option for a negative connotation.[50]

The possibility of positive and negative readings runs like a silken thread through the story. It suffices to recall "came upon," "will bring thee again into this land" (v. 15), "how dreadful" (v. 17), and "so that I come again to my father's house in peace" (v. 21), to be discussed below.[51]

b) *Are two readings possible for the preposition ʿalav ("above it") in v. 13?* From the syntactical viewpoint, based on description as it appears in the text's present form, it is not possible to propose two readings for ʿalav—the term, it seems, refers to the ladder.[52] The description in v. 13,

---

49. Shapira, "Two Readings," 123.
50. Ibid., 24.
51. See below for a discussion of "so that I return in peace" (v. 21) and, separately, of the two readings of the *hapax legomenon* combination "will bring thee again into this land."
52. Interpretations of ʿalav ("on it") have taken the term to mean "on the ladder." Rashi: "standing above it—to protect him," meaning God is standing on the Ladder and Jacob is lying below; see Obadia Sforno (in *Miqraot Gedolot*). See also the Rambam in Klein-Braslavi, "Rambam," 339. Of the more recent commentators, see Houtman, "Dream at Bethel," 345: "In short, Jacob was sleeping on the *sullam*";

which records God's words, clearly has the Deity standing at the head of the ladder. Noteably, however, the term for ladder, *sullam*, occurs in the dream that began in v. 12—as such, v. 12 and v. 13 form part of a single literary unit.[53] Thus, *'alav* ("above it") refers back to the beginning of v. 12, where Jacob is still the subject, while the focus moves to the ladder: "And he dreamed, and behold a ladder set up on the earth, and the top of it reached to heaven, and behold the angels of God ascending and descending upon it." In "and behold, the Lord stood above it" the pronoun refers to the ladder, not to Jacob.[54]

In Lichtenstein's opinion,[55] in contrast to God's actual presence beside Jacob, His appearance above the *sullam* in the dream may be compared with two visions in Amos: "He was standing on a wall..." (Amos 7:7) and "I saw my Lord standing by the altar" (9:1).

By contrast, researchers who maintain that *'alav* should be read as "on him,"[56] as a reference to Jacob, rely on the description of God revealing Himself to Abraham. In Gen 18:2 we read: "Looking up he [Abraham] saw three men standing *'alav (near him)*." For some—especially adherents of source criticism—there are parallels to be seen here with 28:13. Yet Gen 18:2 is different from 28:13. For one thing, God revealed Himself to Abraham during the day—"as the day grew hot"—and not at night, during a dream, as is the case of Jacob. Genesis 18:2 is about Abraham and is linked to the final verses of ch. 17 without any change of

---

Bar-Efrat, *Design*, 123: "The ladder stands on the ground and above it is God"; Y. Zakovitch, *Through the Looking Glass: Reflection Stories in the Bible* (Tel Aviv: Hakibbutz Hameuhad, 1995), 115 n. 5. Savran, *Theophany Narratives*, 75–76, says that the story is unclear about God's presence: "As 'above it' [can also be read as 'above him'] and refer either to the ladder or to Jacob, is God above Jacob's head or above the ladder?" (75). He refers to *Gen. Rab.* 69:3 and 68:12.

53. See the discussion of dream boundaries, above.

54. In the opinion of Fokkelman, *Genesis*, 55, the referent "on it" combines with the other word endings in the previous verse referring to the ladder. Just as "its top" and "on it" refer to the ladder, so does "above it."

55. See Lichtenstein, "E Document," 44 n. 12.

56. Several researchers hold this view: Frazer, *Folklore*, 225–28, derives it from dreams in ANE literature where the god of the holy place reveals himself, standing beside the dreamer; Ehrlich, *Der Traum*, 29, remarks that had the description meant that God was above the ladder, the verb would have been "and He called", not "and He said." Speiser, *Genesis*, 219; Gunkel, *Legends*, 218; and Ehrlich, *Der Traum*, 29, analyzing the dream according to source criticism, see v. 13 as the direct continuation of v. 10, where the subject is Jacob, and there is no ladder. Weisman, *Cycle*, 57–63, writes "The expression 'stood above it' could be interpreted in two ways." However, at p. 66 n. 29 he states explicitly: "above him—above Jacob, following Gen 18:2."

subject. He is the subject of all the verbs, and nothing intervenes between them and the referent of "by," which could refer to no one except Abraham. In Gen 28, however, the central noun changes. In v. 11 it is still Jacob, while in v. 12 the focus moves to the ladder, to which "at the top of it" refers. Verse 13 then reverts back to Jacob. In biblical language, however, a pronoun does not precede the noun to which it refers. Furthermore, the dream vision beginning with "and behold" (v. 12) is presented from Jacob's point of view, not the narrator's, which ends with "and he dreamed." Hence the pronoun in "the Lord stood above it" must refer to "ladder."[57]

Thus, working with the final form of the text results in a perfectly satisfactory and cohesive reading: "above it" refers back to the ladder, and forms a link between vv. 12 and 13. The division of the narrative into distinct sources, which results in it *'alav* referring back to Jacob, is, to my mind, unnecessary. This "reading" by Bible scholars, which assumes that the chapter was created from a variety of sources, ignores the reading of the text in its final form.

2.1.3. *A close reading of the verbal message (vv. 13–14): God's promise.*[58] Scholars tend to divide the divine promise into a long-term part that promises Jacob the Land and progeny (vv. 13–14), and a short-term part that reassures Jacob that God "will watch over you wherever you go and will bring you back to this soil" (v. 15 Fox).

For instance, Brettler notes that "Verse 13 takes place as Jacob flees from his brother, an opportunity for God to reveal His promise to Jacob. Through the promise Jacob is encouraged in the short term in that he is to return to the land, and in the long term that it is to be given 'to thee and to thy seed.'"[59] And Fokkelman argues that "The stylistic means of the chiasmus can embody, symbolize and intimate relation between the entities arranged in the chiasmus…"[60] That is, the chiasmus structure between vv. 13c and 14a, connects the two parts—the two promises, that of *the seed* and that of *the Land*.

---

57. On whether the dream is described from Jacob's or the narrator's viewpoint, see Fidler, "Dream Theophany," 171 and bibliography.

58. A separate section will discuss v. 15 in connection with Jacob's vow.

59. See M. Z. Brettler, "The Promise of the Land of Israel to the Patriarchs in the Pentateuch," *Shnaton: An Annual for Biblical and Ancient Near Eastern Studies* 5–6 (1978–79): 20.

60. Fokkelman, *Genesis*, 57. See also K. Deurloo, "The Way of Abraham," in *Voices from Amsterdam: A Modern Tradition of Reading Biblical Narrative* (ed. and trans. M. Kessler; Atlanta, Ga.: Scholars Press,1994), 96. See also Weisman, *Cycle*, 122.

In my view, it is important to note the connection between the two promises. To my mind, one is dependent on the other: "the promise of the Land" to Jacob can be realized only if Jacob returns to it. This use of "the promise of the Land" in v. 13 is conditional on the promise to return Jacob to the Land in v. 15, and simultaneously explains why Jacob must be returned to the Land.[61]

a) *The link between "and he [Jacob] lay down in that place (*hamaqom*)" (v. 11) and "the land (*haarets*) whereon thou liest" (v. 13).* Verse 13 reminds the reader of v. 11, of Jacob lying down to sleep. A comparison will naturally concentrate in the first instance on the similarities—in this case in language and content—before then looking at the differences—contained here in the message. Below is an illustration of the chiastic structure:

and <u>lay down</u> in ***that place*** to sleep (v. 11)

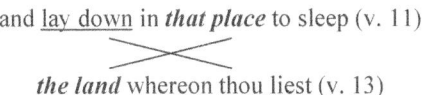

the land whereon <u>thou liest</u> (v. 13)

Similarities in form and content are evident immediately. There is also a chiastic structure in which the two verses are embedded, one that runs through most verses in the story[62] (see section 2.1.2).

It is, I believe, highly significant that the designation of Jacob's sleeping place is changed. While in v. 11 it is "that place," in v. 13 God calls it "the land." Presumably the narrator could simply have said "the place" in v. 13; so why the use of the term "the land"?

By now the reader of the Jabob's Dream will be familiar with the use of "the place," which has been used three times as a keyword, as a literary means of identifying the boundaries of the dream.[63] Yet in the dream there are two other terms, "the land" (vv. 13, 14, 15) and "the earth" (vv. 14, 15), that belong to the same semantic field, and which also seem to serve as literary terms marking the dream boundaries. One may question whether these two specific terms are used deliberately, or as the result of random choice.

---

61. Fokkelman, *Genesis*, 61, argues: "v. 15c ['I shall bring thee again to this land'] can refer to what 13c ['the land whereon thou liest, to thee will I give it'] says: so that this land may be given to Jacob, God will bring him back; the near future serves the remote future."

62. See Fokkelman, *Genesis*, 56–61, for a close reading.

63. As previously noted, "place" appears in the story six times, all in the waking state—three times before Jacob falls asleep (v. 11) and three times after he awakens (vv. 6, 17, 19).

b) *Why specifically* haarets *("the land") and* haadama *("the earth")?* Tracing the use of these and other terms in the story of Jacob's Dream leads one to assume an associative link, namely, the concluding word on one subject introduces by association the first word in the next one. Thus, "he came upon *a place*" points towards "of the stones of *that place*" and to "he lay down in *that place*" in v. 11. In v. 12 we witness the "heaven and earth" a familiar *merismus* in the Bible. An associative link appears to exist between "a ladder set up on the earth (*aretsa*)" (v. 12) and "the land (*haarets*) whereon thou liest" (v. 13). Using this associative reasoning appears to help the narrator harmonize the two parts of the story. Such reasoning is, I would suggest, an integral part of the narrator's style and central to the expression of the story's significance.

We see similar associative reasoning in God's promise of the Land to Jacob, in particular with the use of *haadama* ("the earth") in vv. 14–15. When v. 14b introduces a new subject, the narrator begins by picking up the keyword of the previous one: "in *thy seed* shall all the families of the earth (*haadama*) be blessed." Significantly, it appears that when God says in v. 15, "I will bring thee again into this land (*haadama*)," the terms "land" (*adama*) is preferred over "earth" (*haarets*) because of its associative links to v. 14a.

The same associative links can explain the repeated use of "this" throughout the narrative: "in *this* place" brings in "*this* is none other but the house of God and *this* is the gate of heaven" (v. 17), while "God is in *this* place" (v. 16) introduces by association "is *this* place" (v. 17) and "he called the name of *that* place" (v. 19).

All of this helps to highlight and emphasize the cohesiveness of the narrative. Indeed, Fokkelman, who examined the formal arrangement of the text, defined it as a typical chiastic structure that in his opinion indicates the affinity between the passages.[64]

This formal structure, in my opinion, is a guide to the story's message.[65]

c) *Comparing God's promises to Jacob (28:13b–14) and to Abraham (13:15–17)*. The sensitive reader familiar with the stories of the Patriarchs in the final form of Genesis cannot but sense the similarity in language and content between the two promise of land and seed. In fact, Jacob's link with Abraham and Isaac is created when God introduces Himself

---

64. Fokkelman, *Genesis*, 56–58, 62; see p. 57, where he asserts that the function of the chiasmus is to reinforce the links between the parts.

65. On the link between *form* and *content*, see the introduction to Chapter 1.

specifically as: "I am the Lord God of *Abraham thy father*[66] and of Isaac" (v. 13).

Why "Abraham thy father," when Isaac was Jacob's father and Abraham his grandfather?

Lipton argues:

> The fact that Abraham, and not Isaac, is called "your father" is, at first glance, puzzling. While *avikha* ("your father") may certainly be translated as "your ancestor" in this context, the terminology confuses in a verse that uses the term in its far more familiar sense of "your father," namely with reference to Isaac. It is possible that *Abraham avikha* ("Abraham your father") was a formulaic phrase chosen here, for its power to reassure. Evidence for this reading might be found in God's comforting words to Isaac at the onset of famine in the land (Gen 26:3). Although Abraham is Isaac's father, this use of term implies a lasting security which transcends their biological relationship.[67]

And yet, a further understanding is possible. An important connection between Abraham and Jacob is that they shared an experience that was not afforded Isaac: *God protects both Abraham and Jacob when they sojourned abroad.*

---

66. See D. Lipton, "Revisions of the Night: Politics and Promises in the Patriarchal Dreams of Genesis" (Ph.D. diss., Cambridge University, 1996), 73. The combination "Abraham thy father" is not unique: see, e.g., Gen 29:5, where Laban is mentioned as the son of Nahor who was his grandfather. It rouses reader interest and, like the entire story, stresses Jacob's bond with the God of Abraham and also Isaac. The message and interpretation of Jacob's Dream relates not only to Jacob but to them and to Jacob's future descendants and to making the place a house of God, as in v. 13: "to thee will I give it and to thy seed." Hezkuni's commentary, in *Torat Haim: Five Books of the Law: Genesis* (Jerusalem: Mosad Herav Kook, 1990), states "Abraham thy father, meaning that children's children are as children. So it is too in Radak's commentary in *Torat Haim*: "Your father, as if he were your father and not father of the other children because his inheritance will be yours, and calls my father, Father, and so David his father as was said of Ahaz (2 Kgs 16:2 KJV), and many others (see also 2 Kgs 18:1 and v. 3)." Yet we need not go as far afield as Radak. Genesis 32:10 is sufficient: "Then Jacob said, O God of *my father* Abraham and of *my father* Isaac, O Lord, who said to me, 'Return to your native land and I will deal bountifully with you'."

Possibly referring to Abraham as "your/thy father" serves two purposes. One is merely a repetition of the promise to Abraham in Gen 13:15. The other is that as Isaac his biological father never left the Land of Israel, Jacob resembled Abraham more than Isaac. In v. 21 Jacob says "and if I return safe *to my father's house*." Who is being referred to as "my father"—Isaac or Abraham, or both? See Fidler, "Dream Theophany," 106 n. 36, who mentions Alt's "The God of the Fathers," cited in the discussion of the Sanctuary.

67. Lipton, "Revisions," 73.

In vv. 13–15 God makes Jacob three promises: He promises Jacob "the Land," "the seed,"[68] and His protection: "and will keep thee in all places" (v. 15) and "bring thee again into this land." Noticeably, the promise of the Land and of seed to Jacob in 28:13–14 is identical in terms of content, sequence, and chiastic structure to the one given to Abraham in 13:15–16:[69]

The promise to Jacob *(Gen 28:13b–14)*		*The promise to Abraham* *(Gen 13:15–16; 12:3)*	
v. 13b:	the land (*haarets*) the land whereon thou liest, to thee will I give it, and to thy seed; whereon thou liest[70] to thee and to *thy seed* have I given it	13:15:	for all *the land* (*haarets*) that thou Seest to thee will I give it, and to *thy seed*; Forever
v. 14b: v. 14c:	And *thy seed* shall be shall all the families of *the earth* (*haadama*) be blessed	v. 16: 12:3b:	And I will make *thy seed* shall all the families of *the earth* (*haadama*) be blessed

68. On the link between promises of the land and of seed in the stories of the Patriarchs, see Deurloo, *Abraham*, 96–112. The key phrase "Go forth," he says, refers in the first instance (Gen 12) to land, in the second (Gen 22) to seed.

In modern psychology, ladder and stairs, and ascent and descent, all symbolize sexual intercourse. See Freud, *Dreams*, 221. See also Levin, *Dream*, 78. A. Elizur, *From Within and Without: Psychoanalytical Studies in the Bible and in Judaism* (Tel Aviv: Yarom, 1988), 237–48, gives an extensive discussion of the ladder, ascent and descent as symbols of sexual intercourse. Regarding the psychoanalytical approach, see also Husser, *Narratives*, 96–99.

69. Sarna, *Understanding*, 191, argues: "He then repeated the traditional promise of posterity and land and added, because of Jacob's special situation, an assurance of personal protection in exile and a guarantee of safe return to the land of his birth." Skinner, *Genesis*, 376, argues that vv. 13–16 belong to the J source. See Fidler, "Dream Theophany," 160 n. 150. Fidler cites the parallels 28:14a//13:16; and 28:14b//12:3. See also Carr, *Fractures*, 180–82. Carr, in his chart 9–3, "Correspondence of the Promises to Abraham and Jacob: Gen 13:14–16 and Gen 18:13b–14," argues that: "Just as Abraham received the confirmation of God's promise to him after his split from Lot (Gen 13:2–13), so also Jacob receives similar confirmation of promise after he has separated from Esau" (181, cf. 205). See also idem, "Genesis 28:10–22," 402.

70. See Weisman, *Cycle*, 66; Y. I. Peleg, "The Motif of the Land Promised to the Patriarchs and its Development in the Bible" (M.A. thesis, University of Haifa, 1987), 11–12. I compare the two promises to emphasize an issue perhaps deliberately unclear, namely the size and boundaries of the Promised Land.

These resemblances between the two promises show the narrator's intention to associate them.[71] Jacob receives the promise of the God of Abraham and Isaac just as he is about to leave the Promised Land.

For the narrator of Genesis it was important to stress the connection between Jacob and Abraham. The eternal promise made to Abraham ("forever," 13:15), promised anew to Jacob, is operative even as Jacob is about to leave the Promised Land. Besides, Abraham's promise was not given to him alone but to "thee and to thy seed," thus including Jacob. The association between Abraham and Jacob is reinforced through the repetition of the promise motif, which explicitly recalls Jacob's ancestor, a fellow recipient of God's promise.[72] Were this not enough, the term "the land," similarly used, creates a link between the two blessings, as does "the earth". What is more, the entire statement "shall all the families of the earth be blessed" appears in both promise accounts.

These selected terms, then, are not merely technical and literary instruments used to differentiate between dreaming and waking, but also forged the link between Jacob and Abraham.

d) *Why was it important for the narrator to link Jacob with Abraham and Isaac?* In view of their formulation and ideological outlook, proponents of source criticism identify both blessings with the Yahwistic J source.[73] In their opinion, it reflects a national perspective linking Abraham, Isaac, and Jacob, as father, son, and grandson.[74] "In part of the divine revelation Jacob is perceived as the father of the nation and the heir of his forebears Abraham and Isaac."[75] Weisman, identifies the narrator of vv. 13–14 as Yahwist,

---

71. Fokkelman, *Genesis*, 56–57, says that through God's words to Jacob one hears the formula of His blessing of Abraham.

72. See ibid., 56.

73. This distinction is the means for dividing the text into sources or strata, so that J is an addition to the principal and original E story. According to Weisman, *Cycle*, 64–65, the "national" rather than the personal promise to Abraham makes the verbal message in Jacob's Dream secondary. See also Fidler, "Dream Theophany," 159–60 n. 145, 150, 153, and the accompanying bibliographical citations.

74. Weisman, *Cycle*, 124. Weisman notes that the promise to Jacob was based on a ritual legend of a personal nature attributed to E, in which God accompanies Jacob on his journey and returns him to his father's house.

75. Fidler, "Dream Theophany," 177; see also Fokkelman, *Genesis*, 56, who notes that vv. 13–14 link Jacob to his forebears.

who gave this ritual legend the nature of a story of national promise, by means of typical promises in God's name (vv. 13–14), taking care to weave Jacob's genealogy into that of his ancestors/forebears Abraham and Isaac, by identifying the divinity as "the God of Abraham your father and the God of Isaac." Thus the Yahwist who compiled the stories of the Patriarchs placed his stamp on the stories of Jacob that began and ended at Bethel (ch. 35), by placing the promise as a prologue there, and so giving it national significance.[76]

There is, in my view, no need for such a "locked" definition as to the narrator's identity. With such an approach, one reasonably assumes that his inclination, as described by Weisman, is revealed through God's *verbal message*, especially given the close parallel to the promise of land and seed to Abraham. Yet is my contention that the structure of the story, with its *verbal* and *visual* aspects, also reflects the narrator's aim, of linking Jacob to the other Patriarchs and to their God, through that promise.

Returning to the affinities between the dream vision (v. 12) and God's verbal message (vv. 13–15), the picture now becomes clearer. There is a dialogue between the two and they explain one another. So what does the vision in the dream add or explain about what is missing from the verbal message; and how does the verbal message do the same for the dream vision?

The combination of the visual and verbal, I would maintain, is important for the interpretion Jacob's Dream, a vision that symbolized not only Jacob and his fate, but also the fate of the Patriarchs. Such melding of visual and verbal elements helps to emphasize the connections between them.

The proposed answer to the riddle of the symbolic vision in the dream is so very close to the dream description that one wonders how the research literature has missed it. As already noted, vv. 13–15 function as a continuation of v. 12. Moreover, close reading of the verses reveals that the interpretation of the dream on the symbolic level—i.e. of the vision of the angels of God ascending and descending on the ladder—is found in those verses. I will offer a broader discussion of this later, after I have dealt with whether Jacob's Dream is to be understood as a theophany or a symbolic dream.

76. Weisman, *Cycle*, 124–25.

2.2. The Dream Vision (vv. 12–13a) and Jacob's Verbal Response (vv. 16–17)

2.2.1. *The vision and its (concrete) meaning within a concentric framework.* If one accepts the dream as simply an etiological story[77] explaining how Bethel became a holy place, then v. 17 neatly explains it: "And he was afraid, and said, How dreadful [is] *this place*! this [is] none other but the house of God, and this [is] the gate of heaven."

Rendtorff succinctly described the link between dream and interpretation,[78] asserting that Jacob's verbal response upon awakening contains the three elements relating to the three components of the vision, though in reverse, chiastic order:[79]

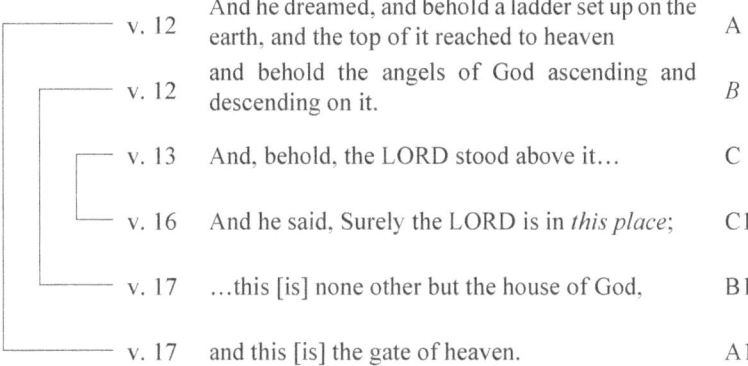

v. 12	And he dreamed, and behold a ladder set up on the earth, and the top of it reached to heaven	A
v. 12	and behold the angels of God ascending and descending on it.	B
v. 13	And, behold, the LORD stood above it…	C
v. 16	And he said, Surely the LORD is in *this place*;	C1
v. 17	…this [is] none other but the house of God,	B1
v. 17	and this [is] the gate of heaven.	A1

---

77. See H. R. Cohen, "The Literary Motif in Jacob's Ladder (Gen 28:12)," in *A Gift for Hadassah: Studies in Hebrew and in Jewish Languages* (ed. J. Ben Tolila; Beer-Sheba: Ben Gurion University, 1997), 16. Cohen maintains that "although there is an etiological aspect in our text…I doubt whether the ladder motif is connected exclusively to it. It certainly has an additional and no less important literary purpose in this context." I agree as to the aspect additional to the etiological one, although my reading differs from his.

78. See Rendtorff, "Bethel," 513. See also Fidler, "Dream Theophany," 172 n. 215. Compare to Fokkelman, *Genesis*, 71.

79. See Fidler, "Dream Theophany," 172. The diagram is hers and I return to it later, explaining the parallel according to which "and behold" characterizes the dream description and "this"—its interpretation, as the short form of Joseph's "This is the interpretation of it" (Gen 40:12). Fidler, "Dream Theophany," 173, defines "this [is] none other but the house of God" as a call for identification as well in the Mahanaim scene (32:2–3), a basis for naming the place Bethel/Mahanaim. Here "this," hinting at a name, signifies identification of both readings of the dream. See the diagram in section 2.2.4.

Fokkelman's impressive analysis of vv. 12–17 similarly identifies chiastic structures that serve as links throughout the story.[80] The link between the vision in the dream (v. 12) and Jacob's response (vv. 16–17) becomes evident when it is recognized as a chiastic structure. The full significance of the link becomes apparent when the structure is designated as a concentric frame.[81]

Repeated use of the chiastic structure, indicating affinity between parts of the story, happens not by chance, but on purpose.[82] While multiple parallelisms indicate links between the story's parts, they raise the question of why the narrator selected this opposing/contrasting chiastic structure. Y. Radai sees chiastic structures in the Bible as evidence of deliberate composition that contradicts source criticism.[83] His concern, however, is not with opposition but with identifying the structural phenomenon and its contribution to understanding the story.

Besides being arranged so as to form a clear chiastic structure, the narrative contains a series of opposites—God and human, heaven and earth—as well as contrasting verbs—"ascend" and "descend," "go" and "come," "give" and "take." I see identifying these as merely one stage in understanding the story. The affinity between them in chiastic parallelism expresses not only the contrast between them but also their linkage in the parallelism frame.

Separating out the verbs in vv. 12–15, we see that they all denote back and forth movement. The angels of God, for instance, not only ascend but descend the ladder, thus seeming to reflect a link and a bridge between heaven and earth. There is, then, affinity between contrasts and opposites, involving movement in two directions. (In this respect, there is a clear difference from the Tower of Babel model, for instance.[84]) As

---

80. Fokkelman, *Genesis*, 56.

81. Ibid., 71–72. See above, n. 28, defining two structural frameworks, the *chiastic* and the *concentric*, which alter the focus of the reader. The diagrams in section 2.2.4 illustrate the distinction.

82. This note is most important in view of the reversal of approach in the present study. While earlier research strove to emphasize and explain the contradictions and tensions in the story and its background, my work emphasizes the text in its present form, with due respect to the narrator. Hence the faith in him, and the effort to find elements unifying the story.

83. See Y. Radai, "Chiasm in the Biblical Story," *Beit Mikra* 20–21 (1964): 48–72. See also idem, "Structures in the Book of Ruth," *Beit Mikra* 24 (1979): 181: "The structures signify that the editor was in full command of the material and planned his opus in advance, a sure sign that the work in question is of a piece, and not patchwork."

84. The concluding section will discuss affinities between the Jacob's Ladder and Tower of Babel stories (Gen 11:1–9).

such, Jacob not only leaves the country but is promised a safe return. The *mal'akei 'elohim* (angels of God) ascend and then descend, while Jacob, like Abraham before him, returns to stay.

Style and structure appear intertwined and help to reveal the story's meaning, or, we might say, the interpretation of the dream. There are contradictions, but they can be bridged. The concentric frame, placing God at the apex of the Jacob's Dream story, thus highlights His centrality and importance there.[85]

Here I propose to identify the ladder whose "top…reached to heaven" (v. 12) as a parallel to "the gate of heaven" (v. 17), and the "angels of God" in v. 12 as a parallel to "the house of God" in v. 17. In the inner circle, the holy of holies, "God stood above it" in v. 13, which parallels "Surely the Lord is in this place" in v. 16. Clearly, then, v. 17 explicates the vision in the dream. We will see later that such parallels have analogies in the wider ANE literature and worldviews, particularly in Mesopotamia and Egypt, with the ziggurat and the root *simmiltu* in Akkadian.[86]

a) *A close reading Jacob's verbal response (vv. 16–17)*. When Jacob awoke, his first word was "surely" (v. 16). One might reasonably have expected him to say "Surely this was a dream"; instead, he says "Surely the Lord is in this place and I knew it not."[87] Possibly the response indicates that Jacob understood the dream as reality, and that the transition from it to the waking state was blurred.

Many researchers—and most notably those advocating the source-critical approach—stress the duplication and repetition in Jacob's responses, resolving the problem by attributing v. 16 to the J source and v. 17 to E.[88] Differently, Rendtorff[89] posits a logical connection between the two, in v. 16: "Jacob recognizes the nature of the place, saying 'Surely the Lord is in this place,' and in v. 17 he derives a conclusion and becomes afraid—a reaction entirely obvious to the ancient hearer."

---

85. See Fidler, "Dream Theophany," 172. I agree that the concentric structure allows us to see that the center of the event is God's appearance and message. Her conclusion that "the ladder and the angels of God are merely a decoration or the backdrop for this revelation," however, is one I reject.

86. See the discussion below on the ladder and its significance.

87. The meaning of both parts of the sentence falls within the question of whether Jacob's Dream is an incubation dream.

88. See Driver's proposal (*Literature*, 16) to divide the passage according to sources.

89. Rendtorff, "Bethel," 513.

b) *The literary function of "place" and "this."* Just as "and behold" has been seen as a literary sign of the dream boundaries, it seems to me that the signal word "this" functions as a literary marker both of linkage between these two verses and as to the meaning of the dream. Discussion of the terms "place," "land," "thy seed," and "earth" raised the assumption that their order of appearance is associative, that is, that a word concluding one subject brings in the next word in a chain of associations. As we saw, "this" and "place" feature within such a chain:

v. 16: and he said, Surely the LORD is in *this place*;
v. 17: ...*this* [is] none other but the house of God,
and *this* [is] the gate of heaven.

That is, the Lord is in "this place," and the conclusions in v. 17 follow:

1. How dreadful
2. this [is] none other but the house of God
3. and this [is] the gate of heaven.

"This," then, is "the house of God," which has a gate called "the gate of heaven." Can it be understood that the heavens are God's dwelling place?[90]

c) *Two readings of the root* yr' *("afraid")*. Rolf Rendtorff has highlighted that while v. 16 states that Jacob recognized the extraordinary nature of the place, v. 17 expresses the result of such recognition, that Jacob is afraid.[91]

The root *yr'* appears twice: once in the words of the narrator—"and he was afraid"—and again in Jacob's utterance, "How dreadful is this place."

When the narrator presents Jacob's response, "and he was afraid and said," after Jacob's waking words, "Surely the Lord is in this place and I knew it not,"[92] he suggests that Jacob was frightened as a result of seeing God. And yet, according to Jacob's own words, "How dreadful is this place!" (v. 17), one may understand that his response is focused on the *place*.

Is this fear (of the place) physical or metaphysical?[93] The combination "How dreadful is this place!" is also ambiguous. On one hand, "dreadful"

---

90. See below for a separate discussion on God's dwelling place.
91. Rendtorff, "Bethel," 513.
92. Proponents of source criticism have focused on Jacob's double response, leading to the contradiction between vv. 16 and 17.
93. Shapira, "Two Readings," 127, notes that *yr'* expresses physical fear, as in "he was afraid to dwell in Ṣoʻar" (Gen 19:30), but also metaphysical fear as in "I heard the sound of you in the garden and I was afraid" (3:10), and "I am a

may have a negative connotation, as in Deut 8:15 and Joel 2:2–11 ("Let all dwellers on earth tremble...the day of the Lord most terrible"). On the other hand, it may have the positive sense of wondrous and exalted, as in "fearful in praises, doing wonders" (Exod 15:11 KJV) and in Deut 10:17.

Since "dreadful" ("awesome" in JPS) appears 44 times in the Bible, 38 times in the divine context and only six times in an earthly one (Deut 1:19; 18:15; Isa 18:2, 7; 21:1; Ezek 1: 22), Shapira concludes that in our text it is to be understood transcendentally.[94] Thus, two readings are possible. Importantly, however, the two possibilities are not mutually exclusive. The first is positive, optimistic, and bodes only good for Jacob, while the second one is negative, expressing Jacob's fears.

2.2.2. *"Behold" and "this" as literary markers identifying the dream and its meaning.* "Behold," I maintain, is the opening formulation identifying the dream, and "this" (shortened from "this is its solution"[95]) indicates the start of the interpretation. As such, the story of Jacob's Dream is intentionally constructed from the two dream types familiar from biblical and ANE literature, *the theophany* and *the symbolic* dream. Hence a double meaning for it must be sought, one of which explains how the site, *maqom*, came to be sacred, and another which, on the symbolic level, relates to the way or road leading away from and towards God's dwelling place.

With this in mind, God's words to Jacob ("I will keep thee in all places whither thou goest"), Jacob's response ("Surely the Lord is in this place"), as well as Jacob's conclusion ("This is none other than the house of God and this is the gate of heaven"), together with the centrality of the dream's double significance, necessitate a separate examination of God's image and dwelling place.

2.2.3. *A proposed second reading: the concentric structure.* The connection between the dream vision and Jacob's response to it reinforces the concept of the dream as an explanation of how Bethel became a sacred site. Additionally, but involving no contradiction, an overview reveals

God-fearing man" (42:18). Was Jacob's fear physical or metaphysical? Shapira points out that of the "20 times that someone fears somebody...only three times does it refer to God (Gen 3:10; 22:12; 42:18). The first probability, then, is that Jacob's fear of 'this place' was physical, and only afterwards becomes: 'this is none other but the house of God and this is the gate of heaven' (28:17b)."

94. Shapira, "Two Readings," 128.

95. See Gen 40:12, 18; and Dan 2:36; 4:15. Note, in particular, Dan 2:36, "this is the dream...and we will tell the interpretation" (KJV); and 5:26, "and this is its meaning."

the story's concentric structure. It places God at the apex, highlighting His centrality and importance. By analogy, the angels in the dream represent drawing closer to God as ascent (and positive), while moving away from God is descent (and negative). It follows that the way to and from God is the essence of the vision. Our interest focuses on the link between reading "the place" (where God dwells) as essence, and reading "the way" (to and from the place) as essence.

2.2.4. *Two readings: the concentric and chiastic vantage points.* For the sake of clarity, I illustrate the distinctions between concentric and chiastic vantage points graphically:

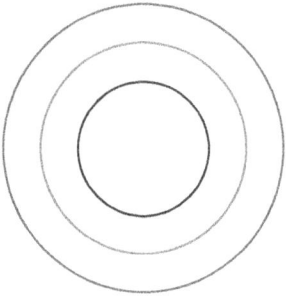

The Concentric Vantage Point

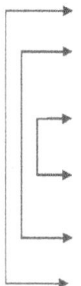

The Chiastic Vantage Point

It is to be noted that the names that research gives to various structures reflect a viewpoint and a desired outcome. When emphasis on change is desired, in my view a structure is preferably called *the chiastic structure*. However, when the central theme is the sacred site of a divine revelation and the divine presence, "And behold, the Lord stood above it," and

"Surely the Lord is in this place," *the concentric structure* is better. While the chiasmus stresses inverted relationships between structural elements, the concentric structure stresses centrality of its apex, and may also be known as apical structure.

The distinction of the structure of the story (as concentric or chiastic) is important in that it changes reader focus and perspective. It also strongly supports the two readings of the Jacob's Dream story, and the view that the story structure reflects its meaning.

2.2.5. *"Surely the Lord is in this place" (v. 16).*

a) *The God of the Patriarchs: "God of wanderings" or "God of the place"?* Biblical scholarship has recognized two principal types of pre-Yahwistic belief reflected in the stories of the Patriarchs.[96] One is the belief in gods of particular places, and the other is a belief in ancestral gods connected to wandering tribes. Weisman argues that "The religious perception stamped into Jacob's life story involves a personal God, his patron and protector in times of danger and crisis, who guides his decisions both existential and elementary in such moments (28:15, 20–22; 31:7, 42; 32:10–13, and elsewhere)."[97] Weisman further notes that "Most of these qualities are typical of the father's God according to Alt."[98]

The story of Jacob's Dream, when examined in the light of these two types, shows that, on one hand, it supports belief in a God of the place. As we have seen, "place" has been seen as a keyword in the story, one which scholars related to local cultic etiology. On the other hand, there is evidence for perceiving God as Jacob's guardian (Gen 28:15, 20) during his wanderings, as Alt defines it. Which type, then, is God, in the story of Jacob's Dream?

Crucially, in my view, the possibility of two readings does not necessitate a decision between them. We need not accept one and reject the other. Indeed, the two readings actually complement one another: God will keep Jacob on his wanderings, but will return him to the place. The linguistic points of contact here are "I will bring thee again to this land" (v. 15), and in Jacob's words, "So that I come again to my father's house in peace" (v. 21).

---

96. A. Alt, "The God of the Fathers," in *Essays on Old Testament History and Religion* (trans. R.A. Wilson; Oxford: Blackwell, 1966), 1–77; see also M. Haran, *Eras and Institutions in the Bible* (Tel Aviv: Am Oved, 1973), 107. See too Pagolu, *Religion*, regarding the faith of the Patriarchs.

97. Weisman, *Cycle*, 46.

98. Ibid.

God appears both to belong to the place, "standing above it," and as the God of wanderings, "in all places whither thou goest." Thus the two aspects of the divinity combine, the first in understanding the etiological nature of the dream, and the second on the symbolic plane, as a *mise en abyme*, of the comings and goings to and from the Land—of Jacob, particularly, and of the Patriarchs, generally. The two are intertwined and interdependent. Jacob leaves the Land, but God is with him and he will return.[99]

b) *Where does God "dwell"?* The apparently technical-geographical question of where God dwells[100] has complex theological aspects connected with the divinity's materialistic or corporeal nature. The issue arose in Lichtenstein's argument over the need to attribute a dream theophany to the E source,[101] representing a more advanced perception of divinity, because God is less material there than in direct revelation attributed to the J source. As to the divinity's material or corporeal nature—does the divine presence abide in the place or only His name? Does God Himself dwell in the heavens and only His name and honor on earth in a particular place of his choosing? If so, is He confined to that place or present everywhere?[102] Is he beyond or within the borders of Canaan, and if within those borders, is he in Bethel or Shechem or Jerusalem?

How does the story of Jacob's Dream answer the questions, and how do they help interpret the story? Psalm 115:16 states: "The heavens belong to the Lord, but the earth he gave over to man." From the standpoint of content, the first line gives the heavens to the Lord. Yet the Hebrew connector *waw* (*wehaarets*) that starts the completing line may be read as either "but" or "and." Whichever way *waw* is understood,

---

99. Fidler, "Dream Theophany," 153, also discerns the local cult aspect of Jacob's Dream, the *hieros logos* of Bethel, and the personal-experiential "Jacob aspect" of his experience when he fled from Esau and was granted a dream theophany with a heartening message. She does not link the Jacob aspect with going from and coming to the Land. Westermann, *Genesis*, 452, argues that "the cult etiology is attached to the place where it is narrated; this is a story told at Bethel about the foundation of this sanctuary."

100. See Baruch, "Deutronomic," 22–27. Later I attempt to show the importance of the question in entering and leaving the Land, and in the two readings of the story of Jacob's Dream.

101. Lichtenstein, "E Document."

102. W. Eichrodt, *Theology of the Old Testament*, vol. 2 (trans. J. A. Baker; OTL; Philadelphia: Westminster, 1967), 188, maintains that the idea of divine revelation in a particular place is by no means restrictive. See, e.g., Job 28:24, "For he sees the ends of the earth, observes all that is beneath the heavens," and Prov 15:3: "The eyes of the Lord are everywhere, observing the bad and the good."

there is a distinction between God and human, and the earth is given over to man.[103] The parallelism, whether completion or contrast ("but"), appears to express what is related in Jacob's Dream, where God stood in heaven while Jacob lay on the ground (Gen 28:13).

As Westermann states, "God's place is in heaven, and there must be a link leading to it like a gate or a stairway."[104] God then promises to give the Land to Jacob and his seed/progeny, the distinctions between the two spheres being expressed by "God stood above it" (the ladder that "the top of it reached to *heaven*") and "*The land* whereon thou liest" (Jacob).

Another reference to humanity's dwelling place on earth, in contrast to God's above in the heavens, is found in 2 Chr 6:18–21: "Does God really dwell with men on earth? Even the heavens to their uttermost reaches cannot contain you… May your eyes be open day and night toward this House, toward the place where you have resolved to make your name abide; may you hear the prayers that your servant offers toward this place…give heed in your heavenly abode and pardon."[105] Humanity's place is on earth, and God's in heaven.[106] God has only placed *His name* in the earthly Temple.[107]

---

103. Both in *form* and *content*, the contrasting parallelism arouses an association in the reader with the Tower of Babel. In both, humans act contrary to God's will. Even Ps 115:1, "Not to us, O Lord, not to us but to your name bring glory," expresses a hidden polemic with the people of Babel, who say "To make a name *for ourselves*" (Gen 11:4). See the separate discussion of the Tower of Babel later in Chapter 4.

104. Westermann, *Genesis*, 460.

105. These verses in 2 Chronicles imply a distinction between God's abode, in heaven, and the ritual site, familiar in the ANE. See G. von Rad, *Genesis: A Commentary* (trans. J. H. Marks; OTL; London: SCM, 1961), 284. However, Lipton, "Revisions," 100, relies on this to interpret Jacob's "this is none other than the house of God and this is the gate of heaven" as differentiating between the place where God dwells, i.e. where gods appear and which becomes a center of ritual, and the gate of heaven, where God dwells.

106. For additional expressions describing God's dwelling place as in heaven, see: "towards this place, give heed in Your heavenly above" (1 Kgs 8:30); "O hear in your heavenly abode" (8:43); "The heaven is my throne, and the earth my footstool (Isa 66:1); "He who is enthroned in heaven laughs" (Ps 2:4); "The Lord has established His throne in heaven" (Ps 103:19).

107. See Y. Zakovitch, "To Abide There, to Place His Name There," *Tarbiz* 41 (1972): 340, maintaining that: "Deuteronomy expresses the accepted view that God dwells in the Sanctuary." Zakovitch's own view is that, according to the Deuteronomist, God is transcendental, and only His name is present. See also G. von Rad, "Theology and the Priestly Document's 'Kabod,'" in *Studies in Deuteronomy* (trans. D. Stalker; SBT 9; London: SCM, 1953), 37–44. Von Rad is aware that one cannot

All of this raises questions about God's corporeality. "The place where the Lord has chosen to put His name there" appears only twice in the Bible, in Deut 12:21 and 14:24. A synonymous expression, "The site where the Lord your God will choose to cause His name to dwell," appears six times (Deut 12:11; 14:23; 16:2, 6, 11; and 26:22). The two combine in Deut 12:5: "to put His name there to have it dwell" (Fox's translation).

The distinction between to "dwell" and "to put His name" relates to God's material nature (his corporeality), and expresses the changed perception of where He dwells, which occurs in Deuteronomy.[108] Knowing that Deuteronomy defines the Temple as the place where God chose to place His name, Weinfeld writes:

> Von Rad was correct in saying that "to place his name" is an ideological innovation to refine and purify the popular belief that God is actually within the temple. The Deuteronomist disputes that popular belief. Innumerable times he repeats "to place his name," to make it known that God placed his name and only his name in the place he chose, while he himself dwells in heaven."[109]

Speaking of Solomon's prayer in 1 Kgs 5, Weinfeld argues: "The Temple does not serve as God's dwelling place, but as the house that the prayers of Israel and of strangers alike pass through on their way to the Lord who dwells in heaven. His heavenly dwelling is stressed in a confrontation to root out the beliefs of those who [still] think His seat is between the cherubim in the Temple."[110]

Comparing Amos and Jeremiah provides another example of the change:[111]

---

suddenly root out established popular beliefs, so recognizes why the biblical narrator preserves the root *shkn*, reflecting God's presence in the Temple, to inculcate that perception. Later the Deuteronomist, whose works appear in Kings, could eliminate the limited corporeality of that root and replace it with an abstract concept: "to place his name there." See Gen 28:16: "Surely the Lord is in this place."

108. M. Weinfeld, "The Change in the Perception of Divinity and Ritual in Deuteronomy," *Tarbiz* 31 (1962): 1–17.

109. Ibid., 10 n. 40.

110. Ibid., 11, notes that adding "heaven" to "your dwelling place" stresses that his place is in heaven, not the in the Temple. See also "Look down from your holy abode" (Deut 26:15), and lest there be any mistake, "from heaven."

111. Ibid., 13. See also M. Weiss, "Following One Biblical Metaphor," *Tarbiz* 34 (1965): 303–18.

Amos 1:2—from Jerusalem	Jer 25:30—from on high (i.e. from heaven)[112]
The Lord roars from Zion Shouts aloud from Jerusalem	The Lord roars from *mimarom* (on high) He makes His voice heard from His holy dwelling

These two texts have an identical structure: "The Lord from...roars, shouts aloud." The difference is in the place from which this emanates. While Amos sees Zion and Jerusalem as the Lord's place, for Jeremiah it is on high (in heaven), from His holy dwelling. Importantly, though, there is no contradiction. The heavenly dwelling is connected to the earthly one, just as a tree growing by a lake is connected to its reflection in the water.

c) *"Surely the Lord is in this place" and "God's dwelling place" and image.* In the light of these distinctions, we return to Jacob's exclamation, one which unquestionably recognizes God's presence. "The house of God" in vv. 17 and 22 reinforces the claim. Given the story's broader narrative—Jacob is on his way out of Israel—Skinner[113] asks whether "Surely the Lord is in this place and I knew it not" expresses the view that the boundaries of Canaan serve also as the boundaries of the Lord's jurisdiction, as it were. (Compare, e.g., Amos 7:17; Hos 9:3–4 with Ezek 4:13, or David's "They have driven me out today so I cannot have a share in the Lord's possession," 1 Sam 26:19, with the idea as reflected in Josh 22.)

Kaufmann[114] maintains that "Holiness is not an intrinsic natural quality of the land, but rather depends on His dwelling there. It was not holy when the Canaanites abode there, but became 'the land of God's inheritance' because it is where 'the Tabernacle of the Lord abides' (Josh 22:19)."[115]

The story of Naaman the Aramean (2 Kgs 5:15–18) is also significant. Cleansed of his leprosy after bathing in the Jordan, Naaman brings to mind Jacob's awakening response:

Gen 28:16 (Jacob)	2 Kgs 5:15–18 (Naaman)
Surely the Lord is in this place And I knew it not.	Now I know That there is no God in the whole world except in Israel

112. See "מרום," BDB 928, 2, "Height of heaven."
113. Skinner, *Genesis*, 377.
114. Kaufmann, *History*, 609.
115. We may implement Kaufman's argument with a minor change, by replacing "dwelt" with "revealed." This seems appropriate to the story of Jacob's Dream. Jacob reached a place by chance ("because the sun was set," v. 11), which afterwards became sacred because God revealed himself to Jacob there in a dream.

Here too form and content complement one another. The two verses in each case create a chiastic structure reflecting reversed significance:

1. God is there ("in this place") as against God is not there ("there is no God"),
2. "In this place" as against "in the whole world."
3. "I knew it not" as against "Now I know."

Significant here is the use of "is" and "is not," as opposed to the material (corporeal) verb "dwell"[116]—not even "where His name dwells." While "is" in Gen 28:16 declares God's presence, it neutralizes his material nature and the question of his permanent or temporary presence,[117] congruent both with the narrator's purpose and Jacob's situation. Jacob is on the way to Haran and God promises to protect him, to give the Land to him and his seed, and to return him to that land.

The story of Jacob's Dream reveals the centrality of the place from which Jacob departs, and to which he later returns. Jacob too comes back to the issue, saying, "so that I come again to my father's house in peace" (v. 21). God will protect Jacob wherever he goes, and will return him to this place.

3. *The Vision in the Dream (Realistic and Symbolic Readings)*

The symbolic interpretation of the dream naturally focuses on Gen 28:12–13a: "And he dreamed, and behold a ladder set up on the earth, and to top of it reached to heaven: and behold the angels of God ascending and descending on it. And behold, the Lord stood above it…" Our attention, then, is on the three elements: the ladder, the angels of God and the verbs denoting ascent (*'alah*) and descent (*yarad*).

3.1. *The First Element: The Ladder (*sullam*):*[118] *Its Nature and Purpose*
The word *sullam* is used only once in the Hebrew Bible—a *hapax legomenon*—which makes its meaning dependent on context. When the context surrounding a *hapax legomenon* is clear, arriving at a satisfactory

---

116. On the significance of this distinction, see above, n. 106.
117. See Baruch, "Deuteronomic," 26. Baruch finds support in the biblical language that distinguishes between "house of God" or *mishkan* ("sanctuary"), and *'ohel moed* ("tent of meeting"). Baruch notes that: "The ancient belief is in the Sanctuary where God dwells, while the tent of meeting implies a place of temporary sojourn."
118. Y. I. Peleg, "What Is the *Sullam* Jacob Saw in his Dream at Bethel?" *Shnaton: An Annual for Biblical and Ancient Near Eastern Studies* 14 (2004): 7–26.

translation is relatively easy; otherwise, more than one reading is possible. Shapira discloses two readings of the Jacob and Esau story, presenting four literary devices that allow for multiple readings. One of these he calls the "linguistic or syntactic uniqueness or rarity"[119] of the particular word or expression. Zakovitch refers to the Midianite's dream in Judg 7:13–15, where the dreamer states, "there was a *tslil* (a commotion)," like "there was a ladder." He argues: "Possibly the unusual word was chosen because it had no unequivocal meaning."[120]

3.1.1. *The etymology of* sullam. Researchers are not unanimous as to the etymology of the *sullam*. A survey of the scholarly literature highlights two prominent understandings for *sullam*.[121] The first one assumes that the Hebrew word derives from the Akkadian *simmiltu*,[122] meaning "ladder," or, by rearranging (transposition of) the letters, "staircase,"[123] indicating that "m" in the word *sullam* is in the root.[124]

The second reading assumes *sullam* is derived from the Hebrew root *sll*,[125] meaning "to throw up a ramp"[126] or "a road."[127] Significantly, the

119. Shapira, "Two Readings," 162.
120. Zakovitch, "Of the Food Came Forth the Eater: On the Dream and its Interpretation," in Kerem, ed., *Varied Opinions*, 37.
121. See, e.g., H. R. Cohen, "The *Sullam*," in *Olam Hatanach: Genesis* (ed. M. Weinfeld; Tel Aviv: Davidson-Atai, 1982), 172. Cohen's methodology is: "with no biblical precedent for the connecting ladder motif, there is no choice but to look into ancient Near East literature…the key to the search is the word *sullam* itself."
122. Cohen, "Motif," 21.
123. See *CAD* 15:173: *simmiltu*. Among researchers suggesting that *sullam* derives from *simmiltu*, see A. R. Millard, "The Celestial Ladder and the Gate of Heaven (Genesis xxviii 12 and 17)," *ET* 78 (1966–67): 86–87. Gnuse, *Samuel*, 68, also mentions the Babylonian story of Nergal and Ereskigal. He also suggests that *sullam* derives from the root *sll*. While he sees a link to the Egyptian stairway in the likeness of the sun's rays, he prefers the Mesopotamian source.
124. Houtman, "Dream at Bethel," 339; Gnuse, *Samuel*, 68. See also Cohen, "Motif," 22, and idem, *Biblical Hapax Legomena in the Light of Akkadian and Ugaritic* (SBLDS 37; Missoula, Mont.: Scholars Press, 1978), 34, 54–56. Cohen does not think *sullam* is derived from *sll*.
125. See "סלל," BDB 699; Houtman, "Dream at Bethel," 336. Among researchers suggesting that *sullam* derives from *sll*, see von Rad, *Genesis*, 279; Speiser, *Genesis*, 218. See S. Mandelkern, "סלם," *VTC* 800. According to Mandelkern, the *m* in *sullam* is only to indicate the verbal structure, while Cohen, "Motif," 120, sees *m* as a root letter. See also Houtman, "Dream at Bethel," 338; Westermann, *Genesis*, 454: "*sullam* is an ascent or stairway, occurs only here; it is from the verb *sll* 'to heap up,' Akkadian *simmiltu*. The verb calls to mind a piled-up (stone) construction, a ramp, which reaches from earth to heaven, from heaven to earth."
126. See von Rad, *Genesis*, 297.

root *sll* in its biblical sense is not found in Akkadian. It follows that *sullam* is best taken as derived from *simmiltu*. One might also say that the proposal to see it as derived from *sll* is *popular etymology*.

Even if *sullam* is not derived in the strict sense from that root, the link is important for the symbolic meaning of Jacob's Dream.

Deciding between the two readings is not easy,[128] nor is it essential for our thesis.

That *sullam* derives from the Akkadian *simmiltu* seems the most plausible explanation, leading to another possible link between that biblical term and ANE literature—the Babylonian ziggurat, with its steps or *simmiltu* leading to the top.

3.1.2. *The biblical* sullam *as an analogy to the Babylonian ziggurat.*

a) *The biblical* sullam *and the Babylonian ziggurat.* Many scholars[129] support the analogy of the *sullam* to the ziggurat.[130] In the late nineteenth

---

127. Houtman, "Dream at Bethel," 338, also notes that *sullam* derives from the verb to pave or to heap up, meaning a raised road of earth and stones. See "they threw up a siege mound against the city, and it stood against the rampart" (2 Sam 20:15).

128. The difficulties of deciding between *sll* and *simmiltu* are evident from changes in F. E. Greenspahn's thinking, in his *Hapax Legomena in Biblical Hebrew* (Chico, Calif.: Scholars Press, 1984), p. 195, cited by Cohen, "Motif," 22 n. 22. Greenspahn included *sullam* in the list of unique words with known roots from other words. But in his article, "A Mesopotamian Proverb and Its Biblical Reverberations," *JAOS* 114 (1994): 37 n. 25, however, Greenspahn preferred *simmiltu*. Although *sullam* has been at times been linked to the root *sll*, it is preferable to compare it to the Akkadian *simmiltu*. Sarna, *Understanding*, 11, derives the etymology of *sullam* from *sll*, alongside *simmilitu*, without deciding between them.

129. E. Stone, "Ziggurat," *OEANE* 5:390–91, describes the ziggurats of the Mesopotamia as follows: "Like modern skyscrapers or medieval cathedrals, Mesopotamian ziggurats served as the visual foci of Mesopotamian cities, providing a symbol of the power of the city and its god visible for miles around... A true ziggurat is a stepped pyramid, square or rectangular in plan, with a temple on top, but this form was not arrived at immediately: the earliest Mesopotamian shrines were built flush with the ground. The sacredness of the shrine structure led to new temples being built on platforms." The ziggurat at Babylon, Stone notes, was dedicated to Marduk and was known as Entemenaki, "The Foundations of Heaven and Earth." This ziggurat possibly inspired the Tower of Babel story (Gen 11:4–9).

130. Von Rad, *Genesis*, 297; A. S. Herbert, *Genesis 50–12: Introduction and Commentary* (TBC; London: SCM, 1962), 85; Speiser, *Genesis*, 218; J. G. Griffiths, "The Celestial Ladder and the Gate of Heaven (Genesis xxviii 12 and 17)," *ET* 76 (1964–65): 229; Millard, "Celestial Ladder," 86–7; Houtman, "Dream at Bethel," 338 n. 4; Fidler, "Dream Theophany," 175. Lipton, "Revisions," 88 n. 40, cites A. Hurowitz's doctoral dissertation, which surveys temples of the ANE, in which

century, Henderson rejected the idea of the *sullam* as a ladder, and proposed identifying it with the "temple-tower" similar to the Mesopotamian ziggurat.[131] Such structures were manmade, stepped towers or ramps, upon which a temple was built. The stepped shape of the ziggurat has naturally encouraged the reading of as *sullam* as a ladder or a staircase.[132] This, together with Jacob's subsequent declaration that "this is none other but the house of God" (Gen 28:17), has encouraged comparison with the ziggurat, a temple "that Babylonians thought of as a bridge between heaven and earth."[133] Stone notes: "The earliest Mesopotamian shrines were built flush with the ground. The sacredness of the shrine structures led to new temples *being built on platforms…*"[134] Hence the comparison between ziggurat and *sullam* is not merely etymological, but is a matter of function and typology as well.

The description of the ziggurat, which is based on Mesopotamian literature as well as on archeological findings, presents us with a shape and structure, and, potentially, a theological worldview, allowing for a comparison to the *sullam*. Importantly, support for this understanding comes not only via the possible derivation from the *simmultu*, but also because of it connection to the Hebrew root *sll*. Indeed, the biblical word *sollelah*, derived from *sll*, appears eleven times in the Bible in the sense

---

dreams were a central means gods used to voice their demands. Lipton, *Revisions*, 90, writes: "It will be suggested here that Genesis 28 is, in fact, a dream authorizing Jacob to build a temple, and that the vision of the *sullam* and the raising of the *masseba* correspond closely to traditional elements of the ancient Near Eastern temple building dreams exemplified by the Gudea accounts." Regarding the *sullam*, see ibid., 89: "Those who regard the *sullam* as a temple tower or ziggurat see it as a symbol of Bethel's holiness rather than as a component of an actual temple…" More than that, Lipton argues: "Although many commentators have recognized in Genesis 28 allusions to temple or sanctuary, few have seen temple building as a central concern of the text, and fewer, if any, have related it to the temple building accounts treated by Hurowitz, 'I Have Built you an Exalted House' (this includes Hurowitz, whose book includes no references to Genesis 28)." Lipton adds on p. 92: "It is clear that the description of a structure reaching from earth to heaven would inevitably have evoked for ancient reader the image of a temple, and there is no obvious reason why Gen 28:12 should have represented an exception to this rule, particularly in view of the subsequent occurrence of the term *beit Elohim* in vv. 17 and 22."

131. A. Henderson, "On Jacob's Vision at Bethel," *ET* 4 (1892–93): 151–52.

132. On a permanent staircase on which angels ascend and descend, see von Rad, *Genesis*, 284–85; Speiser, *Genesis*, 218; Houtman, "Dream at Bethel," 430; Rendtorff, "Bethel," 517; Fidler, "Dream Theophany," 175. See Cohen, "Motif," 26; Lipton, *Revisions*, 91: "The *sullam* is tower rather than a ladder."

133. Von Rad, *Genesis*, 279; Houtman, "Dream at Bethel," 339; Gnuse, *Samuel*, 68; Fidler, "Dream Theophany," 175. See also Cohen, "Motif," 1–45.

134. Stone, *Ziggurat*, 390 (emphasis added).

of an earthwork ramp.[135] Thus, those interpreters who are less convinced by the *simmultu* connection, but who see *sullam* as deriving from the Hebrew root *sll*,[136] can make use of the word *sollelah*,[137] meaning "ramp," and argue for *sullam*'s association with the ziggurat.[138]

The ziggurat's function as a bridge between heaven and earth favors *simmultu*. However, the symbolic interpretation of the ladder favors the *sll* root, even if its connection with the ladder seems to go through an Akkadian word adopted into Hebrew. For accuracy's sake, then, *sullam* should be said to suggest or link to the Hebrew root *sll* rather than to derive from it.

b) *Parallels to the* sullam *in Egyptian and Canaanite literature.* While the analogy of Jacob's Ladder to the ziggurat may not be certain, it does not appear to be unique. Indeed, Griffiths found parallels to the stairway between heaven and earth in Egypt as well.[139] Was our story and the *sullam*, then, influenced by Mesopotamian or Egyptian literature?

Millard does not reject Griffiths' views as to the Egyptian link, but shows that Mesopotamian literature contains a similar idea.[140] In his article, he in fact questions the need to look for Mesopotamian or Egyptian influence in the Jacob story. Millard found that the Canaanite religion practiced *ascent to high places as a means to approach and contact the divinity*, as described in the Ugaritic Kirta Epic (*CTA* 14, iii [Kirta] I 2–9, 20–27[141]). Millard views the Canaanite parallel as more appropriate than the Mesopotamian.[142]

---

135. Houtman, "Dream at Bethel," 339: the root of *sullam* is *sll*, meaning "to heap up earth and stones," "pave." See also Speiser, *Genesis*, 218.

136. Von Rad, *Genesis*, 279, and Speiser, *Genesis*, 218, both identify the biblical *sullam* with the Babylonian ziggurat, while supporting is derivation from *sll*.

137. *Sollelah*, also derived from *sll*, is defined as a road, *mesilla*, winding through mountains, *spiraling up* to the peak, could also resemble ziggurats ascended by circular staircases to the temple at the top.

138. "The staircase is merely a structure of several ramps one above the other." Stone, *Ziggurat*, 390, notes that the ziggurats "appear to have come in two varieties: the generally earlier Babylonian one had rectangular base with stairs providing access to the top; the later one, more often found in Assyria, is square in plan and had more variable access, sometimes including a ramp that spiraled up the building."

139. See Griffiths, "Celestial Ladder," 229–30. Griffiths was the first to raise this assumption in "The Celestial Ladder and the Gate of Heaven in Egyptian Ritual," *ET* 78 (1966–67): 54–55.

140. See Millard, "Celestial Ladder," 86–87.

141. Kirta passage has no ladder. However, this does not impinge on what is important for this research. Let me note that in all the instances the analogy to the literature of the ANE does not view the ladder symbolically. With all due respect to the learned debate between scholars, for our purpose there is no need to decide

Gnuse too preferred the Canaanite parallel.[143] The Sumerian ladder, he maintained, differed from the Egyptian one in that only gods, not human beings, could move on it. This, Gnuse maintains, is a situation more like the one attested in Gen 28, where only the angels of God ascended and descended.[144] Gnuse seeks to trace the path taken by the motif from Mesopotamian to Canaanite mythology, then into the Jacob story cycle, in an attempt to legitimize the sanctuary at Bethel in ancient pre-monarchic times. Fidler too notes that:

> The object called *sullam* is possibly understood better through Canaanite–Ugaritic parallels than through Mesopotamian or Egyptian concepts. Thus, for instance, an Ugaritic text mentions a mountain called *Maslemet*,[145] near mountains linked to the names or abodes of the gods... One may form the impression that the *sullam* in Jacob's dream embodies "the mountain of God."[146]

In all three parallels—the Mesopotamian, the Egyptian and the Canaanite—the *sullam* is a bridge between heaven and earth.

c) *The* sullam *and its role*. More likely to yield a comprehensive answer than the controversial etymology and comparison with the ziggurat are the explanations of Houtman and Cohen.

Houtman notes that,

definitively on the inspiration for the biblical description of the ladder. All the Mesopotamian, Egyptian and Canaanite parallels have a common view of the ladder as a real, vertical bridge between earth and sky. The innovation of the present study is its view of the ladder and its role as symbolic on the horizontal plane, symbolizing the path between the Land and exile.

142. See also R. J. Clifford, *The Cosmic Mountain in Canaan and the Old Testament* (HSM 4; Cambridge, Mass.: Harvard University Press, 1972), 104.

143. Gnuse, *Samuel*, 68.

144. Millard, "Celestial Ladder," 86 n. 4, mentioned by Gnuse, argues: "We may notice, too, that the Babylonian 'ladder' is used for the passage of the divine messengers ('angels'), but not for human beings." See also Cohen, "Motif," 24.

145. Long before Fidler, the Sages saw the *sullam* as a symbol for a mountain, and as was their custom, named it. Shinan, "Dream," 57, maintains that "the Sages offer another solution for Jacob's dream, this time as the giving of law, and all with the help of texts, language hints and surprising word play: 'The Sages explained it [the dream]. The *sullam* is Sinai...the letters of Sinai are those of *sullam*' (the spelling of *sullam* in the Hebrew Bible is without the vowels, and their numerological value is the same)."

146. Fidler, "Dream Theophany," 177, stresses that Maslemet is the name of a mountain mentioned just once, in the tales of Baal and Anat—but who knows what it means? Besides, she argues, could an Ugaritic name from the second millennium B.C.E. really become the basis for Hebrew noun in the first millennium or even later?

> A picture of messengers, going up and down in a steady stream, is hard to reconcile with the concept of an ordinary ladder. On the contrary a (stone) staircase very well fits with the image of messengers going up down at the same time. There is, however, no evidence that *sullam* has this meaning. From Gen 28:12 and the data about *sll* and its *derivate* we can conclude only that a sort of bank or *a sort of way, or path, a "way"* which relates heaven to earth, must be intended.[147]

Later Houtman explains that the *sullam* appears to be the entry way into the sacred space.[148] Cohen, as previously stated, opposes Houtman's view that *sullam* is derived from *sll*, preferring the derivation from *simmultu*.[149] He quotes from Part B, lines 37–38, of the Adapa myth, which leads him to the understanding of *sullam* as a "way": "The messenger of the god Anu led him (Adapa) along *the way* of the heavens, and he *ascended* into heaven; in ascending into heaven and approaching the god Anu…"

Cohen calls our attention to the phrase *simmilat samami*, the *sullam* of the skies in the *Nergal* and *Ereskigal* epic that contains *harran same* ("the way in the skies"). One might say that "way" replaces *sullam*. Using the words interchangeably in this way does not affirm the derivation of *sullam* from *sll*. The Akkadian *harranu* means "way" not only in the physical sense, while *mesillah* means a physical road, and only by extension a way of another type. Apart from this difference, Cohen says, the two examples have much in common: both relate to a mission and in both a *sullam* leads to the gate of heaven.

Even in the Adapa text, then, the *sullam* can be understood as a "way." In the biblical description there is ascent and descent on the *sullam* while in the Akkadian the usual verb connected with the way is "went." There are also several biblical examples of *ascend* used in connected with *way*, as in Num 21:33; Deut 1:22; 3:1; Josh 10:10; 1 Sam 6:8 and 2 Kgs 3:8.

Although Houtman and Cohen do not reach an agreement that *sullam* means "way," they do at least find the common ground that it is a legitimate suggestion. While in the Adapa text, the *way* leads to the gate

---

147. Houtman, "Dream at Bethel," 340 (emphasis added).
148. Ibid., 346–47. Houtman's view is that the *sullam* appears to be the entry *way* into the sacred, which may rouse associations with Pss 120–134, which begin with *shir hamaalot* ("a song of ascents"). O the word "ascents" and the common elements found within the 15 Psalms of Ascent, see M. Fishbane, *Text and Texture: Close Readings of Selected Biblical Texts* (New York: Schocken, 1979), 103
149. See Cohen, "Motif," 37 n. 37. Cohen mentions S. A. Picchioni, *Il poemetto di Adapa* (Budapest: University of Budapest Press, 1981), 18–119. Cf. S. Dalley, *Myths from Mesopotamia: Creation, the Flood, Gilgamesh, and Others* (Oxford: Oxford University Press, 1989), 186.

of heaven, according to Houtman the *sullam*, derived from *sll*, means "way"[150] or "road," and is simply the approach to the holy place.

3.1.3. *Literal and symbolic readings of* sullam. *Sullam* may be understood as a unique term, in its context of the vision of the dream, in two complementary ways. One follows the literal text—a vertical plane connecting the earth and the heavens. This first reading having been discussed at length, the focus now is on the second one. Importantly, this proposal does not contradict the first. Focused on the symbolic level, the question is: What does the *sullam* represent or symbolize?

If we accept the possibility that it recalls and attaches to the biblical *sll*,[151] we discover that its other biblical occurrences may contain interesting symbolic significance.[152]

The *sll* root appears eleven times in the Bible: Exod 9:17; Isa 57:14 (twice); 62:10 (twice); Jer 18:15; Ps 68:5; Prov 15:19; Job 19:12; 30:12. In all of these texts, the nouns connected with *sll* are "highway" (*nativ, orah*) and "path" (*derekh*). These data seemingly reinforce Hautman's assumption that *sullam* means "road" or "path."

The noun *mesillah*[153] also derives from the *sll* root. It appears a total of 28 times in the Bible, including in the unique expression, "And a highway *maslul vaderek* shall appear there" (Isa 35:8).

For the connection between *sullam* and *mesillah*, Jer 31:21 is compared with the Jacob's Dream story:

Jer 31:21	Jacob's Dream—Gen 28:10–22
Erect (*hatsivi*) markers	the verb *nitsav*, "set up":
	"a ladder set up" (*sullam mutsav*, v. 12);
	"the LORD stood above it" (*nitsav*, v. 13);
	"I have set [for] a pillar" (*matseva*, v. 20).
Set up (*simi*) signposts	*wayasem* (vv. 11, 18)
Keep in mind the highway (*mesillah*)	*sullam*
the road (*derekh*) you have traveled	*derekh* (v. 20)
Return (*shuvi*), Maiden Israel	v. 15
Return to these towns of yours	v. 21

---

150. See also BDB 699: סלל.
151. Mandelkern, *VTC* 799. The choice of *sll* as "recalls" and "attaches to," but is not "derived from," is no coincidence. See Greenspahn, "Proverb," 37 n. 25, states that *sullam* "has been linked to the root *sll*."
152. Shapira, "Two Readings," 11, 25–28.
153. See BDB 700: סלל; Houtman, "Dream at Bethel," 339. For *mesillah* in a parallelism, see Num 29:17: "We will follow [ascend] the king's highway." See also BDB 202: דרך.

Both texts contain the verb *nitsav*, "set up," suggesting (i.e. hinting at) a pillar, a *sullam*. Both associate the *sullam* with a road or way (*mesillah*). "The road you traveled" in Jeremiah recalls the way (*derekh*) that Jacob is to go. In both, the verb "return" or "come again" occurs twice.

In his commentary on Jeremiah, Hoffman writes, "the prophet calls on the exiles to set special markers along their way into exile so they may speedily return along the same way."[154]

The imagery is the same, and the language and even the order are similar. Both have similar plot backgrounds of "departure into" exile and "return from" the Land. In the light of this comparison, the Jacob story transmits the message of "Like fathers, like sons"—the fathers being the Patriarchs and their sons the children of Israel.

Additionally, *mesillah*, derived from the *sll* root, in the sense of "paved way," appears 27 times in the Bible, of which half of these occurrence are in the Prophets (ten times in Isaiah, twice in Jeremiah and once in Joel). In most instances, particularly in the Prophets, the word is associated with return to the Land, perhaps pointing out the route from exile to the Land, to God's dwelling place. Thus, for instance, in Isa 57:14: "Build up, Build up (*sollu sollu*) a highway, Clear a road (*derekh*), remove all obstacles from the road of my people."[155] Heltzer, commenting on *sollu* ("Clear a road!") and similar expressions in Isaiah, says:

> Roads (*mesillah*) in Israelite times were no more than mountain trails from their makers threw the stones they had cleared down the mountainside and piled them haphazardly in ramps. As it is said in 62:10: "Pass through, pass through the gates." Isaiah testifies to piling up stones removed from mountain trails: "I will make all My mountains a road, And My highways shall be built up" (49:1). Thus "there shall be a highway (*mesillah*) for the other part of His people out of Assyria, such as there was for Israel when it left the land of Egypt" (11:16).[156]

Thus, understanding *sullam* as suggestive of and connected with *sll*, even though not derived directly from it, may support the legitimacy of the proposal that it is a way, and perhaps even hints at the particular way connecting Israel with the lands of exile. It distances or brings one closer to the dwelling place of God, depending on the direction taken. So we

---

154. Y. Hoffman, *Olam Hatanach: Jeremiah* (ed. Y. Hoffman; Tel Aviv: Davidson-Atai, 1994), 154.
155. See the next verse: "He who high aloft forever dwells, whose name is holy."
156. M. Heltzer, *Olam Hatanch: Isaiah* (ed. Y. Hoffman; Tel Aviv: Davidson-Atai, 1986), 260.

note Isa 40:3, "Clear in the desert a road (*mesillah*) for the Lord,"[157] as well as as 2 Chr 9:11, "and the ramps for the house of the Lord." In the story of Jacob's Dream, however, the Lord promises that He "will keep thee in all places whither thou goest[158] and bring thee again to this land" (Gen 28:15), an idea reiterated by Jacob's vow, "so that I come again to my father's house in peace" (vv. 10–12).

3.1.4. *Summary: The collected data supporting the second, symbolic reading.* Although it is legitimate to link the root *sll* with the *sullam* in the story of Jacob's Dream, such reasoning is not in itself sufficient. For indeed, our concern here is with the *sullam* not as an actual but as a symbolic object—a concept with substantial support:

First, the term *sullam* is a *hapax legomenon* in the Bible, and as such allows for multiple readings determined by context. Second, its appearance in a dream suggests that it is a special, symbolic object.[159] Third, the conclusive argument in support of the symbolic interpretation is the dream structure.[160] As will be seen shortly, Jacob's Dream is reported using a pattern familiar from *symbolic dream* accounts appearing elsewhere in the Bible, as well as in ANE literature. Understanding it in this way (in this genre) influences the interpretation.[161] Fourth, the gigantic object described as joining/linking heaven and earth cannot be an ordinary *sullam*. Fifth, that angels of God, not mortals, ascend and descend on it—a fantastical detail that also further supports the view that this is no mundane object.[162]

---

157. One reading could be to clear the road for the Lord to take, and another to clear a road for the children of Israel on their return to God. A third possibility is a metaphorical road. All three seem simultaneously possible, and enrich the text.

158. The Septuagint adds "the way," although apparently just as a clarification. See *BHK* to Gen 28:15.

159. From this standpoint, the vision in the dream may be interpreted through the promise of seed in God's verbal message, revealing another facet of the analogy to the dream vision. In the broader context of the Jacob story cycle, only after God opened Rachel's womb (Gen 30:22) did Jacob approached Laban, saying: "Give me leave to go back to my own homeland" (30:25). This can be understood as a causal as well as a chronological sequence, the birth acting as a sign and an omen to Jacob.

160. Chapter 1 discusses biblical and ANE attitudes to dreams, and the difference between the two types as does Chapter 4. See also Husser, *Narratives*, 128: "In terms of the accepted class of dreams reports, that of Gen 28:10–22 appears entirely atypical, displaying elements from one category and then the other without really belonging to either of them."

161. On literary genre as a help or a hindrance, see Chapter 1.

162. Speiser, *Genesis*, 218.

What is more, since *mal'akei 'elohim* (the angels of God) are usually messengers with a message in their hands, the absence of a verbal message encourages the search for a symbolic one, whether this be in their very presence, or in their activity, described as ascent and descent.[163] As they do elsewhere in other biblical texts, these verbs— *'alah* ("asecend") and *yarad* ("descend")—contain metaphor and symbolism. We are justified, therefore, to seek the metaphor embodied in the *sullam*.

Nonetheless, the symbolic reading is not the only interpretation possible for the dream, which contains clear structural and linguistic hallmarks of both dream types discussed so far—the theophany and the symbolic dream. The dream should therefore be interpreted on both levels. The present discussion consciously focuses on the symbolic level, since this has received less attention.

Jacob's Dream presents a story that can be understood better through a literary approach involving two simultaneous and complementary readings (the theophany and the symbolic) disclosing all the concealed and revealed strata of the story world. One need not choose between them, especially when they are not contradictory[164] but complementary. Rather, the links between them should be examined in order to understand the rich complexity of the work, and hence to interpret the dream.

The beginning of this chapter stressed the ambiguous nature of the language used in the Jacob narrative. And yet the Jacob story is not undique in making use of ambiguity. In the Joseph story, for instance, the root *nkr* ("know, recognize") indicates both recognition (*makar*) and

---

163. The Hebrew word for angel in this research means "messenger." It is made up of the root *l'k* with the initial letter *m*. See BDB 521: לאך ("messenger, one sent with a message"). On this term and on angels in the Bible, see Rofé, *Angels*, 2. See also D. Elgavish, "The Messenger and the Mission: Diplomacy in Cuneiform Sources in the Ancient East and the Bible" (Ph.D. diss., Bar Ilan University, 1990), 36, where he mentions the word structure. See also Elgavish, *Diplomacy in the Bible from Documents of the Ancient East* (Jerusalem: Magnes, 1998), 30 n. 20. He notes that "the rearranged letters of the *l'k* root are thought to parallel the Akkadian *alakum*, 'to go'…the designation includes going, an important part of the messenger's work"; E. L. Greenstein, "Trans-Semitic Idiomatic Equivalency and the Derivation of Hebrew *ml'kh*," *UF* 11 (1979): 331. See also Mandelkern, *VTC* 625.

164. See H. R. Cohen, "Medieval Commentary on Genesis in the light of Contemporary Biblical Philology—Part 2: Genesis 19–29," in *Masat Aharon: Language Studies Collection Presented to Aron Dotan* (ed. M. Ben-Asher and H. A. Cohen; Jerusalem: Mosad Bialik, 2010), 25–46, especially 31–36. Cohen declares: "I see no justification in this understanding of the vision of the ladder, even as an additional explicatory view" (n. 26). Perhaps the present study will make the symbolic reading seem not only plausible but helpful.

alienation (*nakar, nokhri*): "When Joseph saw his brothers, he *recognized* (*makar*) them, but he pretended *no recognition* (*nakar*) of them" (Gen 42:7 Fox). Similarly, in Greek the word *pharmakos* can mean "poison" or "remedy."[165] The point here is that words can carry multiple meanings, and that at times the biblical author may have knowingly made use of the linguistic possibilities to achieve his purposes. As such, we would do well to keep in mind the possibility of multiple and simultaneous interpretations of the texts before us.

3.1.5. *Conclusion*. The *hapax legomenon sullam* made possible multiple readings. As an object bridging between earth and heaven, between humans and the divinity dwelling on high, it has been understood as a ramp, a ziggurat, a mountain, a rope, the roots of a cosmic tree,[166] and even a ray of the sun (Egypt).[167] All the images correspond with the first reading strategy discussed above, one which sees the *sullam* and the story of Jacob's Dream as cultic etiology.

The second, symbolic reading is less obvious and so requires greater sensitivity to hints within the dream and its closer and remoter surroundings, in "circles of interpretation." Hence, broadening out the reach of interpretation is recommended—from the *sullam*, to the whole dream, to the entire Jacob story cycle, and out to the Patriarchs Narrative.

The first reading appears to lend more structural and functional support to the Akkadian *simmiltu* and the Babylonian ziggurat. The second, by contrast, is more supported by the Hebrew root *sll* and its derivatives, which paved the way to understanding dream and interpretation on the symbolic plane: a way leading to the Land, an approach towards God, and a way leading from the Land, a moving away from Him. Moreover, that *sullam* appears just once not only makes possible, but perhaps suggests, more than one understanding. It is the bridge between heaven and earth, between God and humanity, yet also the way into exile and the way back from it. Thus every approach to the abode of God is considered a (positive) ascent, whether in the Promised Land or outside it, and every distancing from God is a descent, whose ultimate

---

165. See Barzel, *New Interpretations*, 83; Shapira, "Multiple Meanings," 258; Brogan, "Plato's Pharmakon," 8.

166. Fidler, "Dream Theophany," 177. See also B. Margalit, "A *Weltbaum* in Ugaritic Literature?," *JBL* 90 (1971): 481–482; Frazer, *Folklore*, 228.

167. Gnuse, *Samuel*, 68, mentions the heavenly ladder upon which deceased pharaohs were thought to ascend, seeing it as the solar influence reflected on Egyptian belief, the sun's rays indicating the presence of such a ladder. When Jacob called the place "the gate of heaven," in Gnuse's view he may have used Egyptian terminology. See also Griffiths, "Celestial Ladder," 229–30.

manifestation is *Sheol*, the point farthest from God, as in "casts down into *Sheol* and raises up" (1 Sam 2:6). Before us is an analogy between ascending the *sullam* that reaches to heaven, with God standing at the top of it, and the return from exile to the Promised Land. Going towards God is the highly positive common element.

The vertical and horizontal axes of the figure below illustrate two ascents:

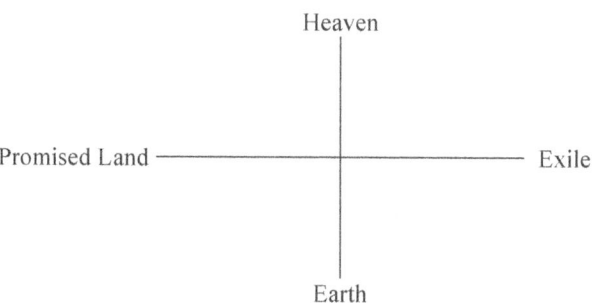

The possibilities, seemingly by design, do not contradict but complement each other. Their common point of departure is the eye of God in His abode. As the ascent of the angels draws them nearer to God, so the approach to the Promised Land is an ascent, *'alah*, a positive act.

Thus the *sullam* not only bridges between heaven and earth, and not only symbolizes the road to and from the Promised Land, but belongs to—and links—the two readings of the story. "Way," then, is the key word in understanding the *sullam*.

On the symbolic plane the "way" is indicated three times. The first is in God's promise: "I am with thee and shall keep thee in all places [ways] that thou goest, and will bring thee again unto this land" (28:15). The second time and third times are in Jacob's vow: "If God be with me and will keep me in *this way* that I go...so that *I come again* to my father's house in peace" (vv. 20–21).

Both the revealed and the concealed dimensions of "the way" in the dream, the vertical and the horizontal, in both directions, are observed from the vantage point of God's abode. Given the reiterated significance of these directions, it does not surprise that in the description of Jonah's flight from God, the key word is *yarad*, "descended": "He *went down* to Joppa... Jonah meanwhile had *gone down* of the vessel" (Jonah 1:3, 5).

Thus, from the divine perspective, the two readings and the revealed and concealed strata in the Jacob's Dream story are all contiguous.

3.2. The Second Element in the Dream Vision: "The Angels of God"— What Are They, and What Is Their Role?

In his dream Jacob sees "angels of God ascending and descending on it" (v. 12b). What is their mission?[168] The question becomes the more pivotal since angels, both in the ANE literature and in the Bible,[169] are generally charged with a mission.

In his doctoral thesis, Rofé notes: "Angel means a messenger. That is clear from the etymology of the word that is valid in Arabic, Ethiopian and Ugaritic and from biblical semantics as well—*mal'akh* appears some 80 times in the Bible to denote mortal messengers sent by mortals…"[170]

Regarding *mal'akei 'elohim* in the story of Jacob's Dream, Rofé argues that "They charge him with no mission and there is no hint that they have any mission whatsoever. And the absence of a mission shows they are of secondary importance."[171]

Fokkelman too regards them, like the ladder to heaven, as having no role except to proclaim God's imminent appearance, which is therefore no surprise.[172] Once their part is over, they appear no more—just like the Burning Bush that served to attract Moses' attention (Exod 3:2). In both revelations, the story is told when God proclaims His promise.

Westermann argues:

> The second part, also beginning with *hinneh* (behold), says nothing new but explains the function of the stairway more clearly by the vision that Jacob has of the *mal'akei 'elohim* going up and down on it. These are heavenly beings, sharply distinct from the singular "angel of God" but like "the sons of God" of Job 1:6; 2:1, who by means of their ascent and descent underscore the link between heaven and earth already described by the stairway.[173]

---

168. See T. W. Cartledge, *Vows in the Hebrew Bible and the Ancient Near East* (JSOTSup 147; Sheffield: JSOT, 1992), 147. Cartledge wrote: "and God's messengers are traveling up and down on their appointed errands" (p. 168).

169. See Elgavish, "Messenger," 35. Elgavish maintains that the term *mal'akh* is fully parallel to the Akadian *mar siprim*, meaning "a messenger."

170. Rofé, *Angels*, 2. See also Cohen, "Motif," 18 n. 10: "The Greek word for angel means messenger." So also Elgavish, "Messenger," 36

171. Rofé, *Angels*, 84, finds the distinction irrelevant, since he is concerned with understanding the text as it is, not in surmises regarding its development.

172. Fokkelman, *Genesis*, 54. See also Sarna, *Unaderstanding*, 198, who said of the angels, "They play no role in the dream."

173. Westermann, *Genesis*, 454.

My point of departure is that the narrator[174] of Gen 28:10–22 used the revealed and explicit verbal message (attributed to the J source) to explain the concealed, symbolic one of the dream vision (attributed to E).[175]

Zakovitch refers to the Midianite's dream in Judg 7:13–15: "The dream is not merely a sign but *a visual enigma* anticipating a resolution."[176] I think Jacob's Dream may also be understood as a visual enigma, one which we, as readers, must try to resolve. The concept of a visual enigma in the context of a symbolic dream appears to put us on track, as it were, towards a fuller appreciation of the narrative, as does the fact that the angels of God bear no message. The very expectation that they should do so leads to the search for their message, even if it is not verbal in nature.

Indeed Cohen, following Ibn Ezra and with the help of ANE literary texts, recognizes the important message of the angels of God in the story by virtue of their activity:[177]

> The *sullam* symbol in Jacob's Dream story seems to function as a bridge. Its source is in a parallel and wide-ranging Mesopotamian literary tradition that the Torah adopted and wove into Gen 28:10–22 after that symbol underwent a process of demythologization. In Jacob's Dream the *sullam* is not merely a background for the message sent to Jacob by his God in heaven: the angels ever ascending and descending make it a symbol of God's perpetual wakefulness and control over what goes on upon the earth.[178]

Cohen explains Ibn Ezra's view that this is an "illustration" or a parable, "as in the prophecies of Zachariah, Amos and Jeremiah, in which the angels' roles is to help God who sends them, his messengers, into the world as though on a ladder that links heaven and earth. Having fulfilled their missions, his servants return heavenward, as if on this same ladder, and report."[179]

---

174. The narrator may possibly be identified with the J source, engaging in dialogue with the E story before him and commenting on it, but there is no resolution to this hypothesis.

175. See the discussion above of the link between the vision and God's message in the dream.

176. Zakovitch, *Dream*, 36 (emphasis added).

177. For our purposes Cohen has an advantage over other scholars previously mentioned in that he recognizes that the angels' message is conveyd in their activity. Up to this point I concur. It is hard, however, either to accept or to reject his view of the message content, which seems based on a first reading of the dream.

178. See Cohen, "Motif," 26.

179. See ibid., 18.

Cohen suggests that "the example of the *sullam* is intended to overcome the natural human sense of an infinite gap that cannot be bridged, that absolutely separates the earth from the divine sphere in the heavens, as in Ps 115:16: 'The heavens belong to the Lord and the human sphere on earth, given over to man.'"[180]

He adds that the motif of the *sullam* as the bridge between two spheres that are naturally unconnected finds expression in ANE literature in the word itself, derived from *simmiltu*, particularly in the two following passages of *Nergal and Ereskigal*. The first passage is the Assyrian version of that myth, already put forth by Millard:[181]

> Nemtar *ascended* the long *sullam* of the heavens /
> Nergal *descended* the long *sullam* from the heavens.[182]

The *sullam*, whose "top reached to heaven" in our text, parallels *simmelat samami*, while the ascending and descending of the angels, messengers of God, parallels the ascent and descent of Nemtar and Nergal, identified in the Assyrian text as envoys (*mar sipri*) between the gods of heaven and those of Sheol.[183] In Mesopotamia, after ascending

---

180. See ibid., 19. On pp. 19–20 he gives biblical examples: Deut 30:11–14; Prov 30:4; Job 11:7–8; Isa 14:12–15; 66:1; Pss 103:10–13; 108:5; Amos 1:1–6. Cohen feels that this could raise doubts as to whether He could actually observe from the heavens what went on on earth. On such doubts, see Job 22:12–14: "God is in the heavenly heights; see the highest stars, how lofty! You say, 'What can God know? Can he govern through the dense cloud? The clouds screen him so he cannot see...'"

181. See Cohen, "Motif," 22–24 (emphasis added). Cohen cites Millard, "Celestial Ladder," 86–87, who discusses the links between the two, but not in the context of the *sullam* as bridge. Cohen, "*Sullam*," 172, mentions this text in connection with Jacob's Dream.

182. Cohen quotes from the Tell el-Amarna epos: "We (the gods of Heaven) are forbidden to descend to you (to *Sheol*) and you (*Ereskigal*, queen of *Sheol*) are forbidden to ascend to us." The only communication permitted between the two spheres is via the messengers. See Cohen, "Motif," 24 n. 33.

183. In Jacob's Dream the *sullam* stands between heaven and earth, not between heaven and Sheol. However, "earth" in the Bible may include the depths (Sheol), as in Jonah 2:7: "I sank to the base of the mountains; the bars of the earth closed upon me forever. Yet you brought my life up from the pit." Y. Zakovitch, *Olam Hatanach: Twelve Prophets A* (ed. N. M. Sarna; Tel Aviv: Davidson-Atai, 1994), 226, writes: "The earth is *Sheol*, as in the Akkadian *ersetu* and e.g. in Exod 15:12: 'The earth swallowed them up.' *The pit* is a name for *Sheol*. See Prov 26:27; Ps 103:4 and elsewhere." In Jonah, use of the verbs "descend" and "ascend" between the opposites "Sheol" and "heaven" is significant (see BDB 982: שאול; Amos 9:2; Job 11:8; Ps 139:8 and Isa 7:11). Descent and ascent appear to be opposites with corresponding values attached to them. The aged Jacob says, "My son must not go

the long *sullam* of heaven, Nemtar and Nergal reach the gate (*babu*) of heaven, obviously identical with "the gate of heaven" in Gen 28:17. Cohen maintains that, according to the myth, the bridge is needed not because of the enormous distance between heaven and earth, but because of a ritual prohibition.[184]

Cohen's second example is "O Sun, open the bolts of the heavens, you have raised a *sullam* of pure lapis." Here again is the motif of the *sullam* as bridge, though not because of some prohibition but rather because of the distance between the horizon and the zenith.[185] If Cohen's reasoning is followed,[186] there is no motif of messages transmitted by envoys.

Rofé, as previously mentioned, sees such perceptions as describing companies of angels ascending and descending on the *sullam* with no special purpose as more congruent with the mythic world than with concepts of angelology.[187] "It is natural," he says, "that the Jewish *midrash* and commentaries should fill in the scanty information by *finding roles for the angels*, missions assigned to them."[188]

His views on these attempts to "explain" angels are not mine, and I do no agree that the Jewish *midrash* and commentaries remained concerned with the mythic world. It was the periphery, then, that dared to commit to writing myth-like statements rejected by the Bible and its commentators, who represented the cultural center.[189] However, angels of God generally have a role that should be sought out even if it is concealed.

Though traditional commentary may sound like simply "filling in gaps" that are not written in the Bible, it is not far from what I propose. It seems that traditional interpretation was deeply sensitive to the story context. Jacob is about to leave the Promised Land, so that the hidden

---

down with you [to Egypt], for his brother is dead and he alone is left. If he meets with disaster…you will send my white head down to Sheol in grief" (Gen 42:38). The verbal link between "go down" and "grief," and between both words and Egypt may signify that to descend into Egypt is like descending into Sheol, identified with evil and grief (42:29).

184. Cohen, "Motif," 24.
185. See ibid., 24–25 n. 35–36.
186. See ibid. Besides twice using *simmiltu*, in n. 37 he mentions another Akkadian text, "The Text of Ag," discussed in the section on the *sullam*.
187. Rofé, *Angels*, 6, on angelology writes: "In this work I use the term as completely synonymous with a belief in angels, not in the sense of…a developed doctrine of angels divided by status and groups, their numbers, roles, qualities and the like."
188. Ibid., 85.
189. See Y. I. Peleg, "When God Began to Create Water (*Maim*) and Earth," *Beit Mikra* 41 (1996): 153–68, where I also define "center" and "periphery."

message of the dream would be in some way connected with that existential situation, a point of departure I share with them in the attempt to resolve the riddle. And yet my approach to the Bible is completely different—or, I should say, the way I read the Bible is completely different. While the Sages attempted to solve problems of their generations by "filling in gaps between what is written in the text and their belief and their expectation from it *drash* (explicating), my interpretation adheres strictly to the text (*close reading*) in its present form and its context, exploring the narrator's direction as I understand it. If I too sound like a *drash*, I would restate my belief that we have here *a symbolic dream* in which symbolism naturally obscures the message. Thus, symbolic meaning may sound like a *drash*, but adherence to the dream situation and comparison with other Genesis stories that dialogue with Jacob's Dream are likely to illustrate and support my proposal (Gen 32:2; 46:1–5 and 11:1–9). The Sages addressed what the story meant to them and their times, whereas I endeavour to adhere to what it states, or what I understand is hidden inside the visual enigma.

Perry and Sternberg[190] rightfully stressed that "filling in blanks by the reader is not arbitrary work. An important criterion for accepting or rejecting a given hypothesis is its relevance for a maximum number of details in the work itself."

For them, and I agree, the Sages' interpretations are not legitimate hypotheses because they come from their own world, not that of the literary work itself. I will offer some examples to illustrate.

3.2.1. *Why, according to the Sages, do the angels first ascend then descend?* Even the medieval Sages asked why the angels of God first ascended, then descended. If they dwelled on high, they would be expected to descend the *sullam* and only afterwards ascend it. Rashi answers: "They first ascend and afterwards descend. Angels accompanying him (Jacob) in the land do not leave it but ascend to heaven, and angels of outside the land descend to accompany him." The Rashbam, by contrast, thinks: "From the literal text one cannot distinguish which came first, for it is customary to mention ascent before descent."[191]

---

190. Perry and Sternberg, "Ironic Eyes," 265, maintain that the process of filling in gaps is directed and restricted by events, thematics, ideas and specific links in the work that follow the inner rules of its world, quoted in the differences between the theophany and the symbolic dream.
191. Nahmanides in the words of Rashbam, *Torat Haim*.

In general the movement of the angels has been interpreted allegorically. For instance, *Tanhuma*[192] states: "The angels represent Babylon, Media, Greece and Edom." Commenting on vv. 12–13, Obadia Sforno says: "And behold the angels of God ascend and descend upon it. And behold God is standing above it, for in the end the ministers of the nations will descend after their ascent, and God blessed be He standing there forever will not abandon His people, as it is said, 'I will make an end of all the nations…But I will not make an end of you' (Jer 46:28)."[193]

Nahmanides (the Ramban) in the name of R. Eliezer the Great says:

> It was as the sight of the Covenant between the Parts with Abraham, for he was shown the rule of four kingdoms, with their rise and fall, and this is the purpose of God's angels. As it is said in Daniel, the minister of the Greek kingdom (Dan 10:20) and of the Persian kingdom (v. 13), and he was promised that he would be raised, and that he would be with him wherever he went among them and be protected and delivered from their hands.[194]

Common to these three readings is that the dream and its interpretation simply express a human view of history, the rise and fall of peoples and cultures until the end of time.[195] Hence, in their opinion, the *sullam* represents the passage of time, history. The angels represent the nations of the earth, who ascend, descend—and disappear. At the top of the *sullam* is God, who controls the world, exalts nations and brings them low, protecting Jacob as an individual and as the symbol of the people of Israel.[196]

---

192. *Tanhuma, vayetse* 2: "Said R. Samuel son of R. Nahman, and behold angels of God ascend and descend, these are the ministers of the idolatrous nations… that the Holy One showed Jacob our father. The minister of Babylon ascends 70 rungs and descends, the minister of Media 52 (and descends), the minister of Greece 100 (rungs) and descends, and the minister of Edom ascends an unknown number. Then Jacob our father became fearful and said: maybe he cannot come down. The Holy One answered (Jer 30:10), Have no fear, my servant Jacob…be not dismayed, O Israel, even if you see him ascend and stay with me—from there I send him down!, as it is said (Obadiah 4) 'Should you nest as high as an eagle, Should your eyrie be lodged among the stars, Even from there I will pull you down declares the Lord.'"

193. See Obadia Sforno (in *Miqraot Gedolot*).

194. Nahmanides on Gen 28:12, in *Miqraot Gedolot*.

195. N. Leibowitz, *Studies in the Book of Genesis* (Jerusalem: World Zionist Organization, 1969), 209.

196. Cohen, "Motif," 18. Cohen cites Ibn Ezra, with explanations and clarifications, who rejected these allegories and defined them as *drash* (not the literal reading).

My belief is that the Sages' allegorical interpretation does not express the message of the story of Jacob's Dream; for me, the Sages' interpretation, which speaks of great nations which rise and fall, expresses their world and time more than it does the world of Jacob's Dream. Having said this, it should be admitted that the Sages did show admirable sensitivity in linking the dream interpretation to the entering and leaving of the Land: Jacob was about to leave it, and God promised to bring him back. Yet the Sages were "filling in gaps." Unlike the Sages, I, as a reader, aim to understand the vision seen in the dream as it is, without adding anything which is not there. I try to understand it via its connection to the biblical story.

Presenting the vision in the framework and context of a *symbolic dream* raises the question of what the vision in all its parts symbolizes. Before setting forth my solutions, I intend to prove that the so-called problems that have dogged generations of commentators—such as the fact that the angels *ascend* before they *descend*[197]—were actually solutions. To put it another way, what the Sages perceived as a revealed problem was in fact a concealed solution containing the narrator's message concerning God's will.

3.2.2. *What is the symbolic meaning of the dream?* The vision is described from the viewpoint of Jacob, who looks and sees:

> And he dreamed, and behold a ladder set up on the earth, and the top of it reached to heaven: and behold the angels of God ascending and descending on it. And, behold, the LORD stood above it… (Gen 28:12–13a)

On the symbolic level, *the angels of God* symbolize the Patriarchs: multiple angels in the Bible generally refer to flesh and blood envoys, while singular angels denote a messenger from heaven,[198] as in "The Angel who has redeemed me from all harm" (Gen 48:16). Multiple

---

197. This device (*hazarah*) is familiar in biblical literature. Polak, *Narrative*, 12–20, writes: "The greatness of art lies in its ability to extricate things from their frameworks… This leads readers to open their eyes and see things as they are. The narrator helps them form an opinion… The device, the phenomenon obliges readers to sense and see the matter, not just to know about it." See also Amit, *Revealed*, 105. Amit writes about using linguistic devices to trap the reader's attention: "They remove readers from their routine, directing their attention to phenomena that interest the narrator, such as hidden polemic."

198. Elgavish, "Messenger," 36, states: "Like *mar siprim* in Akkadian literature, so *mal'akh* [angel] is the most common biblical designation for messengers, whether heavenly or mortal. The first are generally singular, while those linking mortal rulers are designated as plural, *mal'akhim*."

angels as heavenly messengers are exceptional, which therefore may encourage the reader to look for an "exceptional interpretation" for their appearance in plural. Indeed, I do think that the appearance of angels in plural in Jacob's Dream is intentional.

In my view, the angels on one hand represent God,[199] while on the other, in the language of enigma and symbolism, they also represent or symbolize not just Jacob the dreamer but also Abraham and Isaac—hence the appearance in *the plural*. Thus, the promise of the Land is not just to Jacob, but to his seed (28:13),[200] the same promise given earlier to Abraham (12:7; 13:15, 17; 15:18) and to Isaac (26:3–4). (Incidentally, all of these citations are attributed to the J source.)

The heavens on the symbolic plane represent the Promised Land and the place where God dwells, as Jacob says: "This is none other but the house of God and this is the gate of heaven" (v. 17).

The earth symbolizes the lands of exile. As a reflection of the heavens, it represents places to which our ancestors went, or descended to, or were sent down to, like Haran, Ur of the Chaldeans, Egypt and Babylon.

The ladder, the *sullam*,[201] is the symbol or metaphor for the way to and from the Land of Canaan, between heaven and earth, the road the Patriarchs took and will take again—from Aram Naharayim and Haran to Canaan, and back, and the descent into Egypt. Not by chance is Laban in Gen 31 described as analogous to Pharaoh.[202]

---

199. See Rofé, *Angels*.

200. Fishbane, "Composition," 28. Fishbane states that Jacob's ancestry (expressed by "I am the God of Abraham your father"), along with the promise of the land and of seed, indicates that Jacob is the future father of the tribe. It happens, significantly, on the return from Padan, when Jacob is told: "You shall be called Jacob no more…but Israel… A nation, yea, and assembly of nations shall descend from you" (Gen 35:9–13).

201. Note Rashi's commentary on Gen 28:17: "'None other but the house of God': Said R. Elazar in the name of R. Yossi b. Zimra, that *sullam* reached from Beersheba in the south of Judah to Jerusalem in the north of the border between Judah and Benjamin. A *sullam* with its foot in Beersheba and its top in Bethel would touch Jerusalem in the middle… And it is also said (*Pesahim* 88a) 'Jacob called Jerusalem Bethel.'"

202. See also Zakovitch, *Exodus*, 46–48. In the *Passover Haggadah*, which compares Pharaoh with Laban, he finds 14 points of similarity. Both speak of hard labor; Jacob's children multiply both in Haran and in Egypt, as expressed by the root *prts* in Gen 30:43 regarding property, as in Exod 1:13 regarding population; God sees the suffering of the slaves and wants them to return to their country (compare Gen 31:11–13 and Exod 3:6–8); both contain a plea for "send me" (Gen 30:25 and Exod 7:16); they depart with wealth, and the root *ntsl* is used in both in Gen 31:9 and Exod 3:25; 12:6; in both cases the "host" changes his mind—Laban "time and

The continuous ascending and descending of the angels[203] appears to symbolize and to represent what has been and what is yet to be regarding the Patriarchs' and their descendants' attachment to the Promised Land. This is a symbolic dream that predicts things to come, with the knowledge that God has spoken, and controls both the past and the future.

3.2.3. *Why do God's angels first ascend and then descend?* If my supposition is correct and the angels of God represent (symbolize) the Patriarchs, who first immigrate ascended to the Land then descend from it "went down to Egypt" (Gen 12:10), what first appeared a problem (why do God's angels first go up and then go down?) is now seen as its solution. The narrator hints to the reader that the angels symbolize the Patriarchs, so that the vision in Jacob's Dream fits neatly within the wider Genesis story, which tells of the Patriarchs' entry into the Land *before they had left it.*

Zakovitch depicted the Patriarchs' geographical-historical entry and departure as a planned sequence, in what he described as a W-shaped pattern.[204] I see it rather as an M-shaped pattern (neatly, M for migration), with entry represented by an ascending line, and departure by a descending one.

We might also consider the chiastic arrangement of the material:

again" (Gen 31:7) and Pharaoh after each plague; the host-captor is informed of the flight in the same words—"Laban was told that Jacob had fled" (Gen 31:22), while "The king of Egypt was told that the people had fled" (Exod 14:5); pursuit of the fugitives is similarly described—"he pursued him" (Gen 31:23) and "he gave chase to the Israelites" (Exod 14:8); in both instances God intervenes against the pursuer—by warning Laban (Gen 31:11–13) and by drowning Pharaoh and his hosts (Exod 14; 15).

203. Their mission and significance is in their *activity*, legitimizing the theory that they symbolize ascent and descent from the Land. See Elgavish in n. 163 above for linguistic support for the importance of "going" in a messenger's work. Note also Nobelist John Barth, "Tales Within Tales Within Tales," *Antaeus* 43 (1981): 45–63, who studied the story within a story as a literary phenomenon and proposed three categories though which to understand the embedded story's relation to the framework, the third of which is "the dramatic relation in which the embedded story illustrates the theme through action." In *A Thousand and One Nights*, for example, each tale is linked by a return to the framework, animating both. See T. Todorov, *The Poetics of Prose* (trans. R. Howard; Ithaca, N.Y.: Cornell University Press, 1977). Additionally, Greenstein, "Retelling," shows the same linkage between its framework, the Gilgamesh legend, and the embedded story of the Flood that functions as a *mise en abyme*.

204. Zakovitch, *Exodus*, 48.

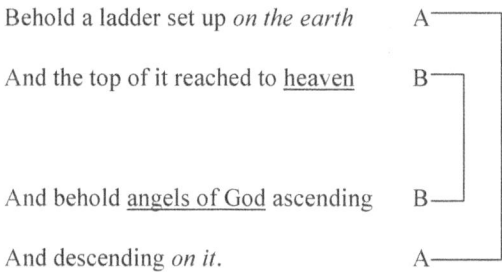

The chiastic structure appears to show two things. First, the chiasmus proves, for me, that there is affinity of two opposites, representing the opposite nature of heaven and of earth. The second aspect becomes clear when we look at the scene from Jacob's vantage point[205] and focus on the movement of the angels of God. We notice the length of the *sullam*, which reaches *from the earth towards the heavens*—that is, from down low to on high. Following Jacob's lead, we bring our gaze back down from the top of the *sullam* to observe the angels of God ascending—so

---

205. The dream vision is described from Jacob perspective (v. 12), as expressed by "and behold." As elsewhere in the Bible, it separates the narrator's viewpoint from that of a protagonist; see A. Berlin, *Poetics and Interpretation of Biblical Narrative* (BLS 9; Sheffield: Almond, 1983), 62. Berlin argues "Of course, not every use of *hinneh* marks a shift in narrative perspective, but it is used often enough for this function to be considered a poetic marker" (p. 91).

Bar-Efrat, *Design*, 64, cites examples of "and behold" following a verb of seeing (Gen 24:63; Judg 3:24; 1 Sam 10:10; 2 Sam 15:32; 16:1; 18:24; 1 Kgs 18:7), emphasizing that "In these examples *and behold* relates the sight in question to the one who sees the thing described, not to the narrator." See also, for instance, Y. Amit, *Judges* (Mikra Leyisrael; Tel Aviv: Am Oved, 1999), 78, who explicates the story of Ehud ben Gera, "And they waited a long time, and behold, he opened not the doors of the parlour; therefore, they took the key and opened them, and behold, their lord was fallen down dead" (Judg 3:25 KJV): "*And behold* [*hinneh*] turns the reader's attention to the figure who sees the event related, bringing the reader closer to the impression of the character in the story." See also p. 90, on "And behold, as Barak pursued Sisera, Jael came out to meet him and said unto him, some and I will show thee the man whom thou seekest, and when he came into her tent, behold, Sisera lay dead... (Judg 4:22): "The first *and behold* turns the reader towards Jael's angle of vision, when she suddenly sees Barak pursuing Sisera. The second *and behold* presents Barak's angle of vision, what he saw when he entered the tent." See also "And Jephthah came to Mitzpeh, unto his house, and behold, his daughter came out to meet him" (Judg 11:34). Amit (p. 206) writes: "*and behold* brings the reader to the character's vantage point. Jephthah sees but one thing, that his daughter is the one coming out to met him." On the syntactic significance of "and behold," see Polak, *Narrative*, 266–67; Kogut, *Hinneh*, 133–54.

our gaze is led in a downwards direction. Then, as we observe the *ascent* and *descent* of the angels, our gaze once again follows and upwards then downwards trajectory.

Thus, by apprehending the *sullam* structure upon which the angels travel, followed by recorded movements of the angels upon it, we, as onlookers with Jacob, witness a two-fold ascent and descent structure—an M-shaped narrative, if you will.

The presence of the M-shaped structure supports my claim that "the angels of God" are first described as "ascending" and then as "descending" in order to hint to the reader that the angels are meant to symbolize the ascending and descending of the patriarchs into and from the Land. The direction of the progression of the angels in the dream—they unexpectedly begin by ascending—causes the reader to ponder the meaning of this unexpected order. My answer is that the unexpected order of the angels' progression is intended to draw the reader's attention to Abraham's journey, which began with his ascension to the Land of Canaan. Once aware of this, the sensitive readers will then experience what Shapira notes in his doctoral dissertation, namely that "a deviation in syntactic or content structure…encourages multiple readings."[206]

3.3. *The Third Component in the Dream Vision: The Verbs* 'alah *(Ascend) and* yarad *(Descend) as a Key to Interpretation*
In the following I will offer two readings—one literal, one metaphorical—of the verbs *'alah* and *yarad*.

3.3.1. *Understanding* 'alah *and* yarad *(in Genesis 28:12) metaphorically*.
The verbs *'alah* and *yarad* indicate movement in opposite directions. Their connotative use in the Bible shows that besides technical direction, metaphoric meaning is common to both.[207] In my reading, the ascent and descent of the angels of God in Jacob's Dream can be understood metaphorically as well as concretely, with their positive and negative connotations.

It is important to note that in Hebrew the verb *'alah* signifies immigration (*'aliyah*) to the land of Israel, while the verb *yarad* denotes emigration (*yeridah*) from the Land, which has negative connotations. Immigrants to the Land of Israel are called *'olim* and emigrants are termed *yordim*.

---

206. N. Leibowitz, *Studies in the Book of Exodus* (Jerusalem: World Zionist Organization, 1973), 402. Leibowitz notes that "verbs of movement such as to ascend, to descend, to retreat, to go before, are frequently used in the Bible…metaphorically." See also Peleg, "Forty Days," 262–74.

207. Shapira, "Two Readings," 162.

The verb *'alah* appears 890 times in the Bible, while *yarad* appears 380 times. Metaphorical use for both verbs is widespread. The fact that they are contradictory/opposing verbs[208] encourages one to concentrate on those instances where the verbs are juxtaposed, presumably not by chance, to stress the contradiction. In my opinion, textual meanings can be uncovered through awareness of this literary technique.

For our purposes it is important to note that exposing the metaphorical meaning of the verbs *'alah* and *yarad* in Jacob's Dream lends serious support to the symbolic interpretation of it. Because of this importance, I shall demonstrate the metaphorical use of these verbs in several biblical stories.

3.3.2. *The verbs* 'alah *and* yarad *in the story of Judah and Tamar (Genesis 38)*. Making extensive use of the verbs *'alah* and *yarad*, the story of Judah and Tamar provides a rich seam of evidence for our understanding of how the two opposing verbs function. Of the 45 occurrences of the verb "ascend" in Genesis, 32 appear in the Joseph story; of the 39 occurrences of "descend" in the same book, 28 are found in the Joseph narrative.[209] The frequency with which these verbs appear together, as well as their locations,[210] encourages examination of whether *'alah* and *yarad* represent a keyword pairing and whether signficance can be seen in their deliberate linkage. Unsurprisingly, such linkage occurs often in the Joseph stories, which describe events taking place both in Canaan and in Egypt.

---

208. The following is a selection of two opposite verbs appearing together: "And behold, angels of God ascending and descending on it" (Gen 28:12); "I Myself will go down with thee into Egypt, and I Myself will also surely bring thee up again" (46:4); "The stranger in your midst shall rise above you higher and higher, while you sink lower and lower" (Deut 28:43); "the Lord…casts down into Sheol and raises up" (1 Sam 2:6). See also 2 Chr 20:16; Job 7:9; Pss 104:8; 107:26; Prov 21:22; 30:4; Eccl 3:21; Amos 2:9. R. Machlin, "Polarity in the [Hebrew] Word *nefesh*," *Beit Mikra* 57 (1974): 410, states: "Polarity runs like a silken thread through all of nature. It is an integral part of our thought. It determines polarity in language." See also R. Gordis, *The Word and the Book* (New York: Ktav, 1976), 137, 271–79.

209. Of these, 16 relate to the descent into Egypt, to be discussed separately.

210. Though used frequently before that, from 16:4 until the end of the Joseph story "descend/go down" is not used. The verb "come" stands in place of "descend/go down": "…and came into Egypt, Jacob and all his seed with him" (46:7); "And these are the names of the children of Israel which came into Egypt" (46:8 KJV). See also 46:26, 27, 32; 47:2 and 1 Sam 1. "Come" is used in the sense of "enter" (see BDB 97: בוא), as in "Jericho was shut up tight, and no one could leave or enter" (Josh 6:1). "Come" seems to indicate a neutral attitude towards entering/coming into Egypt, rather than "go down" with its negative connotation.

2. The Story of Jacob's Dream at Bethel

The first example to be considered is "...Judah *went down* (*yarad*) from his brethren, and turned in to a certain Adullamite whose name was Hirah" (Gen 38:1 KJV). Why was "went down" used to describe what Judah did? Going down from the mountain area to the plane is indeed a matter of topography.[211] However, as Judah "went down" from his brethren, the connotation is that he parted from them. According to Alter, "down from" is an extraordinary expression creating the connection between the separation of one brother from the rest and the separation of Joseph to be described in 39:1: "And Joseph *was taken down* ['was brought down' Fox] into Egypt."[212]

Comparing Joseph and Judah, like any other comparison, involves appreciation of both similarities and differences. Here, the similarity is in the use of the same verb, while the difference lies in its connotation. Judah is the subject of an intransitive verb, Joseph of a passive form: Judah *went down*, while Joseph *was taken down* against his will.[213] Zakovitch and Shinan argue: "The apparent function of ch. 38, placed before [the events of] ch. 39 is to show Joseph's superiority over Judah who fell into the trap Tamar set for him, while Joseph escaped the snare of Potiphar's wife."[214] The comparison, then, between *went down* and *was taken down* reflect negatively on Judah's actions.

A further point relates to the unusual construction "went down from his brethren," which was seemingly chosen to attract the reader's attention and encourage multiple readings of the text.[215] In my opinion, the exceptional phrase "went down from his brethren" invites discussion of *yarad* as a keyword, and particularly the rhetorical role it serves. The inspiration for a second reading, one which looks at the metaphorical significance of the verb,[216] stems from the breadth of meanings that *yarad* seems to carry.

---

211. J. Klein, *Olam Hatanach: Genesis* (ed. M. Weinfeld; Tel Aviv: Davidson-Atai, 1982), 213.

212. Alter, *Biblical Story*, 55–56.

213. See Zakovitch, *Reflection Stories*, 55–56.

214. Y. Zakovitch and A. Shinan, *The Judah and Tamar Story: Genesis 38 in Ancient Translations and in Early Jewish Literature* (RPJSI 15; Jerusalem: The Hebrew University, 1992), 212, 220: "There is a further inverse comparison between Jacob's 'I will go down mourning to my son in *Sheol*' (37: 5) and Judah who when his period of mourning was over, went up to Timnah to his sheepshearers (38:12), shows no grief whatever: shearing was generally a festive occasion..." See the discussion of *mise en abyme* in Bosworth, *Story*, 1.

215. Shapira, "Multiple Meanings," 259.

216. The Sages related to the metaphorical sense of "went down," as did Weinfeld, *Genesis*, 223. Weinfeld noted its technical sense, as well as the word play in 37:1. Judah's isolation is indicated in "Hear O Lord the voice of Judah, And restore him to his people" (Deut 33:7).

3.3.3. *The verbs ʿalah and yarad in the Golden Calf story (Exodus 32)*. In the Golden Calf story the keywords *ʿalah* and *yarad* appear, respectively, seven and three times. They appear to carry both a metaphorical as well as geographical meaning.[217] Buber, in his discussion of keywords, notes that the use of "going up" in connection with the journey from Egypt to the Land of Israel is not related solely to the topographical realities involved in such a movement.[218] According to Buber,

> Some intimations come from the dialectics of *going up* (*ʿalah*), linked to the dialectics of *people* (*ʿam*), which appears some 30 times in our passage, and *going up* not even half as many... Nonetheless it is very important... Even the narrative introduction to the dialogue in Exod 32:1–10 contains: 'Moses, the man who brought us up out of the land of Egypt' (v. 1 KJV) and again, 'These be thy Gods O Israel which brought thee up out of the land of Egypt' (v. 4). And this phrase is repeated four times. It would not surprise were it not that it appears in our text only. To be precise, the causative/affective (*hiphil*) form of *go out*, which is synonymous, is found 24 times outside the text under discussion (and twice within it) while the *hiphil* form of go out in this sense is found only three times in the entire book. That is to say, our story on sin and atonement revolves around a particular subject, which is *going up*.[219]

As I see it, the metaphorical use of these two verbs relates not only to the movement towards the Promised Land, which is described as a "going up," but also to Moses' "going up" on the mountain to God. This is, in my view, opposed to the "going down" from the mountain and from God to the people. In the first verse we are told: "And when the people saw that Moses delayed to come down out of the mount, the people gathered themselves together unto Aaron, and said to him, Up, make us gods, which shall go before us, for this Moses, the man who brought us up out of the land of Egypt, we do not know what has become of him" (Exod 32:7 KJV).

The verbs *ʿalah* and *yarad* confront one another; as the story unfolds, they do so again: "And the Lord said unto Moses, Go, get thee down; for thy people which thou broughtest up from the Land of Egypt have corrupted themselves" (v. 7). There is an analogy here between Moses going down and the people's sinful behavior. "Get thee down" represents motion with a metaphorical significance, as in many other places in the Bible.[220]

---

217. Buber, *The Way*, 304–5.
218. See J. Wijngaard, "*hotsi*' and *heʿelah*: A Twofold Approach to the Exodus," *VT* 15 (1965): 91–102, noting the difference in meaning between the verbs.
219. Buber, *The Way*, 303–4.
220. The Sages too were aware of this, and discussed the descent seen in the Golden Calf story. Of "Get thee down for thy people have corrupted themselves,"

Awareness and recognition of possible metaphoric connotations enriches the understanding of the story.

3.3.4. *The verbs ʿalah and yarad in the Samson Story (Judges 13–15).* Israel Rosenson notes that the Samson stories describe movement between two places, typically making use of the verbs "going up" and "going down."[221] This is by no means rare in the Bible, which refers to "a land of hills and valleys" (Deut 11:11). The location of the biblical narrative, therefore, makes it possible that *ʿalah* and *yarad* are geographically precise technical terms. At the same time, as Garsiel has shown, we may also be dealing with concealed metaphorical meaning.[222]

Zakovitch points out that "the root *yrd* and its parallel opposite *ʿalh* are prominent in the Samson stories. Almost every action of Samson's either begins or ends with his going down or going up."[223] He notes that "Samson's going down to Ashkelon, like other descents before or after any action he undertook (see 14:1, 5, 7; 15:8) on his own initiative, is entirely different from his being brought down[224] to Gaza by the Philistines (16:21) when control of the action passed temporarily to them."[225] Zakovitch argues that "By contrast with Samson's descent, the Philistines *go up* to look for him (Judg 15:9), illustrating that theirs was an opposing intent."[226]

3.3.5. *The verbs ʿalah and yarad in the story of Elijah's ascent to heaven (2 Kings 2:1–2).* Here the two verbs appear opposite one another, the story opening with: "When the Lord was about to take Elijah up to heaven in a whirlwind." Elijah considered parting company from Elisha,

---

Tractate Berakhot says: "What does get thee down mean? Said R. Elazar, 'Get thee down from thy greatness. It seems that greatness is symbolized by height'." Leibowitz, *Exodus*, 402, states: "The *Midrashim* use this possibility in the nature of human speech to enrich and deepen the meaning of the verse about going up and going down physically, geographically, in its metaphorical sense."

221. I. Rosenson, "Ṣorʿah-Timnah, Going Up and Going Down: Geographical Descriptions as Commentary in the Samson Stories," *Beit Mikra* 41 (1996): 135–52.

222. M. Garsiel, "Metonymic and Metaphoric Descriptions in the Bible Story," *Criticism and Interpretation* 23 (1988): 15–20.

223. Zakovitch, *Samson*, 89.

224. The verb *yarad* in Hophal (one of Hebrew's passive forms), like *ʿalah*, opposes *yarad* in Qal (an active Hebrew form), as in the story of Judah who goes down to Adullam of his own will, contrasted with Joseph forcibly taken down to Egypt.

225. Zakovitch, *Samson*, 118.

226. Ibid., 135.

but "Elijah and Elisha set out from Gilgal and…went down to Bethel" (2:1–2). Topographically this is impossible, as one ascends from Gilgal to Bethel. Either they should have "gone down" to Bethel, or a neutral verb like "went" should have been used. The usage we find, deviant as regards content, suggests the reading found in the Septuagint, which replaces *yarad* with "and they came."

Some scholars have provided linguistic solutions for this apparent anomaly. Driver, for instance, located four biblical examples of *yarad* seemingly carrying the meaning of *'alah*, and of *'alah* seemingly carrying the meaning of *yarad*. The present case, 2 Kgs 2:1–2, is one such case.[227] The journey of Elijah and Elisha from Gilgal (813 meters above sea level) to Bethel (963.3 meters) is an ascent and not a descent. In his view, the reference to "ascent" in contexts where the actual journey involves downward movement probably signifies a northward progression; by the same reasoning, "descent" can also signify a southward trajectory. By this logic, "going down" is used instead of "going up" because of the southward nature of the journey from Gilgal to Bethel.

In my view, however, two reasons make this difficult to accept. For one thing, the topographical reality is that Gilgal sits to the southeast of Bethel. An additional counter-argument—one that will be discussed more fully in Chapter 4—is provided by the geographical orientation of the Bible narrative.

My own view, as noted above, is that deviant use of a word or expression serves to make possible and encourage multiple readings. We see this in the phrase "Judah *went down* from his brethren," which make a metaphoric, derived reading possible. Rosenson perceptively shows that "'went down to Bethel' contradicts the opening, 'when the Lord was about to take Elijah up to heaven.' Before us are opposing statements, going up as against going down: in contrast to going up to heaven, going to Bethel is perceived as a descent."[228]

Although the metaphorical reading need not contradict the geographical one, it does so in the present case. The matter arises again in relation to Abraham's descent into Egypt (Gen 12:10).

3.3.6. *The verbs* 'alah *and* yarad *in the book of Jonah: "had gone down…and fell asleep (*vayeradem*)" (Jonah 1:5).*[229] In the book of Jonah we witness the opposition between *'alah* in v. 2 and *yarad* in vv. 3, 5.

---

227. G. R. Driver, "On *'alah* 'Went Up Country' and *yarad* 'Went Down'," *ZAW* 69 (1957): 74–77.
228. Rosenson, "Samson," 147.
229. See Peleg, "Jonah," on two readings of Jonah.

The former verb represents movement in God's direction, while the latter functions as a keyword throughout ch. 1, describing Jonah's flight from God's service, i.e. in the opposite direction, both horizontally and vertically. First "he went down to Joppa" (v. 3a), then "had gone down into the hold of the vessel where he lay down (*vayeradem*, which is phonologically similar to *vayered*, 'went down') and fell asleep." The very use of "down" indicates a negative attitude to Jonah's flight (v. 5). Y. Zakovitch states: "First he went down to the ship, then down into the hold, as if to get as far away from God as possible. As if that were not enough, he falls asleep (note the word play)—mental flight following the physical flight."[230]

The metaphorical use of *going down* not only expresses a negative view of Jonah's action, but is directly connected to the content of fleeing and distancing himself from God. Thus it reinforces the negative metaphorical inferences.

This insight into the role of the verb *yarad* in the book of Jonah strengthens the understanding suggested by present study—namely, that the verb *yarad* in Jacob's Dream has a metaphorical meaning with a negative connotation.

3.3.7. *How the metaphorical meaning of 'alah and yarad originated.* The verb *yarad* indicates motion opposite in direction from *'alah*. Both may have, besides their technical-topographic designation, a metaphoric one that allows *'alah* to express a positive evaluation, while *yarad* has a negative one. One surmise as to how the derived meanings evolved is offered by Rosenson:

> From the dawn of creation, a primeval mold of opposites, heaven and earth has existed. Since the contrast was invested with religious meaning: "The heavens are the heavens of the Lord, but the earth hath He given to the children of men" (Ps 115: 16), activities of going up and going down have become symbolic of rising nearer to God on one hand, and moral degeneration and falling away from Him on the other.[231]

The heaven and earth model of opposites as the basis for the metaphoric meanings of *'alah* and *yarad*, also opposites, seems acceptable, though with a certain reservation. Although the heavens are the Lord's and He gave the earth to humanity, what is common to biblical descriptions of the divine abode is that God is above and humans below. Humans ascend

---

230. Zakovitch, *Twelve*, 220.
231. Rosenson, "Samson," for references and bibliography. Note that the *waw* connector appended to "earth" may be read as either "and" or "but."

to God and God descends to humans. One need not deduce from this that God lives in heaven. That polemic, for all its theological significance, does not add to or detract from the present issue.

From the foregoing it becomes clear that using "went down...and fell asleep"[232] in describing Jonah's flight is not a technical choice: *its metaphorical significance expresses a negative view of the act.*[233]

To conclude, as we have already argued, the derived use of these two verbs in the Bible supports the attempt to reveal their metaphoric meaning in the Jacob's Dream story. That is, besides the vision of the *sullam* described in Gen 28:12, the ascent and descent of the angels of God may be seen as having a positive and a negative connotation. If Canaan ("the Promised Land") is the abode of God, then the metaphoric usage of *'alah* and *yarad* to describe entering and leaving it carries a positive and a negative connotation.

It turns out that entry into the Land is called *'aliyah* and bears a positive connotation, while leaving the Land is termed *yeridah* and bears a negative connotation.

3.4. *Is Jacob's Dream a* Dream Theophany *or a* Symbolic Dream?

We are already familiar with the typological division of biblical and ANE dreams into the dream theophany, where the divinity brings a direct verbal message, and a symbolic dream, where the significance of the vision is often unclear. Oppenheim notes that the distinction dates from a pattern present in Sumerian sources in the third millennium B.C.E., from Homer (ca. 1000 B.C.E.) and on to Ptolemaic Egypt in the late pre-Christian era.[234] Our central issue is which model Jacob's Dream follows.

---

232. On literary devices characteristic of biblical literature, see, e.g., Zakovitch, *Twelve*, 216, 218. Zakovitch notes that "went down...fell asleep" as word play.

233. At the beginning of Jonah, for example, we note the contrast between *'alah* (v. 2), and *yarad* (vv. 3, 5). The former indicates a movement toward God; e.g., "for their wickedness is come up (*'alah*) before Me" (Jonah 1:2). But *yarad* describes how Jonah flees in the opposite direction from the Lord's mission (v. 3), on two planes, horizontal and vertical. The metaphorical *yarad* in the Jonah story does not represent the negative connotation alone, but is directly connected, in terms of content, to leaving the Land and to escaping from God (1:3). This reinforces the supposition regarding the development of the term's negative metaphorical meaning. That is, each *'aliyah*, such as the ascending of the angels in Jacob's Dream, is an act of growing closer to God, in the sky at the top of the *sullam*—and each *yeridah* is an act of growing distant from God, and therefore considered negative.

234. Oppenheim, "*Halom*," 3:144.

3.4.1. Jacob's Dream as a dream theophany.

Most scholars regard Jacob's Dream as a *dream theophany* belonging to the cultic etiology (*hieros logos*) of Bethel, explaining how the place became sacred.[235] The revealed interpretation of the vision in the dream appears in v. 17: "This is none other but the house of God, and this is the gate of heaven."

Oppenheim[236] defines the patterns of the *message dream* (i.e. the *dream theophany*) thus:

Frame	1.	The time and place of the dream: appearance of the divinity or of his messenger
Core	2.	Message from the divinity who appears
Frame	3.	The dream ends as the dreamer awakes, then responds. The message materializes (if this is relevant).

Jacob's Dream at Bethel fits this model.

Frame	1.	The time and place of the dream: appearance of the divinity or of his messenger	Gen 28:10–13a, "angels of God" and "the Lord stood above it."
Core	2.	Verbal message from the divinity who appears	Gen 28:13b–15
Frame	3.	Dream ends, dreamer awakes and responds. The message materializes [or fulfillment] (if this is relevant).[237]	Gen 28:16–17

If indeed Jacob's Dream is a dream theophany, where God reveals Himself and brings a verbal message, how does one explain the vision[238] in the dream? The vision generally is considered an ornament[239] devoid

---

235. Above, n. 14.

236. Oppenheim, *Interpretation*, 186. I have made of use of Fidler's diagram, "Dream Theophany," 16. See also Gnuse, *Samuel*, 75. On p. 64 Gnuse relates it to the Elohistic model, which uses divine revelation in a dream for theological reasons.

237. No message materializes directly from Jacob's Dream, but Fidler, "Dream Theophany," 134, notes that it does so later in the Jacob story cycle, in Gen 31:3; 33:18; 35:1–4.

238. In their research specifically relating to the dream vision and its *sullam*, for Hautmann, Millard, Griffith, Gnuse, Fidler, Lipton and others, effort was concentrated mainly on efforts to identify the *sullam* in Mesopotamian (Hautman, von Rad) or in Egyptian (Griffith) or Canaanite (Millard, Clifford, Gnuse, Fidler) literary sources, assuming apparently that those civilizations inspired the description. For our purposes there has been no focused comprehensive discussion on the symbolic interpretation of the vision in Jacob's Dream at Bethel

239. See Sarna, *Understanding*,193; Fokkelman, *Genesis*, 54; De Pury, *Promesse*, 378; Fidler, "Dream Theophany," 172;

of an intrinsic message,[240] or as an "addition."[241] Westermann, in fact, states, "The second part, also beginning with *hinneh*, says nothing new but explains the function of the stairway more clearly by the vision."[242]

3.4.2. *Jacob's Dream as a* symbolic dream. The dream contains both a divine message in words (vv. 13–15) and a vision (vv. 12–13), which raises the question of whether the vision too is a message and, further, what that message might be. The vision raises its own question as to whether Jacob's Dream follows the symbolic model or attested in the Bible and the ANE literature. If so, its interpretation should be symbolic.

Gnuse, following a five-point model proposed by Richter,[243] understands the Joseph story as follows:

I. Announcement of the dream
II. Introductory formula (*behold*)
III. Dream corpus[244]
    A. Image
    B. Result
IV. Dream interpretation
V. Dream fulfillment (comes later in the plot).

The Richter/Gnuse dream framework is now used to examine the dream at Bethel within the symbolic dream structure:

---

240. Fokkelman, *Genesis*, 54; Sarna, *Understanding*, 198. See Fidler, "Dream Theophany," 155 n. 125. Fidler cites other scholars who support this view.

241. Husser, *Narratives*, 124: "the vision…is perhaps a late addition." Further, on p. 132, Husser ends his discussion on Jacob's Dream by saying: "Paradoxically however, and no doubt by reason of the theological importance of the promise and of the words of salvation expressed in the message (vv. 13–15), the dream regained some of its prestige at a later period with the addition of the *vision* of the staircase and of the angels in v. 12. The aim apparently was to touch up a divine manifestation that no doubt was considered too bland for the taste of the day, and to place the words that follow in a context of greater solemnity."

242. Westermann, *Genesis*, 454–55.

243. Richter, "Traum," 204–5. Richter refers to Jacob's Dream on p. 190. See also Gnuse, *Samuel*, 86–87. Gnuse used Richter's model to analyze the Midianite's symbolic dream in Judg 7:13–15, as well as those in the Joseph story cycle and Daniel, but not those of the Patriarchs, which in Gnuse's opinion, Richter finds more congruent with heard message dreams, following Oppenheim's model. Gnuse appears to have ignored the special structure of Jacob's Dream at Bethel, with its symbolic dream features, which appears to be in keeping with the Richter model.

244. See Oppenheim, "*Halom*." See Richter, "Traum," 204–5. What Oppenheim calls "core of the dream report," Richter calls "dream corpus" (pp. 204–5).

2. The Story of Jacob's Dream at Bethel

Implementing the framework for Gen 28:10–22	Five components of the symbolic dream
I. Announcement of the dream	"And he dreamed" (v. 12)
II. Introductory formula (*behold*)	"and behold"[245] (v. 12)
III. Dream corpus	"and behold a ladder… And behold, the Lord stood above it" (vv. 12–13a)
IV. Dream interpretation	"the house of God" (v. 17); "God…will keep me in this way" (v. 20)
V. Dream fulfillment	Gen 31:13; 33:18; (35:1)

Just as Gnuse examined the Midianite's dream in Judg 7:13–15 according to Richter's model,[246] so now we consider Jacob's Dream in comparison to the Midianite dream:

Jacob's Dream	The Midianite's Dream
I. Announcement of the dream: "And he dreamed" (v. 12)	I. Announcement of the dream: "behold I dreamed a dream" (Judg 7:13)
II. Introductory formula: "and behold" (Gen 28:12)	II. Introductory formula: "and behold" (7:13)
III. Dream corpus: A. Image: "And he dreamed, and behold a ladder set up on the earth, and the top of it reached to heaven" (Gen 28:12) B. Result: (1) "and behold the angels of God ascending and descending on it"; (2) "And, behold, the LORD stood above it" (v. 13)	III. Dream corpus: A. Image: "a cake of barley fell into the camp" (7:13) B. Result: cake overturns the tents (7:13)
IV. Dream interpretation: vv. 17, 20 A. Formula of interpretation: "this [is] none other but the house of God" (v. 17); "in this way" (v. 20) B. Interpretation: (1) Identification: (a) "this [is] none other but the house of God, and this [is] the gate of heaven" (v. 17). (b) " and will keep me in this way that I go" (v. 20)	IV. Dream interpretation (7:14) A. Formula of interpretation: "this is nothing else but" (7:14) B. Interpretation: 1. Identification: "The sword of Gideon" (7:14)

245. Weisman, *Cycle*, 66. While he agreed that "behold" appeared in symbolic dreams, he did not conclude that it served to qualify Jacob's Dream at Bethel as such.
246. Gnuse, *Samuel*, 81.

(2) Meaning: (a) "Surely the LORD is in *this place*" (v. 16); (b) "and will bring thee again into this land" (v. 15); a and b: "So that I come again to my father's house in peace… And this stone…shall be God's house" (vv. 21–22)	2. Meaning: "into his hand God has given Midian" (7:15)

Jacob's Dream, then, is structured—deliberately, it would seem—on both the pattern of dream theophany *and* symbolic dream, raising the possibility that the division into two dream models does not apply in this case (Gen 28:12) nor in Gen 31:10–13.[247] From our standpoint, classification is less important than the understandings derived from the complex structure, which I see as a key to the meaning (the interpretation) of the dream. Ehrlich[248] relates to it as a symbolic dream, although he failed to examine its symbolic significance and declared the vision devoid of meaning.[249]

Some scholars[250] note the complexity of Jacob's Dream and suggest that, in addition to its classification as *dream theophany*, it contains elements that also justify its classification as a *symbolic dream*. However, this distinction did not prompt them to explore the symbolic meaning (interpretation) of Jacob's Dream.[251]

Lipton, for instance, argues that "This dream, although it contains the striking visual image of the ladder…is not *symbolic* in the style of the Joseph dreams."[252] It is unfortunate that Ehrlich, who defined Jacob's Dream as a *symbolic dream*,[253] did not relate to the question of the dream's symbolic meaning, but also claimed that the "vision" lacked meaning.[254]

---

247. Fidler, "Dream Theophany," 29, 40. See also Lichtenstein, "E Document," who cites ANE examples of dreams structured on both models.
248. See Ehrlich, *Der Traum*, 58; idem, "Traum," 3:2023.
249. See Ehrlich, *Der Traum*, 29.
250. Richter, "Traum," 204–5, 209; Baruch, "Deutronomic," 13; Fidler, "Dream Theophany," 154.
251. There is justification for the claim that the knowledge, or rather the conception generally accepted by scholars, that Jacob's Dream is a theophany dream, has prevented scholars from searching for the symbolism in the "vision in the dream," even though they have found in it signs of a symbolic dream.
252. Lipton, "Revisions," 28.
253. See Ehrlich, *Der Traum*, 58, and also "Traum," 3:2023.
254. See Ehrlich, *Der Traum*, 29.

While Fidler recognizes elements of the symbolic dream, rather than look for symbol in the vision in v. 17, she interprets it in "concrete" terms. She notes that while there is a report of a vision, as is in symbolic dreams, particularly in that of the Midianite (Judg 7:14), nevertheless

> It is different only because it does not explicate the dream in symbols, but "concretely," its object being the divine revelation… In the Bethel dream the link between the interpretation of the vision (in v. 17) and the verbal message (vv. 13b–15) is indirect. This is the link between what we defined as the two different facets of the story: the "Bethel facet," centered around identifying the place: "This is none other than the house of God and this is the gate of heaven"; and the "Jacob facet"[255] focused on the verbal message.[256]

Since the dream is structured both on the pattern of dream theophany and symbolic dream, its meaning should be examined on both planes: the revealed plane that sees it as explaining why the place became sacred to Jacob, and on the symbolic, concealed one.

3.4.3. A note on methodology in favor of two readings for the dream and its meaning. My reading approach, which seeks to combine the revealed and concealed interpretations of the dream, resembles that of Perry and Sternberg in "The King Through Ironic Eyes," though it must be emphasized that the decision to analyze the story of Jacob's Dream using the two-pronged methodology is my own initiative and responsibility. Perry and Sternberg regard both the revealed and conceived views within Henry James' novella "The Turn of the Screw" (see Chapter 1, section 2.6) not as contradictory but legitimate within the ambiguity hypothesis. Indeed, if the governess appearing in James' work actually saw ghosts of the dead servants, they were real ghosts and this is a ghost story; yet if, as the authors note, "only she saw them, she was hallucinating and this first and foremost is a psychological drama."[257]

---

255. Richter, "Traum," 210, maintains that Jacob's Dream is "without explication," but adds that after awakening (v. 16) Jacob recognizes the significance of the place, meaning that the dream "has no meaning for the dreamer's future…but for the place." This may have given rise to Fidler's "Bethel facet" and "Jacob facet" above. I shall try to show the second as focused on the way, and the first focused on the place.

256. Fidler, "Dream Theophany," 283, does not explain why a symbolic dream is explained "concretely" and why a dream with all the characteristics of the symbolic is not explained on those lines.

257. Perry and Sternberg, "Ironic Eyes," 183.

The scholarly argument about Jacob's Dream has a similar core. Should it be interpreted on the "concrete" level as *dream theophany*, as Fidler[258] proposes, making it mainly an etiological story regarding Bethel, or symbolically? If the latter, we are left to wonder: What does the dream represent (or symbolize)? Which approach is "right"?[259]

Perry and Sternberg's solution for the Henry James story may help us. They say: "The main compositional principle here is that it is impossible and unnecessary to choose between the two hypotheses… A full reading of the story demands that each hypothesis by itself be rejected, and only the two taken together constitute a legitimate reading."[260]

3.4.4. *Gudea's dream as a theophany dream and symbolic dream.* As J. Ha'efrati does in "The Dead of the Wilderness: A Lyric Poem," so too here I want to examine Jacob's Dream verse-by-verse to see how the two readings or, as he puts it, "impressions," appear there, to avoid distorting the significance of the work through selective interpretation.[261]

Understanding Jacob's Dream on the principle of two simultaneous readings—or two impressions, or interpretations, or meanings—with no need to decide between them, would explain its affinitive links, and particularly those between the dream vision (vv. 12–13a) and the verbal message (vv. 13b–15). In the process, I shall attempt to provide convincing evidence that multiple readings of Bible texts in general and of Jacob's Dream in particular enrich the reader's intellectual world and that of the text. Additionally, I shall look at the question of whether Jacob was aware of the double message in his dream.

This interpretation of the text and especially of Jacob's Dream has support from ANE literature, which provides accounts of dreams that embody both the theophanic and the symbolic.

In the Sumerian literature, the dream of Gudea provides a particularly interesting parallel. In the account of his dream, Gudea saw a figure reaching from earth to heaven. This figure, with the head of a god and wings, appeared with couched lions on either side. The figure ordered Gudea to build his house. Afterwards, there appeared other figures and objects, including a basket for carrying earth and a brick mold with a

---

258. Fidler, "Dream Theophany," 153. Fidler defines it as the "Bethel facet" (p. 283).
259. I agree with Shapira, "Two Readings," 73 n. 73, who stresses that "right" follows the literary reading principle that does not lock down any interpretation of the Bible as the objective or ultimate one.
260. Perry and Sternberg, "Ironic Eyes," 285–86.
261. Ha'efrati, "Wilderness," 101, 124.

brick inside. The goddess Nanashe identifies the figure in the dream as Ningirsu and explicates the divine figures and the symbolic objects linked to building the temple for this god.[262] As Fidler notes: "Gudea's dreams exemplify the variety of the theophany's links to accepted dream varieties."[263]

Just as in Jacob's Dream, but in reverse order, the god delivers a verbal message and a symbolic vision. These are linked not only by consecutive appearance, but because one completes and interprets the other.

Lichtenstein reaches a sweeping conclusion:

> Symbolic dreams, dream-theophanies, corporeal theophanies and the like, are mutually interchangeable both in a given period, and occasionally in the same text.[264]…Indeed, in many cases it would seem that in the ancient Near East the distinction between symbolic dreams, dream-theophanies, and corporeal revelation is more a matter of literary preference than theological necessity."[265]

It seems to me that attempts to find the sources of the story of Jacob's Dream appear to have distanced us from our main concern, which is understanding the story in its present (final) form.[266] Whether accepting or rejecting Lichtenstein's argument that a dream theophany does not distinguish between J and E sources, what is significant for our purposes is that both the "corporeal revelation" and "abstract revelation in a dream" appearing together in ANE literature makes Jacob's Dream in its present form a familiar and recognized literary form.

3.4.5. *Conclusion: "It takes three trees to make a row."* The description of this dream form in ANE literature shows that the complexity of Jacob's Dream, with its theophany (revelatory) and symbolic elements, is not a problem to be resolved but the actual key for unlocking interpretation. As noted, the word "way" (*derekh*) is the keyword in understanding

---

262. See Oppenheim, *Interpretation*, 245–46, for a discussion of Gudea's Dream. Lipton, "Revisions," 90, states: "It will be suggested here that Genesis 28 is, in fact, a dream authorizing Jacob to build a temple, and that the vision of the *sullam* and raising of the monument correspond closely to traditional elements of the ancient Near Eastern temple building dreams exemplified by the Gudea reports."

263. Fidler, "Dream Theophany," 341–43. On p. 2, Fidler argues that "Gudea's dreams exemplify the variety of the theophany's links to accepted dream varieties."

264. Lichtenstein, "E Document," 54; see also Fidler, "Dream Theophany," in her appendix.

265. Lichtenstein, "E Document," 51.

266. Buber, *The way*, 319: "Our eyes behold that critical trends are pushing aside text criticism."

the *sullam*. The ladder, the *sullam*, functions as a symbol for the "way." This is suggested by a number of subtle hints: first, the "way" is mentioned in God's promise—"And behold, I am with thee and will keep thee in all ways whither thou goest and will bring thee again to this land" ("ways," from the Septuagint substituted for "places" in the KJV, 28:15). Secondly, "way" appears again in Jacob's vow: "and will keep me on this way that I go...and I am come again to my father's house" (v. 21). See also "way" in Gen 32:2 and 35:3, and "return" in 31:3, 13 (KJV). The "way," it seems, exists on two planes—the revealed and the concealed, the horizontal and the vertical, the means of access to and from the vantage point of God's abode. Plausibly, then, this is the origin of the metaphoric sense of the roots *'alah* and *yarad* that clarify the concealed message in the dream.

To repeat a point made several times already, the verb for ascent, *'alah*, entails a movement closer to God (literal and metaphorical), while the verb for descent, *yarad*, connotes a movement away from God. Thus, from this viewpoint—i.e. from God's dwelling-place—two interpretations are interwoven: two meanings (open and hidden) to the dream.

Having shown the link between visual and verbal message, the angels of God in action and the *sullam*, showing that Jacob's Dream fills the symbolic model, we have, in the words of linguist M. Joyce, the "three trees that make a row." In fact, more than three trees (= evidences) combine to interpret the dream: looking at it as symbolic, understanding *'alah* and *yarad* as complementary metaphors. To this is added the structural analysis of the text, in particular the link between the dream vision (vv. 12–13a) and the divine verbal message that follows (vv. 13b–15), designed to explain one another. A further structural tier is the result of considering the dream as a *mise en abyme* of the story cycles of Jacob and the Patriarchs, notably Abraham, on the theme of entering and leaving the country (what I termed an M-shaped pattern of movement).

Additional tiers, or "trees," in our "row" (our thesis/our way) are the comparison between the angels of God in 28:12 on the eve of his departure from the Land, and at Mahanaim (32:2–3) on the eve of his return; God's promise on the first occasion and "in a vision by night" as Jacob was about to go down into Egypt (46:2–5); and finally, the *sullam* at Bethel and the Tower of Babel (11:1–9). We have more than the three trees necessary to mark a valid row or way.

3.5. Is There Incubation in Jacob's Dream[267]

As explained in Chapter 1 (section 1.3.1), incubation[268] indicates that the dreamer takes the initiative by sleeping in a holy place and making ritual preparation, in hopes that the god would vouchsafe a revelation. Oppenheim assumes that the incubation dream is the prototype of the theophany dream.[269] Accepting this, it suffices to prove that Jacob's Dream was a theophany dream, and to show that some form of incubation was present, or that the dream resulted from incubation.[270] Even so, the question as to whether the story in its present form describes incubation is still relevant.

Does the dreamer in v. 11 preceding the dream take deliberate steps to be granted a divine revelation? Did Jacob select this particular place knowing that it was holy, and hence that God would be likely to dwell there? Stopping for the night "because the sun was set" indicates that the choice was more a matter of chronological necessity than a premeditated selection of location. Moreover, his startled awakening response—"this is none other but the house of God *and I knew it not*" (v. 16)—proclaims that he neither initiated nor anticipated a divine revelation. Clearly, incubation has no place in his dream.

How, then, do we explain Fidler's long and distinguished list of scholars expressing contrary views?[271] A detailed examination of the subject is necessary.[272]

---

267. Fidler, "Dream Theophany," 166: "While in Bethel there is no example of the incubation ritual, the story might be connected to incubation as prototype or etiology. Following this explanation, the story seeks to explain Jacob's acts at Bethel (sleeping in contact with a stone or close to a monument), adding a historical dimension to emulation of an ancient hero, although the motivation differs." In n. 187 Fidler suggests an analogy with "the etiology of eating *matza* in remembrance of the Israelites' hasty departure from Egypt (Exod 12:34, 39) or of living in booths during Succoth (Lev 23:43)."

268. From the Latin *incubare*, to spend the night in "the place," See Fidler, "Dream Theophany," 17 n. 48.

269. Oppenheim, *Interpretation*, 191.

270. Fidler, "Dream Theophany," 152.

271. See ibid., 166 n. 185, with its list of scholars who found incubation in the story. See also Gaster, *Myth*, 182–84; I. Mendelsohn, "Dream," *IDB*, 868; M. Ottoson, *TDOT* 4:428: חלם חלום; Gnuse, *Samuel*, 109–10 n. 43; see R. Kutcher, "The Mesopotamian God Zaqar and Jacob's Dream," *Beer-Sheba* 3 (1988): 129, asserting that vv. 10–22 describe incubation.

272. Distinguished scholars who reject the incubation view include Ehrlich, Houtman, Gnuse and Fidler.

3.5.1. *Are the four conditions for incubation present in Jacob's Dream?* It is a scholarly commonplace that there are four criteria or conditions for identifying an *incubation dream*.

The first is that it occurs at night, as in Jacob's Dream—"and tarried there all night,[273] because the sun was set" (v. 11).

The second criterion is that the dream results from specific preparations—Jacob "took of the stones of that place[274] and put them for his pillows."

Thirdly, the dream is to occur at a sacred site[275] like Bethel—Jacob's Dream was at Bethel, a well know sacred place.[276]

---

273. Besides "tarried there all night," indicating sleep and meeting the first condition, some commentators link the root *lwn* to the Hebrew for "complain" and "weep," introducing the weeping characteristic of incubation rites and associating it with Jacob. Fidler, "Dream Theophany," 170 n. 206, mentions A. Bentzen, "The Weeping of Jacob: Hos xii 5a," *VT* 1 (1951): 58–59, who noted that weeping is a means of entreating God but related it to the Penuel legend. See E. M. Good, "Hosea and the Jacob Tradition," *VT* 16 (1966): 144, who linked it to *Allon Bekhut*. See Lipton, "Revisions," 84 n. 29, who notes that the *lwn* root may be used either in the sense of sleeping, or of complaining. If Jacob possibly uses a negative connotation for *yfga'*, then he may have grounds for complaint, or else he may be in difficulty. However, in all four biblical instances of *yalun sham* (Gen 28:11; 32:14; Judg 19:71; 1 Kgs 19:20), it means "to spend the night," not "to complain."

Lipton cites *lwn* in Num 22:8, where Balaam invites the Moabite elders: "Spend the night here, and I shall reply to you as God may instruct me." Is Jacob's "lying down to sleep" possibly a paraphrase for spending the night in a manner that will grant him a divine revelation?

BDB 533: לין, לון, translated *lwn* as "lodge, pass the night," and subsequently in the sense of "complain," "murmur," but only in Exod 15:16, 17; Num 14:16, 17; and Lev 9:18.

Lipton, "Revisions," 84 n. 31, quotes Oliva from Madrid, who shed a feeble light on the subject in Jacob's answer to his wives in Gen 35:3: "'and I will build an altar there to the God who answered me when I was in distress,' 'Answered' suggests a question and might be interpreted as seeking an incubation dream." Here the researcher appears to be filling in blanks. The answer could just as easily refer to Jacob's vow; on this matter, see Fidler, "Dream Theophany," 167 n. 192.

274. Gnuse, *Samuel*, 67, quotes Skinner, *Genesis*, 376, as a scholar who thinks the incubation was caused by sleeping on a sacred stone. See my earlier discussion on "the stones of the place."

275. Like the "the site of Shechem" (12:6) and the Arabic *maqam* (*KBL* 560, 7). On v. 11, see Houtman, "Dream at Bethel," 345; Gnuse, *Samuel*, 67, in whose opinion the text describes Bethel as a *maqom*, generally a technical word for a shrine. See also Fidler, "Dream Theophany," 166 n. 179 and bibliography. See also M. Haran, "Miqdash," *EB* 5:322–27.

276. "Bethel…a king's sanctuary and a royal palace" (Amos 7:13); Gnuse, *Samuel*, 67; Fidler, "Dream Theophany," 153 n. 116; Haran, "Miqdash."

The fourth criterion is that the dreamer takes initiative in drawing the attention of the deity.

Looking particularly at the act of taking the ritually significant stone in v. 18, the issue is whether or not Jacob knew that the place was sacred. Is there a contradiction between the chance stopping place (v. 11) and his declaration (v. 16)?

The four above criteria, when applied to the Jacob's Dream, clearly reveal its incubation characteristics, although earlier doubts leave the matter far from clear. I propose a close reading of v. 11 in the light of the last two criteria. Was Bethel known[277] (to whom?) as a sacred site?

3.5.2. Two readings of yfga' bamaqom *in v. 11.* The phrase *yfga' bamaqom* ("encountered a certain place," Fox) is unique in the Hebrew Bible. In discussing multiple readings in the Jacob stories, Shapira proposed "systematic, on-going examination" to disclose the potential of such readings, on the basis of four literary principles:[278]

1. Unclear syntax, language or literary significance—deviation from language norms.
2. Linguistic or literary uniqueness or rarity of a word or expression.
3. An immediate or a general textual link, offering a choice of linkage.
4. Developing a relevant new construction for the word or expression, revealed when an expression with a primary dictionary definition gains a new meaning though studying its other occurrences in the Bible.

The discussion to follow will support the widespread perception that multiple readings help to reveal complexities: such reading, according to Alter, Barth, Geller, Greenstein, Weiss, Miskel, Fokkelman and others, enriches both reader and text. The text is open and carries tension at all times, allowing the reader to understand a complex reality as reflected in the text.[279]

I first discuss separately each of the two Hebrew words, *yfga'*, "chanced/lighted upon," and *bamaqom*, "a place," separately, before then looking at the two terms together.

---

277. See Houtman, "Dream at Bethel," 345: "the cult place which is discovered by Jacob."
278. Shapira, "Two Readings," 230; also idem, "Multiple Meanings," 249. See Fidler, "Dream Theophany," 183 n. 272.
279. Shapira, "Multiple Meanings," 257.

a) *vayfga'*. Why did the narrator choose *vayfga'*, "chanced upon," rather than a neutral verb,[280] like "arrived" or "came"?[281] The phrase *vayfga'* appears only twice in the Jacob stories, the second instance being "…angels of God encountered (*vayfge'u*) him" (Gen 32:2, Fox). We discover that not only are there *angels of God* once again, but they appear as he is about to reenter the Land.

Of the three definitions in the BDB and *KBL* dictionaries[282] for the Hebrew construction *yfga' b-*…, the first is most relevant here: "to chance upon, encounter": a place—"the boundary…touched *pga'* on Jericho (Josh 16:7); people—"you will encounter *pg'ata* a band of prophets" (1 Sam 10:5); or a transcendental entity—"angels of God encountered *pga'* him" (Gen 32:2). Having selected the first definition, rather than "strike and kill" (1 Sam 22:17) or "plead and pray" (Gen 23:8; Jer 7:16), the question nonetheless remains as to the choice of that particular verb rather than "arrived" or "came."

The "plead…pray" definition may suggest that this is an incubation dream, encouraged by the later story (32:2). Shapira views the two as linked, and concludes that "the verb *encounter* is transcendentally defined and has a special link to our verse."

The same reading emerges from the translation of Fox, "and encountered a certain place,"[283] who apparently sensed such a connotation. Accepting this conclusion further supports anticipation of an encounter with the divine. Shapira later states that "the transcendental nature of *encountered* should reflect on our verse as well," so that the verb choice points towards an incubation dream. But was the anticipation Jacob's, or the readers' from hindsight, after the revelation at Mahanaim?

---

280. Ibid.

281. Fidler, "Dream Theophany," 183 n. 272 answers: "In this way the E source sought to show Jacob's arrival at Bethel as entirely a matter of chance. On chance encounter as an E motif, see Weisman, *Cycle*, 65 n. 4. Fokkelman, *Genesis*, 50, states: "What is the effect of the word *wayyifga'*? Compared with the much more neutral *he came* its meaning *to strike upon*, is more sharply profiled, with a certain degree of casualness or unexpectedness."

282. Shapira, "Two Readings," 119; C. Houtman, "Jacob at Mahanaim: Some Remarks on Genesis xxxii 2–3," *VT* 28 (1978): 37. Zakovitch, *Midrashim*, 191, states: "[the Hebrew word] has the double sense of encounter and the more frequent one of inflicting damage." In his view the text of Gen 28:11 contains the first one.

283. Shapira, "Two Readings," 120, notes that Fox appears to have been influenced by "and behold, the angels of God" in v. 12, and perhaps by the dramatic event of Bethel.

2. The Story of Jacob's Dream at Bethel

However, the earlier commentators—and not a few more recent ones—all saw "encountered a certain place" as a sign that Jacob came there purely by chance. Indeed, "the sun was set" explains that the decision was made because of the time, not because of the location; had the sun not been setting, Jacob might well have continued on his journey.

b) *bamaqom*. The use of *bamaqom* also makes two readings possible.[284] In v. 10, Jacob's journey is described in six Hebrew words; v. 11, by contrast, contains much detail using 15 words, six of which are verbs describing just one place where Jacob stopped for the night. "Thus the reader feels that something special will happen there, or the place would not have been mentioned. The anticipation is well founded, as God will be revealed here."[285]

Did Jacob also sense this anticipation?

While v. 10 states the exact point of departure and destination, v. 11 does not mention the location of Jacob's nocturnal sojourn, whereas *place* is mentioned three times. Is this a redundant repetition—an editorial weakness—or has it a purpose? After the dream as well, "place" appears three times, suggesting it functions as a keyword that states the story's essence.

I agree with Fokkelman, who argues:

> We have the point that in one verse the word *maqom* occurs three times. Is that a weakness of the narrator's or is it a justified stylistic of narrator skill? The repetition, if useful, makes the word a key-word, which here would have to serve the purpose, precisely by its seeming redundancy, of proposing the question of what place it was… For *maqom* to be a key-word, integrated in the whole, it must refer to, anticipate, the main theme of the story.[286]

The numerous verbs in v. 11[287] (lighted upon, tarried, set, took, put, lay down) seem to indicate that Jacob was stirred up and excited. If this is

---

284. Fidler, "Dream Theophany," 155–56, defines it thus: "From stage of stating the circumstances (v. 11) one sees a sort of puzzlement regarding the *place*. It is clearly very significant (see the threefold repetition in v. 11). However, the narrator insists that Jacob arrived there entirely by chance." Later she mentions that this "puzzlement" in the dream encouraged Oppenheim to define the link between dream and place as "unintended incubation."

285. Fokkelman, *Genesis*, 50.

286. I agree with Fokkelman, *Genesis*, 49.

287. See Talmon in *Story Telling in the Bible: According to the Lectures of Shemariahu Talmon* (ed. G. Gabriel; Jerusalem: The Hebrew University Press, 1965), 50, on the verb in "the Bible story". See also "numerous verbs" in Gen 25:34: "Jacob then gave Esau bread and lentil stew, he *ate* and *drank* and *rose* and *went away*…"

correct, was he excited over the prospect of a divine revelation? Interestingly, despite its anonymity, "the place" appears three times with the definite article, indicating that it was known and recognized. From the previous verse we understand that it lay between Beersheba and Haran. It seems that Jacob and the reader, unlike the narrator-editor, do not recognize the location as a known ritual site. Jacob finds out only after God reveals Himself, when he awakes and says: "Surely the Lord is in this place and I knew it not." With that, "surely" seems to contradict "I knew it not." That opening word makes it possible to assume some uncertainty and to see the numerous verbs as a sign of tension. Is God in this place? Only after the dream does it turn out to be true.

Shapira[288] calls attention to "in this place" as unique, a *hapax legomenon*. Keeping in mind the second of Shapira's principles mentioned above—i.e. that a unique form may encourage two readings—"in this place" seemingly highlights the tension between the generally known and the anonymous quality of the place.

If the place is known, it supports the reading that incubation took place—were it just an ordinary place, such a reading is ruled out. The hidden tension I indicated in the abundance of verbs and in the designation of the place still does not prove the sacred nature of the place, nor the nature of Jacob's emotion in anticipation of God's appearance.

Shapira, who ignores the incubation issue, sums up by allowing two readings of "and he lighted upon a certain place": the first as the place where he lay down, and the second as the site of a historic event. For our purposes, the second reading, that Jacob chanced upon such a place, indicates its sacred quality and thus makes it possible to anticipate a theophany there.[289] Fidler gainsays the possibility in the text in its present form, suggesting deliberate ambiguity on the part of the narrator, who, unlike Jacob, knows the place is Bethel.[290]

---

288. Shapira, "Two Readings," 121.

289. On understanding "in this place," with its definite article, as indicating a sacred site, like "the site of Shechem" (Gen 12: 6) and the Arabic *maqam*, see *KBL* 560, 7; and Gunkel, Skinner, and Weinfeld's commentaries on v. 11. See also Resch, *Der Traum*, 71. Fidler, "Dream Theophany," 165 n. 176, states: "It is natural to understand the definite as enigmatic, not demonstrative, which makes the place merely some place or other." See Speiser, *Genesis*, 218; Fokkelman, *Genesis*, 63 n. 38; Fidler, "Dream Theophany," 176 n. 178; Rendtorff, "Bethel," 512; and Savran, *Theophany Narratives*, 43–45.

290. Fidler, "Dream Theophany," 166. See also Houtman, "Dream at Bethel," 345: "the cult place which is discovered by Jacob"; Fokkelman, *Genesis*, 63.

3.5.3. *Is this* unintended incubation?[291]

As Oppenheim suggests, a dream theophany may come to one sleeping at a holy site without his initiative or intention, so that he awakes in awe and wonder.[292] Calling such dreams *unintended incubation* may be seen as a compromise between those who recognize incubation in Jacob's Dream and those who deny it. Yet the compromise is self-contradictory, since intent and initiative on the dreamer's part is a condition of incubation. As Gnuse states, "Lack of the dreamer's intent prevents the designation of that dream as a dream of incubation."[293]

Fidler attempts to explain Oppenheim's compromise proposal in the following way: "Since Oppenheim proposes this phenomenon as a prototype description of revelation dreams in holy places (and not as an interpretation of individual dreams), he expands the concept to include cases where the text clearly rules it out, such as Exod 28:10–22 and 1 Sam 3."[294]

Fidler hypothesizes that the Jacob's Dream tradition came down to us from its pre-Israelite "incarnations" or stages, through the ancient tradition of Jacob at Bethel, where incubation was described, through the Elohistic version that rejected it, stressing that entirely by chance Jacob reached Bethel, as in the present version.[295] As to whether "in this place" hints at incubation, she writes: "If the text language still hints at the extraordinary nature of the place, it can be explained by the ambiguity of the narrator who, unlike Jacob, knew it was Bethel."[296]

To conclude: if, as argued by Fokkelman and others,[297] the narrator's purpose is to prove that the location of Jacob's Drean became holy *only after* the divine revelation described in our story, this by definition rules out incubation.[298] Jacob is described as preparing only for sleep, not for a

---

291. Oppenheim, *Interpretation*, 187. See Gnuse, *Samuel*, 109–10 n. 43.
292. Oppenheim, *Interpretation*, 187. Oppenheim found an example of *unintended incubation* in the dream of Tahtomes IV (1400 B.C.E.) beside the Sphinx (*ANET*, 499). Gnuse, *Samuel*, 35, mentions this.
293. Gnuse, *Samuel*, 68.
294. Fidler, "Dream Theophany," 18.
295. Ibid., 181. See Fidler's table of the strata of the Jacob tradition at Bethel on p. 188.
296. Ibid., 166.
297. Fokkelman, *Genesis*, 64: "It is very clear in this case: the place was anonymous and, actually, was not in the least a House of God on its own merits, but could only become one by virtue of an action by God."
298. See Houtman, "Dream at Bethel," 345 n. 36: "We leave out of consideration the question to what extent the concept of the holy place pictured in Genesis xxviii conforms to or differs from the other OT concepts concerning the holy places." Houtman sees no great difference as to whether the place was holy, or

theophany. Thus, without identifying the narrator (the Elohist, according to Fidler, Weisman and others), his efforts to hide all signs and elements of incubation are understandable. But his purpose, undertaken through the hidden polemic, was not fully accomplished and traces of incubation remained. Repetition of "the place,"[299] with the definite article or demonstrative pronoun, directs readers' attention to it, giving the attuned among them the sense of "handwriting on the wall," as in Brecht's poem.[300] Ironically, the narrator highlights precisely what he is trying to conceal.

4. *Two Readings of Jacob's Dream—A Tentative Conclusion*

Jacob's Dream and its interpretation enables, from a literary perspective, two simultaneous readings:

Reading A: The story describes and means to explain how Bethel became a sacred place, a story whose core is the *maqom* ("place")

Reading B: The story tells about Jacob who leaves Israel in order to return in the future; a story whose core is the *derekh* ("way")

The close reading to follow will concentrate on multiple readings of some words and expressions in the story. Shapira (see section 3.5.2)[301] sets forth four principal literary phenomena to disclose the potential for multiple readings in the Bible text.[302] The discussion to follow supports

---

became holy because of a divine revelation. In my opinion he attempts unsuccessfully to circumvent the problem rather than solve it.

299. A similar contrary effect is created by the protagonist of the Song of Songs. Song 1:6, "Don't stare at me because I am swarthy," serves, in fact, to draw attention to her swarthiness.

300. See Berthold Brecht, "An Unconquered Inscription," in *Selected Poems* (trans. M. Avi-Shaul; Tel Aviv: Sifriyat Poalim, 1959), 33. The appearance of "the crocodiles" in the Creation Story (Gen 1:21) is explained in Peleg, "Water," 154–68, in the same way.

301. Shapira, "Multiple Meanings," 249. Shapira lists four types of such readings: the double meaning ($a+b$, where b differs from a); the ambivalent ($a+b$, where a is opposed to b); the double reading of either a or b, and the diacritical reading (a is positive and b negative, or the reverse).

302. Shapira, "Two Readings," cites 51 instances of multiple meanings, of which seven appear in the Jacob stories. This reinforces our assumption, namely that this literary device is typical of the Jacob's Dream narrator, and that, in parallel fashion, revealing the multiple significances in the present study adds a tier to the structure Shapira revealed in the entire Jacob story cycle.

2. *The Story of Jacob's Dream at Bethel* 135

Shapira's perception that multiple readings "make it possible for the reader to understand in greater depth the complexity reflected in the text."[303]

In the previous chapter I noted that, while discussing the David and Bathsheba narrative of 2 Sam 11, Perry and Sternberg advocate an interpretive position quite similar to my own—namely, the interpreting of the revealed and the concealed simultaneously within a narrative. As noted, Perry and Sternberg contend that to understand the world of the literary work, the reader must construct a system of lacunae that correspond to the questions that are not directly answered (i.e. "filling in gaps"). The reader fills in these gaps as s/he reads. In the process of doing this, assumptions and conjectures are made that link details to one another and to the story as a whole, bringing to light the story's complex significance.

In the opinion of Perry and Sternberg, the narrator obliges the reader to propose hypotheses that answer the questions the narrator himself does not answer specifically. This cannot be arbitrary. A hypothesis is accepted or rejected according to its relevance to the greatest number of details in the work itself.[304] I too shall try to show that each hypothesis is supported and affirmed by a number of arguments (i.e. "It takes three trees to make a row"). A criterion for preferring one hypothesis to another is its ability to answer "the maximum number of questions arising in the story, creating the most possible links and affinities among them."

In addition, Perry and Sternberg assert that although the two readings of the David and Bathsheba story contradict one another, one need not choose between them. In contrast, I do not find the two readings of the story of Jacob's Dream contradictory—not only is there no need to decide between them, but each reading in fact contributes to the understanding of the dream's complex message. The arguments in the text are important as proof that both proposed interpretations are plausible and not arbitrary.

The following table presents, in order of appearance, the terms and expressions in the story that allow for two readings (multiple readings) of the story:

---

303. Shapira, "Multiple Meanings," 257.
304. Perry and Sternberg, "Ironic Eyes," 265. They offer a superb example of the importance of genre, quoted in Chapter 1, as to distinctions between theology and symbolic dreams.

Ambiguous terms (metaphor: connotation, uniqueness)	Ambiguous expressions (syntax, uniqueness)
v. 11: "and he encountered upon" (connotation: positive and negative; unique in Jacob story cycle)	
v. 11: "a certain place," "in that place" (definite article or not by chance, spontaneous or planned)	v. 11: "and he encountered upon a place"
	v. 11 "of the stones of that place" (one or several?)
v. 12: "And he dreamed" (a theology or symbolic dream?)	v. 12: "the angels of God" (unique)
v. 12: *sullam* (unique)	
v. 12: the roots *'alah* and *yarad* (metaphor)	
v. 14: "and thou shalt spread abroad" (positive or negative connotation)	
	v. 15: "and will bring thee again to this land" (alive or dead?, unique expression)
v. 17: "this"—short for "this is its meaning"—plus "and behold" (sign of a dream)	v. 16: and he said, "Surely the Lord is in this place, and I knew it not" (Did he know, or not?) v. 17: "How dreadful" (positive or negative?) v. 21: "So that I come again to my father's house in peace" (positive or negative connotation)

From now on, the only words or expressions discussed are those affirming two readings for either "place" or "way." To promote focus on our main goal, any other expression, even if it allows for two readings, will appear only in a footnote.

4.1. *Verse 10*

The story of Jacob's Dream begins: "And Jacob went out from Beersheba, and went toward Haran."[305] The reader begins thinking that

---

305. Fokkelman, *Genesis*, 46, proposes a comparison between v. 10, above, and v. 5: "and Isaac sent Jacob off, and he went to Paddan-Aram to Laban the son of Bethuel the Aramean, the brother of Rebekah, mother of Jacob and Esau." Fokkelman states: "We note a great difference, a long sentence with many proper names opposite a short one with two geographical indications; the great difference in context determines the selection of details… That Jacob is on the way is now the only thing that matters."

the story is about Jacob's departure from Canaan. No opinion is as yet expressed in an open or concealed manner as to whether this is good or bad. In the light of what precedes it, one reasonably assumes that Jacob—and the reader—are concerned about whether Jacob will return to the Land safely, as his mother Rebecca assured him: "Now, my son, listen to me. *Flee* at once to Haran, to my brother Laban. Stay with him a while, until your brother's fury subsides—until your brother's anger against you subsides—and he forgets what you have done to him. Then I will fetch you from there" (27:33–43).

Both verbs in v. 10 depict motion, "went out" and "went toward." The biblical connotations of "went out" in the Bible include "went free,"[306] and indeed the circumstances in Gen 27:43–44 indicate that Jacob was fleeing for his life from Esau. That he "went toward" Haran stresses that Jacob was progressing on the "way."

4.2. *Verse 11*

Two reading of the verb "encountered," *vayfga'*, and the combination "of the stones," *meavnei hamaqom*, were discussed above. I argued that "of the stones of the place" may refer in this verse either to one or several stones, as previously noted, though only v. 18 shows it to be one stone.

The reader of the opening words, "And he *encountered upon* a certain place" might understand that Jacob reached Haran, designated at the end of v. 10. Further reading shows that Jacob spent the night there not because it was his destination, but because "the sun was set," which raises doubts about identifying the place as Haran.

Fokkelman argues: "Presently we are told of a halt in the journey; *place* cannot refer to Haran, so it must be place on the way."[307] Later in the story it becomes clear that it is Bethel. *Harranu* in Akkadian means "way" or "path." The reader, one assumes, when reading that Jacob went toward Haran, might understand that it is a place on his way. Indeed, it was his fate to return. Different levels of understanding are involved here: the "sophisticated reader" will understand the double significance of the name Haran, while the "literal" (naïve) reader will see only the revealed significance.

---

306. BDB 422: יצא ("freed, delivered") See, e.g., "in the seventh year he shall go free" (Exod 21:2); "do not wish to go free" (21:5); "she shall not go free" (21:7) See also 21:3, 7; Lev 25:54.

307. Fokkelman, *Genesis*, 47.

4.3. Verses 12–13a

Jacob dreams. God appears. The first reading of the dream and its interpretation seems to support the accepted scholarly view that its purpose and meaning is to show how "the place" Bethel became a holy site. But the symbolic, concealed meaning of the ascending (*'olim*) and descending (*yordim*) angels of God (*mal'akei 'elohim*), particularly the verbs in that order, may hint that the dream is about the "way."

The deliberate structuring of the story that makes two simultaneous readings[308] possible appears here too. "Ascend" may be read technically/topographically as upward movement from earth to heaven; "descend," meanwhile, can be read as the opposite. Thus the angels create the link between heaven and earth and the divine revelation, making the place holy. Other biblical occurrences of these verbs, however, are metaphorical, "ascend" having a positive and "descend" a negative sense. The vision (v. 12), and in particular v. 13a, where "God is standing at the top," most strongly reinforces the metaphorical sense of the two verbs. This metaphorical reading leads to the second interpretation of the dream.

In a later section I attempted to show that in "Abram *went down* to Egypt" (Gen 12:10), indicating descent, *yerida* suggests criticism of that movement.

In another reading of the vision in Jacob's Dream, the descending angels on the *sullam* symbolize Jacob's leaving (descending from) the Land of Canaan on the way to Haran. This insight requires access to research on biblical and ANE dreams. We have encountered the division into theological and symbolic dreams, where most scholars place Jacob's Dream in the first group and only a few identify its symbolic dream characteristics. In my view it is both, and should be interpreted accordingly. As previously noted, understanding the story of Jacob's Dream as a dream theology strengthens the "place" concept that explains the name of Bethel, while viewing it as symbolic dream, as subsequent readings clarify, leads to a focus on the "way" concept, in which the angels of God represent the actual situation of Jacob's departure from and return to the Land. *Sullam* as object and as symbol of vertical and horizontal movement, of the "way" and its connection with the divine promise to Jacob, is fully explicated in section 2.1.

---

308. This structure typifies the Jacob stories according to Shapira, "Multiple Meanings." In the story of Jacob's Dream the possibility of two readings is not limited to "place" or "way" themes, though that possibility throughout the Jacob stories supports interest in those themes.

4.4. Verses 13b–15

Regarding the question of whether two readings are possible for the preposition *'alav* ("above it") in v. 13, see the discussion above in this chapter.

While vv. 12–13a are visual, this part of the dream is verbal in the main. Unlike advocates of source criticism (and others), who have sought to differentiate between the two, I believe I have succeeded in showing that they complement and explain one another.

Following Weiss's method regarding the consecration of Isaiah (section 2.1), where the visual and verbal parts interpret one another, here too there are verbs describing back and forth movement that do likewise. In the vision it is vertical, between heaven and earth, while (here) in the message it is horizontal, leaving and returning to the Land.

If my assumption is correct that the story of Jacob's Dream is a literary composition in which the vision and the verbal message interpret one another, then the ascending and descending angels should be compared to the divine promise, "I am with thee…and will bring thee again to this land" (v. 15). On the symbolic level, then, the movement of the angels is explained by the divine promise as entering and leaving the Promised Land, while the visual element explains the entering and leaving as ascent (having a positive connotation) and descent (with its negative connotation). That "the Lord stood above it" imparts the positive and negative connotations to such movements. That symbolic reading is additional to, not instead of, interpreting the dream as ritual etiology.

The ambiguous *hapax legomenon* combination "I will bring you back to this soil" (v. 15 Fox) will be discussed below in section 5.3.2. For now, it can be noted that this unique combination may encourage multiple readings. The first one, from the immediate context, is simply a reassurance that God will return Jacob to the Promised Land ("I am with thee"). A broader context, however, to include Jacob's descent into Egypt (46:3–4), could lead to another, ironic reading, where the return to the Land suggests a negative association. God will return Jacob to the earth (soil), in death.

4.5. Verses 16–17

The link between the dream vision in v. 12 and Jacob's verbal response in vv. 16–17[309] supports the view that Jacob's Dream simply explains the etiology of Bethel: "This is none other but the house of God and this is the gate of heaven."

---

309. See previous discussion section 2.2.2, c), in which two readings for "how dreadful" are possible.

Rendtorff aptly described the link between dream and interpretation, saying that Jacob's verbal response on awakening contains three elements relating to the vision in reverse chiastic order.[310] Whether this is the only possible interpretation of Jacob's Dream may become clear in the course of further close reading.

Regarding two readings of root *yara'* ("afraid") in v. 17, see above, section 2.2.1 (b). In addition, it was shown that the combination "How dreadful is this place!" is also ambiguous. On one hand, "dreadful" (*yara'*) may have a negative connotation; on the other hand, it may have the positive sense of wondrous and exalted.

We cannot choose definitively between the two possible readings of Jacob's response—positive, expressing optimism, predicting a good future for Jacob; negative, expressing Jacob's fears.

Savran argues:

> Jacob's response to the dream of the *sullam* in two similar verses (28:16–17) may indicate a double source for the text. As I understand it, however, this double response reflects two separate aspects of human response to a theophany.[311] What appears to be repetitive language describes a complex response comprising contrary feelings that exist side by side, or following one another. Verse 16 expresses fascination, not terror… By contrast, in v. 17, Jacob reflects fear and awe of the divine presence.[312]

4.6. *Verses 18–19: One Reading or Two?*

These verses focus on the sanctity of the place and naming it Bethel, and so support the first reading. Discussing the vow (vv. 20–22),[313] I will show that "place" would be the sole subject if the story ended with v. 19. But since the story of the vow follows, containing both "place" and "way" elements, two readings are possible. Because they are not contradictory but complementary, a legitimate reading must recognize both, and examine the connection between them.

---

310. See Rendtorff, "Bethel," 513. See also Fidler, "Dream Theophany," 172 n. 215. Compare also the analysis of Fokkelman, *Genesis*, 71.

311. See also Y. I. Peleg, "Duality in the Relationship of 'Man–God' in the Book of Job: Two Readings or Two Jobs," *Moed: Annual for Jewish Studies* 21 (2013): 32–55.

312. See Savran, *Theophany Narratives*, 108.

313. See below for discussion of the link between vow and dream. At this point there are two possible readings, for "come again to my father's house in peace" (alive or dead). How "in peace" can be the equivalent of "in death" will be clarified shortly. Nor is the link between the conditions and Jacob's commitments unambiguous. One reading is that he returns on his own initiative, and another is that God initiates the return.

4.7. Conclusion

Research commonly accepts v. 17 as conveying the dream interpretation relating to "place": "This is none other than the house of God." There were reservations, however, as to whether this was the only possibility. Was a metaphorical key to another reading left precisely here?

To prove it was, I refer back to the table in section 2.2.1.

The keyword "this"[314] suggests a second reading. The chiastic structure shows that the dream description uses "and behold" three times, while the interpretation begins three statements with "this." It seems to me that just as "and behold" is a standard linguistic formulation at the beginning of a dream description, particularly where symbolic dreams describe a vision, so "this" is standard for beginning an interpretation. One plausibly assumes that "this" is a shortened form for "this is its solution"[315] (Gen 40:12, 18). In this respect we can note Dan 2:36, "This is the dream, and we will now tell the king its meaning," as well as Dan 4:15, and particularly the expression "and this is its meaning" (Dan 5:26).

Should this inference be correct, then the indicative "this" in Jacob's Dream refers not only to "place" but to "way"; as it is said, "and will keep me *in this way*" (v. 20).[316]

In conclusion, I seek here to add to—not replace—the view of Jacob's Dream as cultic etiology. There is room also for the view that the vision in the dream and its symbolic significance function as a *mise en abyme* of Jacob's entering and leaving the Land. Such a reading does not contradict the accepted one, but rather adds a dimension to the dream and its interpretation.

5. The Vow as a Contribution to Understanding and Interpreting Jacob's Dream

v. 20: And Jacob vowed a vow, saying, If God will be with me, and will keep me *in this way* that I go, and will give me bread to eat, and raiment to put on,

v. 21: So that I come again to my father's house in peace; *then* shall the LORD be my God (Fox: YHWH shall be God to me).

v. 22: *And this stone*, which I have set [for] a pillar, shall be God's house: and of all that thou shalt give me I will surely give the tenth unto thee.

---

314. See discussion in section 2.2.3.
315. See Fishbane, *Text*, 455, as to the combination "this is its meaning."
316. "This" indicates Jacob's "way" from the Land and back to it, and simultaneously hints at the interpretation of the dream. See Y. I. Peleg, "Going Up and Going Down: A Key to Interpreting Jacob's Dream," *ZAW* 116 (2004): 1–11.

5.1. Introduction

The vow,[317] placed immediately after the dream, as well as its content and language, indicate its significance in the story of Jacob's Dream. It relates both to the "way," as Jacob embarks "on this way" in the present, and to his return journey "to my father's house" in the future, and to "the place," referring to the promise that the stone pillar he laid his head upon would become the house of God. He makes His promise to Jacob in v. 15, and Jacob his vow, in the same language, in vv. 20–21.

The comparison raises a theological issue that has engaged both earlier and more recent commentators. The first reading reveals tension between God's promise in vv. 13–15 and Jacob's vow in vv. 20–22. Jacob sets conditions (vv. 20–21)[318] that contradict God's promise in the dream.[319]

Given the divine promise, Jacob's self-righteousness is offensive: he makes conditions with God! This casts doubt as to whether he will keep his promise, and his faith seems to rest solely on the prospect of gain.[320] Such issues troubled traditional commentators,[321] and strengthened adherents of source criticism.[322] As noted before, they resolved the

---

317. See Peleg, "The Vow," and Savran, *Theophany Narratives*, 198. On the connection between dream and vow, Savran writes: "Fokkelman maintains that pouring oil over the pillar recalls the *sullam* reaching to heaven, emphasizing the role of pouring the oil as a link between heaven and earth. As Jacob's own head previously came in contact with the stone, the parallel to v. 11 creates a resemblance between anointing the stone and the dream itself. As the dream reveals God's presence to Jacob internally, so anointing the stone and setting up a pillar externalize that experience. The link between the pillar and the erect *sullam* (v. 12) hint at the link between the dream and Jacob's responses. As the *sullam* stood between earth and heaven in his dream, the pillar does so in a ritual and ceremonial sense."

318. See Westermann, *Genesis*, 458. On the end of the conditions and the beginning of the obligations, see Peleg, "The Vow."

319. The foregoing leads some researchers to deduce the legitimacy of the dream in transmitting a divine message. See Fidler, "Dream Theophany," 42.

320. Thus Satan casts doubt over the faith of Job (Job 1:9): "Does not Job have good reason to fear God?"

321. Rashi, and following him the Rashbam, *Torat Haim*, note that "then shall the Lord be my God" is not a condition but means "His name shall be upon me," or, as the Rashbam says, "will help me in all I do." Thus also Radak: "It was not a condition but concern lest his sin would cause God's promise not to be kept, and he would not return to his father's house and be unable to keep his vow." Leibowitz, *Genesis*, 214, clarifies that there is no doubt here regarding God, but rather a plea, "give me a chance to serve You," as in Hannah's vow. According to Leibowitz, it means, "If I am worthy."

322. Skinner, *Genesis*, 379, sees separation by sources as the only way to clear Jacob of the suspicion of making conditions with God and of doubting the divine promise. In fact, apart from O. Procksch, *Die Genesis*: *Ubersetzt und Erklart* (KAT

2. *The Story of Jacob's Dream at Bethel* 143

contradiction/tension between God's promise (in v. 15) and Jacob's vow by attribution to the J and E sources, respectively.

Their solution is on the diachronic level. The scholarly debate between Carr, Blum, and Van Seters is of interest. Carr's attempt at finding a way to "unite" the diachronic and synchronic approaches is also admirable.[323] Yet the debate over Jacob's Dream takes place on the diachronic plane, or, as Carr defines it (following Blum) in his article, a "compositional' rather than redactional layer.[324]

Van Seters' answer illustrates, in my opinion, the difficulty of the diachronic approach. His answer give no attention to the story in its current form. Van Seters writes that

> The problem with Gen 28:10–22…is not that it contains both divine promise and vow, but that the order of these two is reversed from the usual order. One would have expected Jacob's prayer at the beginning of his flight followed by a theophany in which the deity answered his prayer by means of a promise to be with him on his journey. The fact that this is the obvious order raises the question of why it would have been reversed by any author at any level of the composition…[325]

However, the story in its present/final form tells (in v. 12) of the revelation of God to Jacob before the divine promise (v. 13–15). Van Seters, with all due respect, "ignores" this. He assumes that v. 12 belongs to the E source, with which the redactor of vv. 13–15 was not familiar. Yet the contemporary reader notes that there is only one fact: in the text as it currently stands, the Deity has already revealed himself to Jacob in v. 12.

(See the discussion in Chapter 1, "Literary genre—helpful or misleading?" [pp. 9–11].)

Other scholars have found a correspondence between the divine promise (v. 15) and the vow (vv. 20–22) and do not see the vow as expressing doubt over the promise.[326] Fidler, for example, having compared the vow

---

1; Leipzig: W. Scholl, 1913), who attributes v. 21 to J, other advocates of source criticism attribute the vow to E. See S. R. Driver, *Literature*, 16. Fidler, "Dream Theophany," 167, notes: "Jacob's vow…was not in the ancient story and is clearly the contribution of E, who used it to formulate the (Jacob) story cycle." See also the table there, p. 188.

323. Carr, *Fractures*.
324. Carr, "Genesis 28, 10–22."
325. Van Seters, "Encounter," 508.
326. Fokkelman, *Genesis*, 74–75; Cartledge, *Vows*, 170. Lipton, "Revisions," 82, states: "His vow does not show that he doubts God, but rather that he wishes to clarify precisely how His promise will be fulfilled… The account of life in Laban's house provides a graphic illustration for active divine intervention in Jacob's daily affairs."

in Kirta from Ugaritic literature, proposed that "the narrator of the vow, who also narrated the dream, sensed no particular theological difficulty. God promises in the dream, and the dreamer on his part acts to hasten fulfillment of the promise by making a vow."[327] Indeed, mentioning the vow (Gen 31:13) by God Himself implies no criticism of Jacob.[328]

Even proponents of the synchronic approach who see the present form of the story as an expression of its meaning, stress the problem created by the vow. Rendtorff, for instance, sees vv. 20–22 as separate and independent, unlinked to vv. 11–19, which "deal with the…establishment of the pillar sanctuary at Beth-el."[329] In his opinion, the story is made up of two separate formal units each complete in itself, vv. 11–19 and 20–22.

Rendtorff and others,[330] as noted, regard "place" as a keyword, revealing the boundaries within which they discerned the concentric structure of the story (vv. 11–19a).[331] Seeing "place" as a keyword and given the transformation that the place undergoes, many scholars[332] concluded that the purpose of the Jacob's Dream story was to explain the cultic etiology, the *hieros logos*, of Bethel. The story's end reinforces that understanding: "and he called the name of that place Bethel."[333] Thus, anything after that detracts.[334]

---

327. See Fidler, "Dream Theophany," 43: "King Keret…when the god Il promised him the princess Hari as a wife and told him how he would bring her to his home, Keret sets out on a journey under Il's guidance but also vows: if he succeeds…he will dedicate two and three times Hari's weight in silver and gold to the goddess Ashrat of the Sidonians." Oppenheim, *Interpretation*, 192–93, notes that despite the verisimilitude of the dream the divine promise is not necessarily a foregone conclusion. See also Fidler, "Dream Theophany," 178.

328. See below for a discussion of Gen 31:13. On its many links to the vow and to the broader Jacob story, of which it is seen as a part, see Cartledge, *Vows*, 166.

329. Rendtorff, "Bethel," 512.

330. Ibid., 512, 521. See also Fokkelman, *Genesis*, 49; Fidler, "Dream Theophany," 165.

331. Rendtorff, "Bethel," 512–13. See Otto, "Bet El," 172–73. He sees vv. 11–19a as a unit with a conspicuous chiastic structure. Fidler, "Dream Theophany," 152 n. 108. See also Radai, "Chiasm," 48–72.

332. See Sarna, *Understanding*, 192. Otto, "Bet El," 174, identifies the story structure's center of gravity with recognizing the sanctity of the place, and the story's purpose as the etiology of the Bethel sanctuary. See also Rendtorff, "Bethel," 512. Westermann, *Genesis*, 452, also asserts the purpose of cultic etiology. Cf. also Fidler, "Dream Theophany," 153, 458; Gunkel, *Legends*, 4, 31–37.

333. See the Appendix to Chapter 1 for division of the story, particularly v. 19, according to its sources.

334. Other researchers, including Westermann, *Genesis*, 460, maintain that the vow is an addition. Considering the contradictions between it and the divine promise, it is a hindrance, not a help, both on structure and content levels.

Now I propose to show that, rather than the vow detracting from the story, it in fact helps to reveal its double interpretation. Problems arise for researchers because each one is "locked" into his or her own method, and with that the concept that supports the hypothesis[335] with which they began. Having assumed that the story of Jacob's Dream was "cultic etiology" that aims to show how this place became a holy one, logically the vow was not part of the original story.

However, my literary approach, involving close reading of biblical texts in general and of the Jacob's Dream story in particular, makes multiple readings of a text possible and reveals previously hidden meanings. While the accepted reading refers to "place," and in that context the vow might be seen as an addition detracting from story structure and significance, an additional symbolic reading may reveal the vow as a help in understanding the dream's double message (vv. 10–19). Such a reading[336] relates to Jacob setting out on a journey and God's promise to return him to his point of departure. The vow relates to *both* the "place" and the "way" to and from it.

Had the story ended in v. 19, its main theme would be the transformation of "a place" to a holy place, and the "way" would have been "secondary." But the story in its present form continues, describing Jacob's vow after he awakes from his dream, reintroducing the "way" he has gone and by which he will return to the Promised Land. Hence, describing the vow helps reveal the twofold dream message that includes both the sanctity of the "place" and of the "way"[337] from and to it, that is, to the Promised Land.

5.2. *"So that I come again to my father's house in peace" (v. 21a)*

Verse 21a, relating to the "way," helps to understand the link between dream and vow, and, consequently, the dream and its (symbolic) interpretation, revealing the importance of the "way." What, then, is the role (and the place) of this verse in the vow?

---

335. See Chapter 1 on reading for multiple meanings.
336. Fidler, "Dream Theophany," 153, relates to "the Jacob facet and the Bethel facet."
337. See Carr, *Fractures*, 263. Even though Carr argues that "Jacob's oath in Gen 28:20–22 appears to be an addition to an earlier epiphany report designed to legitimate the sanctuary at Bethel," he notes that "Whereas the early, originally independent epiphany report focused exclusively on legitimating the Bethel sanctuary, the author of Gen 28:10–22 made that tradition into a description of Jacob's encounter with God upon exiting the land. This encounter then balances the later narrative of Jacob's encounter with God upon reentry into the land at Penuel (Gen 32:23–32)."

5.2.1. *The structure of the vow: its condition (protasis) and its promise (apodosis)*. Jacob's vow is the only one in the stories of the Patriarch, but not the only one in the Bible.[338] Significantly for our purposes, it is built on the model familiar from both the Bible and the ANE literature,[339] and particularly resembles the vow in the Ugaritic Kirta epic.[340]

The vow has two parts, one following the other: the protasis or condition, and the apodosis or promise, in which the maker of the vow states his undertaking to God.[341] The opening word of the condition is "if," making it logical to anticipate the promise.

At this point it would be logical to expect that the beginning of the apodosis will be identified via the word *az* ("then"). However, the beginning of the apodosis/promise is difficult to recognize in Jacob's vow as each of his eight promises is introduced by the connecting *waw* rather than *az*. In that case, does "So that I come again to my father's house in peace" (v. 21a) belong to the conditions or the promises? Differing from the accepted research view, if it is accepted as promises and not as a condition, the thorny theological issue of the tension between God's promise (v. 15) and Jacob's vow is resolved. According to this reading, God's promise is congruent with Jacob's stated obligation to return to the Land. Following that answer model,[342] Jacob responded appropriately[343] to God's promise.

338. These are the Israelite vows: of (the people of) Israel (Num 21:2); of Jephthah (Judg 11:31); of Hannah (1 Sam 1:11); and of Absalom (2 Sam 15:7–8). Cartledge, *Vows*, 143–50, deals with vows beyond the scope of our discussion, especially their literary structure. See also pp. 133–73.

339. L. R. Fisher, "Literary Genres in The Ugaritic Texts," in *Ras Shamra Parallels: The Texts from Ugarit and the Hebrew Bible*, vol. 2 (ed. L. R. Fisher; AnOr 50; Rome: Pontificium Istitutum Biblicum, 1975), 131–52 (149–50 = "Two Projects at Claremont," *UF* 3 [1971]: 27–31); S. B. Parker, "The Vow in Ugaritic and Israelite Narrative Literature," *UF* 11 (1979): 694; Westermann, *Genesis*, 458: "The structure corresponds to that of other vows: v. 20 always the same introduction; vv. 20–21b, the conditions; vv. 21b–22, the promises." D. Marcus, *Jephthah and his Vow* (Lubbock, Tex.: Texas Tech Press, 1986), 18, presents characteristic elements in the structure of vows in the Bible, including the introduction: "And Jacob vowed a vow, saying…" By contrast, see Parker, "Ugaritic," 699, and Cartledge, *Vows*, 166–75, who discuss the connection between the biblical and the ANE vow. On the same topic, see also Pagolu, *Religion*, 199, 203. For discussion of ANE vows in detail, see Cartledge, *Vows*, 73–133, and Pagolu, *Religion*, 193–98.

340. Fisher, "Genres," 27–31; Parker, "Ugaritic," 693–700.

341. Cartledge, *Vows*, 12, notes that all biblical vows are addressed to God, not to man.

342. See Bar-Efrat, *Design*, 122, and Polak, *Narrative*, 223–24. There views will be compared later.

343. See Fokkelman, *Genesis*, 74.

Before discussing where the apodosis (obligation) begins, I consider the link between conditions and obligations: which does the dream emphasize/stress? Shapira[344] raises an additional important question: What does one stress in reading Jacob's vow—protasis or apodosis?[345]

In his view, Jacob's vow is of a dual or contradictory nature. On one hand there is the phrase "If God will be with me," which seems to be a conditioned promise. On the other hand, the internal content of the promise depends on no external variable factor, but is an absolute undertaking that in essence forms of vow. Jacob promises that the Lord will be his god, that the stone he raises as a pillar will be the house of God, and he vows a tithe as a gift.[346] As to the link between "If God will be with me" and "then shall the Lord be my God,"[347] is the emphasis on the condition[348] or on the resolute vow?[349]

Shapira replies[350] that the vow should be read as ambiguous: the first reading is the conditional vow that creates theological problems; the second is that "if God will be with me"[351] is not a condition but a plea that all the conditions be met to enable Jacob to serve God. The author concludes that "both readings recognize the conditional element, the 'if,' but the second one mutes it."[352]

---

344. Shapira, "Two Readings," 150–51.
345. M. Haran, "Neder," *EB* 5:786, defines "vow" as an "undertaking entered into without being previously ordered to do so, and on which one thinks God will look with favor… There is no primary need for the vow to be accompanied by any condition, but most vows are made under conditions specified by the one who vows."
346. Shapira, "Two Readings," 150–51.
347. Fidler, "Dream Theophany," 160 n. 25, asserts that "then shall the Lord be my God" is an addition. See the bibliography given by Fidler.
348. As asserted, e.g., by Radak; Parker, "Ugaritic," 693–700. Some, however, regarded the conditions as requests. See Cartledge, *Vows*, 171, who states: "Vows, of course, involve promises as well as requests."
349. As maintained, e.g., by Nahmanides. See Fokkelman, *Genesis*, 74; von Rad, *Genesis*, 280–81; Fisher, "Genres" 147–52.
350. Shapira, "Two Readings," 152.
351. Shapira, ibid., 154, shows that the two readings are expressed in two editions of the JPS English translation: JPS, "if God will be with me…then shall the Lord be my God"; NJPS, "if God remains with me…the Lord shall be my God." While the first stresses the condition with "then," the second omits it, as do Buber's German translation and Fox's English translations.
352. Here Shapira refers to Marcus, *Jephthah*, who reveals the ambiguity in Jephthah's vow.

148   *Going Up and Going Down*

The divine response to Jacob's vow helps answer the question of whether emphasis is on the condition or the promise. It comes as Jacob's story continues, when in Gen 31:13 an angel identifies himself to him, "I am the God of Bethel," going on to mention the pillar and the vow with no hint of criticism. What this means is that the theological problem appears to exist more for researchers and commentators than in the literal text.[353] Most significantly for our purposes, from the divine perspective the vow is linked to the return to the Land, an aspect scholarship has hitherto overlooked.[354]

5.2.2. *Where does the promise (apodosis) begin?* Both earlier and later scholars are divided as to whether the promise/apodosis begins in v. 21b,[355] "and the Lord shall be my God," or in v. 22,[356] "And this stone, which I have set for a pillar, will be God's house."[357] The proposal that

353.   Fidler, "Dream Theophany," 43 n. 7.
354.   It seems to me that if "vow" in 31:13b is replaced by "promise," then God is reminding Jacob of his promise to Him to return to the Land, and that the time has come to keep the promise: "Now arise and leave this land, and return to your native land." This is not simply a linear continuation of "where you made me a vow," but interprets and explains that statement. See Fidler, "Dream Theophany," 147, 151: "In determining the right time for Jacob's return, God responds to Jacob's plea in the vow, to be returned in peace to his father's house (28:21), or is keeping His own promise in the dream to return Jacob 'into this land' (28:15)."
355.   Among its supporters are Nahmanides: "If I return to my father's house I will serve the Lord." See also Marcus, *Jephthah*, 79; I. Avishur, *Olam Hatanach: Genesis* (ed. M. Weinfeld; Tel Aviv: Davidson-Atai, 1982), 174. See also Fisher, "Genres," 79; Parker, "Ugaritic," 698. See too Weisman, *Cycle*, 59; Westermann, *Genesis*, 458; Cartledge, *Vows*, 167, 171; Pagolu, *Religion*, 204.
356.   Among supporters of the thesis that the promise begins in v. 22 are Rashi: "And this stone...if these [things] are done for me, I will do thus." See also Rashbam. Fokkelman, *Genesis*, 75, states: "Before we can start comparing vow and promise, it should be decided whether the main clause in the vow starts in v. 21b or in 22a. We observe the following...the verb comes first in 20b–21a, whereas 22a opens with the subject...[therefore] probable that 21b belongs to the protasis." See also Lipton, "Revisions," 80–81.
357.   Proponents of source criticism have found it especially difficult to explain the use of "Yahweh" alongside "Elohim" in the verse: "the Lord shall be my God" (v. 21b). By contrast, Fokkelman, *Genesis*, 76, states: "The fundamental question is that concerning the names Yhwh and Elohim, and the relationship between Yhwh/God and Jacob. V. 13b implicitly posed the question whether the God of Abraham and Isaac would also be the God of Jacob. For Jacob there was no question that Yhwh is God, certainly not after his vision of God..." According to Weisman, *Cycle*, 60, "The main difficulty in v. 21b has not been resolved. Its context makes it part of the vow, attributed to the E source, while the form of the divine name used

"so that I come again to my father's house in peace" (v. 21a) reflects Jacob's promise—meaning that the promise begins here—does not seem to have been adequately examined.

a) *The "promise" (apodosis) begins in v. 21b: the symmetry between the two parts of the vow as a sign of the dividing point.* Supporters of this view stress the affinity between the two parts of the vow as a characteristic of its structure. Parker speaks of a similarity between the two marked by a special relationship between the condition and what is promised.[358] Marcus, referring to Jephthah's vow, states the case differently: "the four other vows and in the Ugaritic vow examined, there is a parallel between protasis and apodosis. In all cases there is a specific relationship between the condition and the promise."[359] Avishur says, "The conditions of Jacob's vow are in symmetric parallel to his promise. In both there are three items that create a symmetric structure on the principle of measure for measure."[360] Marcus adds that this link occurs "sometimes in the same language," as in Jacob's vow: "If God will be with me" is linguistically parallel to "then shall the Lord be my God."[361] Cartledge[362] and, following him, Pagolu[363] note the place and role of the parallel and the symmetry between the protasis and the apodosis. The latter is not only the first promise but the summation of all Jacob's promises to build the Lord's house and to bring tithes. In view of the foregoing, one recognizes another literary sign that helps support the accepted division of the vow into condition and promise in v. 21b.

---

there, places it with the J source." For solutions Weisman rejects, see *Cycle*, 160 n. 153. Fidler, "Dream Theophany," 160 n. 153, cites numerous commentators who consider v. 21b an editorial addition, among them Dilmann, Wellhausen, Gunkel, Kautsch, Skinner, following De Pury, *Promesse*, 33–35 n. 5, which appears in the Appendix to Chapter 1. See Rendtorff, "Bethel," 519.

358. Parker, "Ugaritic," 699.
359. Marcus, *Jephthah*, 18.
360. Avishur, *Genesis*, 18.
361. A linguistic parallel between conditions and promise is found in the Israelite vow (Num 21:2–3): "If you deliver this people into our hands" (protasis), [then] "we will proscribe their towns" (apodosis). Hannah too vows (1 Sam 1:11): "If you will grant your maidservant a male child" (protasis) [then] "I will dedicate him to the Lord all the days of his life" (apodosis). Van Seters, "Encounter," 508, argues that "If it is necessary to associate the vow closely with the theophany, which in my view must have included 28:13–15, it is still a fair question to ask what is the relationship of vow to divine promise…in 1 Sam 1:9–18 in response to Hannah's prayer in which she offers a vow she does receive a divine promise of its fulfilment…"
362. Cartledge, *Vows*, 149.
363. Pagolu, *Religion*, 207.

b) *Or does the promise begin in v. 22?* Lipton,[364] apparently following Fokkelman,[365] maintains:

> The grammatical construction strongly suggests that the shift from *if* to *then* should take place at the beginning of v. 22. The initial "*If* God will be with me" is followed by four *waw* consecutives in which the verb, of course, precedes the noun. Verse 22, in contrast, opens with the noun (the stone), while the verb (will be) is in the imperfect. It may reasonably be assumed that this grammatical change marks the shift from protasis to apodosis.[366]

c) *Or in verse 21a? Two readings of "so that I come again (*shavti*) to my father's house in peace."* Another linguistic basis suggests a transition in v. 21. Had Jacob said, "He returns (*heshivani*) me" (in Hiphil, the causative in Hebrew), as in the Septuagint translation,[367] "so that I come again in peace to my father's house" would belong unequivocally to the conditions of the vow. There God is the subject: if God is with him, if God keeps him on his way, if God gives him bread to eat and raiment to put on, then "so that I come again in peace to my father's house" (v. 21a) fits into the list of those conditions. But should the verb be read "if I come again" (*shavti*), as it is in the present Hebrew text, then two readings are possible, since it is not explicitly stated thanks to whom, or on whose initiative, Jacob returned. In the first reading it is Jacob's,[368] in the second it is God's.

d) *In conclusion.* The precise location of the protasis in the vow does not significantly affect my main contention, namely that Jacob's "way" from the Land and his return, together with the "place" becoming a sanctuary, the house of God, appearing side by side, complement one another. Possibly, too, the difficulty in determining the transition from conditions to promise is not a matter of chance, but deliberate.

364. Lipton, "Revisions," 80–81.
365. See above, n. 349.
366. See Lipton, "Revisions," 80–81. Lipton's proposal to see v. 22 as the opening of Jacob's promise fits in with her thesis: "It will be suggested here that the dream at Bethel may belong to that class of dreams in which a king (here a patriarch) receives divine authorisation for the construction of a temple, thus confirming that he is held in high esteem by the gods" (p. 67).
367. See *BHK* on 28:21. The vow will later be compared to Absalom's (2 Sam 15:7–8. The causative verb form indicates that God will effect the return. In Absalom's vow it is a condition.
368. On the question of human or divine initiative, see in Chapter 4 on "Abram's versus Terah's departure." See also Y. Gitay, "Geography and Theology in the Biblical Narrative: The Question of Genesis 2–12," in *Prophets and Paradigms: Essays in Honor of Gene M. Tucker* (ed. S. B. Reid; JSOTSup 229; Sheffield: JSOT, 1996), 205–16.

2. The Story of Jacob's Dream at Bethel

5.3. The Link of the Vow to God's Promise (v. 15)

The connection between "so that I come again in peace to my father's house" (v. 21a) and the divine promise (v. 15) is the source of an ongoing polemic. If, however, the two are compared, possibilities open up, some of which resolve the theological issue mentioned earlier. Jacob does not relate to the divine promises (vv. 13–14).[369] Despite the similarity in language and in the order of Jacob's vow (vv. 20–21a), features that bear witness to linkage, there are differences that indicate another message.

5.3.1. *A table of comparison.*
Before going into differences, a table is presented to show the similarities between them.[370]

God's promise (28:15)	Jacob's conditions (28:20a–22)
And, behold, I [am] with thee	If God will be with me,[371] and will give me bread to eat, and raiment to put on,
and will keep thee in all [places] whither thou goest,	and will keep me in this way that I go
	and will give me bread to eat, and raiment to put on,
And I will bring thee again[372] (*vehashivotikh*) into this land [soil, *adama*].	So that I come again (*veshavti*) to my father's house in peace;

369. Fokkelman, *Genesis*, 75, sees no problem. On the contrary, according to Fokkelman, "Jacob's vow is an answer to the second half of God's promise, not to the first half of vv. 13b–14. But patriarchs never answer promises made them by God, so that it is not remarkable that Jacob does not engage with God's words in vv. 13–14, especially as they refer to the remote future. What is remarkable is that he responds at all, and then it is not surprising that he should go into the part of God's promise that refers to the present and the near future."

Nor is Jacob the first biblical figure who reacts and even protests in the face of a divine revelation. See, e.g., Abraham (Gen 18:22–33; 33:12–17); Moses (Exod 33:18); Gideon (Judg 6:13), asking for a sign (vv. 17–18, 36–40). See Cartledge, *Vows*, 171.

370. Fidler, "Dream Theophany," 158 n. 138, shows the similarities, disclosing the difficulties and weaknesses of source criticism, which relates v. 15 to J and vv. 20–21 to E.

371. Pagolu, *Religion*, 207, sees the expression as summing up the conditions that follow. It appears later in the story too when Jacob announces his intention to erect an altar to "the God who has answered me when I was in distress, and who has been with me wherever I have gone" (35: 3). Fidler, "Dream Theophany," 167, relates to the link of 35:2–3 with Jacob's vow.

372. Two readings are possible for the connecting *waw*, in both of which it relates back to "will keep thee in all [places] whither thou goest." In one it means

Jacob's words after God's promise (v. 15) may be understood as a response to it. Fokkelman states: "Jacob gives the one adequate response... Jacob's vow is an answer to the second half of God's promise, not to the first half of v. 13b–14."[373] It may also be regarded as Jacob's attempt to focus on his worries and doubts.[374] God makes him a general promise in v. 15 and Jacob adds "in peace"; God promises to be with Jacob and keep him and Jacob adds "give me bread to eat[375] and raiment to put on." Now for the comparison of expressions in vv. 15[376] and 21a that is the center of my interest:

Gen 28:15	Gen 28:21a
I will bring thee again (or "back") into this land (or "the soil")	So that I come again to my father's house *in peace*

The difference in the form of the verb *shwb*—causative (in Hiphil) in v. 15 and the simple intransitive (in Qal) in v. 21a—has been mentioned already. Hence I focus here on two other differences. One is "in peace,"

"and" and clarifies "all" in "all places whither thou goest," including the return to the Land. But the connector may also be attached to the beginning of the verse and read as a contrast, highlighting the return in contrast to all other routes Jacob takes.

373. Fokkelman, *Genesis*, 74, examining the chain of repeating key words in the second half of the story, helps identify the parallels that creates a structure of action and reaction. In his view it reveals the story's main idea: God enters into a dialogue with Jacob, whose response is thoroughly in keeping with his situation. Polak, *Narrative*, 224, following Fokkelman, divides the story into two subsections structured on the answer model.

374. Fokkelman, *Genesis*, 76: "The parallelism with v. 15 inspired us to this rendering; what God says in 15b means to Jacob: Yhwh will also be *my* God." Cartledge, *Vows*, 170: "Jacob now wishes to remove all doubt...Jacob is taking no chances... He has not only placed the deity under more certain obligations...but also has clarified and expanded on them."

375. On the link between "will not leave thee" and "bread to eat," see Rashi's commentary on v. 20, "I have never seen a righteous man abandoned, or his children seeking bread" (Ps 37:25). See also Fidler, "Dream Theophany," 158 n. 138. Jacob, undemanding, makes do with bread and raiment.

376. Fokkelman, *Genesis*, 61: "Verse 15c can refer to 13c, so that this land may be given to Jacob, God will bring him back; the near future serves the remote future." Westermann, *Genesis*, 198, maintains that v. 15 is a continuation of 27:41–45: "...Then I will fetch you from there," v. 15b "until I have done that which I have promised," refers back to vv. 13–14." The Septuagint reads: "all that which I have promised." See Isa 46:10–11 for its fulfillment. According to Cartledge, *Vows*, 170 n. 55, Jacob interprets the promise as "I will bring thee again into this land," meaning the Promised Land or perhaps even to Bethel. Clarifying v. 21a, Cartledge feels that the contrast between the divine promise and Jacob's response accentuates Jacob's egoistic nature and "adds color to the author's portrayal of Jacob's character."

present in Jacob's vow but absent in God's promise; the other is that God promises Jacob to return him "into this land (soil)," while for Jacob the place is "my father's house." What can be learned from the differences?[377]

5.3.2. *Two readings of the unique phrase "into this land" ("to this soil"—Fox; v. 15)" (*adama*)*. Why did God—or the narrator—select that unique combination?[378] Why not "this land" (*haarets hazot*),[379] used so frequently in the context of the promise of the Land? First, one may use the distinction between "earth" (soil) and "land" to tie it to the previous passage, "all the families of the earth" (v. 14). Second, the unique[380] "into this land" may encourage multiple readings. The first one, from the immediate context, is simply a reassurance that God will return Jacob to the Promised Land[381] ("I am with thee"). A broader context, however, to include Jacob's descent into Egypt (46:3–4) could lead to another, ironic reading, where the return to the Land suggests a negative association.

---

377. Fokkelman, *Genesis*, 77, states: "For what God calls 'this land', neutral and wide words, Jacob's words are, 'the house of my father,' familiar, intimate, close." Cartledge, *Vows*, 170, sees in Jacob's formulation a wish to ascertain God's promise, which also expresses Jacob's egoism.

378. Fidler, "Dream Theophany," 163, sees the promise of return "to this land" as "the work of one already familiar with the story's place within the Jacob story cycle." See also Rendtorff, "Bethel," 513.

379. In all twelve instances where the Land is promised to the Patriarchs (Gen 12:7; 13:15, 17; 15:7, 18; 17:8; 24:7; 25:3–4; 28:3–4, 13; 35:9–12; 48:4), nine times "land" is modified by "this." See Y. I. Peleg, "What Do the Declaration of Independence and the Promise of the Land to the Patriarchs Have in Common?," *Al Haperek* 16 (1999): 145–53.

380. Shapira, "Two Readings," 23, 338, shows in nn. 1, 2, 4, 29, 41, 43 the use of the unique word or expression that encourages "reading for multiple meanings."

381. Does "land" (*'adama*) in v. 13 indicate that God's words to Jacob apply to his descendants, "to thee and to thy seed" (v. 13)? For the use of "earth" (*'adama*) for "land" (*'erets*) in connection with the return from exile, see Jer 16:15: "For I will bring them back (*heshivotim*) to their land (*'adama*) which I gave to their fathers". See also Jer 24:10, 25:5, 35:15. In these and other Bible verses there is no distinction between earth and land in either KJV or JPS. Lipton, "Revisions," 127, examines the connection between the symbolic meaning of Jacob's Dream and return from exile: "The points of contacts between Jacob's situation preceding and subsequent to the dream at Beth-El and the situation of the exiles in Babylon are obvious; both are expelled from their native lands, both enter service to a foreign power, both have brothers who remain at home, and both return in a position of superiority… The dream confirms both that the time spent in service to Laban is part of God's plan for Jacob, and, still more to the point, that Jacob's destiny will be shared by his descendants." Regarding the verbs *'alah* and *yarad* in Gen 28:12 in connection with entering and leaving the Land may support this thesis.

Though it may seem to stretch a point, I go back to Adam, created from the dust of the earth (Gen 2:7) and fated to return to it.[382] In the Eden story, God tells Adam, "By the sweat of your brow shall you get bread to eat, until you return to the ground—for from it were you taken (3:19). Moreover, in that story, bread and clothing appear consecutively: "God made garments...and clothed them," just as in Jacob's vow (28:21c).

Consequently there are two contradictory readings for "I will bring thee again into this land," one encouraging and the other deeply worrying to Jacob. In the first, God will protect Jacob and bring him back alive to the Land. In the second, He will return Jacob to the earth (*adama*) in death.[383]

Indeed, in the context of the story Jacob is existentially worried,[384] fleeing for his life. The second reading comes to mind retrospectively in Jacob's old age. As he is descending into Egypt, God appears to him again "in a vision by night" (46:1–5) and promises him: "Fear not to go down into Egypt...I Myself will go down with you into Egypt, and I Myself will bring you back." Here too God promises to return him, as in 28:15, the causative (Hiphil) verb forms used in both cases, but Jacob did not return alive. Did Jacob understand God's words as encouragement or with foreboding? Assuming that Jacob's vow was a response to the divine promise, is Jacob trying to comprehend unequivocally what is essentially ambiguous?[385] Jacob's, or the narrator's, choice of "to my father's house" (v. 21) instead of "to this land" (v. 15), and the use of the Qal form of the verb *shwb* rather than the causative Hiphil (v. 15), appear to support the first reading that encourages Jacob to believe he will return home in peace. What can be inferred from the absence of "in peace" from the divine promise (v. 15)?

---

382. See also Ps 104:29; Job 10:9; 34:15; Eccl 3:20.

383. Westermann, *Genesis*, 455–56, 460, argues: "The promise in v. 15 differs from that of vv. 13–14 inasmuch as it is not only adapted to the situation of Jacob in flight but also is fulfilled in his lifetime and accords with the life-style of the patriarchs... [I]n origin it is a promise for the road. Its setting in life is the start of a journey or migration... In Genesis 28 the promise of v. 15, which concerns the journey and the story of the patriarch Jacob, is added to the experience of the holy; thus there are brought together those two basic religious phenomena."

384. On distress as a background for vows in the Bible and the ANE, see Parker, "Ugaritic," 699. See also Pagolu, *Religion*, 199: "Vows in Israel generally arose in time of distress just as in the ancient Near East."

385. Doubt might have arisen with the addition of "if" in v. 15: "I will not leave thee if I have not done that which I have promised."

5.3.3. *Two readings of "in peace"* (beshalom) *(v. 21a)*. "In peace" most often, but not always, occurs in positive contexts,[386] Consider for instance "As for you, you shall go to your fathers *in peace*; you shall be buried at a ripe old age (Gen 15:15); "You will be laid in your tomb *in peace*" (2 Kgs 22:20 = 2 Chr 34:28), and "You will die a peaceful death" (Jer 34:5). Their essentially negative connotations may be supported by the divine promise to Jacob: "and will bring thee again into this land." Jacob's subsequent vow becomes ironic. It appears to have sought a positive meaning in God's too general promise, which could be understood either for good or for ill.

Thus the close reading process arouses interest due to its richness and complexity. The reader is in suspense as to whether Jacob will return alive or dead. Moreover, each hindrance Jacob overcomes in his life in Haran increases the reader's concern for him. Only when "Jacob arrived safely (*beshalem*) in the city of Shechem which is in Canaan" (33:18) will these concerns be assuaged, and the choice between the two readings be resolved.[387]

5.4. *Return to the Homeland: A Comparison with Absalom's Vow (2 Samuel 15:7–8)*
5.4.1. *One of three formulations of the vow's content.* Since the expression "if I come again to my father's house in peace" (Gen 28:21a) appears elsewhere in the vows of the Bible and of ANE literature, a comparison to other vows concerning the return from abroad, or to the homeland, seems worthwhile.

As examples of a literary genre, Parker classifies biblical vows as to content in three types: (1) safe return from abroad,[388] (2) military victory, and (3) acquiring a family—all seen as "conditions." Fear is characteristic,

---

386. See, e.g., Judg 8:9; 11:31; 1 Kgs 22:17; 2 Chr 18:16, 26–28; 19:33.
387. Fokkelman, *Genesis*, 77: "In that part of the sentence, v. 21a, Jacob adds: $b^e \check{s}\bar{a}l\hat{o}m$... More than the journey it will worry him to see Esau again. Because the story of Beth-El presupposes the presence of the Penuel scene, as appears at several points later on (we shall come across a verbal connection, in addition to those already mentioned), and because a leading motif in the Penuel scene is how frightened Jacob is of seeing Esau again, and because in Gen. 33, after the reunion, the stem *šlm* is explicitly used once more (v. 18), it is necessary for $b^e \check{s}\bar{a}l\hat{o}m$ to be read against the background of Jacob's flight from his brother's wrath." See also Y. Zakovitch and A. Shinan, *"And Jacob arrived safely in the city of Shechem": Genesis 33:18–20 in Ancient Translations and in Early Jewish Literature* (RPJSI 5; Jerusalem: The Hebrew University, 1985).
388. Parker, "Ugaritic," 699, although the definition of Pagolu, *Religion*, 206, seems preferable.

particularly of the first type. In return for a safe repatriation from abroad, the divinity is promised the service, as a ritual act, of the maker of the vow.[389] Jacob's vow, then, belongs both as regards content and literary context, to the first type. Jacob, journeying to Haran (to abroad), fears both his brother Esau and the unknown situation before him. Hence his concern over being able to return in safety in order to fulfill the promise that was given to him in the dream: "the land whereon thou liest, to thee will I give it, to thee and to thy seed" (v. 13).[390] With that, from the standpoint of a safe return from exile, Absalom's vow is the most like Jacob's.

5.4.2. *Returning from exile—Absalom's vow.* Parker points out two common elements in the vows of Jacob and of Absalom.[391] Both indicate concern for safe return from exile, and both undertake to serve the divinity:

	Jacob's vow (Gen 28:20–22)	*Absalom's vow* (2 Sam 15:7–8)[392]
Background, introduction	And Jacob vowed a vow, saying	Let me go to Hebron and fulfill a vow I made to the Lord
the conditional word	If	If
	I come again to my father's house in peace	God ever brings me back to Jerusalem
The undertaking (apodosis)	v. 22: Then shall the Lord be my God… And this stone… shall be God's house and of all Thou shalt give me I will surely give the tenth unto Thee	I will worship the Lord

389. Pagolu calls this repatriation, fitting in perfectly with God's promise to Jacob in 31:13: "…return to your native land." It also ties in with the exiled hero motif familiar from ANE literature. See the separate discussion of the dream as *mise en abyme* of the Jacob story cycle.

390. While family, "seed," is present in the narrative context, it is even hinted at in the vow.

391. Parker, "Ugaritic," 699; Cartledge, *Vows*, 12, 197; Pagolu, *Religion*, 206.

392. "In peace" is absent from the vow, though in v. 9 the king says "Go in peace" to Absalom. The preceding verses lend irony through word play on the root *shlm*, beginning with Absalom's name, continuing with *leshalem* in. v. 7 (payment of his vow), and with the plea to return to Jeru*salem* (v. 8). The sensitive reader familiar with Jacob's vow, which pleads specifically to return in peace, expects to find that word here. David's "Go in peace" fills the gap, but Absalom goes to war. Cartledge, *Vows*, 197, refers to Fokkelman, *Genesis*, 171.

The utterance "If God ever brings me back to Jerusalem" in Absalom's vow is an unequivocal condition. Likewise, who is to return him is clear, since God is the subject of *shwb* in its causative (Hiphil) form. The same can hardly be inferred from Jacob's "If I come again to my father's house in peace," since it is a condition (part of the protasis). The verb is in Qal and not in Hiphil and its subject is not explicitly stated. Marcus too designates Absalom's "If God…Jerusalem" as a condition (protasis).[393]

Common to the first subjects of both vows, according to Parker, is the fear and the hope of its maker regarding a safe return. However, while "in peace" is not found in Absalom's vow, Jephthah places conditions on his: "on my safe return."

5.5. *Returning in Peace: A Comparison with Jephthah's Vow (Judges 11:31)*

The subject of return in Jephthah's vow, appears, according to Marcus, as an obligation, not as a condition.[394] Can the same be inferred for Jacob's "If I come again…in peace"? The two are here compared:

	Jacob's vow (Gen 28:20–22)	Jephthah's vow (Judg 11:30–31)
Introduction	And Jacob vowed a vow, saying,	And Jephthah made the following vow to the Lord
Condition (protasis)	*If* God will be with me, and will keep me in this way that I go, and will give me bread to eat, and raiment to put on, so that I come again to my father's house in peace	*If* you deliver the Ammonites into my hands
The promise (apodosis)	Then shall the Lord be my God…and this stone…shall be God's house and of all that thou shalt give me I will surely give the tenth unto thee.	Then shall whatever comes out of the door of my house to meet me on my safe [in peace] return from the Ammonites shall be the Lord's, and shall be offered up[395] by me as a burnt offering.

---

393. See Marcus, *Jephthah*, 20. See also Cartledge, *Vows*, 177.

394. Marcus, *Jephthah*, 20, compares Jephthah's vow to Hannah's in 1 Sam 1:11. If she is given a son she will return him: "If you will grant your maidservant a son" (protasis) [then] "I will dedicate him to the Lord for all the days of his life" (apodosis).

395. Given this comparison, one would expect Jephthah to vow: "I will dedicate my daughter to the Lord all the days of her life." This would allow the assumption that Jephthah did not sacrifice his daughter, reducing the tragedy of the story. Four

Differently from Absalom's vow, the grammatical use of the *shwb* root in Jephthah's resembles Jacob's "so that I come again to my father's house in peace." Both use the Qal form of the verb rather than the Hiphil. Both stress concern over the safe return ("in peace"), while neither states whether God or man is responsible for it. Hence there are two possible readings of both, as previously indicated vis-à-vis Jacob's vow, regarding whether he returned on his own initiative or through God's. In the first reading it is Jacob's own initiative.[396] In the second reading Jacob's return is God's initiative. In this sense Jacob's vow is closer to Jephthah's than to Absalom's.[397]

The attempt to resolve definitively, through study of other biblical vows, whether the safe return (*beshalom*) belongs to the conditions, as in Absalom's case, or to the promises as regards Jephthah's, has not succeeded and the issue remains unresolved.

Nonetheless, from Marcus's analysis of Jephthah's vow, an inference can be made regarding Jacob's. Unable to decide between the two, Marcus proposes two readings[398] for the words "shall be offered by me as

---

times the keyword, the verb *'asah* ("do, make") appears, but it is unclear who did or promised to do what. See J. Berman, "Medieval Monasticism and the Evolution of Jewish Interpretation of the Story of Jephthah's Daughter," *JQR* 95 (2005): 228–56. Berman rejects this reading.

396. That vows are addressed to God affirms the assumption that both Jacob and Jephthah attribute a safe return to Him. Yet its absence from Absalom's vow reinforces my right at least to raise the second possibility. On the "division of labor" between man and God in performing the miracle, see Y. Zakovitch, *The Perception of Miracle* (Tel Aviv: misrad habitahon, 1987), esp. 69–77.

397. Avishur, *Genesis*, 174. Avishur notes the structural similarity between Jacob's vow and Jephthah's.

398. One version of the Septuagint translation (see *BHK* on Judg 11:31) suggests, differently from the Masoretic text, that "he had no other son or daughter" (v. 34) means no son or daughter from her *mimena*, i.e. no grandchild to continue his line. If accepted, this could support the figurative reading, that human sacrifice was not involved, but that the daughter, like Samuel, was dedicated to God's service. It fits in well with the daughter's request to "bewail her maidenhood" (v. 37), not her imminent death. Thus Jephthah "rent his clothes" (v. 35), mourning for his own bitter fate in not having a grandchild from his only daughter. Further support for the figurative reading comes from the frequent use of *'asah* (vv. 36 [twice], 37, 39). The daughter says, "do (*'aseh*) to me as you have vowed" (v. 36), and at the end of the story: "he did (*'asah*) to her as he had vowed" (v. 39). What he did, *'asah*, is not stated. That "she had never known a man" (v. 39) allows for the understanding that this was the force of Jephthah's promise, an ambiguous realization of an ambiguous vow.

a burnt offering" (Judg 11:31). One is literal—"he will belong to the Lord" (shall be the Lord's)—the other figurative[399]—"shall be offered as a burnt offering (*'olah*)." In his opinion, the narrator deliberately chose to allow the reader to decide[400] whether the intention was a literal or a figurative sacrifice.

5.6. *Conclusion: Two Readings of the Vow*
Regarding the affinity of the themes of "place" and "way" in Jacob's vow in particular and the dream story as a whole (Gen 28:10–22), the narrator appears to allow the reader to decide[401] whether the main theme is the return to the homeland (first reading) or the establishment of God's house (second reading). The decision is not cardinal, as the decisions are complementary, not contradictory. The return as the central theme of Jacob's Dream appears to have been sidelined—although reinstated through the vow, revealing its importance to the dream as a whole.

The vow, then, heightens understanding of the Jacob's Dream story, by presenting the two themes and the links between them. The order of their appearance (it is immaterial whether "I come again in peace to my father's house" is a condition or a promise),[402] where the return to the homeland is mentioned before the building of God's house, is not only a time sequence but a statement of interdependence. If Jacob does not

---

399. "Alas, daughter!" (v. 35). "Alas" occurs but 15 times in the entire Bible, always in a direct or indirect appeal to God, 11 times as a standard formulation, "Ah/alas Lord God" (Josh 7:7; Judg 6:22; 2 Kgs 3:10; Jer 1:6; 4:10; 14:13; 32:17; Ezek 4:14; 9:8; 11:13; 21:5). Twice the appeal is to Elisha "the man of God" (2 Kgs 6:5, 15) and once to "For the day of the Lord": "Alas for the day! For the day of the Lord is near" (Joel 1:15). Perhaps Jephthah too, then, is addressing God indirectly. The sensitive reader may feel that here as well the "addressee" is not the daughter but God: "*You* have brought me low, you have become my troubler, for I have uttered a vow to the Lord and I cannot retract." Was there a scribal misunderstanding, apparently in "you (f.) *at hayit* have brought me low" when it should have been "you (m.) *atah hayita*," so that Jephthah, like Job in ch. 9, complains against God, like Naomi: "Shaddai has made my lot very bitter" (Ruth 1:20). Suddenly another likeness of Jephthah emerges—more humane towards his daughter and protesting more against God. How does this view help resolve the question of sacrificing his daughter on the altar versus dedicating her to God?

400. Perry and Sternberg, "Ironic Eyes."

401. The narrator may have left the reader to decide also where Jacob went from his conditions to his promises.

402. The not unambiguous proposal that the two themes are present in the apodosis of the vow could not only solve the theological problem, but also hints that Jacob understood that his dream dealt with both themes.

return, be that by means of his own initiative or God's,[403] God's house cannot be built.

After analyzing the entire story in Gen 28:10–22, and in view of the clear links that exist between them, taking the two readings together seems the only "legitimate approach to the Jacob's Dream story with its complex significance."[404] The vow is no add-on that mars the story's integrity. Instead, it illuminates the dream's significance and interpretation in the light of the two proposed readings.

---

403. Later I shall deal with the question of divine versus human initiative. As Gitay, "Geography," 205–16, maintains, only when the two are coordinated and in agreement will humanity's way succeed. In the Jacob story generally, and in the story of the vow in particular, that agreement prevails.

404. See Perry and Sternberg, "Ironic Eyes," 286, for the analogy and paraphrase of these authors.

Chapter 3

THE JACOB'S DREAM STORY AS *MISE EN ABYME* OF THE JACOB STORY CYCLE

1. *Subject and Boundaries*

This chapter discusses Jacob's Dream at Bethel as a story within the Jacob story cycle ("a story within a story"), focusing on the literary and ideological formulation of the dream and its meaning. A good amount of space has already been devoted to the vision in the dream (Gen 28:12–13a) as a symbolic *mise en abyme* of the Jacob's Dream story. Now I shall try to show how that vision reflects the Jacob story cycle as a compact miniature of his descents from and ascents to the Promised Land. Gammie[1] sees departing and returning as an important motif in the Jacob cycle. He and Westermann[2] see *flight–return* as a bridging theme that frames the Jacob story cycle.

Fishbane[3] sees the paired terms *land–exile* as one of the three themes, besides *birth–barrenness* and *curse–blessing* that span the Jacob story cycle. According to Fishbane, "Land functions in this cycle as subject of the binary pair exile/homeland."[4]

---

1. Gammie, "Theological," 120.
2. Westermann, *Genesis 12–36*, 406–7.
3. See M. Fishbane, *Text and Texture: Close Readings of Selected Biblical Texts* (New York: Schocken, 1979), 60, who argues: "Three issues are of primary importance in Gen 25:19–35:22: birth, blessing, and land." See also Westermann, *Genesis*, 406–7. Fishbane and Westermann saw the bridge element in the Jacob story cycle, as in the Abraham cycle. Later, Fishbane's *land–exile* (*ascent–descent*) theme will be studied in connection with Abraham.
4. See Fishbane, *Text*, 61: "The actions of Gen 25:19–35:22 can thus be viewed along a spatial axis. Jacob flees from Canaan and has an encounter with the divine at the border shrine of Bethel (28:10ff.); he stays in Aram until Rachel gives birth, whereupon he returns and encounters the divine at the border shrines of Mahanayim and Penuel (ch. 32)… Only when Jacob resettles in Canaan is his patriarchal destiny confirmed (ch. 35)."

Understanding Jacob's Dream as a *mise en abyme* may help the interpretation of the vision in the dream on the symbolic level. Perceiving the story of Jacob's Dream at Bethel (Gen 28:10–22) in its literary context, stressing its role in the Jacob story cycle—its *mise en abyme* function—sheds light both on the meaning of the dream, and its role vis-à-vis entering and leaving the Land.

Every literary unit, and especially the story of Jacob's Dream, should be studied in the light of its place in the concentric circles structure, as an independent unit, then within its immediate (juxtaposition)[5] and then its broader context—the Jacob story cycle, and the journeys of the Patriarchs, including Abraham, to and from the Land.

2. Defining "Jacob Story Cycle" Boundaries and Place in the Discussion

It is useful here to give a definition of what is meant by "story cycle." To do this, I take up the words of Weisman:

> The term *story cycle*[6] serves two different approaches to the study of the stories of the Patriarchs. According to one, the story cycle is part of a larger work, that is, the entire book of Genesis, or a link in a chain of many links (Gen 12–50). Defining it as a cycle and separating it from others in the chain of Patriarchal stories is determined by the central figure[7] in the stories and not by the narrator. The cycle's place in the literature of the Patriarchs is genealogically determined…according to linear development over three or four generations.[8]

---

5. On the principle of Juxtaposition in the Bible, see the subsequent discussion on Abraham's descent into Egypt. See also M. D. Cassuto, *Biblical and Oriental Studies: Biblical Literature and Canaanite Literature*, vol. 1 (Jerusalem: Magnes, 1974), 200–204; Y. Zakovitch, "Juxtaposition in the Abraham Cycle," in *Pomegranates and Golden Bells: Studies in Biblical, Jewish, and Near Eastern Ritual, Law, and Literature in Honor of Jacob Milgrom* (ed. D. P. Wright, D. N. Freedman and A. Hurvitz; Winona Lake, Ind.: Eisenbrauns, 1995), 509–24; M. Fishbane, *Biblical Interpretation in Ancient Israel* (Oxford: Clarendon, 1985), 399–407; Y. Zakovitch, "The Associative Principle in the Order of the Book of Judges: Its Use in Discerning Stages in the Book's Development," in *Isac Leo Seeligmann Volume: Essays on the Bible and the Ancient World*, vol. 1 (ed. A. Rofé and Y. Zakovitch; Jerusalem: Rubinstein, 1983), 161–83. On the importance of juxtaposition in the Bible as a meaningful editorial device, see Y. Zakovitch and A. Shinan, "Midrash on Scripture and Midrash within Scripture," in Japhet, ed., *Studies in Bible*, 267–270.

6. Weisman, *Cycle*, 7, notes that "story cycle" is a general literary term.

7. Fokkelman, *Genesis*, 238.

8. Weisman, *Cycle*, 38.

Such biblical genealogies generally begin with "These are the generations,"[9] indicating a "biography" relating to the Patriarchs.

Based on collections from medieval Iceland and from the Bedouin, De Pury[10] differentiates between linear and cyclic orders of tales. Other scholars,[11] adhering to the structural approach, describe the Jacob story cycle as a planned structure, usually in chiastic form, in which the first scene parallels the last, the second the penultimate scene, and so on. In this structure, the Jacob's Dream story is presented as parallel to the one in ch. 32.[12]

Fishbane defines both stories as "encounter (verb *paga'*) with the divine at sacred site, near border."[13] The chiastic structure reflects the chiastic, i.e. contrasting, significance according to which departure from the Land, for instance, is contrasted with the return to it. I shall thus compare the story of Jacob's Dream at Bethel, where he encountered angels of God (*mal'akhei 'elohim*) on the eve of his departure from the Land, to the story of Mahanaim, who encountered such figures on the eve of his return.

According to Fishbane, "the Jacob Cycle and its components reflect complete symmetry both in content and in language."[14] Perhaps this stress on "complete symmetry" is the main obstacle to full acceptance of his approach. In the words of Shapira, "The deconstruction established and nurtured by Jacques Derrida is avowedly anti-structuralist, and rejected the idea of structure as an objective fact in the text, and as well, the assumption of any 'objective' text."[15] My own approach is close to that of Fishbane, who summed up is structuralist approach thus:

> The structuralist approach, with all its significance and fascination, cannot replace intense listening to the word and to word combinations, which belongs to another type of literary analysis called *The New Criticism*. It

---

9. See especially "Now these are the generations of Terah" (Gen 11:27); "These are the generations of Isaac" (25:19); "These are the generations of Jacob" (37:2 KJV).
10. De Pury, *Promesse*, 607–9.
11. See Fishbane, *Text*, 40–62; Gammie, *Theological*, 117–34.
12. See Fishbane, *Text*, 53–54, especially "The first (Gen 28:10ff.) occasion is on his flight out of the land, the second (Gen 32:25–33) is on his way in" (p. 54). See also Zakovitch, "Jabbok," 191. Zakovitch posits "a reincarnation of traditions regarding Jacob's struggle with the Divinity."
13. See M. Fishbane, "Composition and Structure in the Jacob Cycle (Gen 25:19–35:22)," *JJS* 26 (1975): 20.
14. See ibid., 19.
15. Shapira, "Multiple Meanings."

insists on the need to isolate, to find the unique feature and to find the secret in each text. The new approach is seen as an addition, not a replacement for the existing literary approach, according to the structuralists.[16]

In connection with the Jacob stories, Weisman stresses:

> I have noticed the difference between the cycle, whose significance is mainly the departure from (Genesis 28) and return to Bethel (Genesis 35), and the biographical cycle[17] that includes the birth story (prolog), his descent into Egypt, his death in Egypt and burial in Canaan (epilog). While my work is focused on the first, I did not avoid the last, assuming that in some stage of the stories of the Patriarchs there would be a complete biographical cycle on Jacob, some parts of which were separated from the composition and editing of the others stories and arranged according to different principles of composition and editing.[18]

Our main interest here is not on surmises as to the story's origin but on the story as it now exists. At the same time, from the synchronic standpoint, one has to be aware of the dangers confronting the structuralists that may lock[19] their attitudes to the text.

Nor need one fully accept the chiastic structure of the Jacob story cycle. It suffices to identify the analogies in it,[20] and our focus is on those aspects that are connected with entering and leaving the Land. To me, the contribution of the structural approach lies in the assistance it offers for the identification of these connections. The chiastic structure, formal in essence, shows the reflective, contrasting link between the revelation story on the eve of Jacob's departure and the one on the eve of his return, which is essentially one of content and values. That both are included in

---

16. A. H. Fish, "A Structuralist Approach to the Stories of Ruth and Boaz," *Beit Mikra* 24 (1979): 265.

17. Possibly in the Jacob stories one may replace "biographic cycle" with "biographic story," although a biography may be understood as a life cycle, as, for example, in Job: "Naked came I out of my mother's womb, and naked shall I return there" (1:21). "Biographic story," however, is preferable.

18. Weisman, *Cycle*, 13, 41–44.

19. Barzel, *New Interpretations of Literary Texts*, 19, notes: "In the *New Criticism* commentary that opens is preferred to commentary that locks."

20. Hendel, "Patterns," 141 n. 20: "…I find unconvincing the recent attempts of M. Fishbane [*Text*, 40–62] and Gammie [*Theological*, 120–24] describing the Jacob structure as an elaborated chiasm. While there are symmetries, as in the encounters with the deity at sacred sites (Bethel, Penuel) on the flight from and the return to the Land, the story as a whole does not conform to a rigorous chiastic scheme." See also Garsiel, "Literary Structure," 65, relating to Fishbane and others, does not rule out parallelism. In Garsiel's opinion, however, "The parallelism is not complete, and one can dispute the source of the literary structure units. In any case, there is chiastic symmetry, even if incomplete, as scholars have suggested."

3. *The Jacob's Dream Story as* Mise en Abyme

the Jacob story cycle that begins with the departure from Bethel and concludes with his return there, heightens the analogy and the symmetry between them.

In section 2.6 of Chapter 1, "Broadening Circles of Commentary," I wrote: "Every literary unit, and Jacob's Dream in particular (Gen 28:10–22), is examined in the context of its place in widening circles—as an independent unit, within its immediate environment (i.e. juxtaposition), and in its broader context." I agree with Zakovitch that "even if the reader is sure he has found the beginning and the end of the story, he must decide whether it is an independent literary unit that can be explicated without reference to its literary surroundings, or whether it radiates into a broader system from which it gets its own light..." He compares the independent story to "a tile in a broad literary mosaic... As an isolated gem it appears differently than it does in a jewel composed of many gems!"[21]

I agree with Fokkelman's conclusion:

> Following Jacob so closely can easily involve too narrow a range of vision; in tracing the Story of Jacob we have not yet taken in account the broader perspective requisite to the investigation of the Story of Jacob, together with Gen 26:34 and 36, into its context, viz. the book of Genesis as inner circle and the Hexateuch as outer circle. At a distance, thus, with a wider range of vision, the texts appear to us in perspective; the themes of land and of family-history are functions of even larger perspective that God's plan of salvation means to a chosen people on its way to a promised land.[22]

In my view, understanding of the Jacob's Dream story in the *mise en abyme* framework reinforces its link to the stories of the Patriarchs.

Therefore, besides examining the stories contiguous to the Jacob cycle (ch. 25–35), in parallel one can also look at the linear description in Genesis from the standpoint of entering and leaving the Land. This perspective not only fills Jacob's life from birth till death, but the stories of the Patriarchs as a whole.

Fidler points out that Jacob's three dreams at Bethel (Gen 28:10–22; at Laban's home (31:10–13) and at Beer-Sheba (46:1–5) appear at three biographical-geographical turning points in his life story, which is told from birth (25:19–27) up to his death and burial (49:29–50:13). My understanding of "Jacob story cycle" follows Fidler's, not the more limited definition generally accepted in biblical scholarship.[23]

---

21. See Zakovitch, *Interpretation*, 57.
22. See Fokkelman, *Genesis*, 241.
23. Fidler, "Dream Theophany," 132, 178.

Fidler points out the strong resemblance between God's revelation to Jacob in Gen 46:1–5, and to Isaac at Beer-Sheba in 26:24.[24] This is shown in the following table:

Revelation to Isaac *(Genesis 26:23–24)*	*Revelation to Jacob* *(Genesis 46:1–5)*
From there he went up to Beer-Sheba	He came to Beer-Sheba
That night the Lord appeared to him	In a vision by night
And said, I am the God of your father Abraham	I am God, the God of your father
Fear not	Fear not to go down to Egypt
For I am with you and increase your offspring	For I will make you there into a great nation

Here too a hidden significance creates the similarity between the two and reminds Jacob and the reader of God's warning to Isaac, "Do not go down to Egypt" (26:2). This explains not only why Jacob was afraid, but that descent into Egypt required God's explicit permission.[25]

3. Mise en Abyme *in the Bible and in Ancient Near Eastern Literature*

As indicated in Chapter 1, *mise en abyme* is a term borrowed for use in studying biblical literature.[26] We examine some methodological and theoretical questions that help clarify the place and role of the story within a story. Then we address the place, role and contribution of the term to the study of biblical narratives in general, and of the Jacob's Dream story and its interpretation in particular.

3.1. *What Is the* Mise en Abyme*'s Place in "the Story Within a Story"?*
The question of where the embedded story is located precedes the question of its role, since, according to Bal,[27] the location of the embedded

---

24. Fidler, ibid., 193, surveys points common to both revelations, and her n. 310 explains the term for a divine message encouraging a person in distress.

25. A later section deals with the connection between the revelation to Jacob at Beer-Sheba (46:1–4) and the story of Jacob's Dream. God's words to Jacob in his dream (28:13–15) may be understood as legitimizing his journey to Haran, given the promise to "bring you back to this land" (v. 15).

26. It is not the only borrowed term, nor is such borrowing new. Close reading, keywords, metaphor, chiasmus and holistic interpretation are other widely used terms that help to understand the Bible story and its world. May *mise en abyme* do so as well.

27. See M. Bal, *Narratology: Introduction to the Theory of Narrative* (trans. C. van Boheemen; Toronto: University of Toronto, 1985), 145–7: "In French the

story influences the role and importance of the *mise en abyme* in the narrative. One problem of what Bal calls the subordinate story is that when it appears near the beginning of the framework or primary story, the reader can guess from the beginning how the framework story will end,[28] detracting at once from readers' interest and suspense. Moreover, if its end is what gives meaning to the entire story, then the idea of *mise en abyme* as the miniature reflecting the framework story is flawed, offering no help in understanding the story. How does one deal with it?

First, for the reader to determine that the embedded story is a *mise en abyme* he/she has to read the entire framework story. Only after that, in retrospect will the resemblance between the two become clear, so that the reader's suspense is preserved. Indeed, another type of suspense is created. The reader no longer asks how the story will end, but whether the hero will find out in time.[29] Besides, "The advance hint gives the reader a handhold, as it were, and a direction that may increase their involvement in the story process.[30]

Secondly, the two stories are never completely identical. As Bal notes, "Resemblance, however, can never be absolute... Even in passport photographs, taken with the express intention to show resemblance to the person portrayed, there may be different degree of likeness."[31] While this is no longer true of passport photos, we can even now not be sure that before us is the *mise en abyme* that will predict or reveal the end of the

---

term *is mise en abyme*... I suggest we use the term *mirror-text* for *mise en abyme*... The place of the embedded text—the mirror-text—in the primary text determines the function of the reader. When the mirror-text occurs near the beginning the reader may, on the basis of the mirror-text, predict the end of the primary fabula. To maintain suspense, the resemblance is often veiled... When the mirror-text is added more towards the end of the primary text, the suspense problem presents itself less emphatically."

28. See A. Jefferson, "*Mise en abyme* and the Prophetic in Narrative," *Style* 17 (1983): 196–208. Jefferson (196) noted that "As an element of the chronology in the narrative...*mise en abyme* has a largely negative function: it pre-empts the ending and spoils its effects by revealing the story *in toto*."

29. Rimmon-Kenan, *Poetics*, 50, discussing *prolepsis* (placing matters before their time) is less common than *analepsis* (flashback), at least in the Western framework. Prolepsis like the *mise en abyme* replaces suspense arising from the question, "What's going to happen?" As for suspense regarding "How did that happen?" (p. 51), one may regard the dream, including Jacob's Dream, as prolepsis. On this (the anticipation, according to Polak), see Polak, *Narrative*, 175, 188. Later we discuss whether Jacob himself understood the symbolic message of his Bethel dream.

30. Polak, *Narrative*, 175.

31. Bal, *Narratology*, 145.

story. Moreover, to preserve the reader's suspense, it appears with a veiled or symbolized resemblance to the framework text, so that damage to the suspense element is small.[32]

3.2. *The* Mise en Abyme *Role in the Story*

Like Bal,[33] Rimmon-Kenan discusses the relationship between the stories as "subordinate relationships: story levels." She considers a figure from Genette's tale "Diegesis," who herself tells a tale. As Rimmon-Kenan notes, "Such stories within stories create layers of levels in which each inner story is subordinate to the one in which it is embedded."[34] According to Genette, in this hierarchic structure[35] the highest level appears right after the first story in which narration is carried out. Understanding the embedded story as subordinate is reinforced with Todorov's enlightening analogy[36] to the story within a story he suggests:

> Let us take a German example, since German syntax permits much more spectacular examples of embedding than English or French:
>
> *Derjenige, der den Mann, der den Pfahl, der auf der Brucke, der auf dem Weg, der nach Worms fuhrt, liegt, steht, umgeworfen hat, anzeigt, bekommt eine Belohnung.*
>
> Whoever identifies the one who upset the post which was placed on the bridge which is on the road which goes to Worms will get a reward.

Todorov argues:

> In the German sentence, the appearance of a noun immediately provoked a subordinate clause which, so to speak, tells its story; but since this second clause also contains a noun, it requires in its turn a subordinate clause, and so on, until an arbitrary interruption, at which point each of the interrupted clauses is completed one after the other. The narrative of embedding has precisely the same structure, the role of the noun being played by the character: each new character involves a new story.[37]

---

32. In Jacob's Dream, the verbs *'alah* and *yarad* are used in their symbolic sense, concealing the resemblance of the dream, and hence its link, to the framework story.

33. Bal, *Narratology*, 49.

34. Rimmon-Kenan, *Poetics*, 89, bases her discussion to a great extent on Genette, whose definitions are cited in G. Genette, *Narrative Discourse: An Essay in Method* (trans. J. E. Lewin; Ithaca, N.Y.: Cornell University Press, 1980), 33–57, about the *mise en abyme* as an embedded story within a framework story.

35. See Bal, *Narratology*, 142.

36. Todorov, *Prose*, 66–79; Barth, "Tales." See also Greenstein, "Flood," 199. Greenstein applies the third of Barth's main observations.

37. Todorov, *Prose*, 70–71.

Barth also considers the appeal of the story within a story.[38] Rimmon-Kenan adds that the "[hypodiegetic =] embedded stories" may fill functions different to those of the stories in which they are imbedded, separately or in combination.[39] These functions are:

1. Function of Activity: sometimes embedded stories contribute to the action of the first story, or advance the story simply by being told, without any connection to their content. Thus in *A Thousand and One Nights*, Scheherezade's life depends on her activity as a narrator.
2. Explanatory Function: the embedded level explains the diegetic level when it answers questions like those about events leading to the existing situation. In this case, the content of the tale, and not the narration *per se*, is of the first importance.
3. Thematic Function: the hypodieget (embedded) and the dieget framework levels are analogous, i.e. are related by similarity and contrast. This type of analogy borders on identity, where the embedded level is transparent and duplicates the framework level is, in French, *mise en abyme*.[40]

Regarding the relations between primary and embedded fabula, Bal argues: "Another possible relationship between the two texts presents itself when the two fabulas are related to each other. Then there are two possibilities. The embedded story can explain the primary story, or it may resemble the primary story."[41]

I argue that the story of Jacob's Dream resembles the story of the Patriarchs in Genesis regarding the question of going up to and going down from the Promised Land. In this case, Bal notes regarding the embedded story (Jacob's Dream), "the explanation is usually left to the reader, or merely hinted at in the fibula."[42]

This remark is important as we discuss the symbolic vision in Jacob's Dream as a *mise en abyme*. Bal expresses the possibility that the fabulas may resemble one another.[43] One example of the explanatory role of the

---

38. Barth, "Tales," 59, citing Todorov's analogy, adds: "The German analogy… is built more dramatically than most framework stories. What is postponed in the sentence are the verbs: if the nouns are 'the figures', the subordinate clauses are the stories within a framework story. The verbs are the dramatic climax…"

39. See Rimmon-Kenan, *Poetics*, 90.

40. The thematic *mise en abyme* may mislead because it may also have an activity function, as shown later.

41. Bal, *Narratology*, 144.

42. Ibid.

43. Ibid., 145.

embedded story is from Todorov: "The appearance of a new character invariably involves the interruption of the preceding story, so that a new story, the one which explains the 'now I am here' of the new character may be told to us."[44] The second example is from Bal, who states that the embedded story not only explains, but may determine the primary one. In "The Embedded Fabula Explains and Determines the Primary Fabula," she argues: "The embedded text may take up the larger part of a book..."[45]

To put it another way, sometimes the embedded story may seem more important to the reader. Such distinctions alert readers to embedded strory, and through it to the uniqueness of the *mise en abyme* as an embedded story, and its relationship to its framework story. We shall use this understanding as a result of identifying Jacob's Dream as a *mise en abyme* of the Jacob story cycle and of the Patriarchs' narrative in which it is embedded, on the theme of entering into and departing from the Land.

3.3. *Jacob's Dream as Anticipation and Retrospection*

In Rimmon-Kenan's opinion, the preliminary story, which is prophetic in nature, appears in prophetic writings in the Bible and "tends to appear in stories within stories in the form of prophecies, curses or dreams..."[46]

Bar Efrat adds:

> Announcing what is to happen serves an important purpose. By interpreting the event as known in advance, the reader's eyes are open not only to see but to understand developments. It sheds light on the deep significance of the happening, giving us a key that allows us, as we read to penetrate beyond events to the causal connections between them and the forces concealed behind them.[47]

---

44. Todorov, *Prose*, 70: "The Arabian Nights affords us...others: for example, in 'The fisherman and the genie,' the embedded story serves as argument. The fisherman justifies his pitilessness toward the genie by the story of Duban."

45. Bal, *Narratology*, 144–45, gives a stereotypical example: "A boy asks a girl to marry him. She loves him, and would rise in the social scale by marrying him. Still she cannot accept him because in the past, she was seduced by a ruthless villain with the usual consequences. Since then she carries the stain of her contact with a perfidious man who took advantage of her innocence. He seduced her in the following manner... The girl retires to a nunnery, and the boy soon forgets her... But...if the young man had been moved by the sad account of his beloved's past, and recognized her innocence, he might have concluded that he wished to forget the past, and give her a second chance. The function of the embedded fabula is then no longer merely explanatory. The exposition influences the primary fabula."

46. Rimmon-Kenan, *Poetics*, 88; Dallenbach, *Mirror*, 60.

47. Bar-Efrat, *Design*, 184.

Anticipation may open not only the reader's eyes but those of the hero, in our case Jacob—if he understands the message in the dream. Understanding the vision of Jacob's Dream symbolically as a *mise en abyme* of the Jacob story cycle on the theme of entering and leaving the Land is a key to and a spotlight upon not only the interpretation of the dream but the Jacob story as well.

An example Polak gives of God offering an anticipatory view is Jacob's Dream at Bethel: "At the beginning of the section on Jacob and Laban is the dream at Bethel in which God promises Jacob help and protection wherever he goes (28:15, 20). This is hinted at once again at the beginning of his escape from Laban's house (31:3, 12–13)."[48]

Bar Efrat notes: "In the great majority of cases where the author wants to hint at future events, he makes it an integral part of the plot. A figure in the plot with the gift of seeing into the future—a prophet, an angel or God Himself—directly *or in a dream*—announces to another participant what is about to happen."[49]

Jacob's Dream exemplifies not only looking forward, but looking back (Janus-like). On one hand, the dream theophany shows that Bethel is a holy place. In this respect it serves the role of ritual etiology. On the other, and at the same time, it is a *mise en abyme* of the Jacob story cycle and the stories of Abraham, depicted in a bird's-eye view by the angels of God who look down not only on Jacob's future life, but also hint at Abraham's life of ascent to and descent from the Land. The verbal message reflects and explains the dream theophany (28:12–13a), repeating the promise of the Land and of seed to his ancestors and his descendants, particularly as God identifies Himself: "I am the Lord, the God of your father Abraham." This supports the interpretation of a simultaneous looking backwards and forwards, and the possibility of relating to it as a *mise en abyme*.[50]

Regarding the dream as an anticipatory look, Polak argues: "The dream [generally] is considered a divine announcement, as in Joseph's words: 'God has told Pharaoh what he is about to do' (41:25). This belief

---

48. Polak, *Narative*, 179.
49. Bar-Efrat, *Design*, 183 (emphasis added).
50. Dallenbach, *Mirror*, 60, states: "One only has to consider the placing of the duplication in the narrative sequence to be able to confirm that all fictional *mise en abyme* have an anachronic form. Logically, one can therefore distinguish three sorts…corresponding to the three forms of dissonance between the time of the narrative and the time of the figure: the first (prospective) reflects the story to come the second (retrospective) reflects the story already completed, and the third (retroprospective) reflects the story by revealing events both before and after its point of insertion in the narrative."

was common to Israel, to most ancient cultures, and to those of the Ancient Near East in particular."[51]

3.4. *The Dream of Utanapishtim as* Mise en Abyme *of the Gilgamesh Epic*

Greenstein[52] asserts that the Mesopotamian Flood Story functions as a *mise en abyme* of the Gilgamesh Epic since it helps broadcast the knowledge contained there.[53] Moreover, knowledge regarding the Mesopotamian Flood Story is disclosed in a dream, which provides important evidence from ANE literature not only of the *mise en abyme*, but also that dreams can also serve this function. This may support my contention that the description of Jacob's Dream also functions as a *mise en abyme* within its framework story. In the Jacob story cycle, as in the Gilgamesh Epic, several dreams appear. In both, the dreams are open or concealed announcements of things to come: in both there are theophanies as well as symbolic dreams.

3.5. *Utanpishtim's and Jacob's Dreams: Their Literary Function as* Mise en Abyme

While *Utanapishtim*'s dream is the last of ten[54] in the Gilgamesh Epic, Jacob's Dream at Bethel is the first of three. Both are *mises en abyme* for their framework stories. Similarly, as Jacob's Dream does not fit in either the symbolic dream or theophany category, neither does Utanapishtim's.

It should be noted that not all versions of the Mesopotamian Flood Story contain an account of the divine announcement coming to the hero in a dream.[55] When the dream is mentioned, as in the Gilgamesh Epic,[56]

---

51. Polak, *Narative*, 188.
52. Greenstein, "Flood," 197–204.
53. Ibid.
54. Gilgamesh had eight dreams, two mentioned in retrospect in the dedication, five in the woods are described as they occur, and an additional dream in which the god attempts to prevent him from embarking on his journey to Utanapishtim. The ninth dream is Enki's, the theophany that predicts his death.
55. Shin Shifra and J. Klein, *In Those Distant Days: Anthology of Mesopotamian Literature* (Tel Aviv: Am Oved, 1996), 88. The authors cite, for instance, the version (Tablet 2, lines 119–20) in which Atra-hasis, hero of the Flood, says "Enki (= Ea) {not} speak to me! for he was sworn—announced to me in dreams." The authors (in their n. 47) state that Ea, god of fresh waters advises Atra-hasis in dreams, not directly, to evade the oath to destroy humanity to which all the great gods were bound (in lines 257–58). See also the Sumerian version from Nippur. See Fidler, "Dream Theophany," 3, in her dissertation's appendix
56. Ibid., 283, lines 194–95: "I revealed not the secret of the great gods; Atra-hasis—a dream I showed him, the secret of the gods he heard."

only at the end of the story can the reader recognize it as such. Ea, accused of revealing the gods' secret to Utanapishtim and of saving humankind, defends himself by saying that he disclosed no secret, but merely showed Atra-hasis (= Utanapishtim) a dream through which he heard the secret. When Utanapishtim tells Gilgamesh how it became known to him, he does not utter the word "dream."[57] Although the message is given at the beginning of the story, no mention is made of whether this was delivered directly or in a dream. Only at the end of the Flood story are we told how the hero got the message, whose details remain undisclosed.[58]

Even though "dream" is not specifically mentioned, disclosure of the gods' plan may have been hinted at by the word *sukkah* in lines 19–20: "The prince Ea swore with them and said their words to *sukkah*." According to Shifra and Klein:

> It appears to refer to a ceremonial reed booth (*sukkah*) that Utanapishtim built in the field, sleeping there at night to dream the message dream. Ea reveals to him in a dream the gods' plan to bring on a flood. Speaking indirectly through the reed wall, Ea can maintain that he did not reveal the gods' secret to Utanapishtim. Compare with Atra-hasis, Tablet 3: lines 20–21.[59] That *sukkah* parallels the "dream house"[60] Enki builds for Gilgamesh on the mountain top in Tablet 4, lines 9 ff.[61]

From the description, Fidler assumes the dream is a theophany, not a symbolic dream.[62] Nevertheless, some scholars maintain it had to be

---

57. Ibid., 276, lines 13–25.
58. A similar literary phenomenon is found in the book of Jonah, who receives two calls from God. In the first (1:1–3) Jonah is given a reason in v. 2—"their wickedness has come before me"—but is not given a message for the people of Nineveh, while the second (3:4) contains the substance of the prophecy—"Yet forty days and Nineveh shall be overthrown"—though the reason is absent. See my article, "Jonah," 262–74.
59. Shifra and Klein, *Anthology*, 120, lines 20–21, explain in n. 60: "Atra-hasis built a hut out in the open to sleep in and [there] to dream prophetic dreams [seemingly indicating an incubation dream, Y. P.]. Ea speaks to him in a dream, through the wall to circumvent his oath to the gods not to disclose the secret of the coming Flood." Fidler, "Dream Theophany," Excursus, 4, explains that from Ea's words it should be understood that "the episode, simply stated, shows the dream as an open means of disclosing the gods' intentions through direct speech."
60. Shifra and Klein, *Anthology*, 216, lines 9–10: "Mountain, grant me a dream, may I see good tidings! Enkido made {his friend} a house for dreams."
61. Ibid., 276, n. 110; Fidler, "Dream Theophany," Excursus, 4 n. 16.
62. Fidler, "Dream Theophany," Excursus, 4.

symbolic.[63] For our purpose of comparing the Gilgamesh Epic with Jacob's Dream as a *mise en abyme*, this is not critically important. That the message came in a dream, and that it is difficult to decide what type of dream it was, like Jacob's Dream at Bethel, simply highlights the similarities between them.

In conclusion, it is possible to argue (along with Greenstein) that there are links between the Gilgamesh Epic and the embedded Story of the Flood. Greenstein's work has shed light on the role and significance of the epic, and also discloses the role of the *mise en abyme* in ANE literature. If this literary phenomenon is found in ANE literature as well, then the hero's dream in the Flood story is a *mise en abyme* for the Gilgamish Epic.

3.6. *Biblical Examples of the* Mise en Abyme

The discovery and presentation of the *mise en abyme* literary structure in the Bible is in its early stages and requires further research. In the work just discussed, Greenstein[64] has presented several recognizable examples:

a. Rachel and Leah building the House of Israel in Ruth 4:11. (Note that M. Bal reads this as a *mise en abyme* mirroring a major theme both of the book of Ruth and of the Hebrew Bible as a whole.[65])

b. A more obvious example is the Levite's cutting up of his concubine's body in Judg 19:29–30, which emblematizes the dissolution of the Israelite tribal league, which theme forms the center of gravity in Judg 19–21.[66]

c. Saul's clutching the hem of Samuel's robe to beg his indulgence and then ironically tearing it, just as Saul had intended to please God but ended up offending him, prompts God to "tear" his kingdom away from him (1 Sam 15:27–28).[67]

---

63. Oppenheim, *Dreams*, 207; Lichtenstein, "Dream Theophany," 49–50.
64. Greenstein, "Flood," 199–200.
65. Bal, *Narratology*, 76.
66. See S. Niditch, *The Symbolic Vision in Biblical Tradition* (HSM 30; Chico, Ca.: Scholars Press, 1983), 371. The author points out the phenomenon without using the term *mise en abyme*.
67. See R. A. Brauner, "'To Grasp the Hem' and 1 Samuel 15:27," *JANES* 6 (1974): 35–38. Brauner does not use the term *mise en abyme*.

d. The "two prostitutes came to the king" in 1 Kgs 3:16–28 (the judgment of Solomon)[68] functions as a *mise en abyme* reflecting the future splitting of the kingdom.[69]
e. Three more examples appear in Gen 38, 1 Sam 25, and 1 Kgs 13.

Berman wrote in 2004: "no full-length treatment of the *mise en abyme* has been conducted within biblical studies."[70] In 2008 Bosworth wrote: "The present work seeks to fill this gap. I will argue that biblical Hebrew narrative includes three *mise en abyme*, specifically Genesis 38, I Samuel 25, and I Kings 13... I am not convinced that there are any additional examples."[71]

While accepting that study of *mises en abyme* in biblical literature is in its early stages, and while also acknowledging that no scholar has yet identified the Jacob story cycle as an obvious candidate for featuring in a *mise en abyme*, I maintain that the evidence I have presented thus far more than justifies a further consideration of the possibilities.

4. *The Dream Vision as* Mise en Abyme *of Entering and Leaving the Land in the Jacob Story Cycle*

4.1. *The Two-directional Path of Entering and Leaving the Land*

The vision in Jacob's Dream of the ascending and descending angels of God[72] is a compact, symbolic reflection of Jacob's departures (*yeridot*, descents) from the Land and of his returns (*'aliot*, ascents) to the Land, and of the attitude to them.

---

68. From an example given by Dr. Seth Rimer, Professor Greenstein's former student, it refers not to the judgment of Solomon but to his dream in Gibeon. Polak, *Narative*, 179, on the dream as anticipation, notes: "God's revelation to Solomon in a dream at Gibeon is imprinted on everything he says, from the story of the prostitutes' trial to the Queen of Sheba episode." Polak does not use the term *mise en abyme*. On the link between the dream at Gibeon and the judgment of Solomon as reflecting events in Solomon's reign, see Fidler, "Dream Theophany," 254 n. 10 and bibliography. Fidler refers to the doctoral thesis of Z. Weisman, "The Charismatic Personality in the Bible" (Ph.D. diss., The Hebrew University, 1972), 223, 235.

69. The list is longer than research has yet shown. For example, the *mise en abyme* possibility should be examined for the following: "the two-edged dagger" (Judg 3:16); "I have a secret message for you" (3:19); and the prophecy "Forty more days and Nineveh shall be overthrown!" (Jon 3:4). See also Peleg, "Jonah," 262–74.

70. Berman, *Narrative Analogy*, 25.

71. Bosworth, *Story Within a Story*, 1.

72. Peleg, "Going Up and Going Down," 1–11.

The story begins: "Jacob left Beer-Sheba, and set out for Haran" (28:10).[73] The direction is important: the narrator reports that he is leaving the Land, his first but not his only departure. Eventually Jacob returns to Canaan: "Jacob arrived safely in the city of Shechem, which is in the Land of Canaan" (31:18). Towards the end of his life, Jacob leaves again: "...to go down to Egypt..." (46:3). God then reveals Himself, giving His "approval" and promising to return him to the Land (46:3–4).[74] Jacob dies in Egypt, and his sons return his remains for burial to the Land (50:4–14).

The Jacob story cycle, from this point of view, is depicted graphically below, the arrowheads showing the up or down direction of the journeys.

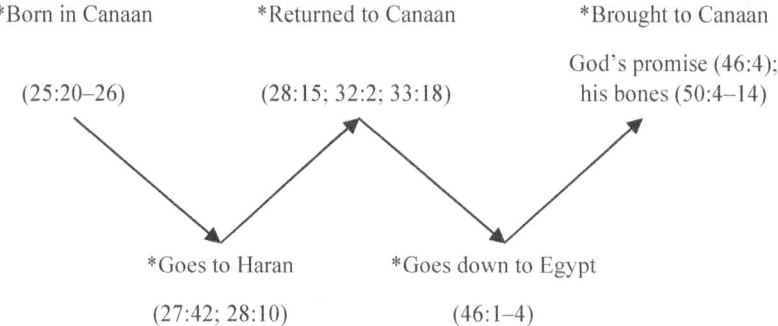

Following Jacob's route, an attempt is made to understand his open and hidden motives for undertaking the journey, as we seek links to Jacob's Dream and especially to the vision in the dream (28:12–13a), assumed to be a compact, symbolic reflection of Jacob's journeys, defined with the help of 2 Sam 3:25: "to learn of your comings and your goings and to find out all..."

---

73. Fokkelman, *Genesis*, 46, draws attention to a great difference between vv. 5 and 10. Verse 5: "Then Isaac sent Jacob off, and he went to Paddan-Aram to Laban the son of Bethuel the Aramean, the brother of Rebekah, the mother of Jacob and Esau." Verse 10: "Jacob left Beer-Sheba, and set out for Haran." One immediately sees that v. 5 is long and v. 10 very short. Verse 5 goes into family connections, while v. 10 merely states the points of departure and arrival. Important there, says Fokkelman, is that Jacob is on his way. Verse 5 states to whom he is going, and v. 10, beginning the Jacob's Dream story, stresses only where he comes from and where he is going, making this the important information and highlighting this vantage point on the story.

74. Similar approval seems to have been given in 28:15 before Jacob's first departure. The two stories (28:10–22 and 46:2–5) will be compared later.

4.2. *The Journey to Haran: Three Readings of Reasons for Jacob's First Departure*

4.2.1. *Jacob is fleeing from his brother (27:43)*. The account of Jacob's first departure comes from Rebekah his mother: "Now, my son, listen to me. *Flee* at once to Haran…until your brother's anger subsides… Then I will fetch you from there."

4.2.2. *Jacob goes to take a wife (28:1)*.[75] Isaac, Jacob's father, after Rebekah's manipulations in 27:46, says to him: "You shall not take a wife from among the Canaanite women. Up, go to Paddan-Aram, to the house of Bethuel, your mother's father, and take a wife from among the daughters of Laban, your mother's brother" (28:1–2). Adherents of source criticism maintain that the difference arises from two separate, independent stories (27:43–45; 28:2, 5) attributed to P and JE sources.[76]

Fokkelman,[77] who considers Rebekah manipulative, regards her as exploiting her husband's blindness when she raises the subject of marriage and at the same time shields the beloved son from Esau's vengeance. The author explains that when the Matriarch says, "I am disgusted with my life because of the Hittite women. If Jacob marries a Hittite…what good will life be to me?" (27:46), she is killing two birds with one stone in that Jacob's flight will not only save him, but lead to a traditional religious marriage. While the first reason is negative and relates to the past, to the theft of the firstborn's blessing, the second is more positive, relating to Jacob's future. Both are linked to real persons acting within earthly reality.

Zakovitch assumes two stories duplicated due to commentary, blurring the force of elements in ch. 27 that do no honor either to Rebekah or to Jacob.[78] With that, in Zakovitch's opinion, "Between the two reasons for Jacob's leaving the Land, there is no actual contradiction. Naturally, Rebekah would tell Jacob about her fears for his life because of Esau his

---

75. The Sages in their time perceived the link between Jacob's Dream and the search for a wife because of the proximity of the dream to his finding Rachel. See the *Gen. Rab.* on *Vayetse* (28:10). See also Lipton, "Revisions," 83: "Ancient Near Eastern dream incubation is often associated with the lack of wife or an heir, and the presence in ch. 28 of several elements of incubation (namely sleep in a holy place with the intention of summoning a dream in response to uncertainty) lends it the appearance of an incubated dream report…"

76. Skinner, *Genesis*, 368.

77. Fokkelman, *Genesis*, 100–101.

78. Zakovitch, *Looking Glass*, 43. The issue is discussed in a chapter titled "Two Stories Explain Each Other."

brother, and in parallel would cause Isaac to send Jacob to Haran because of Esau's marriages to Canaanites."[79]

One statement of the narrator appears to join the two possibilities: "Jacob had obeyed his father and his mother and had gone to Paddan-Aram" (28:7). Harmony is created between the two reasons, improving the image of Jacob, who now appears as a dutiful son honoring his father and his mother, as in the Commandments (Exod 20:12; Num 5:16).

(A methodological note: The two reasons that Jacob left for Haran do not necessarily indicate two separate sources that created the story in its present form, but the realistic possibility that people may have several reasons for what they do. This leads me as a reader to seek two readings of a story, as I try to understand the link between them and its contribution to understanding the story.)

4.2.3. *The third reading: Jacob goes to Haran with God's approval (28:15)*. In addition to the two previous reasons for Jacob's departure from the Land, we also find God's promise: "Remember, I am with you: I will protect you wherever you go" (28:15). This seemingly offers another possible justification for the departure. Fidler states: "The promise in Jacob's Dream might be seen as legitimizing Jacob's flight after stealing the birthright from Esau, and thus even as an apology for his immoral behavior."[80]

Notwithstanding, Fidler rejects the idea because "No reference is made to the theft of the blessing itself."[81] Fidler's rejection of the apologetic tendency since the theft goes unmentioned, may, as I see it, be a deliberate omission that actually strengthens that apologetic tendency.

Such a reading of the divine words and its connection to the other earthly explanations is supported by extensive use of the *double causation* principle[82] in the Jacob story cycle, and not only there. Amit argues: "All biblical literature as we have received it—all its parts and its layers—expresses the double causation principle. In other words, it

---

79. Ibid., 44. Fishbane, *Composition*, 26, finds it reasonable to assume fears both from Esau and from marriages to Canaanites.
80. Fidler, "Dream Theophany," 207.
81. Ibid.
82. The term "double causation" appears to have been coined by Y. Kaufmann in his *The Book of Joshua* (Jerusalem: Kiriat Sefer, 1963), 67. See also I. L. Seeligmann, "Man's Heroism and Divine Deliverance: Double Causation in Israelite Historical Thinking," in *Studies in Biblical Literature: Isac Arie Seeligmann* (ed. A. Horowitz, E. Tov and S. Japhet; Jerusalem: Magnes, 1992), 62–81.

reflects the interaction between two explanatory systems—the divine and the human."[83]

In his doctoral dissertation, Shapira writes:

> Reading for multiple meanings helps disclose complex levels of the story. Thus, for instance, the conflict between Jacob and Esau reflects a story on overt and hidden levels. The first is open and is usually identified with the first reading of the text and the facts about those involved, it is on the human level...following the rules of our world. A second level, however, divulges the story's theological depth... the divine plan.[84]

The literary elements of *double causation* and *dual readings* appear to combine.[85] Both make it possible to read a text in *multiple readings* and require readers' awareness of the importance of the links between readings. Later, in contrasting Terah's departure on his own initiative for Canaan with Abraham's, on God's initiative, we recognize the distinction's theological importance.

4.3. *Jacob's Return Journey from Haran: Three Readings*

Only at the end of Jacob's journey do the words "Jacob arrived safely [*beshalom*]" (Gen 33:18) appear to determine the appropriate reading and affirm his safe arrival. Fokkelman argues:

> More than the journey it will worry him to see Esau again. Because the story of Bethel presupposes the presence of the Penuel scene, as appears at several points later on (we shall come across a verbal connection, besides those already mentioned), and because a leading motif in the Penuel scene is how frightened Jacob is of seeing Esau again, and because in Gen. 33, after the reunion, the stem *šlm* is explicitly used once more (v. 18!), it is necessary for $b^e\check{s}\bar{a}l\bar{o}m$ to be read against the background of Jacob's flight from his brother's wrath.[86]

Like the story of Jacob's first departure from the Land,[87] the story of his return from Haran gives rise to more than one reading. While it seems possible to explain Jacob's return by double causation, as Zakovitch

---

83. Y. Amit, "Double Causation: An Additional Aspect," *Beit Mikra* 38 (1993): 44.

84. Shapira, "Multiple Meanings," 257; Fidler, "Dream Theophany," 136–37.

85. See the extensive discussion in Chapter 1 and my support of this approach.

86. Fokkelman, *Genesis*, 77. See also Zakovitch and Shinan, *Shechem*. We will return to the report on Jacob's return to Canaan in 33:18: "Jacob arrived safely in the city of Shechem which is in the land of Canaan."

87. Fokkelman, *Genesis*, 162, points out the symmetry between the two: both the departure for Haran (27:42) and the return are described as escapes (31:17–21).

puts it: "The Bible preserves two versions of Jacob's decision to return to the Land, and his departure with great wealth (Gen 30:25-43; 31:1-18). Looking at each separately, we shall see how each tradition explains that wealth and attempt to understand the link between the two.[88]

Proponents of sources criticism[89] explain the differences on the basis that ch. 30 belongs to the J source, while ch. 31 belongs to the E source. In fact, the first reference to Jacob's return comes in God's promise in the dream at Bethel as he leaves the Land, where we read, "I...will bring you back to this land" (28:15), and Jacob responds, vowing, "If I return safe to my father's house" (28:21).

4.3.1. *The first reading: Jacob returns on his own initiative (ch. 30).* Immediately after the story of Jacob's Dream we read: "Jacob resumed his journey, and came to the land of the Easterners" (29:1). After years in Haran Jacob tells Laban that he demands to leave (30:25b). Why precisely then?

Just before, we are told that "Rachel had borne Joseph" (v. 25a). Then Jacob tells Laban, "Give me leave to go back to my homeland" (v. 25b). Is there a causal relationship between the two? Did Jacob decide to return because Rachel had given birth to their son? Is the link simply linear-chronological,[90] or did Jacob see Rachel's giving birth as a sign that he should return to the Land?[91] If Jacob did see that event as the fulfillment

---

88. Zakovitch, *Looking Glass*, 45.
89. E.g. Speiser, *Genesis*, 234, 240.
90. Bar-Efrat, *Design*, 146-47, states: "The order in which the smaller story units are organized is both chronological and causal." That is, events are arranged in order of occurrence, and also in a causal sequence where one occurrence is the result of the previous one and the cause of the following one.
91. In Chapter 1, I stated that Jacob's Dream would be studied by literary methods as a story, but that at times I would introduce modern psychology and the dream research of Freud and Jung in a note because of the ambivalent attitudes involved. S. Freud, "The Dream," in *Introduction to Psychoanalysis* (trans. H. Isac; vol. 1 in *Collected Works of Sigmund Freud*; Tel Aviv: Dvir, 1968), 151-63, maintains that ladders, stairs, ascents and descents are typical symbols of sexual intercourse. For an expansion, see Elizur, *Within and Without*, 247. Elizur also cites examples with clearly sexual connotations from the *Zohar*, a core text of Jewish mysticism. He reports too on Frazer's research on the fertility festival on some islands in the Indian Ocean (see J. G. Frazer, *The Golden Bough: A Study in Magic and Religion* [3d ed.; New York: Macmillan, 1935]). Frazer records that the natives on these islands, at the onset of the rainy season, pay homage to the sun god as the supreme male deity, who fertilizes the goddess earth. For this purpose he descends on a sacred fig tree, helped down to earth by the natives, who provide a seven-step

of God's promise of seed (28:14), this is evidence of double causation principle. The open, earthly one is his own decision, the hidden one God's.[92]

4.3.2. *The second reading: Jacob returns on God's initiative (ch. 31).* There is another explanation or reading for Jacob's decision to return to the Land: "Jacob also saw that Laban's manner (*pnei Lavan*)[93] toward him was not as it had been in the past" (31:2). One might expect the next verse to explain that Laban's changed attitude led Jacob to decide to return to the Land, creating a cause and effect relationship between vv. 1 and 2. But instead, and perhaps to illustrate *double causation*, come God's words: "Return to the land of your fathers where you were born" (31:3). In the following verse, what Jacob tells Rachel and Leah combines both: "I see that your father's manner towards me is not as it has been in the past" (31:4), and later comes the divine element, "but the God of my father has been with me" (31:5b). His wives declare on the earthly plane, "Have we still a share in the inheritance of our father's house? Surely he regards us as outsiders, now that he has sold us" (31:15). And on the divine plane they say, "Now, then, do just as God told you" (31:16).

The language seems to position Laban against God. While Laban is their father,[94] he is "not toward me"—or, as the narrator implies, God is

---

ladder. The Arabic *halama* expresses both suitability and sexual maturity (see "חלם," BDB 321). See Fidler, "Dream Theophany," 24 n. 85.

In view of the foregoing, and accepting the verbal message (28:13b–15) of God as interpreting the vision (28:12–13a), the ascending and descending angels may be regarded as linked to God's promise: "your offspring shall be as the dust of the earth" (28:14). Promises of seed and of the Land are linked in several instances in Genesis. Hence Jacob may have seen Rachel's giving birth as a fulfilled promise, and that the time had come to return to the Land.

Fishbane, "Composition," 20, and Gammie, *Theological*, 121, adherents of the structural approach, divide the Jacob story cycle into a chiastic structure, at the center of which stands the report of Rachel bearing Joseph (30:24). This may explain its centrality in the cycle.

92. There is still an unresolved question: Why was Rachel's bearing Joseph the signal to return, and not the births of Jacob's other eleven children?

93. In Hebrew, "Laban's manner", *pnei Lavan* (31:1), sounds much like "Laban's sons," *bnei Lavan* (31:2). This could hint at what the sons said in 31:1: "Jacob has taken all that was our father's," another reason for Jacob's decision to return. See Fokkelman, *Genesis*, 151.

94. The word "father" appears twelve times as a keyword: 31:1 (twice), 3 (twice), 5 (twice), 7, 9, 14, 16, 18, and 19. This could be a concealed hint at Jacob's vow, "and I return safe to my father's house" (28:21).

not with him. By contrast, it is said, "But the God[95] of my father has been with me" (31:5).[96] Jacob then tells his wives about the dream of the he-goats, in which the angel of God (31:11), who later, in v. 13, declares "I am the God of Bethel," says, "Now rise and leave this land and return to your native land" (31:13).[97]

It appears, then, that in ch. 30 the initiative to return to Canaan on the revealed level was Jacob's and involved no divine intervention. By contrast, in ch. 31 the return received divine affirmation.[98]

Zakovitch is not content to mention the earthly and the heavenly reasons for Jacob's return that function together as double causation. Seeking out their interrelationship, he posits a hidden dialogue between them:

> In the version in ch. 31, Jacob thus requires no cleverness: he is a righteous man whose work is done by God, not by his own hand. This perception has another advantage: What Jacob does in ch. 30 is magical in all respects: "Jacob then got rods…" (30:37–39). Then the formulation of ch. 31 takes us from the magical…to the world of miracle, the work of the hand of God.[99]

4.3.3. *Third reading: Jacob flees from Laban to his father's house (31:17–21)*.

There is another aspect to Jacob's return from Haran—that he fled from Laban. As if it were not enough that "fled" is used in 31:20, 21, 24 and 27 to describe his leaving Haran, Jacob is also declared to have deceived Laban. According to the narrator, "And Jacob stole away unawares to Laban" (31:20 KJV), and in Laban's own words, "What hast

---

95. The *waw* prefix in the Hebrew may be either "and" or "but." In the latter case, Laban, father of Leah and Rachel, is contrasted with God. "But (or *and*) the God of my father has been with me" (31:5), as contrasted with "Laban's manner was not what it had been" (31:2). The contrast appears to be on several related planes: Haran as against Canaan, leaving the country as against returning to it, Laban as against God, and "has been with me" as against "is not toward me."

96. "With me" (31:5) directs attention to the same expression in 28:20. A detailed discussion follows later.

97. "The God of Bethel" (31:13) specifically mentions Jacob's vow. Therefore, God's words in Gen 31:3, "Return to the land of your fathers where you were born, and *I will be with you*," hint at the Bethel dream "Remember *I am with you*" (28:15). The comparison of God's words to Jacob (31:3) with Jacob's before encountering Esau shows that Jacob interpreted "I will be with you" to mean "I will deal bountifully with you" (32:10).

98. Fidler, "Dream Theophany," 206, argues "The order to return to his native land (31:3) legitimizes Jacob's leaving Laban."

99. Zakovitch, *Looking Glass*, 46. See Fokkelman, *Genesis*, 158–62, on the differences between chs. 30 and 31.

thou done, that thou hast stolen away unawares to me... Where didst thou flee...and steal away from me" (31:26, 27 KJV).

Calling both "the flight," Fokkelman[100] points out the symmetry between the description of Jacob's departure for Haran (27:42) and of his return to his native land (31:17–21). In both cases the flight is from a family member, and in both cases[101] from a "brother", *'ah*. When they first meet, "Laban said to Jacob...you are a kinsman (*'ahi*)" (29:15), reinforcing the link between the two descriptions. Their relationship is inverse (i.e., it is a reflection). While in the first instance Jacob's direction was away from the country, in the second journey it was the very opposite: returning to the Land. Additionally, the verb "left" describes his departure (28:10), while the "return" is depicted as "arrived safely" (33:18).

Besides their reverse directions, Fokkelman points out another difference between the two flights: the first was brought about by deceit, the second by an act of God.[102]

Then Laban pursues the fleeing Jacob (31:23). After a confrontation, the two characters are described as entering into a covenant (31:44), raising a mound of stones as a witness between them (v. 52), following which the story between the two ends when "Laban left on his journey homeward" (32:1) and "Jacob went on his way" (31:2). As regards Jacob's return, one notes that in a single verse the earthly and the divine motive for an event may be entwined. It reflects the narrator's tendency to harmonize the divine with the human desire for the return to the Land, seeming to assure his safe arrival even when Jacob is still "on his way."

4.4. *Returning to Canaan: "And Jacob went on his way"*
Commenting on stories in cycles, S. Bar-Efrat argues:

> In some instances stories in cycles are ordered in a ring. The Jacob stories are an example. It begins with several stories on Jacob and Esau in Canaan, followed by stories of Jacob and Laban in Haran and, finally, again Jacob and Esau in the land of Canaan. The first two are separated by the Bethel episode and the second and third by the episode of Penuel and its Mahanaim.[103]

---

100. Fokkelman, *Genesis*, 162.
101. Ibid., 163.
102. Regarding the possible link between Jacob's flight from Laban Moses' flight from Pharaoh ("Moses fled from Pharaoh," Exod 2:15), the escape of the Israelites ("the king of Egypt was told that the people had fled," 14:5), and the tradition of the Exodus, see Y. Zakovitch, "The Exodus from Egypt in Genesis," *Al Haperek* 3 (1987): 25–34.
103. Bar-Efrat, *Design*, 146

Another significant issue is the distinction between the revelation where God is heard, and one where He is seen.[104] Gitay stresses that God revealed Himself visually to Abraham only after he entered Canaan (Gen 12:7). Before that he only "heard" God. In the author's opinion, the active form of "see" leads to more intimate communication of God with human beings (e.g. Job 42:5–6). Moriel argues further that God did not reveal Himself to the Patriarchs outside Canaan:

> Note that when he [Jacob] was outside Canaan, God's message came to him only verbally: "Then the Lord said unto Jacob, 'Return to the land of your fathers'" (Gen 31:3), and only when he returned from exile to the Land, "God appeared again (*vayera*) to Jacob on his arrival from Paddan-Aram, and He blessed him" (35:9). Jacob went down into Egypt. In all his years in Egyptian exile we hear nothing of a prophetic revelation, even as no such revelation was given to Abraham in Egypt. However, speaking to his son Joseph before his [own] death he recalls the visions vouchsafed him in Canaan: "El Shaddai appeared (*nir'a*) to me in Luz in the land of Canaan, and He blessed me" (48:3).[105]

Moriel notes further:

> From the foregoing we learn that to reveal his closeness to his children God chose that land, giving it its special quality...called holiness... On the holiness of the Land as God's inheritance, see Num 35:33–34. From this text we learn that you live in a land wherein I dwell, and its uniqueness stems from the combination of Israel and God as its inhabitants.[106]

4.4.1. *The angels of God in Jacob's Dream (28:12) and angels of God at Mahanaim (32:2)*. Even if the link between the vision of the ascending and descending angels in Jacob's Dream, and his journey to and from Haran, do not convince, it seems difficult to ignore the link of the vision to "the angels of God" at Mahanaim as he approaches Canaan: "Jacob went on his way and angels of God encountered him. When he saw them Jacob said, 'This is God's camp.' So he named the place Mahanaim" (Gen 32:2–3).[107]

---

104. See Gitay, "Geography," 208.
105. Y. Moriel, *Israel and Its Land in the Torah* (Jerusalem: World Zionist Organization, 1988), 147.
106. Ibid.
107. On the Septuagint version, see Rofé, *Angels*, 194: "Such importance need not be attached to the Septuagint version. I assume that the original version was: 'When he saw them Jacob said, this is God's camp. So he named the place Mahanaim.'" Zakovitch, "Jabbok," 194, sees the errors as originating from dittography, apparently by a scribe, by chance.

3. *The Jacob's Dream Story as* Mise en Abyme

In Chapter 2 (see section 4, "Two Readings of Jacob's Dream—A Tentative Conclusion"), I pointed out that the descending and ascending of the angels of God symbolize Jacob's departure from and return to the Land. Similarly, understating the vision as a *mise en abyme* not only of the Jacob stories but of departure and return in all stories of the Patriarchs in Genesis may support this thesis.

As noted before, the expression "angels of God," *mal'akhei 'elohim*, appears only twice in the Bible.[108] That both are in the Jacob story cycle calls attention to the similarity and the connection between the two stories where "angels of God" apears. In combination with other elements, the "angels of God" (28:12) make possible two readings of Jacob's Dream and its interpretation. One reading is that it explains how Bethel became a holy place—a story of a place; the other reading that it is the story of Jacob's departure from and return to the Land—a story about a way, a journey.

Now I attempt to show that the appearance of the "angels of God" in Gen 32:2–3 also supports these two readings. Regarding the first, some scholars[109] note that both the Bethel and Mahanaim stories follow the familiar ANE model of the *hieros logos*[110] that explains how a place became regarded as holy. Our main interest, however, is in the second symbolic reading. Indeed, the story of the angels of God at Mahanaim comes within the Jacob story cycle as he journeys back to the Land (*ascent*), as it did at Bethel on his departure (*descent*).

---

108. "Angels of God," *mal'akhei 'elohim*, is a keyword (because of its rarity, or as Buber calls it, "a rare guiding word"). See also Amit, "Multiple Uses," esp. 37–38: there she quotes M. Weiss, "In the Secret of Biblical Dialogue," introduction to Buber, *Way of the Bible*, 26: "There may be a rare expression, or a common one used in a special sense that brings to mind a separate, distant text, and, coming to the reader's mind it deciphers or illuminates one or both [types of] texts." According to Buber, *Way of the Bible*, 284, "We call a guiding word a word or linguistic root repeated in a text or series or group of texts in a significant manner…" Buber (p. 293) gives *lekh lekhah*, "go-you-forth" (Fox), as an example, found only twice in the Torah (Gen 12:1; 22:2).

109. G. W. Coats, *Genesis: With an Introduction to Narrative Literature* (FOTL 1; Grand Rapids, Mich.: Eerdamns, 1983), 223–24, on 32:2–3 (32:1–2 RSV); Gunkel, *Genesis*. Houtman, "Mahanaim," 40, argues: "It is probably not too hazardous to suppose that Gen xxxii 2–3 is to be regarded as the *Hieros Logos* of Mahanaim. It is true that nowhere in the OT is a sanctuary at Mahanaim mentioned, but it is unlikely that an important city as Mahanaim (see e.g. 2 Sam 2:12, 29; 17:24, 27; 19:32) would not have had a significant sanctuary (according to Josh 21:38 it was a city of Gad assigned to the priestly clan of Merari)."

110. Fidler, "Dream Theophany," 153, writes of the "Bethel aspect" that is the *hieros logos* of Bethel (see also pp. 163–64).

A comparison necessarily relates to similarity and difference in both language and content. While similarity displays the connection that justifies the comparison, the difference provides the reason for it—to express the message to be derived. The similarities, moreover, highlight the differences, especially in the present case where the difference involves both opposite and opposition. The Mahanaim scene relates to and is built on the one at Bethel. Fokkelman argues: "From the beginning to the end the Mahanaim scene refers to and builds on the Bethel scene."[111] Zakovitch notes: "There seems to be a link and even dependence between the two stories."[112]

As regards time, the first story took place at night, the second in the morning. As to place and direction, the first happened as Jacob was about to leave the country—the second on the eve of his return. The table below shows similarities and differences, and indicates support of the second, symbolic reading.

Genesis 28:11-12, 16, 19—in Bethel	*Genesis 32:1-3[113]—in Mahanaim*
	Early *in the morning* Laban left
	And Jacob went on his way
He came upon (*paga'*) a certain place	And encountered (*paga'*)[114] him
And stopped there for *the night*,	
for the sun had set	
He had a dream; a stairway was set	
on the ground	

111. See Fokkelman, *Genesis*, 198.

112. Zakovitch, "Midrashim," 194. Elsewhere, Zakovitch, *Looking Glass*, 9, states: "This book deals with 'Reflection Stories' in the Bible, where a situation or character and action are structured as contrasts to those already existing." See also idem, "Reflection Stories: Another Dimension of the Evaluation of Characters in Biblical Narrative," *Tarbiz* 54 (1985): 165–76.

113. Where does the previous story end and the one about *angels of God* begin? Is it in 32:1? Supporters of the source criticism attribute vv. 1–3 to source E, the end of the Jacob and Laban story. See, e.g., R. E. Friedman, *Who Wrote the Bible?* (ed. and trans. S. Abulafia and D. Rubinstein; Tel Aviv: Dvir, 1995), 221. Or does it end in v. 2a? See Fokkelman, *Genesis*, 197; vod Rad, *Genesis*, 308. The differing opinions as to whether this episode closes the story cycle of Jacob and Laban or opens the Jacob–Esau cycle show that it is in exactly the right place, linked to both, to what is said before and after. It thus resembles the symbolic message in the Jacob's Dream vision, which reflects what is related before and after it. The focus is now on the link of the Mahanaim dream to what went before, particularly on Jacob's Dream.

114. On the root *pg'* ("encounter") in 28:11 as identified with the transcendental (linked with 32:2), see Shapira, "Two Readings," in Chapter 3: "Is There Incubation in Jacob's Dream?"

3. *The Jacob's Dream Story as* Mise en Abyme

And angels of God (*mal'akhei 'elohim*) Were going up and going down on it Jacob awoke from his sleep And said	Angels of God (*mal'akhei 'elohim*) Jacob said When he saw them
Surely the Lord is in this place This is (*zeh*) none other than the abode of God That is (*zeh*) the gateway to heaven He named the site Bethel	This is (*zeh*) God's camp (*mahaneh*) He named the place Mahanaim

a) *Similarities between the two.*[115]

1. In both, "Angels of God," *mal'akhei 'elohim*, appear.
2. In both, Jacob reacts similarly to the vision. In ch. 28 he says "Surely the Lord is in this place" and "This is none other than the abode of God." In ch. 32 we read: "When he saw them, Jacob said: 'This is God's camp.'"[116]
3. In both the "etymological legend" of the place name is explained.
4. In both, Jacob names the place.
5. In both, place name is linked to divine revelation.
6. In both, the verb *yfga'* is used.[117]
7. In both, the angels are revealed but have no verbal message.
8. In both, the site of the encounter on the journey may be seen as coincidental, unplanned by Jacob.

---

115. Westermann, *Genesis*, 452, compares the stories' structure: "This structure is confirmed by many points of contact with the close parallel, Gen 32:1–2, which belongs to the same group of narratives. Gen 32:1–2 is also a story which concerns Jacob only and has the same function in the structure of Gen 25–36; the texts 28:10–22 and 32:1–2 frame Gen 29–31. Moreover the two texts agree in the following ways: (1) The narrative happens in the course of a journey; (2) It is an encounter (the verb *paga'* is used in both cases); (3) In both cases the expression *mal'akhei 'elohim* occurs, which is not found elsewhere. (4) The naming of the place. The parallels confirm that the narrative, 28:10–12, 16–19, corresponding to this structure, is a self-contained unity." Fokkelman, *Genesis*, 147 (cf. 208), argues that "the Jacob story cycle structure—Canaan/Bethel/Haran/Penuel—derives in this way."

116. Westermann, *Genesis*, 505. See Houtman, "Mahanaim," 39. See also Fidler, "Dream Theophany," 173, who points out that the identification "This" + "the house of God//God's camp" common to both stories. The importance of the wording is discussed in section 4 of Chapter 2, "Two Readings of Jacob's Dream—A Tentative Conclusion."

117. Zakovitch, "Midrashim," 191, writes that in both dreams *yfga'* means "met." The narrator, to obliterate the struggle between Divinity and Patriarch, uses the ambiguous word as if to say the encounter was simply a meeting. Here as in ch. 28, Jacob saw the angels but no more than that.

9. In both places Jacob learns of God's presence only through a revelation he has there.[118]
10. In both, Jacob is on the way from or to the Land of Canaan.[119]

b) *Differences between the two.*

1. In ch. 28 the revelation took place at night, in ch. 32 it occurred in the morning.
2. The revelation in ch. 28 was in a dream, while in ch. 32 it apparently was not.
3. While in ch. 28, Jacob came upon (*pagaʻ*) a place, in ch. 32 angels came upon (*pagaʻ*) him.
4. In ch. 28 Jacob was journeying out of the Land, whereas in ch. 32 he was on journeying back to it.
5. While the angels' activity in ch. 28 was ascending and descending, in ch. 32 they encountered Jacob.
6. While in ch. 28 the encounter *pagaʻ* was with a place, in ch. 32 it was with Jacob.
7. In ch. 28 the sun sets, while in ch. 32 the sun rises.[120] Nature, here represented by the sun, participates in and expresses other biblical events like the giving of the Law at Sinai. The sun's movements are correlated with those of Jacob and the angels of God.

---

118. The term "camp," *mahaneh*, may relate to a military or a residential site. See "מחנה," BDB 334; von Rad, *Genesis*, 309, also notes that it is not necessarily related to warfare. See Houtman, "Mahanaim," 39: "In the view of the use of *mahaneh* in relation to the name of a place and with regard to Gen xxviii 17, 19, it is self-evident that *mahaneh* refers to a locality, namely, a 'camp,' an 'encampment.' It is the place where the messengers of God, the servants of the King of the world, have their home; from there they go out to fulfill orders everywhere on earth; thither they return after finishing their tasks."

119. Westermann, *Genesis*, 452: "It is not a narrative in the strict sense, but an account of an experience on a journey (28:10) expanded to narrative." On p. 504, regarding 32:2b, he notes that: "What is narrated here is an event on the way." A point of similarity, he points out, is that both encounters were during a journey. Cf. Fishbane, "Composition," 173. Houtman, "Mahanaim," 40 n. 12, states: "It is an ancient interpretation given as early as Nahmanides (= Ramban). According to Rashi, following the *Tanhuma*, the reference is to the band of messengers who accompanied Jacob outside the land of Israel and the band of messengers who were to escort him within Canaan."

120. Fokkelman, *Genesis*, 49: "So the happenings of nature attend, underline and symbolize what happens between God and man." In n. 6 Fokkelman argues: "In both cases [unnecessary] with a contrary effect: the sun sets, but God appears to him and promise to support him; the sun rises, but Jacob limps."

c) *What can the comparison teach?* That "angels of God" appear only in these two instances in the Bible heightens the connection between the two stories where "angels of God" appear. It focuses attention on the theme of the discussion: Jacob's departure from and entry into the Land.

These facts may well have influenced Rashi[121] and other commentators previously mentioned to describe the task of the angels of God as guardians of Jacob in his going from and coming to the Land. Rashi interprets the name Mahanaim: "two camps, those from abroad who had escorted him thus far, and those from the Land of Israel who came to meet him."[122] Clearly, this completes his interpretation of the ascending and descending angels in Jacob's Dream.

Psalm 91:11[123] speaks of angels as guardians on a journey:[124] "For he will order his angels to guard you wherever you go." The link between this verse and Gen 28 can be seen in the selfsame language in 28:15: "I will protect you wherever you go."

Rofé emphasizes that angels of God generally have a task, but not in Gen 28 and 32. "In their characteristics and nature," he says, "the angels of Bethel and Mahanaim lack the typical features of angels."[125] For our purposes, Rofé contributes by pointing out an additional similarity between the two stories.

---

121. Rashi, on 32:2, writes: "Angels of God encountered him means that the angels of the land of Israel came toward him to accompany him into the Land."

122. The name Mahanaim is problematic. Jacob mentions it but once, in the singular—"This is God's camp" (32:3)—but uses the name that means "two camps." See, e.g., Shapira, "Two Readings," 170, and bibliography.

123. Leibowitz, *Genesis*, 210.

124. The God as guardian motif is simply an expression of individual providence. On this J. Klein, *Olam Hatanach: Genesis* (ed. M. Weinfeld; Tel Aviv: Davidson-Atai, 1982), 245, writes: "Jacob's plea to God 'The Angel who has redeemed me from all harm' (48:16) blends with the previous verse: 'The God who has been my shepherd from my birth to this day' who is also the God in whose ways my fathers Abraham and Isaac walked'... Jacob certainly is not seeking to reduce the divinity concept from Creator and Ruler of the world to a tribal or family god. Rather he stresses the divine attribute of special significance to him: the God revealed to him and to his fathers watched over them as individuals, sometimes revealed in the image of an angel... The emphasis is repeated especially in the stories about Jacob, who was obliged more than once to leave his father's house for foreign parts, and hence in particular need of divine guardianship wherever he went. Thus Jacob often addresses Him as 'God of my father' (31:5, 42) or 'God of my father Abraham and God of my father Isaac' (32:9; 27:20; 31:42)." For additional material on God as guardian, see Rofé, *Angels*, 84, and especially 232.

125. For additional material, see Rofé, *Angels*, 84.

As shown above, the opening words of the Mahanaim story—"Laban left on his journey homeward...and Jacob went on his way"—raise questions relating to time and to place. While the story at Bethel begins at sunset, the Mahanaim story begins in the morning.

The present discussion is about the question of *place*. Jacob parts from Laban on his way back to Canaan, saying: "Give me leave to go back to my own homeland" (30:25b). God too tells Jacob, "Return to the land of your fathers, where you were born, and I will be with you" (31:3; see also 31:13b). Jacob not only speaks, but acts, preparing to "go to his father Isaac in the Land of Canaan" (31:18; see also v. 21). Thus one expects symmetry between the two parts of the verse, in which "Laban left on his journey homeward" is followed by "Jacob returned to his place." Thus the story of Jacob and Laban would have ended in the accepted manner. Bar-Efrat writes:

> In many biblical stories the end is stated expressly. For instance, when the beginning or the course of a story states that someone left his place for another one, the end of the story often states that this person returned to his place. The reader then feels that the episode is over (see e.g. 1 Sam 16:1–13; 2 Sam 20:1–22). The story of Balaam is almost identical with ours. 'Then Balaam set out on his journey back home, and Balak also went his way' (Num 24:25). Similarly in the meeting between Saul and David in the wilderness of Ziph: "David then went his way, and Saul returned home" (1 Sam 26:25).[126]

The language of 32:1–2—"Laban left on his journey homeward (*meqomo* = his place). Jacob went on his way"—is formulated to show the end of the story of Jacob in Laban's house, with the same linguistic pattern.[127] Additionally, anticipation of the use of "place" (*maqom*) increases because it ties in well with the entire story. First, it serves as a keyword in the story of Jacob's Dream, especially in "he came upon *a* place" (28:11), and again when Laban says, "It is not the practice in our place" (29:26). It appears for the third time when Jacob tells Laban, "Send me away, that I may go back to mine own place" (30:25b KJV). Why, then, is the text not "Jacob returned to his place"?

The narrator appears to have used the asymmetrical expression deliberately, perhaps to stress that Jacob was still on the way, *derekh*.[128]

---

126. Bar-Efrat, *Design*, 142–43.
127. The phrase that ends the story of Jacob in Laban's house ("Laban left on his journey homeward") can be assumed to have been used to begin the description of Jacob's encounter with the angels of God on his way to Canaan: "And Jacob went on his way."
128. Fokkelman, *Genesis*, 77–78: "In 20c the word *derek* has been inserted, so for the third time we note a more concrete phrase of Jacob's. He will use it again,

3. *The Jacob's Dream Story as* Mise en Abyme

The theophany in ch. 28 was also in a certain *place*, but Jacob had "left Beer-Sheba and set out for Haran," the story ending when "Jacob resumed his journey and came to the land of the Easterners" (29:1).

The absence of the expected symmetry appears to accentuate the fact that Jacob is still on his way, that the destination, the *place*, has not yet been reached. Hence this asymmetrical reading supports the thesis that the Hebrew prefix *waw* in 32:2—"*waw*-Jacob returned to his place"— should be read here as "but," not as "and." Jacob is on the way to the homeland, but has not reached it.[129] The hidden dialogue between *the way* and *the place*, and the two readings of Jacob's Dream, is present here as well.

Significantly, Fokkelman[130] notes that the combination "went on his way," that is, "going" together with "way," appears in the Jacob story only twice: here and in the story of the vow in 28:20.[131] This raises the question of whether God will keep (*shmr*) Jacob as a fulfillment of His promise in 28:15.[132]

Something may be present beyond the literary intention of connecting episodes of the story, possibly a message for Jacob and not only for him, since he and Abraham his grandfather throughout their lives were "on the way" to the homeland and from it.[133] "The way," however, is not the

---

when looking back to the Bethel episode in Gen 35:3; but for the rest the combination occurs only in one other place in the history of Jacob, again in the story that leads up to Penuel—and to that another word, *pg'*, had already led us… When in Gen 32:2f for the first time after Genesis 28 it says: 'Jacob went on his way…' It also emphasizes the Bethel scene as a milestone in the movement out of the country, after which the movement back to it will be marked in 32:2."

129. In describing Jacob's journey, the word "return" is not used, which is in contrast with its repeated occurrence when God talks to him: "Return to the land of your father" (31:3), "return to your native land" (31:13). Apparently the significance is that Jacob is still on the way and has not reached his place, his native land.

130. See Fokkelman, *Genesis*, 197.

131. In the Septuagint version of v. 15 as well, "went" and "way" appear together.

132. Shapira, "Two Readings," 163, also recognizes the doubt as to whether God will support Jacob, not through the use of this combination but through "encountered," which can be read two ways, as shown in discussing Jacob's Dream. There seems to be no contradiction between the two, and that Jacob "went on his way" signals to the reader that God's promise to Jacob in 28:15 and 20 is being kept. Encounter in the Mahanaim story strengthens its link to Jacob's Dream at Bethel, and the reality of God's promise to protect Jacob.

133. A bird's-eye view of the generations reinforces the sense of "like father, like son," as the nation's fathers', like their descendants, are ever "on the way to…" Moriel, *Land*, 59, states: "The history of the relationship between the people of

whole story. The Patriarchs on the way to Canaan proceeded in a positive direction, and the departing way was negative. It will be shown in this study that the use of *'alah* and *yarad* is one literary means to this end.

To conclude, the differences between the Bethel and Mahanaim stories reveal them as mirror images of each other, as shown in the table and lists above. For our purposes, leaving the Land is the mirror image of the return, the opposite geographical directions reflecting opposite values. Although Gen 32:2–3 does not say specifically that to return is better than to leave the Land,[134] and while the *'alah* and *yarad* verbs do not appear, presenting the two stories as opposites determines the attitude to each one separately. That "the angels of God" appear in the entire Bible only in the symbolic dream of ascent and descent as Jacob is about to leave, and again on his homeward journey, supports the theory of their symbolic role.

We may infer, then, contrary to Rofé's argument, that in both stories the angels have a mission and a message. These are not verbal and revealed, but visual and concealed. Their mission is evident from their very appearance, from the time and place of departure from and return to the homeland, from their ascent and descent on the *sullam*. If this last is symbolic, Jacob has been answered on a personal level, even as Israel has been answered at the national level[135] that includes the nation's fathers before him and his descendants after him. As Weisman notes: "The reader who returns to the stories of the Patriarchs cannot but sense their double image: the private person on one hand changing to the group-national figure on the other, at a stroke of the pen."

4.4.2. *Jacob's return to the homeland: "Jacob arrived safely (*shalem*) in the city of Shechem, which is in the Land of Canaan" (33:18)*. Jacob's return journey appears to be a series of ups and downs, a kind of obstacle course that he overcomes with God's help, which was promised to him at Bethel (28:15). Now (in Gen 33:18) at long last he reaches home.

Israel and their land begins with the first steps of the father of the nation in Canaan, and to this day we see ascents and descents… Leaving the country and returning to it dates from the time of Abraham. It continued through the time of Jacob and his sons, and goes on till this day." See also A. B. Yehoshua, *In Praise of Normalcy: Five Essays on Zionism* (Jerusalem: Schocken, 1980), 31–35.

134. In the narrative context, however, the return represents God's will, "Return to the land of your fathers where you were born" (31:3), and His earlier promise, "And will bring you back to this land" (28:15).

135. Weisman, *Cycle*, 9.

"He arrived," *vayavo* (23:18), in this context—where "in Canaan" is emphasized—is the opposite of "Jacob left," *vayetse'*, in 28:10, when he left Canaan. The content of the sentence about his arrival, with the word "safe," *shalem*, which can be interpreted as a place name for Shechem as well, reminds the reader of Jacob's vow in 28:21—"and if I return safe (*beshalom*) to my father's house"—and is understood as its fulfillment. But the return trip is not complete, for we expected him to return to his father's house, whence he set out,[136] while he returns to Shechem. However, immediately in 35:1 God tells Jacob, "Arise, go up (*'aleh*) to Bethel and remain there." Later (35:6) "Jacob came to Luz—that is, Bethel—in the Land of Canaan." The table below shows how very similar the description is to that of his arrival in Shechem.

Arrival in Shechem (33:18)	Arrival in Bethel (35:6)
Jacob arrived (*vayavo*)	Jacob came (*vayavo*)
Safely (*shalem*) in Shechem	To Luz
In the Land of Canaan	In the Land of Canaan
	That is, Bethel
He set up	He built
An altar there	An altar there
And called it El-elohei-yisrael	And called it El-bethel.

According to Zakovitch and Shinan, "The Jacob stories appear to express two perceptions as to fulfilling the vow in Genesis 28, and the traditions in their present form reflect a struggle between two holy sites, Shechem and *Bethel*, a struggle as to their holiness and as to Jacob's link to them."[137]

Our concern is with the link between the description of Jacob's safe (*shlm*) return to the Land of Canaan and the story of Jacob's Dream, which includes his vow. Two readings seem possible for the Hebrew *shlm*. The first could be a city's name,[138] which may answer the question

---

136. See Fokkelman, *Genesis*, 232: "Jacob does not go to Bethel until God himself ordered him to go. He reacts with an adequate attitude of faith, for his journey is to be a pilgrimage. Therefore he orders the whole household to 'purify yourselves and change your garments' (Gen 35:2)."

137. Zakovitch and Shinan, *Shechem*, 68, illustrate the similarities between the two traditions: (1) building an altar in Bethel (35:1, 3, 7) as in Shechem; (2) giving a name—in Shechem it is *El-elohei-yisrael* (33:20), while in Bethel too there is the naming component *El-bethel*. On p. 54 the authors write: "Clearly, then, the tradition before us disputes the perception that Shechem is the holy place where the vow was fulfilled."

138. Zakovitch and Shinan, *Shechem*, 76: "In the struggle between the Jews and the Samaritans, identifying 'safe,' *shlm*, with Shechem, was to the Samaritan advantage."

of where Jacob arrived. In the second reading, *shlm* might serve as an adjective, stating that Jacob arrived safely[139]—that is, it refers to his state upon arrival.[140] A third reading could include both: that Jacob arrived safely, at a place called *shlm*, which would now answer the questions of both where and how.[141]

An important point for our purposes relates to Gen 33:18 as the fulfillment of Jacob's Dream in 28:10–22. In describing the five components of symbolic dreams, I showed that Jacob's Dream fits that model.[142] The fifth component there is fulfillment of the dream,[143] which is found in Gen 33:13, 18 and 35:1–5.

Zakovitch and Shinan note:

> A search for the place of our story among all those concerning Jacob cannot ignore its link to the beginning of the journey to Paddan-Aram, and the vow at Bethel when he leaves the homeland (Gen 28:20–22). Jacob says: "If God remains with me, If He protects me on this journey that I am making…if I return safe to my father's house." Here in our story, after safely evading all the dangers, from the fear of his brother and the personal encounter with "a man," *'ish* (32:25 ff.), he returns safe, *shlm*, to Shechem. In his vow he promises: "the Lord shall be my God," and in Gen 33:20 Jacob declares that God is "*El-eloheu-yisrael*" (Israel = Jacob)."[144]

4.4.3. *Jacob's return to Bethel in 35:1–8 (attributed to the E source).*

Besides the verbs "return," *shub* (28:15, 21; 31:3, 13; 32:10), and "come," *bo'* (33:18; 35:6), in Jacob's return to Bethel, there is "go up,"

---

139. Rashi links "safe," *shlm*, to the vow: "immediately upon his return to the land of Canaan, as it is said, 'if I return safely to my father's house' (28:21)."

140. According to Rashi, "sound, *shlm*, in body in learning and in resources." A scribal error may have occurred: the final *bet* in Jacob's name is similar to the *bet* omitted before *shlm* (*beshalem* = in peace). M. Weinfeld, ed., *Olam Hatanach: Genesis* (Tel Aviv: Davidson-Atai, 1982), 193, states: "Jacob came to Shechem with a message of peace and friendship: 'These people are our friends' (34:21). The biblical *shlm* like the Akkadian *salimu* may also mean covenant and agreement (Josh 9:15)."

141. In *Jub.* 30:1–2, in A. Kahana, *The Apocrypha*, vol. 1 (Tel Aviv: mekorot, 1937), 297–313. See also Zakovitch and Shinan, *Shechem*, 8: "*Shlm* is a place name, but immediately introduces the tradition interpreting it as an adjective meaning safe, unharmed, which also links it to Jacob's vow (Gen 28:21)."

142. See Chapter 1, on components of the symbolic dream.

143. See Fokkelman, *Genesis*, 232: "Then Jacob quotes the identical words from the Bethel scene of Gen 28 to emphasize the fulfillment: 'He has been with me on the way that I have gone' (Gen 35:3)… The attention we paid to 'way and 'go' in 32:2 and 33:17 proves justified."

144. Zakovitch and Shinan, *Shechem*, 67.

'aleh—from the mouth of God Himself: "Arise, go up (*'aleh*) to Bethel" (35:1). To his family, Jacob repeats, "let us go up to Bethel" (v. 3).

Here at the end of the journey, the circle seems to close. Jacob went up to Bethel as God commanded, built the altar to God who had appeared and answered him as he fled from Esau his brother (35:2, 6–8). Jacob erected another pillar and poured oil over it (35:14–15), and then: "Jacob gave the site, where God had spoken to him, the name of Bethel" (35:15).

Fokkelman[145] describes Gen 35:1–15 as the fourteenth of fifteen scenes in the Jacob story cycle as "Bethel revisited, home-coming." Here Jacob completes the symmetry of the dream in Gen 28 by erecting the pillar, anointing it with oil and giving the name Bethel.

From the beginning, when God tells Jacob to return to Bethel, it suggests Jacob's Dream there in ch. 28. God orders Jacob to erect an altar to "the God who appeared to you when you were fleeing from Esau your brother" (35:1). Afterwards, Jacob tells his household, "Come, let us go up to Bethel and I will build an altar there to the God who answered me when I was in distress,[146] and who has been with me wherever I have gone" (35:3).

In Fidler's opinion,[147] "and who has been with me wherever I have gone" refers to Jacob's vow: "If God remains with me and if He protects me on this journey that I am making" (28:20).

Weinfeld adds that "God who answered me" (35:3) may be understood in the sense of Ps 20:2, "May the Lord answer you in time of trouble" and elsewhere in the Psalms (34:5; 81:8; 91:15).[148] Similar language is used on thanksgiving steles in the Phoenician-Punic and Aramean regions.

But Jacob's journey does not end with the return to Bethel, for in the very next verse we are told that "They set out from Bethel" (35:16). Within the Joseph story cycle Jacob again leaves the homeland, this time for Egypt (46:1–5). Unbeknownst to his father, Joseph had been sold (37:25), taken down (39:1) and kidnapped into Egypt (40:15).

The selling of Joseph also follows the omnipresent dual causation principle. Joseph elucidates it for his brothers: "Have no fear. Am I a substitute for God? Besides, although you intended me harm, God intended it for good" (50:19–20).

---

145. Fokkelman, *Genesis*, 231.
146. Fidler, "Dream Theophany," 168, says that the combination "when I was in distress" (*beyom tsarati*) refers to Jacob's flight from Esau (compare 35:7 and 27:43) and the occasion when God answered him was when He revealed Himself at Bethel when Jacob was fleeing.
147. Fidler, "Dream Theophany," 167–68.
148. Weinfeld, *Genesis*, 196, commenting on Gen 35:3.

The ascending and descending angels of God in Jacob's Dream appear to symbolize not only Jacob's journey to and from the homeland, but also his rising and falling condition on the way, and changes in the reader's attitude to what he does.

4.5. *Jacob's Second Departure from the Homeland: The Descent into Egypt Story (46:2–5) and Its Link to 28:12*

Again there is a famine in the Land, and on their father's initiative—"Go down and procure rations for us there, that we may live and not die" (42:2)—Jacob's sons go down to Egypt. After Jacob learns that Joseph is alive in Egypt, he says, "I must go and see him before I die" (45:28). This is Jacob's second (departure) descent from the Land. On the way, at Beer-Sheba God reveals Himself, saying: "Fear not to go down to Egypt" (45:3). Here again is the dual causation principle. Jacob decides to go down to Egypt and, in parallel, God gives His approval. There recurs the familiar pattern of God's promise to return him to the homeland: "I Myself will go down (*yarad*) with you into Egypt and I Myself will bring you back (*'alah*)" (46:4). In the comparison below, I indicate the link between Jacob's Dream at Bethel (28:10–22) and the vision by night in Beer-Sheba (46:1–5).

The point of departure is that in both stories, revelation came as Jacob was about to leave the homeland, God promising to return him there. The comparison shows the plausible interpretation, that Jacob's departure in 46:4 is a *descent, yarad*, and his return an *ascent, 'alah*, clarifying the symbolic meaning of the ascending and descending angels of God in Gen 28.

Jacob's Dream *(Genesis 28:10–18)*	*Jacob's "vision by night"* *(Genesis 46:1–5)*
	Jacob and all that was his
Jacob left	And came
From Beer-Sheba	To Beer-Sheba
	Where he offered sacrifices to the
	God of his father Isaac
For the sun had set	
He had a dream	In a vision by night
He said, I am the Lord	And he said, I am God[149]
The God of your father Abraham and the God of Isaac	The God of your father
How awesome is this place	Fear not to go down to Egypt

---

149. "I am God," like "angels of God," appears in the Bible only once more, in 31:13, when God orders Jacob to return to the homeland.

Your descendants shall be as the dust of the earth	I will make you there into a great nation
Remember I am with you	Myself I will go down with you to Egypt
I will protect you wherever you go	
And will bring you back *'alah* to this land	I Myself will bring you back (*hashivotikha*)

a) *Similarities between the two.*

1. In both, God reveals Himself in a dream or vision in the night.
2. In both, God reveals Himself on the eve of Jacob's departure from the homeland.
3. In both, the verb for *leaving* is in the Qal form, while the verb for returning is in the Hiphil.
4. In both, God promises Jacob to bring him back to the homeland.
5. In both, God identifies Himself as Jacob's ancestral God: "The God of your father Abraham and the God of Isaac" (28:13); "The God of your father" (46:3).
6. In both, God promises Jacob: "I am with you."
7. In both cases Jacob poured oil/offered sacrifices to his father's God.

Similarity in language and content links the two stories. There is also additional if concealed support for dialogue between the two in God's promise to Jacob: "Remember, I am with you and I will protect you wherever you go" (28:15). "Wherever" is the keyword, suggesting that God will be with Jacob not only on his way to Haran but anywhere he went, including "down to Egypt." The encouragement in ch. 46: "Fear not to go down to Egypt... I Myself will go down with you...and also bring you back," absent from ch. 28,[150] speaks of and explains the need for God's promise in the earlier revelation: "I will protect you wherever you go" (28:15).[151]

---

150. "Fear not" appears in the Septuagint in 28:13. Fidler, "Dream Theophany," 193, sees divine encouragement in "Fear not" (46:3), which also appears in stories of the Patriarchs in 15:1; 21:17 and 26:24. In it she sees a sign of the "prophecy of deliverance." See also Fidler's n. 310.

151. While "protect," *shmr*, appears in ch. 28 and not in ch. 46, God promises Jacob to be with him so that he will not fear to go down into Egypt. Hence we sense that the two stories complement one another.

b) *Differences between the two.*

1. While ch. 28 relates a dream, ch. 46 speaks of "a vision by night."[152]
2. In ch. 28 God reveals Himself to Jacob after he leaves Beer-Sheba, while in ch. 46 this happens before his arrival there.
3. In ch. 28 the protagonist's name is "Jacob"; in ch. 46 it is "Israel."[153]
4. In ch. 28 the divine revelation comes as Jacob leaves for Haran; in ch. 46 as he leaves for Egypt.
5. While in ch. 28 Jacob uses "How awesome" relating to the place; in ch. 46 God uses "Fear not" relating to the way, the descent into Egypt.
6. In ch. 28 Jacob pours oil over the stone; in ch. 46 he sacrifices to his father's God.
7. In ch. 28 Jacob sacrifices after the theophany; in ch. 46 he does so before it.[154]

---

152. Weisman, *Cycle*, 20, points out that "'a vision by night' is used nowhere else in the Bible, but typologically represents a theophany similar to those in dreams, and related to the E source" (28:12; 31:11 and 31:24 [to Laban]; compare 20:6 [to Abimelech]); Fidler, "Dream Theophany," 189–90 n. 293, surveys the work of scholars attributing 46:1b–5a to the E source.

153. Fidler, "Dream Theophany," 190: "This is the first and only time Jacob receives a message of a national nature, that in Egypt he is to become a great nation... The story represents the transition from Jacob the man, head of a household, to Jacob/Israel, father of the nation."

154. The sacrifice before the dream has suggested incubation to some scholars. See ibid., 195 n. 318–19. Also McAlpin, *Sleep*, 159. While McAlpin identifies signs of incubation, possibly Jacob's ritual before the revelation in ch. 46, rather than after it as in ch. 28, may be intentional, to improve Jacob's image. The ch. 46 the narrator may well not have liked the suspicious Jacob in ch. 28, whose vow conditioned his faith on God's protection despite the earlier divine promise (v. 15) to protect him wherever he goes. Jacob's conduct in ch. 28 contrasts sharply with that in ch. 46, where sacrifice precedes any revelation. Possibly the narrator of 46, troubled by events unfolding in ch. 28, described Jacob's sacrifice before another departure from the homeland preceding the revelation and the divine promise—of course with no conditions, befitting Jacob the Patriarch. There were doubts as to Jacob's utilitarian character in 28:13–16, which is seen to anticipate benefits from God's promise. Jacob himself reinforces these doubts in 32:10: "O God of my father Abraham and of my father Isaac, O Lord who said to me, 'Return to your native land and I will deal bountifully with you.'" Abarbanel's reasoning is that "In this definition he is working to obtain benefit…" (in Leibowitz, *Genesis*, 212). The story in ch. 46, then, is to remove all such suspicions, an idea integrating with and even supported by additional hidden dialogues in the Jacob story cycle designed to improve our Father

c) *What can be learned from the comparison?* The above comparison seems to indicate a hidden dialogue between the two stories about Jacob's descent or departure from the homeland and God's promise to bring him back.

As the unique combination "angels of God" is used only twice in the Bible, once in advance of Jacob's departure (28:12) and once as he is returning (32:2), so with the unique "I am the Lord God" (46:3). The first time the phrase occurs is in connection with Jacob's return: "I am the God of Bethel where you anointed a pillar and made a vow to Me. Now arise...and return to your native land" (31:13). The second is on the eve of Jacob's second departure: "I am God, the God of your father. Fear not to go down to Egypt, for I will make you there into a great nation" (46:3). That each of the two combinations appears only twice in the entire Bible, both times connected with Jacob's departure or return, is not coincidental. It creates a double association—between the two stories that interpret one another, and also between the Land and the return to it.

The resemblance between the dreams at Bethel (28:10–22) and at Beer-Sheba (46:1–5), as regards the divine message and the use of language, indicates their connection.[155] With that, the differences, especially between "go down," *yarad*, and "bring back," *'alah*, in ch. 46, and "set out" and "return" in ch. 28 are not coincidental. The difference, as I see it, is the interpretation of the dream and shows the symbolic meaning of the angels of God ascending and descending in ch. 28. Thus the story in ch. 46 reinforces the symbolic meaning of Jacob's Dream at Bethel.

The two stories, then, complement, explain and interpret each other:[156]

1. "Go down," *yarad*, and the promise to "bring back," *'alah*, in ch. 46 have a purpose: to interpret leaving the country (in ch. 28) as descent and the return as ascent. This supports my proposal to understand *the vision in the dream* (28:12–13a) and *the verbal message* (28:13b–15) as mutually explanatory.
2. "Fear not" in ch. 46 is absent from ch. 28, but appears to hint back to Jacob's fears as he left for Haran, and why divine encouragement was needed: "I will protect you wherever you go" (28:15).

Jacob's image. See also Y. Zakovitch, "Jacob's Deception: Genesis 25," in *Dr. Baruch Ben Yehuda Volume: Studies in the Bible and in Jewish Thought* (ed. B. Z. Luria; Tel Aviv: Israel Society for Biblical Research, 1981), 121–44; Zakovitch, *Looking Glass*, 68–69.

155. See Fidler, "Dream Theophany," 193.
156. See above, n. 151, on absence of "protect" (*shmr*) in ch. 46.

What was Jacob afraid of in ch. 46? Was it the theophany itself,[157] or the difficulties and dangers of the journey at his advanced age?[158] When God tells Jacob "Fear not," we understand that he has fears, though not what was fearful in Egypt.

In most cases in the Bible "ascend" (*'alah*) and "descend" (*yarad*), respectively, signify positive and negative metaphors. Its use here, particularly by God Himself, would have frightened Jacob. Thus "Fear not to go down[159] into Egypt" embodies two contradictory statements, the first being the negative "go down" and the second, also from the mouth of God, "fear not," intended to banish worry at least in this instance.

Fidler emphasizes: "Only from a broader prospect that includes at least the stories of Isaac, can Jacob be understood to regard the descent into Egypt as negative in God's eyes, or a danger to the promise of the land to his seed."[160]

In an earlier article on Abraham's descent into Egypt,[161] I noted the link between God's command to Isaac, "Do not go down to Egypt" (26:2) and the contrary action taken by his father Abraham "Abram went down to Egypt" (12:10). I see 26:2 as a precaution in which God conceals His message to Isaac: do not repeat your father's mistake. Besides, Abraham descends to Egypt "to sojourn there," while Isaac is told to "Stay in the land," not there in Egypt.

In the light of this evaluation, Jacob's hesitation to go down into Egypt is understandable. Indeed, R. Yoseph Bechor Shor, commenting on v. 3, notes: "As his heart warned him regarding what God said to his father Isaac, Do not go down to Egypt, and since it might have displeased him that he too was going, he made sacrifices to the God of his father Isaac, to which he said: Fear not to go down into Egypt, for I do not object."[162]

---

157. See Fidler, "Dream Theophany," 193 n. 312; J. C. Greenfield, "The Zakir Inscription and the Danklied," in *Proceedings of the Fifth World Congress of Jewish Studies: Jerusalem 1969*, vol. 1 (ed. P. Peli and A. Shinan; Jerusalem: The Hebrew University, 1973), 181. Fidler cites but disagrees with Greenfield's proposal.

158. See Skinner, *Genesis*, interpreting v. 3.

159. This enters into the discussion of Abraham's descent into Egypt in 12:10.

160. See Fidler, "Dream Theophany," 193–94.

161. Y. I. Peleg, "Abraham First the Zionist and the First *Yored*," *Al Haperek* 14 (1998): 25–31.

162. See Fidler, "Dream Theophany," 194 n. 314, quoting Josephus, *Ant.* 2.170–176: "And when he camped near Beer-Sheba, he sacrificed to God… And fear consumed him lest his sons prefer settling in Egypt… He feared his house would be destroyed for descending into Egypt not according to God's will."

The revelation in ch. 46 appears to dialogue, as it were, with the one in ch. 28 (both conventionally attributed to the E source) regarding the attitude to leaving the homeland. "The vision by night" in 46:1 is designed to indicate indirectly that the ascending and descending of the angels of God in 28:12 represent and symbolize the Patriarchs' ascents to and descents from the homeland, thus bringing closer the symbolic interpretation of the Bethel dream. The verb *yarad*, "go down," in ch. 46 fills two literary functions: it explains Jacob's departure negatively, and clarifies that Jacob's Dream of the descending angels on the *sullam* is a symbol of Jacob's (Abraham's) descent from the homeland.

Additionally, the vision of the ascending and descending angels (28:12) hints at the fate of the Patriarchs' descendants. We look at the book of Joshua, where besides the suggestions hidden in the text itself,[163] is the sense of "Like father, like son" in what the people say to Joshua: "For it was the Lord our God who brought us and our fathers up (*hama'aleh*) out of the Land of Egypt, the house of bondage...and guarded us all along the way that we traveled..." (Josh 24:17).

The similarity between these three verses (Gen 28:15, 20; Josh 24:17) shows their connection:

Genesis 28:15	*Genesis 28:20*	*Joshua 24:17*
And I will bring you back To this land	And if I return safe (*beshalom*) To my father's house	Who brought (*hama'aleh*) us and our fathers up from the Land of Egypt, from the house of bondage
And I will *protect* you Wherever you go	If he *protects* me On this journey That I am making	And *guarded* us All along the way That we traveled

The connection between God's promise (28:15) and Jacob's vow (28:20–22) is discussed in section 5 of Chapter 2. The text from Josh 24:17 too recalls Jacob's vow to serve God if He protects him on his journey (28:21).[164] Most significantly, in Joshua, "In reply, the people declared, 'Far be it from us to forsake the Lord and serve other gods'" (Josh 24:16). Similarly, Jacob concludes with a vow: "the Lord shall be my God" (Gen 28:21), and in Josh 24:17 language and content both recall the promise to Jacob in Gen 28:15.

---

163. See Fidler, "Dream Theophany," 198, regarding the two readings of Gen 46:4. Fidler says that the promise relates to "a great nation, not only to Jacob."

164. Y. Zakovitch, *Olam Hatanach: Joshua* (ed. G. Galil; Tel Aviv: Davidson-Atai, 1994), 218.

In Jacob's Dream (in Gen 28), God's promise is given as he is leaving (*descending* from) the homeland, while in Josh 24 the people make their declaration as they are about to enter (*ascend*). Another contrast is the divine promise to protect Jacob in the future is met with a vow, while the Israelites of Joshua's time praise God for protecting them in the past. This can be seen to bring together the promise to Jacob ("I will assign to you and to your offspring," Gen 28:13) and its fulfillment to his descendants in Joshua's time.

In conclusion, the verb in 28:15, *vehashivotikha*, "I will bring you back" (that is, God promises to return Jacob to the homeland), is changed/replaced in Josh 24:17 to *hama'aleh*, "God brought us up from," which has a positive connotation in the Bible. So too in Gen 46:4. The return, then, is not only God's will but carried out under His responsibility. In a literal translation from Hebrew, he is "raising," *ma'aleh*, Jacob and his descendants to the Land.

5. *Jacob's Dream as* Mise en Abyme *for the Patriarchal Narrative*

> The *yarad* concept (leaving the Promised Land—in Hebrew) came into the world with Abraham's narrative. [Abraham] the first Jew is both the first *'oleh* (entering the Promised Land—in Hebrew) and the first *yored*. Throughout history the Jew has carried within him the elements of both.[165]

Until now we have considered the dream vision in Gen 28:12–13a as *mise en abyme* for the story of Jacob's Dream, then as one reflecting the Jacob story cycle in compact miniature as descent from and ascent to the homeland. We now go on to consider it, particularly the vision as a *mise en abyme* for the stories of the Patriarchs, as reflecting the attitude towards their entering and leaving the homeland.

As in the Jacob story cycle, here too we follow descriptions of Abraham as he enters and leaves. We require far greater altitude to follow Abraham across the entire world known to him and probably to the story's early hearers:

1. Abraham's ascent journey (*'oleh*) from Ur of the Chaldees to Canaan.
2. "Abram went down (*yarad*) to Egypt" (12:10).
3. "From Egypt Abram went up (*'oleh*) into the Negeb" (13:1)

---

165. Yehoshua, *In Praise of Normalcy*, 31.

5.1. *Abraham the Patriarch, the First Immigrant (ʿoleh): Two Readings or Two Sources?*

Jacob's journey to and from the Land begins with the story of departure from Ur of the Chaldees, or Haran according to Gen 15:7, for the Land of Canaan. Right after that, with famine in Canaan, Abraham goes down (*yarad*) to Egypt (12:10), then he returns, ascends (*ʿalah*) to Canaan (13:1).

Genesis offers three reports of Abraham's departure for Canaan. According to the first (11:31), Terah took his son Abraham away from Ur of the Chaldees. The second (12:1–5) states that God commanded Abraham at Haran (not Ur) to leave his home and native land and go to the Land of Canaan, and Abraham went. In the third version (15:7)[166] God, not Terah, ordered Abraham to leave Ur of the Chaldees,[167] not Haran.

Can these differences be bridged, or are they different because they come from different literary sources,[168] or from different originally oral traditions regarding Abraham's journey to Canaan? In my view, the three possibilities/reports do not contradict but complement one another, showing the complexity of the story. They raise two questions: Who removed Abraham from his original home—God or Terah? And where from—Ur of the Chaldees or Haran? The first question is our present focus.[169]

The first account of Abraham's departure from Ur of the Chaldees is in Gen 11:31. He seems to have been taken by Terah: "Terah took his son Abram, his grandson Lot the son of Haran, and his daughter-in-law Sarai, the wife of his son Abram, and they set out together from Ur of the

---

166. Peleg, "Who Brought," 22–40.

167. That God revealed Himself to Abraham at Ur of the Chaldees, apparently based on 15:7, is post biblical, from Acts 7:3–4 (KJV): "The God of Glory appeared unto our father Abraham when he was in Mesopotamia, before he dwelt in Haran, And said to him, Get thee out of thy country, and from thy kindred, and come into the land which I shall show thee. Then came he out of the land of the Chaldeans and dwelt in Haran; and from thence, after his father was dead, he removed him into this land." On Acts in this context see Y. Zakovitch, "The Exodus from Ur of the Chaldees: A Chapter in Literary Archaeology," in *Ki Baruch Hu: Ancient Near Eastern, Biblical, and Judaic Studies in Honor of Baruch A. Levine* (ed. R. Chazan, W. W. Hallo and L. H. Schiffman; Winona Lake, Ind.: Eisenbrauns, 1999), 423.

168. On the source criticism approach, see T. L. Thompson, *The Historicity of the Patriarchal Narratives: The Quest for the Historical Abraham* (Berlin: de Gruyter, 1974), 310.

169. The answer to the first question may help to answer the second.

Chaldees for the Land of Canaan, but when they came as far as Haran, they settled there" (11:31).

This raises two central questions: Why did Terah leave his home? And why did he go only as far as Haran, not to Canaan?

5.1.1. *Four readings as to why Terah left Ur of the Chaldees.*[170]

> Why does a person move from one home to another? It is not from a surfeit of good, from fullness where one has everything, from where it is safe, warm and protected, with a family radiating light and kindness. Nothing will induce one to leave such a home... For one to leave home there has to be a change in the home itself... Emigration journeys begin when a flaw appears in the primary habitat.[171]

Nothing is said about Terah's motives for leaving. A motive is expected, as people do not leave home and country for a distant land for no reason. There should be either a push from the point of departure or an attraction towards the destination, or both.[172] The lack of explanation in Terah's case is the more conspicuous because of a particular explanation regarding Abraham: he follows the divine command in "Go forth from your native land and from your father's house to the Land that I will show you..." (Gen 12:1).

Below are four possible readings or understandings of Terah's departure.

1. The first possible reading is that there is no explanation for his departure because biblical language is spare and economical in discussing characters.
2. The second possible reading is a complement to the first: there is no explanation because Terah is a "secondary character."
3. The third reading allows that, while it is not explicitly mentioned, Terah may have left because of his son Haran's death.
4. The fourth possibility is that God is behind the departure. This becomes known to readers only in retrospect in 15:7: "I am the Lord who brought you out from Ur of the Chaldees to assign this land to you as a possession."

---

170. Chapter 2 of the present book explains that *two readings* refers to multiple readings generally, i.e. more than one reading. That principle guides the present discussion.

171. H. Naveh, *Male and Female Travelers: Travel Stories in the Hebrew Literature* (Tel Aviv: Misrad Habitahon, 2002), 46–47.

172. Ibid., 42–43, notes: "Emigration may be summed up in four words: 'from home to home'... In the modern world it is permanently and finally leaving one home in the hope of creating and establishing a new permanent and final home..."

a) *Biblical language is spare and economical, so Terah's departure is not explained.* Is this really the reason for restricted and limited character description? There is some support from Gunkel, in *The Legends of Genesis*:

> Many stories in Genesis contain no more than ten verses… The extent depends on the narrator's artistic ability and the listening capacity of the hearers. Ancient narrators were unable to create more comprehensive stories and equally, they could not anticipate that their hearers would listen longer… In ancient times [people listened to] very short stories that took no more than a quarter of an hour to relate… Written stories are naturally more comprehensive than oral ones because the eye can take in more material than the ear."[173]

As stated before, the brief, terse nature of Bible stories is no sign they are meager, but indicates an advantage. Gunkel himself writes of "the simplicity and clarity in the art of the ancient story," and that "this ancient form of legend attests to the sparse nature of ancient composition." Then, in the same breath, he adds: "These narrow borders…bring forth the essence of its poetic quality…"[174] Yairah Amit, in a chapter titled "Formulating Characters Using Economical Means," mentions Gunkel's ambivalence.[175] Alter mentions "the ability to create characters from scanty means, leaving gaps *that create a sense of depth and complexity.*"[176]

Our awareness as readers as to restriction and reduction creates an obligation to close, attentive and sensitive reading out of respect for the author, as we relate in all seriousness to the biblical literary work with its depths, its gaps and its silences. This is no simple, meager work, but rather a highly complex one whose silences are part of its complexity. The double meaning and ambiguity of the biblical story only increase the pleasure of reading it.[177] The preceding analysis indicates that the

---

173. Gunkel, *Legends*, 7, 44, 46.
174. Ibid., 46–50.
175. Amit, *Reading*, 76–87. Cf. Alter, *Biblical Story*, 131. See also Polak, *Narative*, 16: "Despite the relatively condensed nature of the Bible story, its vocabulary includes a broad, rich variety of expressions. That wealth is the more noticeable…because the limited framework contains the same [language] variety as a larger work." The relatively narrow space does not cause a sense of paucity, but intensifies and concentrates the strength of the words.
176. Alter, *Biblical Story*, 133 (emphasis added). See also S. Bahar, "Silence Is the Message," *Moed: Annual for Jewish Studies* 17 (2007): 1–21.
177. Y. I. Peleg, "A Time to Know the Biblical Text," *Al Haperek* 19 (2002): 176–89. See also Shapira, "Multiple Meanings," 249–82.

absence of a motive for Terah's departure is no sign of the poverty of the work, but rather seems to show that he is a secondary character in the story.

b) *A second possible reading: Terah was a secondary character in the story so no reason was given for his leaving Ur of the Chaldees.* What is *a secondary character*? Uriel Simon notes that, among other functions,

> it may serve as "a means for moral evaluation of the main character"... It is almost never expressed in specific words, but indirectly by means of acts and their consequences... Broadly speaking, *the secondary character is spoken of only as necessary to advance the plot or to illuminate another character, not solely for its own sake.*[178]

Besides Simon's explanation why no reason for Terah's departure is stated, the absence may be seen to emphasize the departure of Abraham at God's command, and hence why Abraham arrived in Canaan while Terah did not.

There is some irony in a story where the father is secondary to the son. Possibly the comparison between the two overshadows Terah, although it becomes evident that its purpose is to glorify and strengthen Abraham. I do not see Terah as a negative figure. It may even be maintained that Terah started the journey to Canaan and Abraham continued it in the dual geographical/spiritual sense. Yet the story is about Abraham's image and ascent to the homeland.

Defining a story character as secondary in this case has both an advantage and a disadvantage. The advantage lies in explaining Terah's lack of motive to leave. The disadvantage is that so defining[179] him as secondary may prevent the search for such a motive, though it may not be stated explicitly. Even if he is defined as a secondary character, we still have to read about Terah sensitively and carefully in the search for concealed hints about his motives. The approach that respects the biblical literary work and rejects even accepted labels requires that much.

Indeed, the short report on Terah's departure after his son Haran's death suggests that this may be the reason the father left. Did the undisclosed reasons for the son's death influence the father's decision to leave? As I see it, the death and departure not only followed each other,

---

178. U. Simon, *Reading Prophetic Narrative* (BEL 15; Jerusalem: Mosad Bialik, 1997), 323.

179. The issue is similar to labeling biblical and ANE dreams as one of two types. While this may explain a motive or reveal its links to or among components, it rules out the possibility of finding an additional, not necessarily contradictory, meaning. Furthermore, it limits and leads to errors, "locking" the meaning of a text or dream, so significant a factor in multiple readings.

3. The Jacob's Dream Story as Mise en Abyme 207

but one occurred because of the other.[180] This leads, at least in concealed fashion, to an earthly human reason for Terah's leaving Ur of the Chaldees, which leads to a third reading.

c) *A third reading allows that Terah left Ur of the Chaldees because of Haran's death, though without stating so. How did that happen?*

1) *"Haran died in the lifetime of his father Terah": literal and metaphoric readings.* The son's death is described at some length: "Haran died in the living-presence of Terah (*al pnei Terah*) his father, in the land of his kindred in Ur of the Chaldees" (Fox), or according to KJV: "And Haran died before his father Terah," or according to JPS: "Haran died in the lifetime of his father Terah" (11:28). The expanded first part of the sentence—*al pnei Terah*—stands out against the typical terseness of the Bible story (*hazarah*, defamiliarization), a device familiar in biblical literature: the biblical narrator is typically most economical with words. The narrator might simply have said that Haran died, and so Terah took his now fatherless grandson Lot with him. The purpose of the expanded text, one assumes, was to call the reader's attention to Terah's suffering as a bereaved father.

The English "in the lifetime of his father Terah" is a metaphoric rendition of the Hebrew (as in Num 3:4).[181] In literal Hebrew that phrase has another even harsher meaning—before the eyes of Terah his father,[182] (according to Fox: "Haran died in the living-presence of Terah [*al pnei*

---

180. See Bar-Efrat, *Design*, 146. The subject touches on the Sages' view of juxtaposition in the Bible. Even Zakovitch, *Inner-Biblical*, 34, offers a chapter titled "Juxtaposition in Literature as an Interpretive Instrument." He writes: "The reason for her [Sara's] death was that when they told her about the binding of Isaac and that he was almost slaughtered, she expired. Can Moses have died of grief and heartbreak after God told him, 'This is the land of which I swore to Abraham, Isaac, and Jacob… I have let you see it with your own eyes, but you shall not cross there. So Moses the servant of the Lord died there, in the land of Moab, at the command of the Lord' (Deut 34:4–5). Does v. 5 report that Moses died because the Lord told him he would not cross? Although Moses would have known of this before. In Deut 32:49–52 God told him: 'Ascend these heights…in the land of Moab facing Jericho, and view the land of Canaan, which I am giving to the Israelites… You shall die on the mountain that you are about to ascend.'" Perhaps, though, Moses hoped that if he reached the lookout point, God might allow him to enter.

181. "But Nadav and Avihu died by the will of the Lord…so it was Eleazar and Ithamar who served as priests in the lifetime of their father Aaron (*al pnei Aharon*)" (Num 3:4).

182. For "before" as the literal reading of *al pnei*, see, e.g., Elisha the Prophet's instruction to Gehazi: "Gehazi had gone before them and had placed the staff on the boy's face ['before the boy,' *al pnei*]" (2 Kgs 4:31).

Terah] his father"), explaining the bereaved father's agony. The sight of his dead son gave him no rest, so he left his native place.

Josephus too relates Terah's departure to his son's death. In his *Jewish Antiquities*, Josephus states: "Because Terah hated the land of the Chaldeans in his grief over Haran, they all left for Haran in Aram Naharaim."[183] Thus we have a causal relationship between Haran's death and Terah's departure.

Presenting Terah as a minor or secondary character, then, served to show why his departure from Ur of the Chaldees went unexplained. When one is not content to affix that designation, however, a motive must be sought, even a concealed one. When it is found, the depth and complexity of the story is suddenly revealed. Precisely that awareness of sparse writing and condensation led me to examine *al pnei Terah* and to discover the tragic human motive for Terah's departure.

2) *Haran's death in the book of Jubilees*.[184] The Bible story does not disclose how Haran died. Zakovitch suggests using post-biblical literature to fill in the details missing in the "condensed" biblical version:

> The condensed tradition is expanded and expounded in the condensed biblical version, as regards Abram's war against the idol makers and the burning of Haran in the fire (a *midrash* on the Hebrew *Ur*). The earliest known version is in the *Book of Jubilees*: "At night Abram burned the house of the idols, and the house and all inside it burned down, and nobody knew. And they arose at night and sought to save their gods from the fire. Haran hastened to save them, the fire burned upon him and he was burned in the fire, and died in Ur of the Chaldees before Terah his father, and they buried him in Ur. And Terah left Ur of the Chaldees, he and his sons, to go to the land of Lebanon and the land of Canaan" (12:12–15).[185]

The obvious question is whether the post-biblical information on Haran's death and Abraham's struggle with the idol makers is a later version filling gaps in the biblical story, or is it a case of using an old tradition to repair "censorship" on the earlier version? According to Zakovitch,

---

183. Josephus, *Ant.* 1.152.
184. See Peleg, "Who Brought," 22–42; Zakovitch, "Exodus from Ur," 429–43. On Haran's death by fire and Abraham's escape in the literature of the Sages, see Louis Ginzberg, *The Legends of the Jews*, vol. 2 (trans. and ed. M. Hacohen; Ramat Gan: Masada, 1967), 1–22. *Jubilees* comments on the literary meaning of "before Terah his father."
185. Zakovitch, "Exodus from Ur," 438. Zakovitch summarizes material on Haran's death: "The tradition that preceded P was rejected and disappeared from the book of Genesis, but stayed alive in the oral mode."

the tradition of Haran's death in the fire in Ur of the Chaldees and Abraham's rescue from it "became known to the P source who decided to reject it from the Bible."[186] According to Zakovitch and Shinan, "This is no late composition, but the surfacing of an ancient tradition."[187] They assume the story was kept out of the Torah because "the Torah seeks to minimize and distance the slightest 'dust' of idolatry from the fathers of the nation. The Torah presents Abraham as one who never knew and never saw idolatry in his life, and so elects to begin his life story in Canaan, making do with only the most essential details of his previous life."[188]

As I see it, the dramatic phrase "before Terah his father" and the name of the city, "Ur of the Chaldees" (*Ura* in Aramaic means "fire"), are rescued from an ancient tale. They were left as a "sign" in the Hebrew Bible like *the writing on the wall*, like "the great dragons"—*hataninim hagedolim*—in the Creation story in Gen 1:21.[189]

For our purposes, the story of the fire in Ur raises the possibility of divulging the complex relationships between Terah and his household. Haran's death, according to the *Jubilees* story, was Abraham's fault because he burned the idols. Horror wells up at the thought of what went through Terah's mind when one son caused the other's death.[190] What were Abraham's thoughts after he caused Haran's death, though not deliberately? Can feelings of guilt explain the responsibility he assumed

---

186. Cf. Cassuto, *Genesis*, 2:186: "is what midrashic literature relates about Haran and his death, a remnant of an ancient tradition, but we have no possibility of clarifying the details."

187. Y. Zakovitch and A. Shinan, *That's Not What the Good Book Says* (Tel Aviv: Yediot Aharonot, 2004), 136; See also Y. Hoffman, *Olam Hatanach: Isaiah* (Tel Aviv: Davidson-Atai, 1986), 239. On "Who redeemed Abraham?" (Isa 29:22), Hoffman writes: "The event to which this refers is not clear. Rashi and Radak, *Torat Haim: Five Books of the Law: Genesis* (Jeusalem: Mosad Harav Kook, 1990), interpret it as the redemption from Ur of the Chaldees, but it may hint at another event in Abraham's life: deliverance in the war of the kings (Genesis 14) or from Pharaoh (12:10–20)."

188. Zakovitch and Shinan, *That's Not What the Good Book Says*, 136.

189. On the expression "the great sea monsters," JPS in Gen 1:21, see Peleg, "Water," 153–68.

190. The same fate befell Adam and Eve when Cain killed Abel. One might assume an analogy to "before (*al pnei*) Terah his father" in God's words to Cain: "Why are you distressed, and why is your face fallen (*naflu panekha*)?" (4:6). One assumes Terah's face fell when his son died, though the absence of "fell" mars the analogy, though surely not Terah's suffering. For the bereaved parent's standpoint, see Rebekah's words to Jacob: "Let me not lose you both in one day!" (27:45).

for Lot, Haran's son?[191] The narrator's insistence on calling Lot "his brother's son" (12:5) is not merely information, but rather stresses a closeness that reminds the reader of Abraham's guilty feelings. If we accept Zakovitch's proposal that the fire in Ur is an original but censored Bible story, we better understand Terah as a bereaved father. Not only did he lose Haran, but the other son Abraham caused the loss and bereavement. Was this why Terah left Ur of the Chaldees?[192]

5.1.2. Why Terah only reached Haran and did not continue to Canaan: two readings. Our discussion begins with the naïve informative reading, followed by an explanation of the importance of when Terah died—was it right after arriving in Haran or not? Following this, Terah's departure (11:31) is compared with Abraham's (12:5) and conclusions are drawn. Finally, God's command to Abraham in 12:1 reveals the second reading.

a) *Is Genesis 11:31 chronological, descriptive and naïve, or do causality and tendentiousness make it a criticism?*[193] Genesis 11:31 presents the first report of Abraham's departure for Canaan from Ur of the Chaldees. It raises two questions. The first is why Terah left Ur, for which four possibilities have just been presented. The second, now discussed, is why Terah traveled only as far as Haran (and did not continue to Canaan) and the narrator's attitude to the halt there.

A careful reading discloses two consecutive reports. The first is that Terah and his household leave Ur of the Chaldees "for the Land of Canaan." The second is "and (or *but*, according to Fox) when they came as far as Haran, they settled there"—that is, they did not reach Canaan.

---

191. Zakovitch and Shinan, *That's Not What the Good Book Says*, 135, draw an analogy between the story of Haran's death by fire in Ur and Lot's deliverance from the fire in Sodom: "An echo can be found in the story of what happened to Haran's son, Lot. Haran was burned by fire because of sin, but Lot, who had not sinned, was shown mercy (19:24), but was delivered from the burning city by divine messengers…" The circle of Abraham's guilty feelings due to Haran's death now closes. Regarding the special relationship between Abraham and Lot, see Y. I. Peleg, "Was Lot a Good Host? Was Lot Saved from Sodom as a Reward for His Hospitality?," in *Universalism and Particularism at Sodom and Gomorrah: Essays in Memory of Ron Pirson* (ed. D. Lipton; SBLAIL 11; Atlanta, Ga.: SBL, 2012), 134–62.

192. A fourth possible reading is that God brought Abraham out. It emerges only in retrospect, after entering Canaan, in 15:7: "I am the Lord who brought you out from Ur of the Chaldees…," discussed after comparing Terah's departure with Abraham.

193. See Perry and Sternberg, "King," 263–92, explaining the difference between a straightforward (naïve) report and an ironical/critical one, in the beginning of the David and Bathsheba story (2 Sam 11:1).

Is there a causal relationship between the two or just a chronological one? Immediately, in v. 32 the narrator reports: "Terah died in Haran." The impression is that Terah died upon arrival there, so did not continue to Canaan. Is this *really* what happened?

The story goes on to report the divine revelation to Abraham: "The Lord said to him, "Go forth from your native land and from your father's house to the land that I will show you" (12:1). The report appears to follow the course of events: after Terah's death in Haran, Abraham continues on to the Land of Canaan. A more careful reading, however, indicates otherwise.

b) *Two readings of Terah's death: Did he really die upon arrival in Haran, and hence did not reach Canaan? How are the reports in 11:31 linked to the one in 11:32?* One reading is simply chronological (naïve), reporting events in the order of occurrence, according to which the household departed from Ur of the Chaldees for Canaan: Terah and his family settled in Haran, where Terah died at a good old age: "The days of Terah came to 205 years" (Gen 11:32). A second reading allows for *a more critical approach* with a less naïve description, based on the causation principle.[194] That is to say, because they left for Canaan *but* only reached Haran, and settled there, Terah died. Had he reached the Land of Canaan as planned, he would not have died. This implied criticism is discussed below.

Several reasons support the critical reading, even if not explicitly. The first is linguistic. The connecting *waw* of the Hebrew can be read as either "and" or "but": Is it "and reached Haran" or "but reached Haran"?[195] The second option introduces causality and, with it, criticism of Terah. He left for Canaan but did not continue the journey, so therefore he died in Haran. That is, his death there could be seen as a punishment.[196] If so, was his sin not continuing to the new homeland?

---

194. See Bar-Efrat, *Design*, 146–47, for definitions of the causality principle.

195. Both readings appear in English translations. The KJV reads "And they came unto Haran and dwelt there," while the NJPS Bible (1985) and Fox (1977) offer "But when they had come as far as Haran, they settled there." While in Hebrew both options are open, translating serves to "lock" the interpretation.

196. It resembles the book of Ruth in another sense. In Ruth, Elimelech died after he left the homeland, while here a father died on his way there. The point is discussed relating to Abraham's descent into Egypt. Terah and Elimelech remained outside Canaan: "they settled there" (Gen 11:31) and "they...remained there" (Ruth 1:2, 5). Did Terah, Elimelech, and his sons die because they remained outside the Promised Land? The *Tosefta* (*Nezikin, Avoda Zara* 4:4) reads: "And so Rabbi Simeon would say, Elimelech was a great man in his generation, a community leader, and because he left the country he and his sons died of hunger."

From another standpoint, he may not have reached Canaan because he died, meaning that his death is not a punishment for not reaching that country but rather its consequence. Is that really so?

Against the reading in which Terah dies—for whatever reason[197]—upon arrival in Haran stand the following chronological data:

1. Terah, at seventy years of age, begot Abraham: "When Terah had lived seventy years, he begot Abram" (11:26).[198]
2. Abraham, at seventy-five, received the order to go forth and did so (12:1, 4): "Abram was seventy-five years old when he left Haran" (12:4).
3. Terah, then, was 145 years old (70+75)[199] when he reached Haran (11:32).
4. If Terah died at 205, he must have stayed sixty years in Haran.

The chronological data show, even if not explicitly, that Terah stayed in Haran for another sixty years, so that his death there was not what kept him from reaching the Promised Land. This concealed criticism is not designed to fault Terah so much as to exalt Abraham for reaching their original destination. Had the narrator wished to criticize Terah openly, he almost certainly would have said that he lived another sixty years in Haran.

We can look at this from another angle: it can be claimed that the Bible does not clearly state that Terah continued to live in Haran in order to defend Abraham, lest the reader might criticize him for not honoring his elderly father, and leaving him behind in Haran.

In my opinion the narrator focuses on Abraham as the main character. Terah's role, secondary but not negative, is to highlight Abraham's entry into the Land.[200] Comparing Terah's departure (11:31) with Abraham's departure (12:5) will support this notion. Therefore, we will postpone the additional reading—the fourth one.

---

197. Two readings would seem possible not only as to when, but also as to why Terah died.

198. When Abraham was 99, God revealed Himself, telling him: "You shall no longer be called Abram, but your name shall be Abraham, for I will make you the father of a multitude of nations" (17:5).

199. Zakovitch, "Exodus from Ur," 423: "In the Samaritan version of the Torah, Terah died immediately on arriving in Haran, at the age of 'five and forty and a hundred years,' not at the age of 205 as in the Masoretic text." Zakovitch prefers the Samaritan version.

200. Peleg, "Who Brought," 22–42.

5.1.3. Comparing Terah's departure with Abraham's.[201]

a) *Presenting them as reflections of each other*. The description of Terah's departure highlights Abraham's positive image, or, more specifically, the actions of Terah his father, as shown in the following table.[202]

Terah's departure (11:31)	*Abraham's departure (12:5)*
Terah took	Abraham took
His son Abram and Lot the son of Haran and his daughter-in-law Sarai	His wife Sarai *and* his brother's son Lot
	And all of the wealth that they had amassed, *and* the persons they had acquired in Haran
And they set out together from Ur of the Chaldees	And they set out
For the Land of Canaan	For the Land of Canaan
When *they came* (*vayavo'u*) to Haran "*but* when they had come as far as Haran" (Fox) They settled there	They arrived (*vayavo'u*) in the Land of Canaan

1) *Similarities between the two*.

1. In both, Terah and Abraham take their family members.
2. Both leave from Ur to go to Canaan.
3. Both descriptions have a similar language structure:
   a. "He took this and that one"
   b. "And they set out"
   c. "For the Land of Canaan"
   d. "And they came to (or they arrived to) (a place)"

The similarity of structure, language and content appears to indicate a concealed dialogue link between the two. The differences may point to the nature of the dialogue.

---

201. Some scholars see these two descriptions of a journey to be familiar formula from the Bible and from ANE literature (Ugaritic). On these passages as examples of those formulae, see Cassuto, *Canaanite*, 26–27. Avishur, *Genesis*, 91, adds: "Among the descriptive formulae common to biblical and Ugaritic literature is that of a man departing from home with his family and possessions on a journey to reach another place. Such fixed forms may be schematically described thus: Someone takes this one, that one and the other one and their possessions and departs (or comes or goes) to some place. In descriptions of such journeys the departing individual takes a certain number of people or property items or both. The numbers are always whole: seven or three or ten items."

202. From Peleg, "Abraham," 25–31.

2) *Differences between the two.*

1. Who went first, and from where? While Terah left Ur of the Chaldees, taking his son Abraham with him to Haran, Abraham continued to the Land of Canaan.[203]
2. Who and what did each take with him? Terah took only his family, while Abraham took "all the wealth they had amassed… in Haran."
3. Where did they get to? While Terah reached only as far as Haran, Abraham reached the Land of Canaan.
4. Dream and realization: Terah set out for the Land of Canaan but only reached Haran, while Abraham set out for Canaan and reached it.

The first two differences relate to the departure, while the second one raises a question: Did Terah, unlike Abraham, leave his property behind in Ur of the Chaldees because he intended to return at some time? The third difference relates to the place reached by each man. The fourth is about the whole enterprise in the light of plan and realization, and seems to reinforce the hidden and most significant purpose of the story.

For our purposes, the most significant difference concerns the places where Terah and Abraham ended their journeys. That Terah did not reach Canaan highlights the fact that Abraham did. This calls to mind a phenomenon that Zakovitch calls "description as reflection."[204] Terah sets out for Canaan but does not arrive (11:31); Abraham, on the other hand, sets out, but, unlike Terah, who settles in Haran, arrives there (12:5).

Possibly the narrator wanted to flatter Abraham by describing his father's conduct. Possibly too the reader is being asked to judge Abraham's act in the light of Terah's, and to understand that what his father could not or would not achieve, Abraham achieved. That Terah did not reach Canaan despite efforts to do so, but settled in Haran, reinforces the impression made by Abraham's achievement.[205]

---

203. Haran is on the way from Ur of the Chaldees to Canaan. The name, from the Akkadian *Haranu*, meaning "way," makes possible a hidden midrash on the name that exposes its role in the story.

204. Zakovitch, "Reflection Stories," 165: "…The reflection reverses the descriptive lines of the original, and the reader who notes the deliberate link between original and reflection understands that the new image acts in an opposite fashion from the one it was based on, and will evaluate the hero of the story in the light of the one in its parallel, for good or ill."

205. The comparison between the two journeys is made from two complementary literary vantage points. One considers them as *reflected stories*, and the other looks at Terah as the secondary character to Abraham's principal one. Both indicate the intent to criticize Terah in order to praise Abraham.

3. *The Jacob's Dream Story as* Mise en Abyme

b) *A second reading of the question: Why did Terah not reach the homeland?* The human initiative of Terah is contrasted with the divine initiative of Abraham. While the *waw* prefixed to "they came" may be read either as "and" or "but," in the latter case it becomes ironic and criticizes Terah,[206] who did not carry out his intent.

Significantly, between the departures in Gen 11:31 and 12:5, God reveals Himself to Abraham, commanding: "Go forth from your native land and from your father's house to the land that I will show you" (12:1). That the divine revelation did not occur before Terah's departure invites the question of whether this is why Terah did not reach Canaan, while God's command to Abraham brought him to the Land. (The reader wonders whether without the divine command Abraham would have gone on to Canaan or remained in Haran.) The sense is that while Terah's departure is unexplained and on his own initiative, Abraham's was planned and initiated by God. Deurloo maintains that the difference between Terah's "incidental initiative" was that if [the situation] seemed good in Haran they would stay there, while "the intentional initiative of Abram" directed them to Canaan.[207] As Gitay sees it, the main difference between the two departures is that Abraham the son answered God's command to leave, while Terah the father left on his own initiative.[208] Abraham, unlike Terah, relied completely on God's word—Divine guidance that showed him a new land.

Terah's journey is formulated as emigration, like Esau's move from Canaan to the hill country of Seir (Gen 36:6), and is similar to descriptions appearing in the Ugaritic literature.[209] The difference between all these migrations and Abraham's is the divine command that preceded it. This comparison between Abraham and Terah may also sharpen the distinction between one who dreams of entering the homeland and one who realizes that dream.

Differently, it may be said that Terah left for the place to which God specifically ordered his son Abraham (12:1). How then did he sin? Was he forcing the day of deliverance,[210] while Abraham started out for

---

206. Terah is contrasted with Abraham in Josh 24:2: "Then Joshua said to all the people… Terah the father of Abraham and the father of Nahor lived beyond the Euphrates and worshipped other gods. But I took your father Abraham from beyond the Euphrates and led him through the whole land of Canaan."

207. Deurloo, "Abraham," 86. This assumption may explain why Terah did not take his possessions with him while Abraham did (Gen 12:5).

208. Gitay, "Geography," 205–16.

209. See Avishur, *Genesis*, 91.

210. Jacob's acting against Esau is similar. See Y. Zakovitch, "The Exemplary and the Perfect Character in the Bible," in *Surely There is Not a Righteous Man on*

Canaan upon the divine command and so reached it? The main difference may be that Terah did not receive God's blessing given to one who obeys, and his death frees Abraham, the new founding father.

5.1.4. A fourth, retrospective, reading: God is the One who brought Abraham out of Ur of the Chaldees by means of Terah. The fourth reading for Terah's departure comes to light as God tells Abraham "I am the Lord who brought you out from Ur of the Chaldees" (15:7).[211] It comes in retrospect, years later, when repeated after Abraham's descent into Egypt and return to Canaan.

Further on in Genesis, there is a change in the way events and causes are perceived. This takes place after Abraham enters the homeland. Suddenly and in retrospect, we become aware that God Himself took Terah out from Ur of the Chaldees (15:7).[212] This verse makes it necessary to reread the story of Terah's departure with his household as it repeats the promise of "this land"[213] to Abraham for the third time. (See 12:7 and 13:14–17.)

a) *God's words in Genesis 15:7: A simultaneous polemic with the stories of the Exodus and of Terah's departure.* To understand God's message to Abraham, it should be interpreted in a broader context. As Todorov says, "There is no utterance without relation to other utterances."[214] My thesis is that God's words, as the narrator presents them, relate at one and the same time to two Bible stories, or rather dialogue and argue with them simultaneously. For the sake of focus, the analogy to the Exodus story will be omitted.[215]

Earth Who Does Good and Never Sins (Jerusalem: President's Residence, 1997), 25. According to Zakovitch, as against the forces trying to save Jacob's honor and place responsibility for his acts on his mother, for example, there is also a force "trying to teach us of the sin of forcing the hour of deliverance, for which Jacob paid in full. Did not God tell Rebekah before her sons' birth, the older shall serve the younger?" (25:23).

211. See Gen 1:2: "...a wind from God sweeping over the water." I propose that "a wind from God" (as in Gen 1:2) swept over the Land, particularly over Ur of the Chaldees, in Gen 11:31.

212. The reader comes to understand Terah and his deeds in the second reading, noting that Terah lived 60 years after Abraham left for Canaan.

213. See Peleg, "Declaration," 145–53.

214. The comparison of Bible texts is from the standpoint of Bakhtin. See Todorov, *Bakhtin*, 60.

215. For more details, see also Peleg, "Who Brought," 22. Gen 15:7 is worded almost identically to Exod 20:2—"I am the Lord your God who brought you out of the Land of Egypt" (cf. Deut 5:6)—save that the departure is from Egypt not from

3. *The Jacob's Dream Story as* Mise en Abyme

b) *The analogy to the story of Terah's departure.* God's words to Abraham (15:7), "I am the Lord who brought you out of Ur of the Chaldees," contradict the previous description of the departure (11:31) as initiated by Terah: "Terah took his son Abram, his grandson Lot...and they set out together for the Land of Canaan..." Who, then, took Abraham from Ur of the Chaldees—Terah or God?

The divine promise of the Land to Abraham in 15:7 is just one of three references to his departure for the Land of Canaan. The differences amongst them raise another question as to whether Abraham was taken from Ur of the Chaldees or from Haran. We focus on the first question, which will help answer the second one.

Can these differences be resolved, or do they stem from three different literary sources or traditions[216] relating to Abraham's journey to Canaan? I see them as not contradictory but complementary, indicating the complexity of the story.

Zakovitch's proposal regarding the link between the three references is reasonable, since Gen 15:7 does not represent a tradition that is additional to and independent from 11:31 and 12:1–5.[217] Rather, it links to and suggests the story in 11:31.

As I see it, 15:7 looks back on hitherto unknown material regarding God's intervention in Abraham's departure from Ur of the Chaldees for Canaan. Polak has discerned such a view "in certain biblical stories that in a series of events repeat events mentioned before."[218]

That text opens a window[219] onto events already described in 11:31. It reveals the Lord acting within events, and determines that not Terah but God Himself took Abraham from Ur of the Chaldees. More precisely, while Terah took his son Abraham, he did so because of God's initiative, even if neither Terah nor the reader were exposed to the knowledge that God initiated Terah's departure was aware of it.

Three other texts support the theory that God took Abraham out from Ur. Two are entirely explicit, while the third relies largely on style and context:

Ur. On the similarity between Exodus and Abraham's departure, see Van Seters, *Abraham*, 216, 264. See also Westermann, *Genesis*, 243.

216. As posited by source critics. See Thompson, *Historicity*, 310.

217. Zakovitch, "Exodus from Ur," 439: "The third tradition on the grace shown to Abraham—taking him from Ur of the Chaldees—is simply the continuation of a now hidden/lost tradition."

218. Polak, *Narative*, 167, provides examples.

219. One recalls the divine stratum revealed in the Job framework story: "One day the divine beings presented themselves before the Lord, and the Adversary (*hasatan*) came along with them" (Job 1:6).

In Gen 24:7, Abraham himself tells the senior servant of his household: "The Lord, the God of heaven, who took me from my father's house and from my native land, who promised me on oath saying, I will assign this land to your offspring..." The word "took" here seems to link with "And Terah took Abram his son" in 11:31. However, there Terah took Abram, while in ch. 24, God took him.

In Neh 9:7, "You are the Lord God who chose Abram, who brought him out of Ur of the Chaldees..."—that is, God and not Terah did so.

The Ten Commandments too reinforce "I the Lord" (not Terah) in Gen 15:7, as shown by comparing it with that of the Commandments (Exod 20:6; Deut 5:6). Both state: "I am the Lord your God who brought you out of the Land of Egypt, out of the house of bondage," identifying and arguing with what follows: "You shall have no other gods beside Me." Thus "I am the Lord your God" appears to dispute with "other gods," as if to say, I not other gods am your God.

c) *Summarizing the readings regarding Terah's journey.* There are four readings as to why Terah left Ur of the Chaldees. These arise because:

1. The terse and economic Bible story omits details.
2. Terah is a secondary character in the story.
3. Terah left because his son Haran died "before his father," which allows for two readings—one stressing that Terah is a bereaved father, the other that Haran died before Terah's eyes, stressing the tragic circumstances of the son's death.
4. It was God who took Terah and his household out of Ur of the Chaldees, as indicated in 15:7.

There are further readings, both of which are connected with Terah's death and the location of that death outside of the Promised Land of Canaan. According to one reading, Terah did not reach Canaan because he died in Haran; according to the other, he died there as punishment for deciding not to go on to Canaan.

An additional reason discloses the significant feature of double causality in the biblical story. Since that concept is so important here, it is further exemplified with the story of the sale of Joseph. The analogy, it seems to me, elucidates and explains both stories.

d) *Joseph and his brothers: double causation in retrospect.* Parallels to the formulations of Abraham's journey from Ur of the Chaldees to Canaan are found in the account of Joseph's journey from Canaan into Egypt. In the Abraham story, the question is who removed Abraham from Ur, while in the Joseph story it is who sold Joseph to whom.

As the story begins, Judah says to his brothers, "Come, let us sell him to the Ishmaelites... His brothers agreed" (Gen 37:26–27). Later, "When the Midianite traders passed by they pulled Joseph up out of the pit. They sold Joseph for twenty pieces of silver to the Ishmaelites, who brought Joseph to Egypt" (v. 28). The Hebrew is unclear as to who "pulled up," "raised" and "sold" Joseph to the Ishmaelites. Was it the brothers, as suggested by v. 27, or the Midianites, according to v. 28? Furthermore, v. 28, and even more explicitly 39:1, state that the Ishmaelites brought Joseph to Egypt: "When Joseph was taken down into Egypt, a certain Egyptian, Potiphar, a courtier of Pharaoh and his chief steward, bought him from the Ishmaelites, who had brought him there." But this is not congruent with 37:36: "The Midianites, meanwhile, sold him in Egypt to Potiphar, a courtier of Pharaoh and his chief steward." Who, then, sold Joseph to Potiphar?

Here as in the Abraham story, one asks if the differences can be reconciled, or if they indicate different literary sources.

Towards the story's end, when Joseph meets his brothers and identifies himself to them, he tells them, retrospectively, that God had a hand in the matter: "*I am Joseph* your brother, he whom you sold into Egypt. Now, do not be distressed or reproach yourselves because you have sold me hither: it was to save life that *God sent me ahead of you*" (45:4–5). Only in retrospect does Joseph disclose the divine element in the story of his sale, to his brothers and to the reader.

Such points find expression not only in the Jacob and the Joseph stories, but in others relating to the Patriarchs throughout Genesis. Shapira points out:

> Reading for multiple meanings helps disclose the complex strata of the story. Thus, for instance, in the episode of the conflict between Jacob and Esau there are two parallel levels: the revealed and the concealed one. The first, generally identified in the first reading of the text and the actuality of its characters, is on the human level...operating by earthly rules. The other level, however, reveals the theological depth of the story...a divine plan.[220]

Greenstein too calls our attention to the double significance of 37:28.[221] In his opinion, the differing versions (38:21, 28, 36; 39:1; 45:4–5) confuse the account of what in fact happened:

> By blurring the human factors leading to the enslavement of Joseph, the narrative sharpens our image of the divine factor in bringing it about. The brothers, who had denied divine providence by belittling Joseph's dream

---

220. Shapira, "Multiple Meanings," 257 nn. 31–34.
221. Greenstein, "Joseph," 114–25.

(which in the ancient Near East in general and in our narrative in particular have the status of revelations), learn that Joseph's descent to Egypt was part of God's larger design… An equivocal reading of the sale of Joseph leads to the realization that, in the view of our narrative, it is not crucial to our understanding of the story whether the brothers sold Joseph to the Ishmaelites or the Midianites kidnapped him. It is important, rather, to perceive that the descent of Joseph to Egypt and his subsequent rise to power there reveal divine providence in history.[222]

We can conclude, then, that God's word to Abraham after he reached Canaan (15:7), like what Joseph said to his brothers in 45:4–5, is designed to state in retrospect the place and role of God in Abraham's journey to the Land of Canaan.

1) *Formulations of double causation in Bible stories.* From the analogy with the story of Joseph on the way from Canaan to Egypt and its message, we return to Abraham's journey to Canaan, specifically to identifying the two components behind the events. The first is human, in the form of his biological father Terah, and the second is God, his spiritual father, revealed in retrospect only after the journey.

One may recognize double causation in, for instance, the dividing of the Red Sea: "Then *Moses* held out his arm over the sea and (or *but*) *the Lord* drove back the sea with a strong east wind all that night, and turned the sea into dry ground" (Exod 14:21). That is, while Moses held his arm or his staff, God with the east wind performed the miracle and dried the sea. In Hebrew, the *waw*[223] prefixed to "Lord" can function in a contrastive ("but") as well as conjuctive sense ("and").[224]

---

222. Ibid., 123.
223. Thus, e.g., the visitors tell Lot: "Whom else have you here, sons-in-law, your sons and daughters, or anyone else that you have in the city—bring them out of the place. For we are about to destroy it" (Gen 19:12–13). Later, however, "The Lord rained upon Sodom and Gomorrah sulfurous fire from the Lord out of heaven" (19:24). The link between God's angels' responsibility for destroying Sodom (in v. 12), and that of God himself appears in v. 13, where the angels tell Lot: "because the outcry against them before the Lord has become so great that He has sent us to destroy it" (19:13b). The angels are God's messengers, acting in His name.
224. The division of labor, as it were, between God and Moses, or mortal man in general, has been likened to a teacher and pupil standing by the chalkboard, the pupil with chalk in hand. The teacher guides the hand so that it writes something in accordance with his own will. Who, then, wrote on the chalkboard—the teacher or the pupil? There is no attempt here to depict the complexity of the biblical human–God relationship, so that despite its great importance, the issue has no place in our discussion.
There is a similar metaphor in Isa 45:1: "Thus aid the Lord to Cyrus, His appointed one—*whose right hand He has grasped*, treading down nations before

3. *The Jacob's Dream Story as* Mise en Abyme

2) *Why is God's role related only in retrospect?* If the divine stratum is so important, why is it not stated specifically at the beginning of the story? Why even does Gen 11:31 not declare that God initiated the departure? Amit's answer is that God's role in the biblical story reflects beliefs and opinions contained in it: "The tendency to stress the concept of a distant divinity, in which the Temple is where His name, not God Himself dwells, leads to different confrontations within the story as well. If God remains in heaven, then He must be removed from the characters on stage."[225] Closer to our present theme, Amit adds: "Thus arose the stories in which God remains behind the scenes, and intervenes indirectly *through dreams* or prophets." Or as in our story, He appears in a retrospective account. Amit continues:

> God's appearance in the stories has a clear purpose—to show how He rules the world: intervenes or looks on, from within or from above, acts or simply watches. The more anthropomorphic and concrete the perception, the more God is pictured as intervening, dwelling among us and taking action. The greater the tendency to distance Him from the human sphere and not to attribute flesh and blood characteristics to Him, the more God is depicted as watching from above.[226]

To me, God was made known to the protagonist and the reader as directing events only in retrospect. This represents a middle point between the anthropomorphic and concrete view and the one that distances God from the human sphere.

3) *Conclusion*. The versions of the story of Abraham's departure for the Promised Land express the narrator's view, designed to teach two important points. One is that Abraham's point of departure is not as important as his destination: whether he left from Ur of the Chaldees or from Haran is of less consequence than that he left in order to reach Canaan. The second point, now central, is that the first reading might indicate that Terah left on his own initiative (11:31);[227] retrospectively (15:7), it becomes clear that the initiative was God's, to bring Abraham to the Promised Land. Terah, like Joseph's brothers or the Ishmaelites in

---

him…" This example of a division of labor between God and Cyrus also helps to understand "I the Lord." This verbal combination, which appears eight times in Isa 45, directs us to the main point that God is identified within a polemic.

225. Amit, *Reading*, 88.
226. Ibid., 89.
227. Personal initiative is not necessarily to Terah's credit, as a modern reader might suppose. On the contrary, absence of God's assent might be negatively interpreted, even if no openly critical word was expressed. Gitay, "Geography," 206, examines Terah's act in the light of earlier human initiatives in Genesis.

the Joseph story, or like Assyrian (Isa 10:5) and/or Cyrus in Isa 45, was an instrument in God's hands.

The three descriptions of Abraham's departure for Canaan (11:31; 12:1–5; 15:7) have, I trust, convinced readers that the differences do not necessarily derive from different literary sources, but show double causation at work within the story. This explains the seeming contradictions, and reflects the narrator's view recognizing divine intervention, even retrospectively, in human affairs.

5.2. *"Abram Went Down to Egypt" (12:10)*

5.2.1. *Abraham the first emigrant (*yored*): two readings of Genesis 12:10.* Abraham the Patriarch, the first immigrant, *'oleh* (going up) to the Promised Land, was also the first emigrant, *yored* (going down).[228] Is this emigrant of the Promised Land a problem for the narrator?

Genesis 12:10 states: "Abram went down to Egypt to sojourn there, for the famine was severe in the land." Two readings are possible due to hidden tensions between two seemingly contradictory forces. The first seems to explain and excuse Abraham's descent, the second criticizes it. They are intertwined, and so sensitive, attentive reading[229] is required to distinguish between them. A second look reveals the two readings as seemingly contradictory, because both, uncomfortable about Abraham's descent, confront it differently. While the first attempts to excuse and explain the undesired act, the second disapproves of it. The first seems to soften the criticism of Abraham's descent from the Promised Land in the second.

The narrator, I think, experiences discomfort and perhaps even shame[230] regarding the descent into Egypt, which leads to the need both to justify and to excuse, and to a sense of anger and censure.

a) *The first reading explains and justifies Abraham's descent into Egypt.* Verse 12 begins by describing, and so emphasizing, the famine, explaining why Abraham had to leave. The narrator appears to have enlisted several literary techniques to this end. For example, the verse is structured in a "closed" ring structure: a, b, b', a'.

---

228. I have since learned that A. B. Yehoshua wrote similarly; see his *Normalcy*, 31.

229. It is worth repeating that besides discerning the two readings, their link and its contribution to understanding the story must be examined and understood. The story itself includes and encourages two readings, independent of the reader's arbitrary literary decision.

230. K. A. Deurloo, "Narrative Geography in the Abraham Cycle," in *In Quest of the Past: Studies on Israelite Religion, Literature and Prophetism* (ed. A. S. van der Woude; OtSt 26; Leiden: Brill, 1990), 54.

a	There was a famine in the Land	
b	And Abram went down into Egypt	
b'	to sojourn there	
a'	for the famine was severe in the Land	

Thus the verse is within an *inclusio* framework that opens and closes by describing the famine, which creates a sense of stifling. It is meant to stress the famine,[231] which is described at its second mention as "severe."

As *a'*, "for the famine was severe in the Land," explains the famine in *a*, so "sojourn" in *b'* explains and softens "went down into Egypt" in *b*, especially the verb *vayered*, "and/but went down."[232] That is, Abraham went down temporarily[233] "to sojourn" there as a stranger[234] because of "a famine in the Land." As in the other links, the famine in *a* is designed to justify the descent from the Land in *b*.[235] The very need for justification indicates a negative attitude to Abraham's act.

b) *The second reading as criticism of Genesis 12:10.*

1) *Two readings of* gur—*sojourn and permanent settlement.* According to the first reading,[236] the word *gur* it means to sojourn for a time,

---

231. Bar-Efrat, *Design*, 26–27; The double use of "famine" as repetition is another literary device for emphasis. So we note that "in the Land" is used twice, reinforced by contrast with Egypt, mentioned the second time indirectly by "there."

232. As "there" refers to Egypt, so "sojourn" refers to "went down."

233. See "גור," BDB 157 as reside or sojourn somewhere temporarily; Kellermann, "גור," *TDOT* 2:439; Y. Dor, *Were the Foreign Wives Actually Expelled? The Separation Issue During the Return to Zion* (Jerusalem: Magnes, 2006), 15. She exemplifies the temporary quality in the root *gur* by comparing "the land you sojourn in" to "an everlasting holding" in God's promise to Abraham (17:8), which she regards as diametrically opposed.

234. I. L. Seeligman, "*Ger*," *EB* 2:546: "In the Bible the root *gwr* signifies living outside the native land"; Gitay, "Geography," 212–13: "The Hebrew verb *gur* signifies the stranger's status (see Gen 19:9)."

235. Drought and resulting famine were part of the Patriarchs' lives on the frontier of the desert. Significant for our purposes is how the biblical story reflects the way the people themselves saw famine. See S. E. Loewenstamm, "Measure for Measure," *EB* 4:840–46. Loewenstamm points to Deut 11:13–17, contrasting plentiful harvests as the result of keeping God's commandments, with terrible drought to follow as His wrath against disobedience. Thus famine there in Deuteronomy is God's punishment for sin, or a trial of faith, as in Job and the binding of Isaac (22:1). Neither issue, however, seems to apply specifically in the stories of the Patriarchs to the famine. The Patriarchs descent and return seems to apply to it.

236. See n. 233, above.

and according to the second, it means to settle permanently. Gitay[237] notes that it may signify permanence, as in 2 Sam 4:3, "where they have sojourned to this day," and in Jer 35:7. Moreover, God tells Isaac, "Sojourn in this land" (26:3 KJV) in relation to Canaan, understood as a reference to permanent habitation there.

In this reading, although Abraham is said to have gone down into Egypt because of the famine, it was not "until better times" but permanently, supporting the critical view. Additionally, "there" referring to Egypt indicates distance and alienation—opposite of "here" in the Land—suggesting that the narrator emphasizes and prefers the latter. *The ring structure* beginning and ending with "in the country" supports such a reading.

2) *Juxtaposition expresses criticism of Abraham (12:10 and 12:1).* As Jacob is seen to have divine approval (46:3–4) whenever he left the Land, so one assumes that its absence in Abraham's case is concealed criticism. The juxtaposition of Abraham's descent into Egypt and the previous episode where God orders him to go forth to the Land of Canaan (12:1) reinforces the assumption. Criticism of the descent into Egypt is highlighted by "Go forth from your native land, and from your father's house to the land that I will show you" (12:1).

In his book *Inner-Biblical Interpretation*,[238] Zakovitch also examines the proximity of texts. Further, in an article, Zakovitch notes, "The placement of two texts one after the other is designed to influence our reading of them,"[239] and may clarify the narrator's intent[240] for the reader. What, then, is shown by the juxtaposing two texts, one stating that Abraham goes to the unknown land of Canaan in absolute obedience to God (12:1–9), and the other that Abraham leaves that country because of the severe famine (12:10–20)?

In Zakovitch's opinion, "Abram's disregarding of God and his impulsive decision to go to Egypt at once, after God brought him to the promised land, is considered a failure by the editor, for which his descendants will have to pay by enslavement in Egypt."[241]

---

237. Gitay, "Geography," 213–14.
238. Zakovitch, *Inner-Biblical Interpretation*, 9: "In 'Inner-Biblical Interpretation' we refer to the light one biblical text sheds on another—whether as regards the close or remote context, or whether to adapt the text to the commentator's beliefs and opinions."
239. Zakovitch, "Juxtaposition," 509. Zakovitch prefers the terms "editor" or "editors" to "narrator."
240. Ibid., 511.
241. Ibid., 518.

Nahmanides too regards Abraham's descent into Egypt, even because of the famine, as a sin for which the children of Israel will later suffer: "His (Abram's) departure from the land to which he was previously ordered, because of the famine, is a sin he committed. For God in famine will redeem from death, and for this act upon his seed was decreed exile in the Land of Egypt under Pharaoh." Nahmanides also hints at juxtaposition when he notes "the land to which he was previously ordered," apparently referring to "Go forth...to the land that I will show you" (12:1–3).[242]

Juxtaposition also raises the question as to why Abraham, whom God spoke to twice (12:1, 7), does not cry out asking Him what to do.[243] Instead, he gets up and leaves the Promised Land (12:7), contradicting the previous order to go there.

c) *The meaning of "and Abram went down to Egypt" (Genesis 12:10).* Research is thoroughly familiar with the view that "went down" reflects criticism.[244] Criticism is expressed in the choice of that verb rather than, for example, simply "went."

α) *Three possible readings of "went down" (*yarad*).*[245] There are several readings of that verb in 12:10:

1. The first reading assumes that "went down" signifies Abraham's *geographical route into Egypt.* One descends on the map to travel south. Egypt is at the bottom of the map, so to get there from Canaan one descends. It is simply a verb of motion indicating direction.
2. The second reading assumes the verb was chosen for *topographical* reasons, to indicate Abraham's route from a high place in Canaan to a lower one in Egypt.[246]

---

242. Nahmanides, *Torat Haim*, 156. Gitay, "Geography," 211–12, refers to the literary link between the two: 12:10, which tells of Abraham's descent, opposes 12:1, which tells of Abraham going up to Canaan.

243. Consider Abraham vis-à-vis Isaiah: "O disloyal sons...who set out to go down to Egypt without asking me" (Isa 30:1–2).

244. See Nahmanides, *Torat Haim*, 200, cf. 156. See Y. Zakovitch and A. Shinan, *Abram and Sarai in Egypt: Genesis 12:10–20 in Ancient Translations and in Early Jewish Literature* (RPJSI 2; Jerusalem: The Hebrew University, 1983); Deurloo, "Narrative Geography," 48–62; idem, "Way of Abraham," 95–112. See also Gitay, "Geography," 205–16. Such criticism on Abraham for going down to Egypt is not new. Our research points out the tendentious choice of *yarad* expressing criticism, thus supporting a second reading.

245. The verb *yarad* appears 380 times in the Bible: 307 times in Qal form, twice in Hiphil, in the causative form (an active one), and six times in Hophal (a passive form).

3. The third reading assumes that "went down" appears here in the *metaphorical* sense that seems to regard Abraham's journey to Egypt as a negative act.

The first two readings contain no value judgments, while the third regards the journey into Egypt negatively. Given the widespread metaphorical use of "went down" in negative contexts in the Bible, it can reasonably be assumed in this case. I propose that its use instead of the more simple "went," reveals criticism of the descent from the Promised Land.

The first two readings are reasonable at first sight. "Went down" is simply a technical term related to geography and topography, especially when the land is compared to a map. G. R. Driver and others assert that in the Bible every southward journey is a descent.[247] With that, as regards leaving the Promised Land, "went down" is used largely in connection with Egypt[248] to the south.

It is also logical to relate "going down" for journeying south and "going up" for northward travel to the position of north and south at the bottom and top on modern-day maps.[249] This was not always so. Since placing the north at the top of the map follows from the use of the

---

246. G. Mayer, "ירד," *TDOT* 6:317; Y. Keel, *The Book of Genesis* (Daat Mikra; Jerusalem: Mosad Harav Kook, 1997), 336, states: "Since the settled part of Egypt (the Nile Valley and the Delta) are lower than the land of Canaan...'and Abraham went up' we have already explained that every departure from Egypt to the land [of Canaan] is called 'going up' in the text and every departure from there to Egypt is 'going down,' while for departure for any other land—Aram Naharayim for example—the texts uses 'go' (24:10; 28:10)." See section 5.3.1 for a discussion of "went up (from Babylon)" in the time of Ezra and Nehemiah.

247. G. R. Driver, "Went Up," 74–77; "ירד," BDB 432; Mayer, "ירד," *TDOT* 6:315-22.

248. "Going down" to Egypt appears 26 times in the Bible. Of these, 20 are in Genesis, while 18 occur in the Joseph stories: 37:25; 39:1; 42:2–3, 38; 43:4–5, 7, 15, 20, 22; 44:21, 23, 26; 45:9, 13; 46:3, 4. It appears in connection with Abraham only in 12:10 and once with Isaac (26:2). Outside Genesis it appears six times: Exod 3:8; Num 20:15; Deut 10:22; 26:5; Josh 24:4 and Isa 52:4. Additionally, that verb is used in connection with Philistine cities: Judg 14:19 ("He went down to Ashkelon"); 1 Sam 13:20 ("so all the Israelites had to go down [to = *el* in Hebrew] the Philistines," in the Septuagint and in the Targum of Jonathan, "the land of the Philistines"; there may be haplography = dropping *el* [= to] from Israel), Amos 6:2. See "ירד," BDB 432, item 1d, in the sense of going down to Egypt.

249. See C. H. Brown, "Where Do Cardinal Direction Terms Come From?," *Anthropological Linguistics* 25 (1983): 135. He sees a Western prejudice in the ubiquitous aligning of north with the top of map. His reasoning is based on modern languages and the use of the magnetic compass to identify the north, so is not relevant to the biblical times.

3. *The Jacob's Dream Story as* Mise en Abyme

magnetic compass, it could have begun only in the fourteenth century C.E.![250] We are left to ponder, therefore, what was done in ancient times.

β) *Directional terms in the Bible: how were they determined?* O'Connor,[251] basing himself on Brown's research,[252] notes four criteria for determining the principal biblical terms denoting direction.[253]

The first is cosmological, using east, the direction from which the sun rises, and west,[254] from which the sun sets.

The second makes use of atmospheric features, as in "the whole remnant of thee will I scatter to all the winds" (Ezek 5:10 KJV).[255] The "east wind" is a frequent verbal combination for directions as in "Does a wise man…fill his belly with the *east wind*?" (Job 15:2).[256]

The third criterion makes use of general directional terms like "above," "below," "before," "behind," "left" and "right," with the place of the rising sun as the point of departure. The Hebrew word for "forward," *qedma*, is the direction of the rising sun, the east,[257] so that the biblical Eastern Sea is apparently the Dead Sea. The Mediterranean in biblical Hebrew is called "the sea behind,"[258] as in "In that day, fresh

---

250. Y. Shimoni, "Navigation," *EH* 24:930, explains that a Viking device from the eighth to tenth centuries C.E., based on a groove carved into the thwart of the ship to locate the North Star, preceded the magnetic compass.

251. M. O'Connor, "Cardinal Direction Terms in Biblical Hebrew," *Semitic Studies in Honor of Wolf Leslau on the Occasion of His Eighty-fifth Birthday*, vol. 2 (ed. A. S. Kaye; Wiesbaden: O. Harrassowitz, 1991), 1143.

252. Brown, *Direction Terms*, 121–61.

253. See B. S. Childs, "Orientation," *IDB* 3:608–9. Childs presents criteria that he calls "some methods of orientation that developed historically before the discovery of the compass: a) basic directions; b) local geography; c) solar—the sun; d) "polar orientation" that came into use only with the invention of the compass.

254. The Bible contains additional terms for this criterion to indicate the "east," for instance "(Now) the sun was going out upon (*yatsa'*) the earth" (Gen 19:23 Fox; see also Judg 5:31; Isa 13:10), and to indicate the west, for instance "at the setting-time (*erev*) when the sun comes in (*bo'*)" (Deut 16:6 Fox; see also Exod 22:25; Josh 8:29; 10:27) and in Jacob's Dream "for the sun (*ba'*) had come in" (Gen 28:11 Fox); It should be noted that "evening," *erev*, or in Akkadian *erebu*, means "enter" (see "ערב," BDB 787), i.e., the sun enters (into the Mediterranean Sea). That leads to the meaning of the term "west," *ma'arav* in Hebrew.

255. Also "I shall bring four winds against Elam from the four quarters of heaven" (Jer 49:36)

256. See O'Connor, "Cardinal Direction," 1143 n. 13.

257. I. Efal, "*Qedem*," *EB* 7:26; "קדם," BDB 869, "front" (before) the opposite of behind *ahor*; see, e.g., "You hedge me before and behind (*ahor*)" (Ps 139:5).

258. For "behind," *ahor*, as a Hebrew synonym for "the west," see Isa 9:11: "Aram from the east (*qedem*) and Philistia from the west (*ahor*)." See also Ps 139:5; Job 23:8.

water shall flow from Jerusalem, part of it to the *qadmomi* and part of it to the Western Sea *aharon*..." (Zech 14:8; see also Deut 11:24; 34:2; Joel 2:20).

The ancients, looking east,[259] saw the Dead Sea before them and the Mediterranean behind them, with the north to the left and the south to the right.[260] Thus "left" indicated the "north," as in "...he pursued them as far back as Hobah, which is north[261] ('left,' *smol* in Hebrew) of Damascus" (Gen 14:15). Addition corroboration is found in the Arabic for north, *shimal*. To the "right"[262] (*yemin, teman* in Hebrew) was the south (Deut 3:27; Hab 3:3), opposite the "left" or "north" (Gen 13:9, 14; Exod 26:18; Isa 21:2; 40:24; Eccl 11:3).

All four directions appear in Job 23:8–9:

> But if I go East (*qedem*)—He is not there;
> West (*ahor*), I do not perceive Him;
> North (*smol*)—since He is concealed, I do not behold Him;
> South (*yamin*)—He is hidden and I cannot see Him.

The fourth criterion comprises directional terms based on topographical features in Canaan,[263] such as mountain, region, or sea. The "north (mountain)"[264] represents north; "south land,"[265] the south, and "sea," the west.

---

259. M. Weinfeld, *Olam Hatanach: Deuteronomy* (ed. G. Galil; Tel Aviv: Davidson-Atai, 1994), 107.
260. O'Connor, "Cardinal Direction," 1144 n. 15, writes: "The model of the land as human being created such metaphors as *Tabbur-erets* (navel of the earth)." See Judg 9:37; Ezek 38:12.
261. See Klein, *Genesis*, 106. On "left," *smol*, meaning "north," see also Job 23:9.
262. See "North and South (*yamin*) You created them" (Ps 89:13). Cf. also 1 Sam 23:19.
263. Brown, "Direction Terms," 138.
264. See, e.g., M. Garsiel's commentary on Isa 14:14 in *Isaiah*, 79–80: "The king of Babylon's bragging is in Canaanite mythological terms. He would establish himself in the holy mountain in the north, the seat of *Baal* son of *El*, father of the gods in Ugarit mythology (*tsafan* in Ugaritic), identified today with Jebel Arka (the bald mountain) in the Turkish border... Scholars estimate that that the Canaanites began to identify mountain names by their direction, so that the abstract geographical definition *north* replaced the ancient term *left, smol*. The north mountain was a ritual center for the god Baal, and hence Baal of the North in Assyrian documents."
265. The Negeb indicates a region (Gen 20:1; 24:62); or the southern part of the country, according to the context, a distinction important in translation. For instance, though *negbah* is translated as "south," in Gen 13:1, when Abraham "went up into the Negeb" from Egypt it would have been a geographical error to translate "Negeb" as "south." Of course, the Land of Israel was, as now, north of Egypt.

3. *The Jacob's Dream Story as* Mise en Abyme

Most significantly, the point of orientation is in fact the east,[266] where the sun rises, not the north.[267] The English word "orientation"[268] derives from the Latin *oriens*, meaning "east." One assumes a causal element in the similarity between the two languages as to the origin of that particular word.

Additional support for *east* as the primary biblical direction lies in the frequency of "east" appearing first whenever the four winds of heaven[269] are named. "East" is mentioned first in seven of the 14 instances, while on only four occasions is "north" given first.[270] In describing the tribes' inheritances in Joshua, too, the east is the point of departure.[271] The tribal borders mentioned by Joab the military commander in David's time begin with Moab and Gilead, which are *easterly* locations (2 Sam 24:4–8).

Decisive proof of the importance of the east in determining direction lies in the Madaba Map, the earliest one that depicts the Land of Israel.[272]

---

266. Y. Aharoni, *Atlas Carta for the Biblical Period* (vol. 1 of the *Atlas Carta for the History of the Land of Israel*; Jerusalem: Carta, 1972), 11, writes: "In our hands there is no ancient map from the biblical period. If there were, we could assume that it faced east because the Bible uses *qedmah* or *qadimah* only in the sense of east, *ahor or aharon* is west, right is south and left is east." Benjamin in the south land is the southernmost of Rachel's tribes.

267. M. Harel, "*Qedmah*—South or East?," *Mada: Popular Science Magazine for All* 25 (1981): 9, writes that the essential need for orientation within the village, the city and uninhabited spaces led the ancients in Bible times to use first and foremost the sun, rising in the east, for this purpose. So did the other Semitic peoples.

268. R. Reich, "Gazing Forward, to the East...," *Ladaat* 20 (1989): 33; D. Pines, "Orientation," *DFWH* 24.

269. The seven instances are: "east, west, north and south" (1 Chr 9:24); "east...north...south...west" (26:14–16, 17–18); "east and west...north...south" (Zech 14:4); "east...west...north...south" (Isa 43:5–6); "east to the east...south... west...north" (Num 2:3, 10, 18, 25; Josh 19:13); "east...south...west... north" (Num 35:5); "east...north...south...west" (Ezek 42:16–19).

270. "North and south, east and west" (Gen 13:14); "north...south...east... west" (Ezek 48:16–17); "north...west...south...east..." (1 Kgs 7:25 = 2 Chr 4:4).

271. Harel, "*Qedmah*," 9: "The Bible calls drawing a map 'writing down a description of the land' (*tikhtevu*, Josh 18:6–8; 19:12–13)." Indeed, in mapping the inheritances of the seven tribes—Benjamin, Simeon, Zebulon, Issachar, Asher, Naphtali and Dan (Josh 19:1–40)—the boundary descriptions begin in the east and end in the west. The same is true for the three other tribes: Judah, Ephraim and Manasseh. Maps of Reuben's and Gad's inheritances across the Jordan (ch. 13) were also described from the east.

272. See Y. Hoffman, *Olam Hatanach: Jeremiah* (Tel Aviv: Davidson-Atai, 1994), 154, notes that this is the most ancient map of *Erets Israel*.

There too the east, not the north, is at the top.²⁷³ During the centuries during which the Bible was composed, and indeed for many centuries that followed, "north" was not used as the primary directional reference point. Instead, *orient*ation was to the east—or the *Orient*—where the sun rises.

This fundamental and important difference in spatial/geographical/topographical understanding supports the thesis that going east, not north, entailed "ascent" on the (psychological) maps of the ancients. Concomitantly, going west, not south, was "descent."

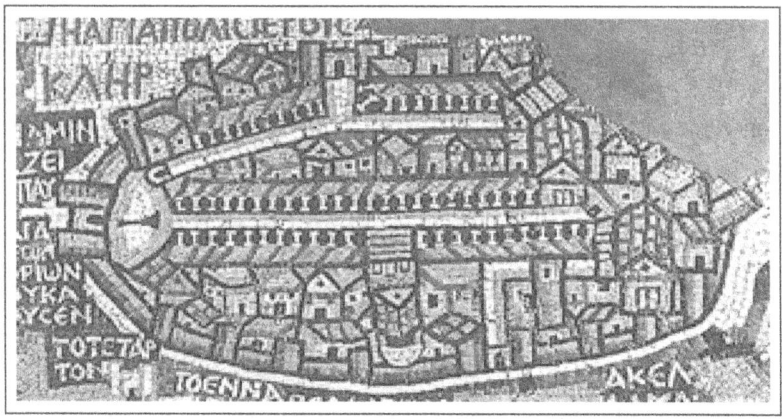

The Madaba Map
(with the East appearing at the top of the map)

Hence the prevailing idea found in Bible scholarship²⁷⁴—namely, that "Abram went down to Egypt" is simply a technical statement about going south, because Egypt is south of Canaan—is erroneous. The biblical understanding of direction meant that to "go down" meant to go west, not south, for the east was at the top of the "ideological/mental map."

273. Harel, "*Qedmah*," 11: "The Madaba map is considered the most ancient one to describe *Erets Israel*...[created in] Byzantine times in the sixth century C.E. It is to be seen in a mosaic in the floor of the church at Mount Nebo, northeast of the Dead Sea. The top of the map faces east, *qadimah* or *qedmah*, the bottom the Mediterranean Sea. The right is the south and the left, the north. Similarly, maps of the world from Roman and medieval times are oriented to the east, *oriens* inscribed at the top and Jerusalem at the center." Aharoni, *Atlas*, 11, explains that this map's main purpose is to "describe *Erets Israel* according to the Bible." See also M. Avi-Yonah, "The Madaba Map," *EB* 4:839–40, mentioning that the mosaic map was discovered in 1884, oriented to the east.

274. See "ירד," BDB 432; Mayer, "ירד," *TDOT* 6:315–22; G. R. Driver, "Went Up," 75–77.

If the present study correctly asserts that "went down to Egypt" cannot be a technical statement of direction, then it has a derived, metaphorical meaning expressing a sense of negativity, as evident in many biblical instances. Its inherent value judgment is more about Abraham's leaving the Land (12:1, 7) than about his destination, Egypt.

γ) *Three readings of* yarad *summarized.* The term *yarad* in Gen 12:10 is used metaphorically, expressing a critical negative attitude to Abraham's journey to Egypt. Even if it is said to be used only technically, for a journey to the south or the southwest, or for a topographical descent from Canaan to Egypt, that still does not rule out an additional negative reading. Going down to Egypt means going away from the Land of Canaan, and away from God's command (12:1), away from God in the literal and metaphorical sense. No wonder it is perceived as negative and disturbing.[275]

Comparing it to God's instruction to Isaac in a similar situation, "Do not go down to Egypt" (26:2), enhances that perception.

δ) *Abraham goes down to Egypt and Isaac is told "Do not go down" (26:2).* Verse 10:12 opens with the first of three versions of the "She's my sister" stories, reflecting discomfort over Abraham's descent into Egypt. In the second story, descent is not mentioned. Abraham simply "journeyed to the region of the Negeb and settled between Qadesh and Shur…sojourning in Gerar" (20:1).

The narrator's purpose in ch. 20 appears to be, as it was vis-à-vis other problems in 12:10–20, to mitigate the severity of Abraham's descent from the Land. If so, then ch. 20 may support the first excusing and justifying reading. In ch. 20 Abraham not only does not leave the country, but acts on the divine command, "Up, walk about the land" (13:17).[276]

Criticism of Abraham for descending into Egypt becomes sharper in the third version, when God commands Isaac, "Do not go down into Egypt" (Gen 26:2), which apparently stands in polemic dialogue[277] with

---

275. Methodologically, the foregoing discussion shows the importance of the reader's knowing how to compare biblical and extra-biblical texts and having sensitivity to the links between them. It seems that without the attempt above to justify the descent with the ring structure of repetition, for example, of the famine in the Land, the naïve reader might not appreciate the descent was negative.

276. Aharoni, *Atlas*, 213–23.

277. This is no initiative of the modern scholar-reader. Hints, concealed or revealed, are found in the writing of the biblical story itself, where they reflect an important element of the story's formulation. The stories interpret, argue with and highlight one another. They function as image and background, black on white. Just as black and white, when compared, define one another, so does each story vis-à-vis the other, encouraging readers to judge how its characters behave.

"Abram went down into Egypt" (12:10). This is reflected in the following table:

Genesis 12:10 (Abraham)	Genesis 26:1–2 (Isaac)
There was a famine in the Land	*There was a* famine *in the Land*
	Aside from the previous famine that occurred in the days of Abraham…
	The Lord appeared to him and said
And Abram *went down* into Egypt	*Do not go down* to Egypt
To sojourn (*gwr*)	Stay (*gwr*)
There	In the Land that I point out to you
The famine was severe in the Land	

Indeed, "aside from the previous famine that occurred in the days of Abraham" (26:1) invites the reader to make comparisons, linking as it does the two stories. When God tells Isaac, "Do not go down to Egypt" (26:2), he and the reader are told that he should not act like his father. The contrast continues. Abraham is said to have gone to sojourn "there" while Isaac is told expressly to stay in "this land" that God points out. The contrast of Abraham and Isaac[278] in their response to famine is clearly a concealed criticism of Abraham, supporting the view gained from the second, critical reading of 12:10. One notes that Isaac, born in the Land (and "bound" there on the altar), never left it in his life.

ε) *Conclusion: the meaning of "And Abram went down to Egypt."* Discussion of Abraham so far has focused on two comparisons: between him and his father Terah, and between him and his son Isaac. While the first revolved around the issue of ascending to the Promised Land, the second related to descent from it. In both there is a hidden dialogue between human and divine initiative. When Terah initiated the departure from Ur of the Chaldees without God's approval it came to a halt at Haran, where he died. Abraham, differently, left by divine command to go to Canaan and reached it. In retrospect, however, it turns out that even Terah's departure too was divinely initiated: "I am the Lord who brought you out of Ur of the Chaldees (15:7).

God's command to Isaac—"do not go down to Egypt" (26:2)—seems addressed not only to the past and to Abraham's descent, but also to the future. We find an echo of this in the divine message to Jacob before he descended into Egypt (46:2), where Jacob receives ad hoc approval,

---

278. Concealed criticism of Abraham's descent into Egypt is perceptible too in Jacob's response to famine. Abraham goes to sojourn, while Jacob sends his sons to procure food in Egypt and return to Canaan with it (Gen 42:1–2). See also Gitay, "Geography," 213.

showing that, without it, leaving the country was forbidden. Abraham's life in Egypt was far from easy and, accepting the idea that leaving the country is itself a transgression, we can say that in Egypt one sin led Abraham to another,[279] until he returned to the Promised Land.

5.2.2. Two readings of the story of Sarah in Pharaoh's house.

a) *Was Israel's ancestress in danger?*[280] *Did Pharaoh touch (*naga'*) Sarai?* We have seen that Abraham's and Sarah's journey from the Promised Land to Egypt—as a result of the famine in the Land—is viewed as descending from the Land. In other words, the narrator sees descent as a negative act. Moreover, we have noted that in the Bible the verb *yarad* ("to descend") bears a negative metaphorical connotation. We shall now show that Abraham—and mainly Sarah—are exposed to dangers which strengthen the message that descending from the Promised Land is a negative and dangerous act.

---

279. Moreover, Abraham in 12:10–20 is described as a liar who abandons his wife and maintains his right to silence when accused by Pharaoh. Why Abraham is portrayed negatively is beyond the scope of this discussion, so suffice it to say that it explained a no less difficult issue: why the Israelites became slaves in Egypt. This seems to be why Nahmanides complained against Abraham for leaving the country, considered a sin, the punishment for which fell upon his descendants enslaved in Egypt. On this issue, see Zakovitch and Shinan, *Abram and Sarai*. On Gen 12:10 as a "mini Exodus," see P. D. Miscall, *The Workings of Old Testament Narrative* (Semeia Studies; Chico, Ca.: Scholars Press, 1983), 42–45. On the perception of exile as punishment, see M. Weinfeld, "Right and Duty: Perception of the Promise in Sources from the First and Second Temple Periods," *Zion* 29 (1984): 115–26; I. Rosenson, "Exile in Haran and the Exile of Generations: Like Fathers, Like Sons," *Annual of Orot Israel College* 1 (1989): 11–24 See below for a discussion of the Patriarchs' route according to the "W-shaped model."

280. This section is based on a paper presented at the International Conference of the SBL in Cambridge, July 2003. In preparing the present version I received assistance and advice from Dr. Nancy Rosenfeld, to whom I express my gratitude. Formative material appearing in this section was first published in Y. I. Peleg, "Was the Ancestress of Israel in Danger? Did Pharaoh Touch Sarai?," *Beit Mikra* 48 (2003): 54–64. Another version appeared under the same title in *ZAW* 118 (2006): 197–208. The section title "Was the Ancestress of Israel in Danger?" reflects the viewpoint of the article. Cf. Fidler, "Dream Theophany," 109–20; K. Koch, "The Ancestress of Israel in Danger," in *The Growth of the Biblical Tradition: The Form-Critical Method* (trans. S. M. Cupitt; New York: Scribner's Sons, 1969), 111–28; R. Polzin, "The Ancestress of Israel in Danger," *Semeia* 3–4 (1975): 81–97. According to Cassuto, *Genesis*, 232, "The triple repetition of saving the ancestresses emphasizes the value and constancy of the Deity's assistance to those loyal to him."

When a grievous famine plagues the Land, Abram and Sarai go down to Egypt. On the way, Abram tells his wife: "Please say that you are my sister" (Gen 12:11). Abram fears that if she is known to be his wife, "They [the Egyptians] will kill me and let you live" (v. 12). We do not know how Sarai responds. Nor does the narrator say what happens to her as a result, but the reason for Abram's request is clear: "that it may go well with me because of you" (v. 13).

Abram's character in this story raises moral questions: he lies; he behaves selfishly, abandoning his wife to the mercy of others;[281] and he does not even try to justify himself and his motives to Pharaoh, who eventually confronts him: "Why did you not tell me that she was your wife? Why did you say 'she is my sister'?" (vv. 18–19).

When Abram and Sarai arrive in Egypt, the Egyptians see "how beautiful the woman[282] Sarai was" (v. 14), "and praised her to Pharaoh" (v. 15). As a result, "the woman was taken into Pharaoh's palace" (v. 15). What if anything happened between Pharaoh and Sarah the Ancestress of Israel? The question has intrigued generations of commentators, modern and ancient.

1) *The repetition as an inner-biblical interpretation.* We note a similar meeting between Sarah and Abraham and a foreign king, this time Abimelech, king of Gerar (Gen 20). The similarity between these two stories, and similarities in both content and language between them and a third one, of Isaac and Rebekah in Gen 26, make comparisons inevitable.

There are several possible reasons. Supporters of source criticism,[283] for example, attribute the story in ch. 12 to the J source, the one in 20:1–18 to the E source, and the story in 26:1–14 to the J source. However, according to Zakovitch and Shinan,[284] who are identified with the school of inner-biblical interpretation, ch. 12 contains the earlier story, while the stories in chs. 20 and 26 are later interpretations of it. I accept their suggestion that ch. 12 contains the earlier version, while the stories in chs. 20 and 26 were meant to interpret and improve the moral characters of the major figures in ch. 12. Two examples should suffice for justification.

---

281. On the idea that "Abraham wishes to prevent Sarah from being raped," see G. Hepner, "Abraham's Incestuous Marriage with Sarah: A Violation of the Holiness Code," *VT* 53 (2003): 143–55.

282. "The woman" appears nine times as a *leitwort* in the story, apparently pointing out the centrality of Sarai.

283. Skinner, *Genesis*; Gunkel, *Genesis*. For more about scholarly attention to the so-called wife–sister texts, see Lipton, "Revisions," 31–47.

284. Zakovitch and Shinan, *Abram and Sarai*, 333.

3. *The Jacob's Dream Story as* Mise en Abyme

First is the handling of the moral issue raised by Abram's lie when he asks Sarai to say she is his sister. This is elegantly solved in 20:12 when Sarai is shown in fact to be Abraham's half-sister, as he tells Abimelech: "And besides, she is in truth my sister, my father's daughter though not my mother's; and she became my wife" (v. 12).

Secondly, and more pertinent to my claim, the story as found in ch. 12 does not state clearly that the king "touched"[285] Sarai, but rather that he took her for his wife. There is, with that, no direct denial that he touched her, and the ambiguous formulation in ch. 12 allows us to conclude that Pharaoh did indeed touch Sarai. In ch. 20, by contrast, there is a clear statement that Abimelech king of Gerar took Sarah (v. 2), but we are immediately informed that God intervened in time: "But God came to Abimelech in a dream by night," telling him "You will die because of the woman that you have taken, because she is a married woman." As a result, and to dispel all doubt and concern, we are told: "Now Abimelech did not approach her" (v. 4).[286]

The juxtaposition between Sarah's stay in Abimelech's house (Gen 20) and the birth of Isaac (Gen 25) led Rashi to interpret the verse thus: "This is the story of Isaac, son of Abraham. Abraham begot Isaac" (Gen 25:19). Again, we have to wonder why the repetition. Why was the narrator not content with "This is the story of Isaac, son of Abraham"?[287] Rashi answers: "When it is written 'Isaac son of Abraham,' there is an

---

285. The use of the verb "touch" has a sexual meaning. Three of its eight occurrences in Genesis (3:3; 12:17; 20:6; 26:11, 29; 28:2; 32:26, 33) are used in the wife–sister stories. Lipton, "Revisions," 44–47, points out the different use in texts 12:17; 20:6 and 26:11. With that, the common denominator is, in my opinion, the extent to which the verb contains sexual connotations. Since this is not always so (e.g. in Ps 105:15, where the parallelism indicates that "touch" = "harm"), the narrator can create tension as to whether the touch is soft though neutral, or physical with sexual intent. This is even more explicit in the third story: "whoever touches this man or his wife shall be put to death" (Gen 26:11).

In this verse Van Seters, *Abraham*, 181, differentiates between Isaac and his wife Rebekah. Van Seters finds word-play based on the dual usage of *naga'*: "there is an interesting use of the verb *naga'* since vis-à-vis a man it means to inflict bodily injury, but regarding a woman it means to approach sexually."

286. Regarding this phrase and the next one, "...That was why I did not let you touch her" (Gen 20:6), Lipton, "Revisions," 44 n. 35, states: "Pairing these two phrases may explain the unusual use of the preposition אל as opposed to the more common one in v. 6. Possibly *el* may indicate the sexual nature of Abimelech's intended 'touch' here."

287. See also in 21:3: "Abraham gave his newborn son, whom Sarah had borne him, the name of Isaac."

implication that 'Abraham begot Isaac,' lest contemporary wiseacres say that Abimelech got Sarah pregnant. Sarah, after all, had lived with Abraham for many years without becoming pregnant; for this reason God made Isaac resemble Abraham in appearance, as a sign that Abraham begot Isaac. Thus it is written 'Isaac son of Abraham' to show that 'Abraham begot Isaac.'"[288]

What happened to the woman Rebekah in the third story (Gen 26)? There is no cause for concern or for divine intervention since Rebekah was not brought to the king's house: "When some time had passed, Abimelech king of the Philistines, looking out of the window, saw Isaac fondling his wife Rebekah" (v. 8). Yet although Rebekah was not taken to the king's house, from what the king says to Isaac we infer a cause for worry. Abimelech demands of Isaac: "What have you done to us! One of the people might have lain with your wife, and you would have brought guilt upon us." In the context of the verb "lie with" Abimelech declares to his people: "Anyone who molests[289] this man or his wife shall be put to death" (v. 11). The verb "touch" used in this story has also been softened. The touching of Sarah has been played down, and is referred to in passing as an afterthought to the touching of Isaac.

This motif is even more attenuated in Ps 105:12–15: "They [Abraham and Isaac and Jacob] were then few in number…wandering from nation to nation, from one kingdom to another. He [God] allowed no one to oppress them… Do not touch my anointed ones, do not harm my prophets." The imperative verb appears in the plural and its object is the Patriarchs—to Abraham, Isaac and Jacob—rather than to the Ancestresses. "Touch," *naga'*, is synonymous here with "oppress" and "harm," with no sexual connotation.

Despite this tendency to attenuation, and the assurance in ch. 20 that nothing "happened" between Abimelech and Sarah, our concern remains, and with it the need to find out whether Pharaoh indeed touched her, as indicated in ch. 12. Moreover, in the light of ch. 20, clearly stating that Abimelech neither touched Sarah nor approached her, the lack of any reference to the issue in ch. 12 is even more surprising. We wonder whether anything happened, and suspect that something did!

---

288. Rashi, on Gen 25:19. In *Tanhuma, Toldot* A, we find: "When Sarah was being thrown back and forth between Pharaoh and Abimelech and became pregnant with Isaac, the peoples of the world would say: 'Can one who is a hundred years old father a son? (Gen 17:17) Perhaps she is pregnant by Abimelech or Pharaoh.'"

289. I prefer Fox's translation: "whoever touches."

3. *The Jacob's Dream Story as* Mise en Abyme 237

2) *Close reading of the story in chapter 12.* To find clues in ch. 12 as to what "really happened" in Pharaoh's palace necessitates *close reading* of the story, from "and the woman was taken into Pharaoh's palace" (12:15). Significantly, Sarai was taken "to Pharaoh's palace," not "to Pharaoh," a formulation meant to comfort the reader who fears for Sarai. Support for this assumption is found in the "and" appended to "she was taken," which can, however, also be understood as "but." Although Pharaoh's ministers praised her beauty to Pharaoh, Sarai was fortunately not taken to him, but merely to his palace.

Verse 16 brings continued cause for concern that Sarai, Israel's Ancestress, may indeed be in danger. At this point her fate hangs in the balance. Yet instead of telling us what happened, the narrator abandons her temporarily in Pharaoh's palace and focuses the verse on Abram, whose situation improved signally after he allowed his wife to be taken from him. Creating suspense is, of course, a common literary-dramatic device.

The next verse opens with *vayenaga'*, "and he was plagued/touched." Who plagued/touched whom? If the subject of the previous verse was Pharaoh, the reader concerned about Sarai might understand that the subject of the current verse is also Pharaoh.[290] At this stage in the reading process, one suspects that what we feared would happen to Sarai has happened—Pharaoh has indeed touched her. Fortunately the passage then reveals to us that Pharaoh did not touch her; rather, he "was touched/plagued" by God: "But the Lord afflicted Pharaoh with mighty plagues" (12:6a). Sarai, moreover, is the reason for them: "on account of Sarai the wife of Abram" (v. 17).

Why did the biblical author choose the root *ng'*, then repeat it twice (v. 17)? His literary genius is revealed by using *ng'* as a concealed literary tool that hints at the Exodus, as Cassuto[291] and others have noted. The root *ng'* also designates the plagues of Egypt (Exod 1:1). But even if the narrator wished to hint at these plagues, why did he choose *nega'im*?

---

290. Note a similar word order, aimed at increasing tension, in the second story (ch. 20). Immediately after we learn that Abimelech "took Sarah" (*vayqah et Sarah*, 20:2), the verb *vayavo* appears (v. 3a). The biblical uses of *vayavo* indicate that besides the "innocent" meaning, "to enter," it may have a sexual connotation. The sensitive reader may now be confused as to how "he entered" should be understood, How relieved we are again (as in 12:17) that the subject is God, who appears to Abimelech in his dream!

291. Cassuto, *Genesis*, 228: "The story of Abram's and Sarai's descent into Egypt surprisingly parallels the later stories at the end of Genesis and the beginning of Exodus, of the descent of the children of Israel into Egypt." Miscall, *Working*, 42–45, terms the story in Gen 12:10–20 "a mini-Exodus."

He could have employed *'otot* ("signs") or *moftim* ("wonders"), used repeatedly to signify the plagues visited on Egypt, as in Exod 12:3: "But I will harden Pharaoh's heart, that I may multiply My signs and wonders in the Land of Egypt." (See also 10:1, 2; 11:9, 10.) The root *ng'* appears only once with the meaning "to plague" in the Exodus stories, but not in plural (the form is *nega'*): "And the Lord said to Moses: 'I will bring but one more plague (*nega'*) upon Pharaoh" (Exod 11:1).

It is my claim that *nega'im* (in Gen 12:17), with its double meaning (as "touched" and as "plagued"), was chosen to denote the punishment God visited on Pharaoh to hint at both the plagues visited on Egypt and Pharaoh's sin against Sarai. There is no specific description of that sin. Did Pharaoh sin by taking Sarai to his palace, or by what he did to her after she was brought to his house? Did he, in other words, sin against her feminine purity? The verb *naga'* hints at this. As a result, the reader swings back and forth between hope and fear for Sarai during her stay in Pharaoh's house, this pendulum effect appearing to reflect Sarai's own feelings as well. Just when the phrase "to Pharaoh's palace" would enable us to relax, the word *nega'im* renews our fears. Pharaoh's words to Abram, "so that I took her as my wife" (Gen 12:19), then strengthen our sense that there was indeed "something" between the king and the Ancestress of Israel. The opening phrase "and I took her" sounds innocent enough in that it recalls the previous use of *laqah*—"and the woman was *taken*"[292] (v. 15) merely to his palace. Yet the conclusion "for/as my wife" raises our suspicions and fears.[293]

In the context of biblical usage, the combination: "took + her + for/as his wife" indicates a formal intimate relationship,[294] even if, as medieval interpreters argue, the woman is married against her will.[295] The relationship between Abram and Sarai, for example, is described as follows:

---

292. The second story (20:2) reads: "So the King Abimelech of Gerar had Sara brought (*vayiqah*) to him." She is brought not "to his palace" but "to him," without the ending "for/as a wife."

293. Interpreting this passage, Ibn Ezra (in *Miqraot Gedolot*) notes: "'She was taken to be his wife' means that 'he lay with her,'" although in his interpretation of *nega'im gedolim* he writes: "the *nega'im gedolim* impaired Pharaoh's male potency, and he was therefore unable to touch her."

294. See "לקח," BDB 542–43: "be taken in marriage"; G. J. Wenham, *Genesis 1–15* (WBC 1; Waco, Tex.: Word, 1987), 176–83. See also "לקח," *TDOT* 8:19.

295. Traditional commentators, apparently aware of this, claimed that Sarai was taken against her will. See, for example, Radak: "Our teachers say that Sarai was taken against her will because she was married to another man. This contrasts with what they said about Esther; she was taken willingly...she was unmarried and was taken to be the wife of a king."

"Abram and Nahor took to themselves wives" (Gen 11:29; see also 25:20). In the language of the Second Temple period the verb *vayqah* is synonymous with *vaysa' otah le'isha* (see 1 Chr 23:22; 2 Chr 11:21; 13:21; 24:3; Ezra 9:2, 12; 10:44; Neh 3:2).[296] In Modern Hebrew too, *nasa'* refers to marriage.

The formulaic phrase *laqah otah le'ishah* appears elsewhere too. In Exod 6:20–25 we find an abridged formulation: "Amram took to wife his father's sister Jochebed, and she bore him Aaron and Moses" (v. 20), according to which the woman's giving birth is contiguous with, and a direct result of, her being "taken to wife." This short version obviously omits certain necessary steps in the process, such as his "lying with her" and her conceiving a child by him.[297]

In the light of this abridged formulation (Pharaoh says "I took her as my wife," 12:19) we might expect that this "taking" resulted in Sarai's bearing him a son. Are we, then, justified in concluding that because Sarai did not conceive nor bear Pharaoh a son, he had not "touched" her? This is counter indicated, however, by the first statement about Sarai, that "Sarai was barren, she had no child" (Gen 11:30).

At first this description of Sarah as the barren Ancestress sounds both tragic and absurd. The barren mother is an oxymoron. The original

---

296. See also A. Ben-David, *The Language of the Bible and the Language of the Sages* (Tel Aviv: Dvir, 1967), 121, 179, 208; R. Polzin, *Late Biblical Hebrew: Towards an Historical Typology of Biblical Hebrew Prose* (Missoula, Mont.: Scholars Press, 1976), 146; J. M. Sasson, *Ruth* (Baltimore: The Johns Hopkins University Press, 1979), 20; J. Gray, *Joshua, Judges and Ruth* (The Century Bible; London: Nelson, 1967), 40. See also A. Brenner, *Ruth and Naomi: Literary, Stylistic and Linguistic Studies in the Book of Ruth* (Tel Aviv: Hakibbutz Hameuhad, 1988), 132. Brenner discusses the combination: "They married (*vays'u*) Moabite women" (Ruth 1:4). She claims this is a later combination, adding: "The parallel earlier expression is *laqah le'ishah* (Judg 21:22, etc.). Perhaps the earlier *laqah* was replaced by *nasa'* because the former had come to mean 'purchasing.'" H. Ringgren, "נשא," *TDOT* 10:28–29; J. Fleishman, "Socio-Legal Aspects of Genesis 34," *Shenaton: An Annual for Biblical and Ancient Near Eastern Studies* 13 (2002): 150, 152.

297. "So Boaz married (*vayqah*) Ruth, she became his wife, and he cohabited with her. The Lord let her conceive, and she bore a son" (Ruth 4:13). The same sequence is found in Isaiah, using the verb *qarav*: "I was intimate (*va'eqrav*) with the prophetess and she conceived (*vatahar*)" (Isa 8:3). The two verbs *va'eqrav* and *vatahar* not only appear one after the other, but clearly bear a cause and effect relationship. In other words, *va'eqrav* caused her to become pregnant. This is important in the second story in Gen 20. Besides *naga'* (v. 6) we find the expression: "Now Abimelech had not approached (*lo qarav*) her" (20:4). That is, he had not lain with her.

statement of Sarai's barrenness was apparently intended to hint at events to come. It serves as the background for ch. 26, in which her inability to conceive is again noted: "Sarai, Abram's wife, had borne him no children." She then pleads with Abram: "Look, the Lord has kept me from bearing. Consort with my maid, perhaps I shall have a son through her" (16:2). We know well how that story ends: "The Lord took note of Sarah as He promised, and the Lord did for Sarah as He had spoken. Sarah conceived and bore a son to Abraham" (Gen 21:1–2).

That Sarai's barrenness is the first information we receive about the Mother of Israel is highly significant in interpreting the story of her stay in the house of the foreign king, and especially as to what happened between Pharaoh and Sarah the Matriarch. If Sarai is indeed unable to conceive, she would not have become pregnant even if Pharaoh had lain with her, as a willing partner or not. Her barrenness makes it possible not to state what happened to her in Pharaoh's house, thereby protecting the honor of the first Ancestress of Israel. At the same time, Sarah's inability to conceive may remain a source of concern for the reader, who continues to swing back and forth between hope and fear as to Sarai's fate.

b) *The measure for measure principle applied as word for word.* An argument previously hinted at supports the hypothesis that Pharaoh indeed touched Sarah. The second story in ch. 20 is used to clarify the first one, as to whether Pharaoh touched the Matriarch or not.

The verb *naga'* appears in both stories. In Gen 12 *nega'im* describes the punishment visited by God on Pharaoh, while in Gen 20 *naga'* ("touch") describes the sin Abimelech almost committed. Touch in the sense of sin is reflected in Abimelech's dream, where God answers Abimelech's complaint: "I knew that you did this with a blameless heart, and so I kept you from sinning against me. That was why I did not let you touch her" (Gen 20:6). We learn that, had Abimelech in fact touched Sarah, it would have been a sin in God's eyes.

How does God behave in each story? The Deity's intervention in ch. 20, which prevents Abimelech from sinning by "touching" Sarah, focuses attention on its absence in ch. 12. Why did God not prevent Pharaoh from sinning, as he later did with Abimelech? Moreover, why did the Righteous Judge punish Pharaoh? Had the king sinned? What was his sin? The narrator does not answer. The answer lies in the punishment itself, meted out on the principle of *measure for measure*.[298]

---

298. Y. I. Peleg, "The 'Measure for Measure' Principle by Means of 'Word for Word'," *Beit Mikra* 44 (1999): 357–60.

In the Bible, this important literary device, the measure for measure principle, is expressed as "word for word." In current language, "measure for measure" expresses connection and mutual suitability in content and in form, between the act (sin) and its consequence (punishment). The Bible expresses that principle in the literary use of the same word in describing both the sin and its punishment.

Three examples of this literary device should suffice:

First, the use of *ra'a* ("evil") in Jer 26:3: "It may be they will hearken, and turn every man from his evil *way*; that I may repent Me of the evil, which I purpose to do unto them because of the evil of their doings." The word "evil" expresses both the sin and its punishment. Similarly in Jonah 3:10,[299] the use of the word "evil," as in Jeremiah, is a convincing literary device for expressing the linkage between sin and its punishment.

Second, the role of *herev* ("sword") in the prophet Nathan's speech to King David (2 Sam 12:9–10): "You have put Uriah the Hittite to the sword…" (*herev* = the sin). "Therefore the sword shall never depart from your House" (= the punishment). In the depiction of David's sin in ch. 11, an actual sword is not mentioned as the means of Uriah's death. In the parable of the poor man's ewe lamb in ch. 12 Nathan carefully selects the same word, "sword", here functioning as a literary device for expressing both the sin and its punishment, to emphasize the linkage between the two.

Third, the verb *akhal* ("eat") in the story of the Garden of Eden describes the sin and its punishment. Adam's and Eve's sin is that "She took of its fruit and ate. She also gave some to her husband and he ate" (Gen 3:6), and its punishment, "By the sweat of your brow shall you get bread to eat" (3:19). "Eat," used to describe both sin and punishment, emphasizes the link between them.

In view of these examples the reader reasonably concludes that if Pharaoh's punishment was *nega'im*, then his sin also lay in his *negi'a* ("touching") of Sarai. Moreover, the description of the sin Abimelech almost committed by means of the verb *naga'* supports that hypothesis.

The measure for measure principle, as seen in the use of *naga'*, is expounded in Rabbi Berachia's commentary on Gen 12:17: "because he dared to touch the matriarch's body."[300] Lieberman adds:

---

299. Peleg, "Jonah," 231 n. 18.
300. In S. Lieberman's translation from the Aramaic. See S. Lieberman, *Greek and Hellenism in Jewish Palestine* (Jerusalem: Mosad Bialik, 1962), 30–31, also discussing the question: what sin led to Pharaoh's being punished?

> Rabbi Berachia was one of the most famous scriptural expounders of his time, and his contention that God plagued Pharaoh because he dared to touch the Matriarch's body was surely intended to clarify the matter for his listeners. The expounder apparently sensed the phenomenon of measure for measure by means of word for word, without formulating and defining it.

The biblical narrator appears to face a dilemma: Whose honor should he protect, Sarah's or that of God the righteous judge? To protect Sarah's honor he should state that Pharaoh did not touch her. If, however, the king did not touch her, why would a just God punish him with *nega'im*? Conversely, to protect the Deity's reputation as a righteous judge, it should have been stated openly that Pharaoh sinned against Sarai, thus justifying the punishment visited upon him.

The dilemma seems to have led the narrator to employ an ambiguous, even nebulous lexicon, thereby maintaining the honor of both. If the theory developed here has revealed what "really" happened between Sarai and Pharaoh, then the Deity retains His status as a just God who punishes (*nega'im*) Pharaoh according to the principle of measure for measure for the sin of touching (*naga'*) Sarai; on the other hand, Sarah, the Ancestress of Israel, is portrayed as a woman tainted, albeit unwillingly.

5.3. *"From Egypt Abram Went Up" (Genesis 13:1)*[301]

5.3.1. *Why did Abraham return to the Promised Land?*

Before the report on Abraham's return in Gen 13:1 comes one in which Pharaoh, following the deception practiced on him, drives him out: "Now then, here is your wife; take her and be gone!" (12:19). The two are compared:

Genesis 12:20	*Genesis 13:1*
And Pharaoh put men in charge of him And they *sent him off* (*vayeshalhu*) With his wife And all that he possessed	From Egypt Abraham *went up* With his wife And all that he possessed Together with Lot into the Negeb[302]

---

301. In the contrasting parallel, Abraham "went down to Egypt" (12:10); when returning, he "went up" (13:1). On the difference and contrast between the two, see Cassuto, *Genesis*, 246.

302. In the Septuagint and the Peshitta "together with Lot" appears at the end of v. 20 (see *BHK*). "Together with Lot" was probably added to 12:20 to link this verse to 13:1. Moreover, Abraham goes up from Egypt to the Negeb, geographically from south to north, with the additional positive metaphorical meaning. In English

"And all that he possessed," appearing in both reports and the identical situation in which Abram and his wife go from Egypt to Canaan, are intended to demonstrate the link between the two, although attention is focused on the difference. While in 12:10 the reason for his return is hardly to Abram's credit (Pharaoh "sent him off"), the verb choice in 13:1, where "Abram went up" (not "went" or "went out" or "left"), is deliberate. As previously explained at length, "go up" in its frequent metaphorical use in the Bible imparts a positive meaning to the journey. Movement up is understood as drawing nearer to God, which the story context also supports. The step is taken with God's encouragement and His hand is assumed to be involved. "The Lord afflicted Pharaoh and his household with mighty plagues on account of Sarai, wife of Abram" (12:17) and Pharaoh's immediate complaint, "Why did you not tell me that she was your wife?," are cause and effect. That is, God informed Pharaoh, through the plagues, about Sarai. Without His intervention, Sarai would probably have remained in Pharaoh's house and Abraham in Egypt "till this very day."[303] Pharaoh, unaware of all this, appears to function as God's instrument in returning Abraham to Canaan.

Thus, while the first report in 12:19–20 shames Abraham, who is expelled from Egypt, the use of "went up" (13:1) in the second report shows his return to the Land in a favorable light and thus softens the account of his expulsion. Moreover, *vaya'al* at the beginning of the Hebrew sentence heightens the importance of the act, the narrator apparently wanting to stress the word's positive sense.

5.3.2. *Going up ('alah) to the Land, not only from Egypt.*

a) *The Babylonian exiles "go up" in the days of Ezra and Nehemiah.* In discussing the verb *yarad*, we noted the scholarly claim that its principal use is for going down from the Promised Land to Egypt, and *'alah* for going up from Egypt. With that, not always does *'alah*[304] describe a journey from Egypt to Canaan: it is also used for entering the Land from places other than Egypt.

---

translation "Negeb" is a place name, a place in the south of the country, with little rainfall. Some translators, however, always rendered it as "south," including in 13:1 instead of "to the Negev" as in the Fox translation.

303. Gitay, "Geography," 209, contends that God's involvement is linked to the promise to make Abraham father of the people of Israel, a promise threatened by events in Egypt, and so God acted.

304. There are instances where travel from Canaan to Egypt does not use *yarad*: "As he was about to enter (*lavo*) Egypt" (Gen 12:11, 14); "And these are the names of the sons of Jacob who came (*ha-ba'im*) to Egypt" (46:8, 27). Cf. Gen 48:5; Exod 1:1, and elsewhere.

The formulation "brought out," *hotsi'*, for the departure from Egypt stresses the place and especially the condition "the house of bondage"[305] that the children of Israel were freed from, while "brought up," *he'elah*, in its metaphorical sense, highlights the purpose and the destination, the Land of Canaan—a journey in a positive direction.[306]

"Went up" is also used for the return to Zion from the Babylonian exile[307] in numerous examples from Ezra[308] and Nehemiah,[309] so that journey too is *'aliyah*, "going up."

b) *Why going to the Land of Canaan is "going up,"* 'alah, *in Isaiah, Micah and Jeremiah*. Jeremiah describes the days to come when the children of Israel will return to Zion from the Babylonian exile in terms of the Exodus:

> Behold, the days come, saith the LORD, that it shall no more be said, The LORD liveth that brought up (*he'elah*) the children of Israel out of the land of Egypt. But, the LORD liveth, that brought up (*he'elah*) the children of Israel *from the land of the north, and from all the lands*[310] whither He had driven them: and I will bring them again into their land that I gave unto their fathers. (Jer 16:14–15 KJV)

305. See, e.g., "Opening eyes deprived of light, rescuing (*lehotsi'*) prisoners from confinement" (Isa 42:7); See "יצא," BDB 422; D. Daube, *The Exodus Pattern in the Bible* (All Souls Studies 2; London: Faber & Faber, 1963), 24. Daube notes that "went out," *yatsa'*, creates an association with redemption from slavery.

306. *Hotsi' mimitsraim* ("took out of Egypt") appears 87 times in the Bible, and *he'elah* ("brought up") 41 times. See Wijngaard, "Twofold Approach," 91–102.

307. Lipton, "Revisions," 127, argues: "The points of contact between Jacob's situation preceding and subsequent to the dream at Bethel and the situation of the exiles in Babylon are obvious; both are expelled from their native lands, both enter service to a foreign power, both have brothers who remain at home, and both return in a position of superiority. The extent to which these parallels would have reassured the exiled Jews need hardly be spelled out… The dream confirms both that the time spent in service to Laban is part of God's plan for Jacob, and still more to the point, that Jacob's destiny will be shared by his descendants."

308. In Ezra, *'alah* appears 14 times, ten times in connection with the return from the Babylonian exile: 1:3, 5, 11 (twice); 2:1; 7:6, 7, 9, 28; 8:1.

309. Neh 7:5: "the genealogical register of those that come up"; 7:6: "These are the people of the province among those who came up from among the captive exiles"; 7:61: "The following were those that came up from Tel-melah"; 12:1: "These are the priests and the Levites who came up with Zerubbabel." Nehemiah once mentions the exodus from Egypt: "This is your God who brought you up out of Egypt" (9:18).

310. The exiles are brought up from the north, not the south. See Keel, *Genesis*, 336: "The Sages expounded that the land of Israel is higher than all other lands (*Zevahim* 54b). Rashi comments that the Sages derived it from v. 15: "for God lives who brought the children of Israel up from the north and from all the lands…"

We are concerned not only with the use of "went up" to designate the return of the Israelites to Canaan, but its connection with the return from "all the lands," not just Egypt. Furthermore, should anyone maintain that only a journey from south to north is "going up," the text declares specifically that going from the north land to Canaan is also "up." What is important, then, is not the departure point, but the destination—Canaan, the Promised Land.

The End of Days visions[311] of Isaiah and Micah seem to express a similar idea:

> In the days to come, in the Mount of the Lord's House shall stand firm above the mountains and tower above the hills. And all the nations shall gaze upon it with joy. And the many peoples shall go and say: "Come, let us go up to the Mount of the Lord, to the House of the God of Jacob; that he may instruct us in His ways, and that we may walk in His paths." For instruction shall come forth from Zion… (Isa 2:2–3; Mic 4:1–2).

While "going up," '*alah*, on the Mount is topographical, the text immediately continues "To the house of the God of Jacob," which gives the passage its importance and the verb its positive metaphorical significance. Those who say "Come, let us go up" are not only the nations from the south, from Egypt, but all the nations, with emphasis on "all."

Thus '*alah* derives its positive literal and metaphorical significance from the sense of drawing nearer to God. The vantage point is the one from which the travelers are observed, the one where God abides. All approaches to it are positive, all distancing negative. Hence from north, south, east and west, drawing near that abode (the navel of the earth) is designated as "going up." When God's abode is thought to be Bethel, then Bethel is the centre of the earth, and any journey towards it from any direction is positive and designated as "going up." When the abode of God is Jerusalem, it is the earth's navel or "omphalos," all travel in that direction is positive and designated as "going up."[312]

6. *The Departures and Returns of the Patriarch According to the W-Shaped Model*

Research[313] on the Patriarchs' ascents to and descents from the Promised Land has given rise to a model shaped like the letter W (hereafter the

---

311. See Peleg, "End of Days," 7–34.
312. In Chapter 4 it is noted that this understanding is expressed in the epitaph of Rabbi Kook on Mount Scopus in Jerusalem.
313. Zakovitch, "Exodus," 25–34, esp. 28–29. See also idem, *You Shall Tell*, 48–49, when it is described "as part of a carefully planned geographical-historical scheme."

W-shaped model or pattern), according to which Abraham leaves Mesopotamia (Haran) and comes to Canaan (Gen 12:4–5), then descends into Egypt because of famine; he eventually returns to Canaan (Gen 12:10–20). His son Isaac, the second Patriarch, is born in Canaan and does not leave the country despite the famine following the divine prohibition (26:2). Jacob first goes to Mesopotamia/Haran (28:10), returns to Canaan (33:18), and then, driven by famine, descends with his entire family into Egypt in the wake of his son Joseph (ch. 46), having received divine permission to leave the country and the promise they will return (vv. 3–4). The descent of Jacob and his children is not the end of the process. After their return to Canaan and their long, tumultuous history in the Land, they are punished with exile in Mesopotamia, the close of the historical narrative extending from "When God began to create" (Gen 1:1), all the way to the report of the exiled king of Judah, Jehoiachin: "...his prison garments were removed...a regular allotment of food was given him at the instance of the king...all the days of his life" (2 Kgs 25:30).

This, then, is the complete geographical scheme, the W-shaped pattern:[314]

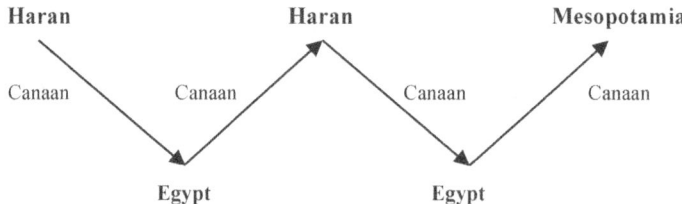

This symmetrical repetition of their journey is no coincidence. According to Zakovitch, "The purpose of creating the impression of repetition or of cycles in history is to teach that coincidence does not rule the world but clear design and fixed patterns controlled by Providence."[315]

---

314. See Zakovitch, *You Shall Tell*, 48. See also idem, "Exodus," 28. The symmetry between Abraham and Jacob as regards leaving and entering the country is shown in that they both sacrificed in the vicinity of Bethel, and again upon their *return* (Abraham 13:3–4; Jacob 35:6–7). Both are said to have made sacrifices again on their *departure* (Abraham 12:8; Jacob 28:10–22). See Lipton, *Revisions*, 123, who discusses this interesting comparison.

315. Zakovitch, "Exodus," 29. In my opinion, symmetry in the W-shaped pattern encourages recognition of *double causality* in the events that were discussed above.

3. *The Jacob's Dream Story as* Mise en Abyme

It seems to me that if the journey of the Patriarchs from and to the Promised Land, so that departure is negative and opposed to God's will, whereas entering is positive and in accordance with it, the W should be inverted to an M model that preserves symmetry and meaning, while graphically expressing the value attitude to that route.

7. *Conclusion: The Vision in Jacob's Dream as* Mise en Abyme *of the M-Shaped Model*

The proposed M-shaped model graphically represents the Patriarchs' journey. A rising line marks each ascent, and a downward line each descent, with arrows indicating direction of travel:

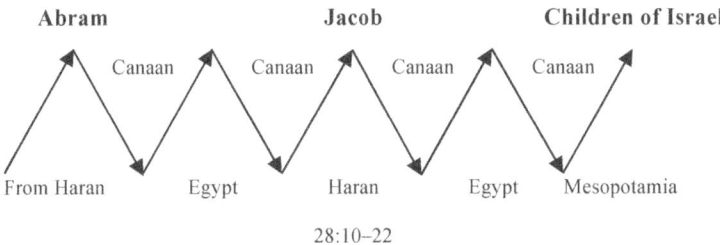

28:10–22

The story cycle of the Patriarchs, as they enter and leave Canaan, then, follows an M-shaped model.[316] In this framework, Jacob's Dream at Bethel takes place on his way to Haran, leaving the country. Placed within the Patriarchs' story cycle, it encourages the idea that it is a story within a story, reflecting the story framework in which it is set.

In my opinion, reading the ascending and descending angels in the dream vision symbolically encourages the understanding that it is a *mise en abyme* of the stories of the Patriarchs on the attitudes to entering and leaving the Land. In other words, every ascent, like that of the angels in Jacob's Dream, is drawing near to God, and every descent is a distancing. This supports both the symbolic reading of the dream and reveals the positive and negative values regarding the Patriarchs' entering and leaving the Land. In the dream, that movement goes through the gate of heaven. Like every gate, it allows entry and departure, ingress and egress.

---

316. The M-shaped model for the journeys of the Patriarchs and their descendants, zigzagging up and down, is preferable to others. It is arranged so that to reach Canaan from the other lands is an ascent, while leaving Canaan is a descent, with the respective positive and negative connotations.

Chapter 4

CONCLUSION AND DEPARTURE POINT:
"THE GATE OF HEAVEN" JOURNEYS FROM BABYLON
TO BETHEL AND TO JERUSALEM CYCLE

*1. Two Readings of Jacob's Dream Summed Up:
Concentrated Data on "Going Up and Going Down—
A Key to Interpreting Jacob's Dream" (Genesis 28:10–22)*

> This is none other than the house of God and this is the gateway to heaven. (Gen 28:17)

Summation as a point of departure characterizes this book as a whole: as the introduction is the starting point for the journey, so the summation or conclusion is the point of departure for another journey.[1] The symbolism carried by "departure" in a conclusion lies in the theory that Jacob's Dream is a *mise en abyme* for the stories of the Patriarchs who came to and left the Promised Land. Thus the structure of the book reflects its theme.

The second part of this summary chapter contains a new element, one comparing the Tower of Babel story with the one of Jacob's Ladder (*sullam*). That, however, is the departure point for a new study beyond the scope of the present book.

The journey ends in this chapter, but is not complete. My hope is that the story of Jacob's Dream has served to combine the two principal foci of the book, namely:

1. *Two readings* as a literary phenomenon, with Jacob's Dream at Bethel showing its function in understanding the Bible. We have seen the two readings for words like *yifga'*, *sullam*, *'alah*, and *yarad*. Two readings are also possible for word combinations, including "stones of the place," "I will return you to this land,"

---

1. This trajectory is taken by Professors Zakovitch and Shinan in several of their co-authored studies. See Y. Zakovitch and A. Shinan, *Abram and Sarai in Egypt: Genesis 12:10–20 in Ancient Translations and in Early Jewish Literature* (RPJSI 2; Jerusalem: The Hebrew University, 1983). See also Zakovitch and Shinan, *Shechem*.

and "How awesome is this place!" In the broader context, the dream may be read in two ways: as a *theophany* and as a *symbolic dream*. In one case it relates to the "place," *maqom*, as a sacred site, and in the other to the "way" to and from that place, leading to the second focus of the story.
2. The focus on the Patriarchs' journeys to and from the Promised Land. The dream is understood as symbolic, as a *mise en abyme* of these journeys. According to Gen 28:10–22, Jacob has the dream when he stops for the night at Bethel on a journey—or flight—to Haran.

For me, the biblical story is the objective, not a means for understanding something extraneous to it. I assume the biblical story is rich and supports more than one interpretation. The immense value ascribed to that story's every word sharpened my awareness of the link between form (*how?*) and content (*what?*), both of which serve the story's purpose. As Meir Weiss says, "Every idea formulated in a language pattern cannot be formulated in any other one."[2]

There follows a summary of the idea of "ascent and descent" (*'alah* and *yarad*), as put forth in this book, as the interpretation of Jacob's Dream.[3]

2. *The* Mise en Abyme *as a Miniature Reflection*

Jacob's Dream, particularly the vision it contains (28:12–13a), serves as a symbolic miniature and compact reflection of all the Patriarchs' journeys, and of the attitudes towards them. As was explained in Chapter 1, it is a *mise en abyme*. Additionally, the vision of the *ascending* ("going up," *'olim*) and *descending* ("going down," *yordim*) angels appears as Jacob is about to leave ("to go down," *yarad*) Canaan, God declaring explicitly, "I will watch over you wherever you go and *will bring you back to this soil*" (28:15 Fox).

3. *Jacob's Dream Is a Theophany and a Symbolic Dream*

In studies of both the Bible and in ANE literature, research divides dreams into two main types: *dream theophanies*, where the divinity has a verbal message, and *symbolic dreams*, which reveal pictures requiring an interpretation.

2. Weiss, *Scripture*, 20.
3. See Peleg, "Going Up and Going Down," 1–11.

Most scholars regard Jacob's Dream as a *dream theophany*—with a verbal message from the Divinity. They see it as ritual etiology explaining how Bethel became a ritual center[4]—the *hieros logos* of Bethel. Nonetheless, there is a vision too (vv. 12–13a), which raises the question of what the vision symbolizes—an issue of interpretation. Indeed, we have shown that while some scholars note symbolic elements in the revelation, they nonetheless regard them as decorative, with no relevance of their own.

My own view in support of the dream's symbolic elements is by no means the sole way to understanding its meaning. Moreover, and importantly, it does not contradict but rather enriches and complements accepted views. That the dream contains both theophany (revealed) and symbolic (concealed) elements, shows its complexity and the need to understand (to interpret) them both.

The literary approach that focuses on the final form to the text, recognizing the legitimacy of the possibility of multiple readings, paves the way to the proposed symbolic interpretation of the dream.

4. *Support for the Symbolic View of Jacob's Dream*

To this end we highlight the components of the vision: the ladder (*sullam*), the angels of God (*mal'akhei 'elohim*), and the verbs "ascend" and "descend" (*'alah* and *yarad*)—all of which appear in Gen 28:12–13a:

> And he dreamed, and behold a ladder set up on the earth, and the top of it reached to heaven: and behold the angels of God ascending (*'olim*) and descending (*yordim*) on it. And behold, the Lord stood above it...

4.1. *What the Ladder (*sullam*) Symbolizes*[5]

The *sullam* is shown as a gigantic object serving as a "way" connecting heaven and earth. In a dream, especially a symbolic one, it may be seen not only as a physical object that links heaven and earth, but also as a symbolic object that links Jacob and God, and with that, humans on earth and God in the heavens.[6]

---

4. Peleg, "Place (*Maqom*)," 83–91.
5. Peleg, "*Sullam*," 7–26.
6. Cohen, "Motif," 16. Citing Ibn Ezra, Cohen adds, "The *sullam* symbol in Jacob's Dream appears to function as a link...not only as background for the divine message to Jacob from his God in heaven, but the angels perpetually ascending and descending on it make it a symbol of God's awareness and complete control of what transpires on earth" (p. 26).

In this study I point out that the *sullam* may also symbolize the "way" between the Promised Land and exile. Indeed, going and coming along this way is mentioned three times in this story. The first is in God's promise: "I will watch over you wherever you go and *will bring you back* (*vehashvotikha*) to this soil" (28:15 Fox). The second time is in Jacob's vow: "If God will be with me and will keep me in the *way* (*derekh*) that I go" (v. 20), and the third "...*I come again* (*veshavti*) to my father's house in peace" (v. 21).

Sullam as a unique word, a *hapax legomenon*, making it difficult to identify. Its meaning depends entirely on the context. In unambiguous contexts the meanings of *hapax legomena* are sometimes easy to establish. In cases such as Gen 28, however, multiple meanings become possible. Such is the case with the *sullam*.

4.1.1. *The etymology of* sullam: *its link to the Babylonian ziggurat*. A survey of the literature indicates that scholars differ on this point, with there being two main ways of understanding the etymology of *sullam*.[7] One view relates the term, via a rearrangement of the letters, to the Akkadian *simmiltu*, meaning "stairway." The other position derives the term from the Hebrew root *sll*, meaning "to throw up a ramp, a pathway"—a word that does not exist in Akkadian. Even if *sullam* is not derived from *sll*, the link between them is most significant in the symbolic understanding of Jacob's Dream.

Considering *sullam* as derived from *simmiltu* creates another link with ANE literature, through the Babylonian ziggurat structure, whose steps (*simmiltu*) lead to its summit. Many scholars identify the *sullam* with the ziggurat on the strength of *its function* as a bridge between heaven and earth. This makes *simmiltu* the more likely origin of *sullam*, reinforcing the revealed interpretation of the dream within the ritual etiology.

The symbolic reading of *sullam* is reinforced by regarding the word as related to, rather than derived from, the *sll* root, which appears in the Bible eleven times with the associated nouns "path," "way" (*derekh*) or "road." Houtman points out the synonymous derivative *mesillah* in Isa 62:10.[8]

---

7. E.g. Cohen, "The *Sullam*," 172; see also S. Bar, *A Letter That Has Not Been Read: Dreams in the Hebrew Bible* (trans. L. J. Schramm; HUCA 25; Cincinnati: Hebrew Union College Press, 2001), 19 n. 49.

8. Houtman, "Bethel," 339. See "מסלה," BDB 700.

Mesillah appears no fewer than 27 times, designating a paved way or road—as, for example, in Isa 35:8: "And a highway *maslul* shall appear there." Nearly half the occurrences of *mesillah* are in the Prophets (ten times in Isaiah, twice in Jeremiah and once in Joel). In most instances, particularly in the Prophets, the *sll* root *appears in connection with the return to Zion, a possibly oblique reference to the return from exile to the land where God abides.* Thus, "Build up, build up (*sollu sollu*) a highway! Clear a road (*derekh*)! Remove all obstacles!" (Isa 57:14).

Hence understanding *sullam* as reminiscent and related to the *sll* root, even if not derived from it, reinforces its interpretation as a road, a "way." It may even be a special road between the Promised Land and exile.

4.1.2. Sullam *in summary*. The unique word *sullam*, as I see it, has two meanings. In the revealed, vertical sense according to the biblical text, it connects heaven and earth. On the symbolic plane, the concealed one, it carries a horizontal sense, indicating the way or road between the Promised Land and exile. In both, *it leads to and from the abode of God.*

4.2. *The Role of the Angels of God (*mal'akkei 'elohim*) in Jacob's Dream*

What do "angels of God" in Jacob's Dream symbolize? What is their mission? In the Bible and in ANE literature angels are emissaries with a message. As Rofé had noted, "The [Hebrew] word *angel* means emissary. This is clear from the etymology of the verb *la'akh* that it derives from in Arabic, Ethiopian and Ugaritic[9] as well as from the biblical semantics..."[10] He notes further, "In the Jacob's Dream story the angels impose no mission on him."[11] Even Fokkelman assumes that the angels have a mission other than to proclaim, with the *sullam* reaching to heaven, that God is about to appear. God's appearance, then, is no surprise. Hence, in his opinion, after the *sullam* and the angels have completed their role, they do not reappear. Just as the burning bush was a means to attract the eye and the attention of Moses—"...and there was a bush all aflame yet the bush was not consumed" (Exod 3:2)—so both revelations continue as God speaks and makes His promise.

---

9. Cohen, "Motif," 18 n. 14, notes that the Greek word *angelos* means "emissary."
10. Rofé, *Angels*, 2.
11. Ibid., 84.

By contrast, I maintain that the very expectation that angels of God, as emmisaries, will have a message leads to the search for a non-verbal one. Their activity, their continuous movement ascending and descending, is that message. As Elgavish has noted, "Some think that the *l'k* root parallels the Akkadian *alakum*, meaning 'to go.' In their opinion, it extends to 'going,' an important element of the emissary's work."[12]

4.3. *The Metaphorical Significance of* 'alah *and* yarad *("Ascend" and "Descend")*

The verbs *'alah* and *yarad* express movement in opposite directions, and both have metaphorical as well as literal significance. Metaphorically, "ascend" has a positive significance and "descend" a negative one. "Ascend" appears in the Bible 890 times, most often in a positive sense, and "descend" 380 times with negative connotations.

The verbs "ascend," *'alah*, and "descend," *yarad*, used metaphorically in the story of Jacob's Dream, support the symbolic reading of the dream. The ascent of the angels of God means drawing closer to God, their descent distancing from Him, in both literal and metaphorical senses. This may reasonably be seen as the beginning of the use of these verbs with positive and negative metaphorical meanings. It does not surprise, then, that in Jonah's fleeing before God, the keyword is "went down," *yarad* (Jonah 1:3).[13]

4.4. *On the Combination: "Angels of God" in Genesis 28:12 and 32:2*

The word combination *mal'akhei 'elohim* appears just twice in the Bible, once in Jacob's Dream at Bethel and the second time at Mahanaim: "Jacob went on his way, and *angels of God* encountered him. When he saw them, Jacob said, this is God's camp. So he named the place Manahaim" (Gen 32:2–3).

The use of this rare expression directs the reader's interest towards a connection between the two stories. Notably, there are other similarities between the two accounts. According to Zackovitch, the Mahanaim story is "a mirror image"[14] of the story of Jacob's Dream at Bethel. In respect of time, the first story takes place at night, the second in the morning. In the Bethel story Jacob encounters upon the place, while at Mahanim *mal'akei 'elohim* encountered him. The most important (reflected) difference for our purpose is that the Bethel story takes place as Jacob is leaving the Land, while at Mahanaim he is about to return to it.

12. Elgavish, "Messenger," 30 n. 20.
13. See Peleg, "Jonah," 262–74.
14. Zakovitch, *Looking Glass*, 9.

The supernatural encounter in these special circumstances is designed to show the reader that the *mal'akei 'elohim* combination appears only upon departure from the Land or return to it. The usage is not coincidental, and supports the symbolic interpretation of the dream.

If the angels of God symbolize the Patriarchs and the *sullam* symbolizes the way between the Promised Land and exile, then—as we know—Abraham first *ascended* to the Land and then *went down* into Egypt. Consequently, what was a problem for generations of commentators—why the angels of God first ascended into heaven and then descended back to earth—becomes its solution: recognizing Jacob's Dream as a symbolic dream in which the angels of God symbolize the Patriarchs.

It seems that, by means of defamiliarization, the narrator hints at the solution. According to this solution, the angels of God, who symbolize the Patriarchs and their link to the Promised Land, tie the dream description (in which the angels of God first ascend and then descend) to the narrative in Genesis, according to which Abraham's ascent into the Land precedes his descent from it.

4.5. *The Verbal Message Supports the Symbolic Vision*

After the description of the vision (Gen 12:12–13a) comes the verbal message from God (vv. 13b–15). Anyone familiar with the stories of the Patriarchs recognizes the similarity in language and content in the promise of land and seed to Jacob here and the promise to Abraham (13:15–17). Jacob is linked to Abraham and Isaac when God presents Himself: "I am the Lord God of Abraham thy father and of Isaac" (28:13). The narrator had to show the reader the link between Jacob and his fathers and so to clarify that the dream related not only to Jacob and his fate but to theirs as well. In v. 15 the divine message relates to Jacob's immediate future: "I will keep thee in all places whither thou goest and bring the again into this land (*ha'adama*)." The vision and the verbal message not only follow but interpret one another.[15]

Research in general, particularly source critcism, opposes this view, stressing differences between the passages and attributing the vision (v. 12) to the E source and the verbal message to a waking revelation in the J source. My point of departure is that the narrator of Gen 28:10–22 used the revealed, explicit verbal message (attributed to the J source) to explain the hidden symbolic message of the vision (attributed to E).

---

15. Y. I. Peleg, "Vision and Message in Jacob's Dream," *Moed: Annual for Jewish Studies* 13 (2003): 55–64.

Weiss points out a similar structure in which *vision* and *verbal message* interpret one another in Isa 6.[16] Indeed, examining the verbs of motion in the two components of Jacob's Dream reveals a common element of back and forth movement, but on different planes. While in the vision the movement is on the vertical axis—up and down, from earth to heaven—in the verbal message it is on the horizontal plane—leaving and returning to the Land. The visual message contributes to the verbal one in that returning to the Land and leaving it (vv. 15, 20) are understood as ascending, *'aliya*, and descending, *yerida*. That is, Jacob's departure for Haran may be understood as a distancing, *yerida*, from God, a negative act, and his return as an ascent, *'aliya*, drawing nearer to Him.

The *verbal message* contributes to the *visual* one by assisting with the understanding of the acts of ascending and descending of the "angels of God." The *mal'akhei 'elohim* symbolize the attitude (positive or negative) to the Patriarchs' entering and leaving the Land.

My hope is that I have presented more than the "three trees it takes to make a row" (M. Joyce), and have offered compelling support for the symbolic interpretation of Jacob's Dream. The *sullam* symbolizes the way to and way from the Promised Land, the ascending and descending angels of God the Patriarchs, ascent drawing them closer to God and descent distancing them. Finally, the divine promise of Jacob's safe return to the Land (recalling similar promises of land and seed to the Patriarchs), and the vision in the dream interpret one another.

5. *The Jacob's Dream Story as* Mise en Abyme *of Patriarchal Journeys*

The concept of *mise en abyme*, first defined at the beginning of Chapter 1, is now applied to the symbolic interpretation of Jacob's Dream. The *mise en abyme* reading is especially compelling when the dream is considered as an embedded story in the stories of the Patriarchs, as part of the narrative in which the dream occurs, and in the broader context, as a *miniature reflection* of all those stories, whose protagonists repeatedly enter and depart from the Land.

The author A. B. Yehoshua states:

> The concept of *yored* (emigrant from Israel) was born in the story of Abraham, who was both the first to go up (*'oleh*) to the land and the first to descend (*yored*) from it. The Jew throughout history carries these two essences—the ascent and descent qualities—within him.[17]

16. Weiss, *Scriptures*, 99.
17. Yehoshua, *Normalcy*, 31.

My earlier article on Abraham reflected Yehoshua's statement in the book of Genesis,[18] and I relate now to the final sentence: "The Jew throughout history carries these two essences—the ascent and descent qualities—within him." Moreover, in biblical research[19] the ascents and descents of Abraham and Jacob have been represented graphically in a historical-geographical diagram in the form of a W.

Analysis of the Patriarchal wanderings from this standpoint does seem to affirm Yehoshua's statement.

To describe the Patriarchs' journeys from and to the Promised Land with the intention to show the first as negative and against God's will—as reflected in his words to Isaac: "Do not go down to Egypt" (26:2)—and the second is positive and accords with His will, the W-shaped model should be inverted, so as to form an M-shape. By so doing, the graphic symmetry and its significance are thus maintained, while the values attached to the journeys are expressed in the appropriate directions.

5.1. *The M-Shaped Model of the Patriarchal Journeys*

Since this model represents and symbolizes not only the Patriarchs' journeys, but also that of their descendants over the generations, it appears to be the preferable one.

Understanding the vision in Jacob's Dream as a *mise en abyme* of the Patriarchs' journeys to and from the Promised Land supports the symbolic interpretation of the dream. Here is an analogy between the ascending the stairway whose top reached to heaven with the Lord standing above it, and the return or ascent from exile to the Promised Land. Both cases, literally as well as metaphorically, represent drawing nearer to God and therefore are evaluated positively.

6. *The Tower of Babel (Genesis 11:1–9) and Jacob's* Sullam

6.1. *Comparing the Two*[20]

6.1.1. *Structure and meaning of the Tower of Babel story*. The Tower of Bable story offers an impressive example of a literary work whose *form* and *content* combine to reveal its message. One may see the *concentric*

---

18. Peleg, "Abraham," 25–31.
19. See Zakovitch, *You Shall Tell*, 46–99.
20. See A. Parrot, *The Tower of Babel* (trans. E. Hudson; London: SCM, 1955), 169; Y. Elitzur, *Israel and the Bible: Studies in Geography, History and Biblical Thought* (Ramat Gan: Bar Ilan University, 1999), 44–48; Cassuto, *Commentary*, 154–69.

structure revealing both content and significance, a story that emphasizes God at its center. The *concentric structure* creates a tower-like narrative structure.

Cassuto, however, has pointed out the contrast between the people and God. He wrote, aptly in my view: "The short story before us is a splendid example of biblical literary art. It contains two word groups of the same length, in contrasting parallel as to form and content."[21] Thus, we observe a *chiastic structure*, a literary construction that contrasts the human will and deeds with those of the Divine. The opposites are ironically structured through the key phrase "Come let us," *havah* (11:3, 4), expressing the first two bursts of human enthusiasm. The keyword appears again in v. 7, but here it expresses God's will: "Let us (*havah*), then, go down and confound their speech"; as a result, the humans stop building the city and the tower. Even the *waw* (*vayered*) that begins the Hebrew description of God's act (in v. 5) can be read to indicate contrast ("but"), enhancing the structure and meaning of the story:[22] God descends (*vayered*) to stop human initiative. The human acts are interpreted as sin on the *measure for measure*, or rather the *word for word*, principle.[23] God punishes humans in ways befitting their sin:[24] the people acted for their own sake, in order "to make a name *for ourselves*." There is irony in God's response: "it was called Babel," a derogatory rather than a distinguished name. We see a further irony when we go on to read that "because there the Lord confounded the speech of the whole earth, and from there the Lord *scattered* (*hefitsam*) them over the face of the whole earth" (v. 8).[25] For indeed, the humans had acted lest "we shall be

---

21. Cassuto, *Genesis*, 158–59.
22. Ibid., 166: "They thought whatever they thought, but God came down and nullified their decision." See Fox's translation: "*But* YHVH came down to look over the city and the tower."
23. The literary structure of the story, with its two passages of equal length, contributes to the understanding of *measure for measure*, or, as I prefer, *word for word*, which combines two terms from biblical research—*measure for measure* and *keyword*. These, as we have seen, reflect the link between *form* and *content*. For example, "ate" signifies Adam's sin in eating the fruit of the tree of knowledge (Gen 3:16), and also his punishment: "In the sweat of your brow shall you get bread to *eat*" (3:19). In Nathan's reproach to David (2 Sam. 12:9–11), "sword" plays the same role, as does "lap up" in Elijah's reproach to Ahab regarding Naboth. See Peleg, "Measure for Measure," 357–60.
24. Zakovitch, *Looking Glass*, 61: "Explication of the name Babel explains the builders' punishment."
25. Cassuto, *Genesis*, 165: "Later the story relates with bitter irony that they won a name (v. 9) but a derogatory one signifying their language that was confounded."

scattered[26] (*nafuts*) all over the world" (v. 4). The people said, "Let us build ourselves a city and a tower" (v. 4 Fox), to which God's response was "Let us, then, go down and confound their speech" (v. 7).

The Tower of Babel story is a source of polemic both vis-à-vis other Bible stories and parallel tales in Babylonian literature. As Zakovitch and Shinan have noted, "The entire Tower story disputes the Babylonian tradition that saw building the temple to Marduk in Babylon as an expression of veneration to that god and to the belief in Babylon as the point of juncture of heaven and earth—the gate of heaven."[27] When readers are aware that the story they are reading is a response to another biblical or extra-biblical story, understanding becomes deeper.

6.1.2. The Tower of Babel story and the story of building the E-sag-ila.[28]
The irony of the Tower of Babel story—the (inverse) linking of human and Divine deeds—are probably present also in the description of the building of the E-sag-ila, which appears in the Babylonian creation myth, *Enuma Elish*. "There seems to be a discrepancy between what the Babylonians thought was grandeur and honor, a sort of parody."[29]

The Babylonian story tells of the decision to build Babel, with its tower, as thanksgiving to their god:

> And now, Lord, who has granted us deliverance
> How shall we give you thanks?…
>
> When Marduk heard this
> His face shone like the light of day
> "Let Babel that you desired, be built…"

---

26. The same linguistic device is used in Exod 1:10 when Pharaoh sought to "deal shrewdly" with the children of Israel lest they "rise up from the ground" (*pen irbeh*, v. 10). But "the more they were oppressed, the more they increased and spread out" (*ken irbeh*, v. 12).

27. Zakovitch and Shinan, *That's Not What the Good Book Says*, 67.

28. Shifra and Klein, *Distant Days*, 41 n. 46 "*E-sag-ila* is the central temple of Marduk king of Babylon. The name is Sumerian and means 'house of raising of the head.'"

29. Cassuto, *Genesis*, 155. Cassuto (p. 157) surmises that the story (Gen 11:1–9) was written "after the city lay in ruins, the Israelites relating to Babylonian pride in irony…'you called your city *Bab-ili*, the gate of God, and your tower foundation of heaven and earth… You did not know that only God Himself—no human being—can determine where the gate of God is, and you did not know that the heavens belong to God and the earth He gave to men.'" Notwithstanding, Jacob understands Bethel to be "the gate of heaven" (28:17). See also Zakovitch, *Looking Glass*, 61.

> For a year they baked her bricks
> Came the second year
> And they raised the E-sag-ila's head to face the *afsu*
> They built the tower, the highest *afsu*.
>
> They established seats for Anu, for Anlil, for Eah and for him (Marduk).[30]

By contrast, construction in Gen 11:1–9 was not designed to exalt God: men built city and tower "to make a name for ourselves." It therefore seemed to dispute the Babylonian story in which Marduk's temple was called "house of the raised head" (*E-sag-ila*) where the tower soared aloft.

6.1.3. Similarities between the Tower of Babel and sullam *of Jacob stories.* The need for comparison arises first when one notes that both stories contain the unique expression "its top in the sky" (Gen 11:4; 28:12). As Buber asserts, "When a word appears only twice in the Bible, it should be regarded as an extraordinary key word linking the two stories in which it appears, as in the case of 'go forth' and 'angels of God.'"[31]

Both stories, moreover, contain the elements *ladder* and *tower* being built between earth and sky, and both conclude by explaining the name of the place. The Akkadian *Bab ili*, "Gate of God," creates an association with Jacob's response, "This is none other but the house of God, and this is *the gate of heaven*" (Gen 28:17).[32]

In both stories, too, events take place along both vertical[33] and horizontal axes. The vertical plane includes movement between heaven and earth (11:4; 28:12, 17) with the motion verbs of ascent and descent (11:5, 7; 28:12). On the horizontal plane, we find "scattered them" (11:9) and "will keep thee…and bring thee again into this land (28:15); "so that I come in peace to my father's house" (28:21). "Scattered" appears in Gen 11:4, 8 and 9. In Gen 28, "spread abroad" and "go" appear respectively in vv. 15 and 20, "come" in v. 21.

30. Shifra and Klein, *Anthology*, 41–42, col. 50–69.
31. Buber, *Way of the Bible*, 293.
32. M. Weinfeld, *From Joshua to Josiah: Turning Points in the History of Israel From the Conquest of the Land Until the Fall of Judah* (Jerusalem: Magnes, 1992), 126. For more similarities between the two stories, see Zakovitch and Shinan, *That's Not What the Good Book Says*, 67–72.
33. Besides vertical movement (= verbs) there are vertical objects (= nouns), such as the *sullam*, the pillar and the tower. See also J. P. Berton, "Sacred Place," *ER* 12:526, stating that a basic role of a sacred place is "a place for contact with God, so that such symbols might be vertical objects that reach from earth toward heaven, such as mountains, trees, ropes, pillars and poles."

Verbs of horizontal motion in the two stories relate to human beings, while those of vertical motion relate to God or angels of God. The two planes appear to be woven together.

6.1.4. *Linking the Tower and the* sullam *with the Babylonian ziggurat.* The similarity between the two stories invites comparison, and the Tower of Babel story has received much attention from von Rad, Griffith, Milard, Fidler, Zakovitch and others. Such research relates in particular to the Babylonian ziggurat.

For our purposes, the threefold connection highlights the ziggurat as a temple that the Babylonians regarded as linking heaven and earth. Stone notes that the inspiration for "the later legend of the tower in Babel (Gen. 11:4–9) derives from the Babylonian ziggurat dedicated to Marduk and known as the Temple of the Foundation of Heaven and Earth."[34]

"In Mesopotamia from the end of the third millennium B.C.E., there are texts relating to the central temple to which people flock from all corners of the land."[35] The first large center was at the Sumerian city of Nippur. Weinfeld writes:

> Babel arose later and regarded itself as replacing Nippur, and adopted this ideology. Nippur and Babylon called themselves *markas same u erseti*, which may be rendered as "navel of the world"… In Greece, at Delphi the temple was perceived as *omphalos*, the center of the world. It appears too that Bethel, a royal shrine in northern Israel (Amos 7:13) was seen in the kingdom of Israel as the point of connection between heaven and earth (Gen 28:22).[36]

Fidler adds: "An argument to this effect is found relating to central ritual sites in Israel (Shechem, Zion), and in the ANE regarding specific structures, especially the ziggurats that were perceived as a cosmic *axis mundi* linking the earth with the abode of the gods."[37]

As Zakovitch puts it, "A close look at the Tower and at the *sullam* shows that the early history of Bethel as a ritual center is a reflection of an act in early Babylon."[38]

---

34. Stone, "Ziggurat," 5:391.
35. Weinfeld, *From Joshua*, 124.
36. Ibid., 125.
37. Fidler, "The Dream Theophany," 175 n. 234.
38. Zakovitch, *Looking Glass*, 60. See also Zakovitch and Shinan, *That's Not What the Good Book Says*, 68–70.

6.1.5. *Points of difference*[39] *between the Tower of Babel and Jacob's* sullam. There are several points of differences between the Tower of Babel and the account of Jacob's *sullam*:

1. Building the tower with its head in the sky was a negative human initiative, while the dream revelation to Jacob of the *sullam* with its top in heaven was the will of God. Humans must remain on earth,[40] and if God wants, humans have a revelation of the link between heaven and earth.
2. The human plan on the vertical axis—building the tower to reach the sky—will not succeed. God stops them: "for nothing they propose will be out of their reach" (11:6). The *sullam*, by contrast, links heaven and earth, with angels of God ascending and descending on it. On the horizontal plane, such human initiative as "they migrated from the east, they and came upon a valley in the Land of Shinar" (11:2), brings to mind Terah's initiative to go to Canaan. Here Gitay[41] proposes that close reading of Gen 2–12 reveals a dominant theme, the idea of the Land. He lists seven events, the fifth being the Tower of Babel story, in which the geographical center is selected by humans, not God. Human initiative in either plane[42] does not accord with God's will and thus leads to a series of disasters.
3. Building the tower was to enhance human prestige: "and let us make *ourselves* a name" (11:4 Fox), in defiance of heaven (v. 6). Differently, the stone in Gen 28:22 was to be the foundation of God's house, to glorify His name.[43]
4. The fear of the Tower of Babel's builders is that they "shall be *scattered* all over the world" (11:8). This, ironically, is precisely what happens in v. 9: "from there the Lord *scattered* them over

---

39. The points of difference are those that prove my argument. For more, see Zakovitch, *Looking Glass*, 60–62.
40. Ibid.
41. Gitay, "Geography," 206.
42. The divine response does not specify precisely what meets with disfavor: "...now there will be no barrier for them in *all* that they scheme to do" (11:6 Fox). The word "all" here may include both planes.
43. Weinfeld, *Genesis*, 5: "Making a name in the Bible and in ANE literature generally involved erecting a monument (cf. 2 Sam 8:13; Isa 56:5), to a particular event." Thus Gen 28:22 may be seen to dispute "making a name for ourselves," for Jacob says: "and this stone which I have set shall be God's house." Weinfeld (p. 85) further notes: "Only the name of God is of value. A man making his own name is in the nature of sin." Compare the prophecy to David: "I will give you great renown, like that of the greatest men on earth" (2 Sam 7:9; also Isa 63:12, 14).

the face of the whole earth."⁴⁴ Everything humans did was intended to prevent what they feared most—wandering of the world. And yet, this was precisely what caused them, as a divine punishment, to be scattered.

5. The wandering they feared—their punishment—was the reward promised Jacob on the journey he was beginning: "And thy seed shall be as the dust of the earth, and thou shalt spread abroad to the west and to the east, to the north and to the south...and I will bring thee again to this land for I will not leave thee..." (28:14–15). In the Tower of Babel story God perceived the human act as a sin, or more precisely as violating his commandment to be fruitful and multiply and fill all the earth (Gen 1:28). Hence humans were scattered over the face of the earth, against their will. Regarding the Jacob's *sullam* story, God promises to return Jacob "to this land," and from the vow too it is understood that Jacob is about to leave *only temporarily*—he intends to return to his father's house (v. 21).

6. In both stories the place name is explicated. Babel indicates the builders' punishment: "That is why it was called Babel, because there the Lord confounded the speech of the whole earth" (11:9). The name Bethel, by contrast, shows that Jacob recognizes God's presence there: "How dreadful is this place! This is none other than the house of God and this is the gate of heaven (28:17; see also 28:7, 19 and 22).

6.2. *The Differences Between the Two Stories Help to Interpret Jacob's Dream*

The picture emerging from the differences shows that the beginning of the Bethel ritual site is a mirror-image of the beginning of Babylon. According to Zakovitch,

> It seems that the narrator of Genesis 28 knew not only Genesis 11 and the Babylonian tradition, but an additional tradition: that the explication of Babel in Genesis 11 is that it was a polemic name given to conceal the

---

44. Pharaoh gives his people similar reasons for oppressing the Israelites—"Let us deal shrewdly with them that they may not increase"—with similar results in both cases. In Gen 11:8, 9, "The Lord scattered them from there over all the face of the earth," while in Exod 1:12 we read: "But the more they were oppressed, the more they spread out." Additionally, Exodus describes hard labor in making bricks, "they made life bitter for them with harsh labor at mortar and bricks" (1:14), which is similar to Gen 11:3, "Let us make bricks...bricks served them as stone and bitumen as mortar."

true meaning of *Bab ili*, meaning the gate of God, or *Bab itani*, gate of the gods. By implying the comparison of Jacob's revelation to the sin of the Mesopotamians, *the narrator transposes the "gate of heaven" from Babylon to Bethel*, as Jacob proclaims in v. 17.[45]

And to avoid misunderstandings, Zakovitch concludes: "This place and not Babylon, i.e. the gate of heaven is Bethel, not in Babylon."[46]

Within our thesis of interwoven vertical and horizontal planes that complement one another, transfer of the *gate of heaven* from Babylon to Bethel symbolizes acceptance of the Patriarchs' movement from Ur of the Chaldees to Canaan, which testified to drawing closer to God, both physically and spiritually. The corridors, as it were, to the gate of heaven moved from Babylon to Bethel following the Patriarchs' journey, which was commanded by Abraham's God: "Go forth from your native land and from your father's house to the land that I will show you" (Gen 12:1).

Strange as it may seem at first sight, the movement of heaven's gate to Bethel in Canaan is noted specifically as Jacob is about to leave that land. Upon reconsideration, however, it is not so strange, for against the background of departure the preference for Canaan over any land outside it is stated. This signifies that Jacob's descent is only for the purpose of ascent, and that he will return, just as his mother had promised (27:44) and as God had promised him (28:15).

6.3. *Establishing the Gate of Heaven at Bethel, Not Babylon*

The *sullam* in Jacob's Dream symbolizes the way between Babylon and Bethel. One end of it is on the ground, representing Babylon, and the other in heaven, representing Bethel in the Land of Canaan, where God stood.[47] Babel's status as a mirror-image of Bethel, is a parallel of the deeds of humans in Gen 11, which are contrary to God's will, reinforces God's preference for Bethel in Canaan, which is now the navel of the world. A metonymic-symbolic relationship is inferred between Babel and foreign lands (the Land of Babylon at least), and Bethel and the Land

---

45. Zakovitch, *Looking Glass*, 60–61 (emphasis added).
46. Ibid. One can maintain, too, that later "this place" moved to Jerusalem, just as "this land," when it relates to "Promised Land," became an ambiguous, flexible term.
47. That Bethel symbolizes Canaan is understood from 35:6: "Thus came Jacob to Luz—that is Bethel—in the land of Canaan." "In the land of Canaan" simply explicates a reflection of the words in Gen 11:2: "and settled there" is distinguished from "here." "There" appears four more times in the Tower of Babel story—in vv. 7, 8 and twice in v. 9—highlighting its significance as a keyword. See Zakovitch, "Reflection Stories," 165–76.

of Israel. Consequently, any journey to Bethel (the abode of God according to Jacob's Dream) is an *ascent*, is positive, while leaving it is *descent*, distancing one from God, and hence negative.

7. *In Conclusion:*[48] *The Gate of Heaven in Jerusalem— A Departure Point for Further Research*

When Jacob declares upon awakening, "This is none other than the house of God, and this is the gate of heaven" (28:17), he refers to the place where he dreamt his dream, Bethel. "This" has been seen to indicate Jacob's polemic with another place, with Babylon's tradition as a site of union between heaven and earth. But the journey of the gate of heaven does not end here.

A similar expression brings our story to mind in the dedication of Jerusalem in 1 Chr 22:1: "David said, 'Here (*zeh*) will be the house of the Lord,[49] and here (*zeh*) the altar of burnt offerings for Israel,'" and the double use of "here," *zeh*, suggests both in form and content the language of Jacob's Dream in Gen 28:17. The two are tabulated below:

Jacob regarding Bethel (Genesis 28:17)	*David regarding Jerusalem (1 Chronicles 22:1)*
This is (*zeh*) none other than the house of God	Here (*zeh*) will be the house of the Lord
And this is (*zeh*) the gate of heaven	And here (*zeh*) the altar of burnt offerings for Israel

According to Zakovitch, "The removal of the gate of heaven from Babylon, unworthy of such a title, to Bethel where God shows Jacob the place of the gate, is not the end of the process. The story of Araunah's threshing floor, the story of Jerusalem's consecration in David's time as

---

48. Will the conclusion come only at the End of Days? See Peleg, "Peace Vision," 7–33.

49. Y. Amit, "Araunah's Threshing Floor: A Lesson in Shaping Historical Memory," in *What Was Authoritative for Chronicles?* (ed. E. Ben-Zvi and D. Edelman; Winona Lake, Ind.: Eisenbrauns, 2011), 133–44: "David states that the place of the altar in Araunah's threshing floor is Israel's legitimate temple, repeating the deictic expression זֶה 'this' twice: '*This* is the house of the Lord, and this is the altar for burnt offerings for Israel…' This phrasing returns us to the Jacob's Dream story, in which Jacob reiterates the sanctity of the place by repeating the deictic expression 'this' four times (Gen 28:16–17). It is difficult to ignore the resemblance between Jacob's words, 'This is none other than the house of God,' and those of David, 'This is the house of the Lord God,' although Jacob was sanctifying Bethel while the Chronicler is discussing Jerusalem."

4. Conclusion and Departure Point

told in Chronicles, the text adds to the account in 2 Sam 24 "David said, here (*zeh*) will be the House of the Lord and here (*zeh*) the altar of burnt offerings for Israel.'"[50] Moreover, in both stories the speaker's reaction stems from his awe: Jacob says, "How dreadful is this place," while David "was terrified by the sword of the angel of the Lord" (1 Chr 21:30).

In Zakovitch's opinion, there seems to be a purpose in formulating the Chronicles text in the spirit of its source, expressing the tendency to see in different ritual sites simply other names for a single place, Jerusalem.[51] Thus, later, the Midrash, which does not recognize the polemic and perhaps not the competition between the two, identifies Bethel with Jerusalem:

> Jacob was seventy seven years old when he left his father's house and the well went before him from Beer-Sheba to Mount Moriah. And he reached there late in the day…and spent the night there, for the sun was setting. Jacob took twelve stones from the stones of the altar on which his father Isaac was bound and set them at his head at that same place… Jacob awoke in great fright and said: the abode of the Holy One is here: "this is the gate of heaven."[52]

The gate of heaven, then, does not cease to wander in the story of Jacob's *sullam*, which appears as a mirror-image or as a reflection story of the Tower of Babel story. The Chronicler moves the gate of heaven at Bethel to the site God chose for the Temple in Jerusalem.

Amit, in her book on the revealed and the concealed in the Bible, discusses Bethel as the subject of a hidden polemic: "Biblical literature has an ambivalent attitude to Bethel. There are traditions that indicate its time-honored sacred status, while other texts are acutely critical of the place."[53] Amit clearly refers to Jacob's Dream (28:21–22) and Abraham's earlier building of an altar there (12:8). Criticism of Bethel is familiar from the Prophets, as in Hos 4:15; 5:8; 10:5; Amos 2:14; 4:4; 5:5; and Jer 48:13. Amit notes: "Ritual at Bethel was criticized particularly at the time of Josiah's reform (1 Kgs 13), in support of ritual concentrated in a single place. Bethel was thus perceived as competing with Jerusalem."[54]

---

50. Zakovitch, *Looking Glass*, 62.
51. Y. Zakovitch, "Biblical Traditions Regarding the Beginnings of Jerusalem's Sacred Status," in *Jerusalem in the First Temple Period* (ed. D. Amit and R. Gonen; Jerusalem: Yad Ben-Zvi, 1990), 12–22.
52. *Pirqe Rabbi Eliezer* 35.
53. Amit, *Polemics*, 120–21.
54. Ibid., 121.

Assuming a link between the symbolic interpretation of Jacob's Dream and the motif of ascent to and descent from the Promised Land, clarifies the comparison between Jacob's Ladder and the Tower of Babel. In the perspective of that motif, Babel as a mirror-image of Bethel shows Bethel as preferred, and so it is the site of the gate of heaven, the entry to the abode of God. Therefore, in order to get closer to God, one should go up to Bethel and not to Babel.

In time, as noted, the abode of God moved from Bethel to Jerusalem, which left the abode of God within Canaan.

Jerusalem's centrality is reflected in Isaiah's vision of Judah and Jerusalem: "In the days to come, The Mount of the Lord's House shall stand firm above the mountains, and tower above the hills… And many peoples shall go and say: Come let us *go up to the mount of the Lord, to the house of the God of Jacob*" (Isa 2:2–3).[55]

Zakovitch correctly asserts a connection between the End of Days vision in Isaiah and the Tower of Babel story.[56] Furthermore, the place of that prophecy in Isaiah tells of human arrogance: "Man's haughty looks shall be brought low and the pride of mortals shall be humbled. None but the Lord shall be exalted in that day" (Isa 2:11–12). This brings to mind the human pride in the Tower of Babel story. Isaiah declares that God's hand will be "on *every soaring tower* and every mighty wall" (v. 15). Zakovitch adds: "The word 'mighty' (*betsurah*) also echoes the Tower of Babel story: "Nothing will be beyond their reach" (*yibbatser*, Gen 11:6). Additionally, one may notice that in Isaiah "every tower" seems to include and indicate the Tower of Babel.

Thus, many threads connect the Tower of Babel story with the story of the *sullam* at Bethel and the vision of the End of Days. The centrally important gate of heaven, as the entrance to the abode of God (or to the abode of His name), moved from Babylon, to Bethel and thence to Jerusalem.

---

55. See Peleg, "Peace Vision," 7–33.
56. Y. Zakovitch, *"Who Proclaims Peace, Who Brings Good Tidings": Seven Visions of Jerusalem's Peace* (Haifa: University of Haifa Press, 2004), 162. Zakovitch adds that Zephaniah understood the link between the two when he said: "For then I will make the peoples pure of speech, so they all invoke the Lord by name" (Zeph 3:9), the peoples referring to those in Isa 2:3–4. "Pure of speech" alludes to the punishment meted out in the Tower of Babel story in Gen 11:9: "That is why it was called Babel, because there the Lord confounded the speech of the whole earth."

4. Conclusion and Departure Point

The centrality[57] of the Land of Israel and of Jerusalem within the Jewish culture is stressed, for example, in *Tanhuma*:

> The land of Israel is at the center of the world.
> Jerusalem is at the center of the Land of Israel
> The Temple is at the center of Jerusalem.
> The Sanctuary is at the center of the Temple.
> The Ark is at the center of the Sanctuary and
> The Foundation Stone before the Ark is that on which the world is founded.[58]

Further, in later Talmudic literature, we read: "The Temple is above all Israel, and Israel is above all the nations."[59]

---

57. Weinfeld, *From Joshua*, 127, notes that the temple's cosmic quality is that it is the heart of the world, at its center. The map of ancient Babylon puts Babylon at the center of the cosmos. So too Jerusalem (in Ezek 5:5): "Thus said the Lord God: I will set Jerusalem in the midst of the nations, with countries round about her." Weinfeld notes that "in the midst" can be understood either as (1) in the middle or (1) among, but the first seems appropriate here, reappearing in v. 6: "the nations that are round about you." Even if Ezekiel was not referring to Jerusalem's location, but only to its connection to the nations, as G. Brin, *Olam Hatanach: Ezekiel* (ed. G. Brin; Tel Aviv: Davidson-Atai, 1993), 37, assumes, Brin's words are worth considering: "following this prophecy and in consequence of other writings, Jerusalem and *Erets Israel* in general was perceived as the navel of the world, as expressed beginning with the ancient translations of the Bible, the Apocrypha, the Dead Sea Scrolls, Philo, Josephus, the New Testament and even in later literature. Jerusalem's centrality and *Erets Israel* as the navel of the world may also be seen on ancient maps."

On Jerusalem perceived as the center of the world, see the *Letter of Aristeas*, Philo, and others, discussed in I. L. Seeligmann, "Jerusalem in the Thought of Hellenistic Judaism," in *Studies in Biblical Literature: Isac Arie Seeligmann* (ed. A. Horowitz, E. Tov and S. Japhet; Jerusalem: Magnes, 1992), 404.

58. *Tanhuma, Kedoshim*. Weinfeld, *From Joshua*, 127, thinks that the central temple is also the starting point of Creation, following Second Temple tradition: "the foundation stone (*even hashtiyah*) from which the navel of the world and from which the whole world extends (*Pirqe Rabbi Eliezer* 35)." Weinfeld (p. 127 n. 3): "Prof. Greenberg pointed out to me that *shtiyah* comes from the weaving domain (*shti va'erev*) and thus corresponds to 'from which the world was woven,' not 'on which the world was founded.'" See also S. Lieberman, *Tosefta kifshuta: Comprehensive Commentary to Tosefta*, vol. 4 (Moed; Newark, N.J.: Jewish Theological Seminary of America, 1955), 772–73.

59. Seeligmann, "Jerusalem," 403, cites this tradition from *Kiddushin* 69a. See the End of Days vision in Isa 2:2: "The Mount of the Lord's House shall stand above the mountains and tower above the hills." Whether in the physical or the spiritual sense, one must ascend to reach it, so that leaving it involves descent.

In conclusion, the title of the present book, *Going Up and Going Down: A Key to Interpreting Jacob's Dream*, indicates its goal. The discussion of ascent and descent as key to the symbolic meaning of Jacob's Dream shows that the vision of ascending and descending is interpreted as entering and leaving the Promised Land. Awakening, Jacob exclaims: "This is none other than the House of God, and this is *the gate of heaven*" (Gen 28:17). That gate, like all others, is intended for entry and departure, ingress and egress. In the course of time, the gate of heaven,[60] the abode of God, moved from Bethel to Jerusalem.

As this study has hopefully demonstrated, a commonly held perspective is that approaching the abode of God—whether from within the Promised Land or outside it—is considered as *ascent* (Hebrew *'aliya*). This idea is most succinctly expressed in the Hebrew epitaph of the revered Chief Rabbi of Israel, Rabbi Abraham Isaac Hacohen Kook (1865–1935), on the Mount of Olives in Jerusalem:

> Ascended (*'alah*) to the Land of Israel, 28th of *Iyar* (1904)
> Ascended (*'alah*) to Jerusalem, 3rd of *Elul* (1919)
> Ascended (*'alah*) to heaven, 3rd of *Elul* (1935).

---

60. See the detailed discussion in Zakovitch, *Looking Glass*, 12–22.

BIBLIOGRAPHY

Aharoni, Y. *Atlas Carta for the Biblical Period*. Vol. 1 of the *Atlas Carta for the History of the Land of Israel*. Jerusalem: Carta, 1972 (Hebrew).
Alt, A. "The God of the Fathers." Pages 1–77 in *Essays on Old Testament History and Religion*. Translated by R. A. Wilson. Oxford: Blackwell, 1966.
Alter, R. *The Art of Biblical Narrative*. New York: Basic, 1981.
———. *The Art of the Biblical Story*. Translated by S. Zingel. Tel Aviv: Adam, 1988 (Hebrew).
Amit, Y. "Araunah's Threshing Floor: A Lesson in Shaping Historical Memory." Pages 133–44 in *What Was Authoritative for Chronicles?* Edited by E. Ben-Zvi and D. Edelman. Winona Lake, Ind.: Eisenbrauns, 2011.
———. *The Book of Judges: The Art of Editing*. Jerusalem: Mosad Bialik, 1992 (Hebrew).
———. "Double Causation: An Additional Aspect." *Beit Mikra* 38 (1993): 41–55 (Hebrew).
———. "'The Glory of Israel Will Not Lie Nor Repent; For He Is Not a Man, That He Should Repent': On the Trustworthiness of Narrators and Spokesmen in the Bible Story." Pages 45–56 in *Or leYa'akov: Research Studies on the Bible and the Dead Sea Scrolls in Memory of Yaakov Shalom Licht*. Edited by Y. Hoffman and F. Polak. Jerusalem: Mosad Bialik, 1997 (Hebrew).
———. *Judges*. Mikra Leyisrael. Tel Aviv: Am Oved, 1999 (Hebrew).
———. "The Problem of Multiple Uses of the Term 'Key Word.'" *Sadan* 1 (1994): 35–47 (Hebrew).
———. *Reading Biblical Stories*. Tel Aviv: Misrad Habitahon, 2000 (Hebrew).
———. *Revealed and Hidden in the Bible: Hidden Polemics in Biblical Narrative*. Tel Aviv: Yediot Aharonot, 2003 (Hebrew).
Arpeli, B. "Caution, Biblical Literature! On the Story of David and Bathsheba and Questions of Poetics in the Biblical Story." *Hasifrut* 2 (1970): 580–97 (Hebrew).
Avi-Yonah, M. "The Madaba Map." Pages 839–40 in vol. 4 of Cassuto et al., eds., *Encyclopaedia Biblica*.
Avishur, I. *Olam Hatanach: Genesis*. Edited by M. Weinfeld. Tel Aviv: Davidson-Atai, 1982 (Hebrew).
Bal, M. *Lethal Love: Feminist Literary Reading of Biblical Love Stories*. Bloomington, Ind.: Indiana University Press, 1987.
———. *Narratology: Introduction to the Theory of Narrative*. Translated by C. van Boheemen. Toronto: University of Toronto Press, 1985.
Bahar, S. "Silence Is the Message." *Moed: Annual for Jewish Studies* 17 (2007): 1–21 (Hebrew).

Bar, S. *A Letter That Has Not Been Read: Dreams in the Hebrew Bible.* Translated by L. J. Schramm. Monographs of the Hebrew Union College 25. Cincinnati: Hebrew Union College Press, 2001.
Bar-Efrat, S. *The Artistic Design of the Biblical Story.* 4th ed. Tel Aviv: Sifriyat Poalim, 1993 (Hebrew).
Barth, J. "Tales Within Tales Within Tales." *Antaeus* 43 (1981): 45–63.
Baruch, E. "The Prophetic Dream and Its Rejection by the Deuteronomic School." M.A. diss., University of Haifa, 1987 (Hebrew).
Barzel, H. *New Interpretations of Literary Texts: From Theory to Method.* Ramat Gan: Bar Ilan University Press, 1990 (Hebrew).
Ben-David, A. *The Language of the Bible and the Language of the Sages.* Tel Aviv: Dvir, 1967 (Hebrew).
Bentzen, A. "The Weeping of Jacob: Hos xii 5a." *Vetus Testamentum* 1 (1951): 58–59.
Berlin, A. *Poetics and Interpretation of Biblical Narrative.* Bible and Literature Series 9. Sheffield: Almond, 1983.
Berman, J. A. "Medieval Monasticism and the Evolution of Jewish Interpretation of the Story of Jephthah's Daughter." *Jewish Quarterly Review* 95 (2005): 228–56.
———. *Narrative Analogy in the Hebrew Bible: Battle Stories and Their Equivalent Non-battle Narratives.* Supplements to Vetus Testamentum 103. Leiden: Brill, 2004.
Berton, J. P. "Sacred Place." Pages 526–35 in vol. 12 of *The Encyclopedia of Religion.* Edited by M. Eliade. 16 vols. New York: Macmillan, 1987.
Blum, E. *Die Komposition der Vatergeschichte.* Wissenschaftliche Monographien zum Alten und Neuen Testament 57. Neukirchen-Vluyn: Neukirchener Verlag, 1984.
Bosworth, D. A. *The Story Within a Story in Biblical Hebrew Narrative.* Catholic Biblical Quarterly Monograph Series 45. Washington, D.C.: Catholic Biblical Association of America, 2008.
Brauner, R. A. "'To Grasp the Hem' and 1 Samuel 15:27." *Journal of the Ancient Near Eastern Society* 6 (1974): 35–38.
Brecht, B. "An Unconquered Inscription." Page 33 in *Selected Poems.* Translated by M. Avi-Shaul. Tel Aviv: Sifriyat Poalim, 1959 (Hebrew).
Brenner, A. *Ruth and Naomi: Literary, Stylistic and Linguistic Studies in the Book of Ruth.* Tel Aviv: Hakibbutz Hameuhad, 1988 (Hebrew).
Brettler, M. Z. "The Promise of the Land of Israel to the Patriarchs in the Pentateuch." *Shnaton: An Annual for Biblical and Ancient Near Eastern Studies* 5–6 (1978–9): 7–24.
Brin, G. *Olam Hatanach: Ezekiel.* Edited by G. Brin. Tel Aviv: Davidson-Atai, 1993 (Hebrew).
Brogan, W. "Plato's Pharmakon: Between Two Repetitions." Pages 7–23 in *Derrida and Deconstruction.* Edited by H. J. Silverman. New York: Routledge, 1978.
Brown, C. H. "Where Do Cardinal Direction Terms Come From?" *Anthropological Linguistics* 25 (1983): 121–61.
Buber, M. *The Way of the Bible.* Jerusalem: Mosad Bialik, 1964 (Hebrew).
Butler, S. A. L. *Mesopotamian Conceptions of Dreams and Dream Rituals.* Münster: Ugarit-Verlag, 1998.
Carr, M. D. "Genesis 28, 10–22 and Transmission-Historical Method: A Reply to John Van Seters." *Zeitschrift für die alttestamentliche Wissenschaft* 111 (1999): 399–403.
———. *Reading the Fractures of Genesis: Historical and Literary Approaches.* Louisville, Ky.: Westminster John Knox, 1996.

Cartledge, T. W. *Vows in the Hebrew Bible and the Ancient Near East*. Journal for the study of the Old Testament: Supplement Series 147. Sheffield: JSOT, 1992.
Cassuto, M. D. *Biblical and Oriental Studies: Biblical Literature and Canaanite Literature*. Vol. 1. Jerusalem: Magnes, 1974 (Hebrew).
———. *The Book of Genesis and Its Structure*. Jerusalem: Magnes, 1990 (Hebrew).
———. *Commentary on the Book of Genesis*. 2 vols. Jerusalem: Magnes, 1964 (Hebrew).
Cassuto, M. D. et al., eds. *Encyclopaedia Biblica*. 8 vols. Jerusalem: Mosad Bialik, 1950–82 (Hebrew).
Clifford, R. J. *The Cosmic Mountain in Canaan and the Old Testament*. Harvard Semitic Monographs 4. Cambridge, Mass.: Harvard University Press, 1972.
Coats, G. W. *Genesis: With an Introduction to Narrative Literature*. The Forms ot the Old Testament Literature 1. Grand Rapids, Mich.: Eerdmans, 1983.
Cohen, H. R. *Biblical Hapax Legomena in the Light of Akkadian and Ugaritic*. Society of Biblical Literature Dissertation Series 37. Missoula, Mont.: Scholars Press, 1978.
———. "Medieval Commentary on Genesis in the Light of Contemporary Biblical Philology—Part 2: Genesis 19–29." Pages 25–46 in *Masat Aharon: Language Studies Collection Presented to Aron Dotan*. Edited by M. Ben-Asher and H. A. Cohen. Jerusalem: Mosad Bialik, 2010 (Hebrew).
———. "The Literary Motif in Jacob's Ladder (Gen 28:12)." Pages 1–45 in *A Gift for Hadassah, Studies in Hebrew and in Jewish Languages*. Edited by J. Ben Tolila. Beer-Sheba: Ben Gurion University, 1997 (Hebrew).
———. "The Sullam." Page 172 in *Olam Hatanach: Genesis*. Edited by M. Weinfeld. Tel Aviv: Davidson-Atai, 1982 (Hebrew).
Dallenbach, L. *The Mirror in The Text*. Translated by J. Whiteley and E. Hughes. Chicago: University of Chicago Press, 1989.
Dalley, S. *Myths from Mesopotamia: Creation, the Flood, Gilgamesh, and Others*. Oxford: Oxford University Press, 1989.
Daube, D. *The Exodus Pattern in the Bible*. All Souls Studies 2. London: Faber & Faber, 1963.
De Pury, A. *Promesse Divine et Légende Culturelle dans le Cycle de Jacob: Genèse 28 et les Traditions Patriarcales*. 2 vols. Paris: Gabalda, 1975.
Deurloo, K. A. "Narrative Geography in the Abraham Cycle." Pages 48–62 in *In Quest of the Past: Studies on Israelite Religion, Literature and Prophetism*. Edited by A. S. van der Woude. Oudtestamentische studiën 26. Leiden: Brill, 1990.
———. "The Way of Abraham." Pages 95–112 in *Voices from Amsterdam: A Modern Tradition of Reading Biblical Narrative*. Edited and translated by M. Kessler. Atlanta, Ga.: Scholars Press, 1994.
Diengott, N. *The Poetics of Fiction*. Tel Aviv: Open University, 1986 (Hebrew).
Dor, Y. *Were the Foreign Wives Actually Expelled? The Separation Issue During the Return to Zion*. Jerusalem: Magnes, 2006 (Hebrew).
Driver, G. R. "On ʿalah 'Went Up Country' and yarad 'Went Down'." *Zeitschrift für die alttestamentliche Wissenschaft* 69 (1957): 74–77.
Driver, S. R. *The Book of Genesis*. 2d ed. Westminster Commentaries. London: Methuen, 1904.
———. *Introduction to the Literature of the Old Testament*. New York: Meridian, 1957.
Efal, I. "*Qedem*." Page 26 in vol. 7 of the *Encyclopaedia Hebraica*. Edited by J. Klausner et al. 32 vols. Jerusalem, 1948–80 (Hebrew).

Ehrlich, L. *Der Traum im Alten Testament*. Beihefte zur Zeitschrift für die alttestamentliche Wissenschaft 73. Berlin: Töpelmann, 1953.

———. "Traum." Pages 20–23 in vol. 3 of the *Biblisch-historisches Handwörterbuch: Landeskunde, Geschichte, Religion, Kultur*. Edited by B. Reicke and L. Rost. 4 vols. Göttingen: Vandenhoeck & Ruprecht, 1962–79.

Eichrodt, W. *Theology of the Old Testament*. Translated by J. A. Baker. 2 vols. Old Testament Library. Philadelphia: Westminster, 1967.

Elgavish, D. *Diplomacy in the Bible from Documents of the Ancient East*. Jerusalem: Magnes, 1998 (Hebrew).

———. "The Messenger and the Mission: Diplomacy in Cuneiform Sources in the Ancient East and the Bible." Ph.D. diss., Bar Ilan University, 1990 (Hebrew).

Eliade, M. *Myths, Dreams and Mysteries: The Encounter Between Contemporary Faiths and Archaic Realities*. Translated by P. Mairet. New York: Harper & Row, 1960.

Elizur, A. *From Within and Without: Psychoanalytical Studies in the Bible and in Judaism*. Tel Aviv: Yarom, 1988 (Hebrew).

Elitzur, Y. *Israel and the Bible: Studies in Geography, History and Biblical Thought*. Ramat Gan: Bar Ilan University, 1999 (Hebrew).

Empson, W. *Seven Types of Ambiguity*. London: Chatto & Windus, 1930.

Fidler, R. *Do Dreams Speak Falsely? Dream Theophanies in the Bible: Their Place in Ancient Israelite Faith and Traditions*. Jerusalem: Magnes, 2005 (Hebrew).

———. "The Dream Theophany in the Bible, Its Place in the History of Biblical Literature and Israelite Religion." Ph.D. diss., The Hebrew University, 1996 (Hebrew).

Fish, A. H. "Eldad and Medad Prophesy Within the Camp: a Structuralist Study of Numbers 11." *Studies in Bible and Exegesis* 5 (1997): 45–55 (Hebrew).

———. "A Structuralist Approach to the Stories of Ruth and Boaz." *Beit Mikra* 24 (1979): 260–65 (Hebrew).

Fishbane, M. *Biblical Interpretation in Ancient Israel*. Oxford: Clarendon, 1985.

———. "Composition and Structure in the Jacob Cycle (Gen 25:19–35:22)." *Journal of Jewish Studies* 26 (1975): 15–38.

———. *Text and Texture: Close Readings of Selected Biblical Texts*. New York: Schocken, 1979.

Fisher, L. R. "Literary Genres in the Ugaritic Texts." Pages 131–52 in *Ras Shamra Parallels: The Texts from Ugarit and the Hebrew Bible*. Edited by L. R. Fisher. Analecta Orientalia 50. Rome: Pontificium Istitutum Biblicum, 1975.

———. "Two Projects at Claremont." *Ugarit-Forschungen* 3 (1971): 27–31.

Fleishman, J. "Socio-Legal Aspects of Genesis 34." *Shenaton: An Annual for Biblical and Ancient Near Eastern Studies* 13 (2002): 141–55 (Hebrew).

Fokkelman, J. P. *Narrative Art in Genesis: Specimens of Stylistic and Structural Analysis*. Studia Semitica Neerlandica 17. Assen: Van Gorcum, 1975.

Fox, E. *The Five Books of Moses: A New Translation with Introductions, Commentary, and Notes*. New York: Schocken, 1995.

Frazer, J. G. *The Golden Bough: A Study in Magic and Religion*. 3d ed. New York: Macmillan, 1935.

———. *Folklore in the Old Testament: Studies in Comparative Religion, Legend and Law*. Abridged ed. London: Macmillan, 1923.

Freud, S. "The Dream." Pages 151–63 in *Introduction to Psychoanalysis*. Translated by H. Isac. Vol. 1 in *Collected Works of Sigmund Freud*. Tel Aviv: Dvir, 1968 (Hebrew).

———. *The Interpretation of Dreams*. Translated by M. Brachiahu. Tel Aviv: Yavneh, 1959 (Hebrew).

Friedman, R. E. *Who Wrote the Bible?* Edited and translated by S. Abulafia and D. Rubinstein. Tel Aviv: Dvir, 1995 (Hebrew).

Gammie, J. G. "Theological Interpretation by Way of Literary and Tradition Analysis: Genesis 25–36." Pages 117–34 in *Encounter with the Text: Form and History in the Hebrew Bible*. Edited by M. J. Buss. Society of Biblical Literature Semeia Studies. Philadelphia: Fortress, 1979.

Garsiel, M. "Literary Structure and Message in the Stories of Jacob and Esau." Pages 63–81 in *Hagut Bamikra: Collected Essays in Memory of Yishai Ron*. Edited by E. Hamenaham. Tel Aviv: Am Oved, 1983 (Hebrew).

———. "Metonymic and Metaphoric Descriptions in the Bible Story." *Criticism and Interpretation* 23 (1988): 5–40 (Hebrew).

———. *Olam Hatanach: Isaiah*. Edited by Y. Hoffman. Tel Aviv: Davidson-Atai, 1986 (Hebrew).

Gaster, T. H. *Myth, Legend, and Custom in the Old Testament: A Comparative Study with Chapters from Sir James G. Frazer's Folklore in the Old Testament*. New York: Harper & Row, 1969.

Geller, S. A. "The Struggle of Jacob: The Uses of Enigma in a Biblical Narrative." *Journal of the Ancient Near Eastern Society* 14 (1982): 37–61.

Genette, G. *Narrative Discourse: An Essay in Method*. Translated by J. E. Lewin. Ithaca, N.Y.: Cornell University Press, 1980.

Ginzberg, L. *The Legends of the Jews*. Translated and edited by M. Hacohen. 2 vols. Ramat Gan: Masada, 1967 (Hebrew).

Gitay, Y. "Geography and Theology in the Biblical Narrative: The Question of Genesis 2–12." Pages 205–16 in *Prophets and Paradigms: Essays in Honor of Gene M. Tucker*. Edited by S. B. Reid. Journal for the study of the Old Testament: Supplement Series 229. Sheffield: JSOT, 1996.

———. "Theories of Literature and the Question of (Hebrew) Biblical Theology: A Prolegomenon." *Scandinavian Journal of the Old Testament* 10 (1996): 61–68.

Gnuse, R. K. *The Dream Theophany of Samuel: Its Structure in Relation to Ancient Near Eastern Dreams and Its Theological Significance*. Lanham, Md.: University Press of America, 1984.

Good, E. M. "Hosea and the Jacob Tradition." *Vetus Testamentum* 16 (1966): 137–51.

Gordis, R. *The Word and the Book*. New York: Ktav, 1976.

Gray, J. *Joshua, Judges and Ruth*. The Century Bible. London: Nelson, 1967.

Greenberg, M. *On the Bible and Judaism: A Collection of Writings*. Tel Aviv: Am Oved, 1984 (Hebrew).

Greenfield, J. C. "The Zakir Inscription and the Danklied." Pages 174–91 in Peli and Shinan, eds., *Proceedings*.

Greenspahn, F. E. *Hapax Legomena in Biblical Hebrew*. Chico, Calif.: Scholars Press, 1984.

———. "A Mesopotamian Proverb and Its Biblical Reverberations." *Journal of the American Oriental Society* 114 (1994): 33–38.

Greenstein, E. L. "An Equivocal Reading of the Sale of Joseph." Pages 114–25 in *Literary Interpretation of Biblical Narrative*, vol. 2. Edited K. R. R. Gros Louis et al. Nashville: Abingdon, 1982.

———. "Job's Wife—Was She Right After All?" *Beit Mikra* 49 (2004): 19–31 (Hebrew).

———. "The Retelling of the Flood Story in the Gilgamesh Epic." Pages 197–204 in *Hesed Ve-Emet: Studies in Honor of Ernest S. Frerichs*. Edited by J. Magness and S. Gitin. Atlanta, Ga.: Scholars Press, 1998.

———. "Theory and Argument in Biblical Criticism." *Hebrew Annual Review* 10 (1986): 77–93.

———. "The Torah as She Is Read." Pages 29–51 in *Essays on Biblical Method and Translation*. Brown Judaic Studies 92. Atlanta, Ga.: Scholars Press, 1989.

———. "Trans-Semitic Idiomatic Equivalency and the Derivation of Hebrew *ml'kh*." *Ugarit-Forschungen* 11 (1979): 329–36.

Griffiths, J. G. "The Celestial Ladder and the Gate of Heaven (Genesis xxviii 12 and 17)." *Expository Times* 76 (1964–65): 229–30.

———. "The Celestial Ladder and the Gate of Heaven in Egyptian Ritual." *Expository Times* 78 (1966–67): 54–55.

Grossman, J. "Ambiguity in the Biblical Narrative and Its Contribution to the Literary Formation." Ph.D. diss., Bar Ilan University, 2006 (Hebrew).

Gunkel, H. *Genesis*. Göttingen: Vandenhoeck & Ruprecht, 1964.

———. *The Legends of Genesis: The Israelite Literature*. Translated by A. Zeron, R. Peled and D. Amara. The Biblical Encyclopaedia Library 16. Jerusalem: Mosad Bialik, 1998 (Hebrew).

Gunn, D. M., and D. N. Fewell. *Narrative in the Hebrew Bible*. Oxford: Oxford University Press, 1993.

Ha'Efrati, J. "The Dead of the Wilderness: A Lyric Poem." *Hasifrut* 1 (1968): 101–29 (Hebrew).

Haran, M. *Eras and Institutions in the Bible*. Tel Aviv: Am Oved, 1973 (Hebrew).

———. "Miqdash." Pages 322–27 in vol. 5 of Cassuto et al., eds., *Encyclopaedia Biblica*.

———. "Neder." Pages 785–90 in vol. 5 of Cassuto et al., eds., *Encyclopaedia Biblica*.

Harel, M. "*Qedmah*—South or East?" *Mada: Popular Science Magazine for All* 25 (1981): 9–11 (Hebrew).

Heltzer, M. *Olam Hatanach: Isaiah*. Edited by Y. Hoffman. Tel Aviv: Davidson-Atai, 1986 (Hebrew).

Hendel, R. S. "Patterns of the Hero in Early Israel: Jacob and Moses." Pages 138–65 in *The Epic of the Patriarch: The Jacob Cycle and the Narrative Traditions of Canaan and Israel*. Harvard Semitic Monographs 42. Atlanta, Ga.: Scholars Press, 1988.

Henderson, A. "On Jacob's Vision at Bethel." *Expository Times* 4 (1892–93): 151–52.

Hepner, G. "Abraham's Incestuous Marriage with Sarah: A Violation of the Holiness Code." *Vetus Testamentum* 53 (2003): 143–55.

Herbert, A. S. *Genesis 50–12: Introduction and Commentary*. Torch Bible commentaries. London: SCM, 1962.

Hezkuni. *Torat Haim: Five Books of the Law: Genesis*. Jerusalem: Mosad Harav Kook, 1990 (Hebrew).

Hoffman, Y. *Olam Hatanach: Isaiah*. Edited by Y. Hoffman. Tel Aviv: Davidson-Atai, 1986 (Hebrew).

———. *Olam Hatanach: Jeremiah*. Edited by Y. Hoffman. Tel Aviv: Davidson-Atai, 1994 (Hebrew).

Houtman, C. "Jacob at Mahanaim: Some Remarks on Genesis xxxii 2–3." *Vetus Testamentum* 28 (1978): 7–44.
———. "What Did Jacob See in His Dream at Bethel?" *Vetus Testamentum* 28 (1977): 337–51.
Husser, J. M. *Dreams and Dream Narratives in the Biblical World.* Sheffield: Sheffield Academic, 1999.
Iser, W. "Indefiniteness and the Response of the Reader of the Short Story to the Structure of Affinity in the Literary Text." *Hasifrut* 21 (1975): 1–15 (Hebrew).
Izhar, S.. *To Read a Story.* Tel Aviv: Am Oved, 1982 (Hebrew).
Japhet. S., ed. *Studies in Bible.* Scripta Hierosolymitana 31. Jerusalem: Magnes, 1986 (Hebrew).
Jefferson, A. "*Mise en abyme* and the Prophetic in Narrative." *Style* 17 (1983): 196–208.
Jenks, A. W. *The Elohist and North Israelite Traditions.* Society of Biblical Literature Monograph Series 22. Missoula, Mont.: Scholars Press, 1977.
Jirku, A. "Materialen zur Volksreligion Israels." Pages 297–313 in *Von Jerusalem nach Ugarit: Gesammelte Schriften.* Graz: Akademische Druck-u. Verlagsanstalt, 1966. Repr. from Leipzig: Deichert, 1914.
Josephus. *The Jewish Antiquities.* Translated by A. Schalit. Jerusalem: Mosad Bialik, 1967 (Hebrew)
Jung, K. G. *On Dreams.* Translated by H. Shoham and I. Toren. Jerusalem: Dvir, 1982 (Hebrew).
Kahana, A. *The Apocrypha.* Vol. 1. Tel Aviv: Mekorot, 1937 (Hebrew).
Kaufmann, Y. *The Book of Joshua.* Jerusalem: Kiriat Sefer, 1963 (Hebrew).
———. *The History of Israelite Belief: From Ancient Times to the End of the Second Temple.* 8 vols. Tel Aviv: Mosad Bialik, 1972 (Hebrew).
Keel, Y. *The Book of Genesis.* Daat Mikra. Jerusalem: Mosad Harav Kook, 1997 (Hebrew).
Kerem, D., ed. *Varied Opinions and Views on Dream in Israelite Culture.* Varied Opinions and Views in Israelite Culture 5. Rehovot: Kibbutz Education Department, 1995 (Hebrew).
Klein, J. *Olam Hatanach: Genesis.* Edited by M. Weinfeld. Tel Aviv: Davidson-Atai, 1982 (Hebrew).
Klein-Braslavi, S. "The Rambam's Commentaries on the Jacob's Dream Story." *Bar Ilan* 22–23 (1988): 329–49 (Hebrew).
Koch, K. "The Ancestress of Israel in Danger." Pages 111–28 in *The Growth of the Biblical Tradition: The Form-Critical Method.* Translated by S. M. Cupitt. New York: Scribner's Sons, 1969.
Kogut, S. "On the Meaning and Syntactical Status of *hinneh* in Biblical Hebrew." Pages 133–54 in Japhet, ed., *Studies in Bible*.
Kselman, J. S. "A Note on Numbers XII 6–8." *Vetus Testamentum* 26 (1976): 500–504.
Kutcher, R. "The Mesopotamian God Zaqar and Jacob's Dream." *Beer-Sheba* 3 (1988): 125–30 (Hebrew).
Lieberman, S. *Greek and Hellenism in Jewish Palestine.* Jerusalem: Mosad Bialik, 1962.
———. *Tosefta kifshuta: Comprehensive Commentary to Tosefta*, vol. 4. Newark, N.J.: Jewish Theological Seminary of America, 1955.
Leibowitz, N. *Studies in the Book of Exodus.* Jerusalem: World Zionist Organization, 1973 (Hebrew).

———. *Studies in the Book of Genesis*. Jerusalem: World Zionist Organization, 1969 (Hebrew).
Levi, Z. *Hermeneutics*. Tel Aviv: Sifriyat Poalim, 1986 (Hebrew).
Levin, Y. *Psychology of the Dream*. Tel Aviv: Dekel, 1980 (Hebrew).
Lévi-Strauss, C. *Structural Anthropology*, vol. 1. Translated by C. Jacobson and B. Grundfest Schoepf. New York: Basic, 1963.
Lichtenstein, M. "Dream Theophany and the E Document." *Journal of the Ancient Near Eastern Society* 1, no. 2 (1969): 45–54.
Lieberman, S. *Greek and Hellenism in Jewish Palestine*. Jerusalem: Mosad Bialik, 1962 (Hebrew).
Lipton, D. "Revisions of the Night: Politics and Promises in the Patriarchal Dreams of Genesis." Ph.D. diss., Cambridge University, 1996.
———. *Revisions of the Night: Politics and Promises in the Patriarchal Dreams of Genesis*. Journal for the Study of the Old Testament: Supplement Series 228. Sheffield: Sheffield Academic Press, 1999.
Loewenstamm, S. E. "Measure for Measure." Pages 840–46 in vol. 4 of Cassuto et al., eds., *Encyclopaedia Biblica*.
Machlin, R. "Polarity in the [Hebrew] Word *nefesh*." *Beit Mikra* 57 (1974): 401–15 (Hebrew).
Malul, M. *The Comparative Method in Ancient Near Eastern and Biblical Legal Studies*. Alter Orient und Altes Testament 227. Kevelaer: Butzon & Bercker, 1990.
———. "Studies in Legal Symbolic Acts in Mesopotamian Law." Ph.D. diss., University of Pennsylvania, 1983.
Mandelkern, S. *Veteris Testamenti Concordantiae*. 6th ed. Jerusalem: Schoken, 1965 (Hebrew).
Marcus, D. *Jephthah and His Vow*. Lubbock, Tex.: Texas Tech Press, 1986.
Margalit, B. "A Weltbaum in Ugaritic Literature?" *Journal of Biblical Literature* 90 (1971): 481–82.
McAlpin, T. H. *Sleep, Divine and Human in the Old Testament*. Journal for the Study of the Old Testament Supplement 38. Sheffield: Sheffield Academic, 1987.
Millard, A. R. "The Celestial Ladder and the Gate of Heaven (Genesis xxviii 12 and 17)." *Expository Times* 78 (1966–67): 86–87.
Miscall, P. D. *The Workings of Old Testament Narrative*. Semeia Studies. Chico, Ca.: Scholars Press, 1983.
Moriel, Y. *Israel and Its Land in the Torah*. Jerusalem: World Zionist Organization, 1988 (Hebrew).
Naveh, H. *Male and Female Travelers: Travel Stories in the Hebrew Literature*. Tel Aviv: Misrad Habitahon, 2002 (Hebrew).
Ne'eman, N. "Bethel and Bet Onn: The Problem of Locating Ancient Ritual Sites in Israel." *Zion* 50 (1985): 15–25 (Hebrew).
Niditch, S. *The Symbolic Vision in Biblical Tradition*. Harvard Semitic Monographs 30. Chico, Ca.: Scholars Press, 1983.
O'Connor, M. "Cardinal Direction Terms in Biblical Hebrew." Pages 1140–57 in vol. 2 of *Semitic Studies in Honor of Wolf Leslau on the Occasion of His Eighty-fifth Birthday*. Edited by A. S. Kaye. Wiesbaden: Harrassowitz, 1991.
Oppenheim, A. L. "Halom." Pages 143–49 in vol. 3 of Cassuto et al., eds., *Encyclopaedia Biblica*.

———. *The Interpretation of Dreams in the Ancient Near East: With a Translation of an Assyrian Dream-Book*. Transactions of the American Philosophical Society 46. Philadelphia: American Philosophical Society, 1956.

Otto, R. *The Idea of The Holy*. Translated by J. W. Harvey. London: Oxford University Press, 1950.

———. "Jakob in Bet El." *Zeitschrift für die alttestamentliche Wissenschaft* 88 (1976): 165–90.

Oz, A. *A Tale of Love and Darkness*. Jerusalem, Keter, 2002 (Hebrew).

Pagolu, A. *The Religion of the Patriarchs*. Journal for the Study of the Old Testament: Supplement Series 277. Sheffield: Sheffield Academic, 1998).

Parker, S. B. "The Vow in Ugaritic and Israelite Narrative Literature." *Ugarit-Forschungen* 11 (1979): 693–700.

Parrot, A. *The Tower of Babel*. Translated by E. Hudson. London: SCM, 1955.

Peleg, Y. I. "Abraham the First Zionist and the First *Yored*." *Al Haperek* 14 (1998): 25–31 (Hebrew).

———. "'And If I Came Back in Peace to My Father's House' (Gen 28:21): The Vow and Its Contribution to Understanding and Interpreting Jacob's Dream." *Beit Mikra* 46 (2001): 335–52.

———. "Duality in the Relationship of 'Man-God' in the Book of Job: Two Readings or Two Jobs." *Moed: Annual for Jewish Studies* 21 (2013), in Press (Hebrew).

———. "Going Up and Going Down: A Key to Interpreting Jacob's Dream." *Zeitschrift für die alttestamentliche Wissenschaft* 116 (2004): 1–11. (A Hebrew version of this article was published in *Hebrew Union College Annual* 76 [2005]: 33–47.)

———. "'I am the Lord Who Brought You Out from Ur of the Chaldeans': Who Brought Abraham Out and from Where?" *Moed: Annual for Jewish Studies* 17 (2007): 22–40 (Hebrew).

———. "The Motif of the Land Promised to the Patriarchs and Its Development in the Bible." M.A. diss., University of Haifa, 1987 (Hebrew).

———. "The Place (*Maqom*) in the Story of Jacob's Dream." *Al Haperek* 18 (2001): 83–91 (Hebrew).

———. "A Time to Know the Biblical Text." *Al Haperek* 19 (2002): 176–89 (Hebrew).

———. "Two Readings of the Story of David, Bathsheba and Uriah." Paper presented at the International Meeting of the SBL. Tartu, Estonia, July 27, 2009.

———. "Two Readings of the Vision of the End of Days: The Peace Vision of the End of Days in Isaiah (2:2–5) and the Peace Vision in Micah (4:1–5)." Pages 7–33 in *End Time and Afterlife in Judaism*. Edited by J. H. Ellens. Vol. 1 of *Heaven, Hell, and the Afterlife: Eternity in Judaism, Christianity, and Islam*. Santa Barbara, Calif.: Praeger, 2013. (An earlier version of this article was published in Hebrew in *Shnaton: An Annual for Biblical and Ancient Near Eastern Studies* 20 [2010]: 27–50.)

———. "Vision and Message in Jacob's Dream." *Moed: Annual for Jewish Studies* 13 (2003): 55–64 (Hebrew).

———. "Was Lot a Good Host? Was Lot Saved from Sodom as a Reward for His Hospitality?" Pages 134–62 in *Universalism and Particularism at Sodom and Gomorrah: Essays in Memory of Ron Pirson*. Edited by D. Lipton. Society of Biblical Literature Ancient Israel and Its Literature 11. Atlanta, Ga.: SBL, 2012.

———. "Was the Ancestress of Israel in Danger? Did Pharaoh Touch Sarai?" *Zeitschrift für die alttestamentliche Wissenschaft* 118 (2006): 197–208. (A Hebrew version of this article was published in *Beit Mikra* 48 [2003]: 54–64.)
———. "What Do the Declaration of Independence and the Promise of the Land to the Patriarchs Have in Common?" *Al Haperek* 16 (1999): 145–53 (Hebrew).
———. "What Is the *Sullam* That Jacob Saw in His Dream at Bethel?" *Shnaton: An Annual for Biblical and Ancient Near Eastern Studies* 14 (2004): 7–26 (Hebrew).
———. "When God Began to Create Water (*maim*) and Earth." *Beit Mikra* 41 (1996): 153–68. (Hebrew).
———. "'Yet Forty Days, and Nineveh Shall Be Overthrown' (Jonah 3:4): Two Readings of the Book of Jonah." Pages 262–74 in *God's Word for Our World: Biblical Studies in Honor of Simon John De Vries*. Edited by J. H. Ellens et al. Journal for the study of the Old Testament: Supplement Series 388. London: T&T Clark, 2004. (A Hebrew version of this article was published in *Beit Mikra* 44 [2000]: 226–43.)
Peli, P., and A. Shinan, eds. *Proceedings of the Fifth World Congress of Jewish Studies: Jerusalem 1969*, vol. 1. Jerusalem: The Hebrew University, 1973 (Hebrew)
Perry, M. "The Dynamics of the Literary Text." *Hasifrut* 28 (1979): 6–46 (Hebrew).
Perry, M., and M. Sternberg. "The King Through Ironic Eyes." *Hasifrut* 1 (1968): 263–92 (Hebrew).
———. "Caution, Literature! On Problems of Interpretation and Poetics in the Bible Story." *Hasifrut* 2 (1970): 608–63 (Hebrew).
Polak, F. *Biblical Narrative: Aspects of Art and Design*. The Biblical Encyclopaedia Library 11. Jerusalem: Mosad Bialik, 1994 (Hebrew).
Polzin, R. "The Ancestress of Israel in Danger." *Semeia* 3–4 (1975): 81–97.
———. *Late Biblical Hebrew: Towards an Historical Typology of Biblical Hebrew Prose*. Missoula, Mont.: Scholars Press, 1976.
Procksch, O. *Die Genesis: Übersetzt und Erklärt*. Kommentar zum Alten Testament 1. Leipzig: Scholl, 1913.
Rad, G. von. *Genesis: A Commentary*. Translated by J. H. Marks. Old Testament Library. London: SCM, 1961.
———. "Theology and the Priestly Document's 'Kabod.'" Pages 37–44 in *Studies in Deuteronomy*. Translated by D. Stalker. Studies in Biblical Theology 9. London: SCM, 1953.
Radai, Y. "Chiasm in the Biblical Story." *Beit Mikra* 20–21 (1974): 48–72 (Hebrew).
———. "Structures in the book of Ruth." *Beit Mikra* 24 (1979): 180–87 (Hebrew).
Radak. *Five Books of the Law: Genesis*. Jerusalem: Mosad Harav Kook, 1990 (Hebrew).
Rashbam. *Torat Haim: Five Books of the Law: Genesis*. Jerusalem: Mosad Harav Kook, 1990 (Hebrew)
Ravid, D. *Joab Son of Zeruiah: Controversial Hero*. Tel Aviv: Hakibbutz Hameuhad, 2009 (Hebrew).
Reich, R. "Gazing forward, to the East." *Ladaat* 20 (1989): 33 (Hebrew).
Rendtorff, R. "Jakob in Bethel." *Zeitschrift für die Alttestamentliche Wissenschaft* 94 (1982): 511–23. (Also published in Pages 115–27 in *Isac Leo Seeligmann Volume: Essays on the Bible and the Ancient World*, vol. 3. Edited by A. Rofé and Y. Zakovitch. Jerusalem: Rubinstein, 1983.)
Resch, A. *Der Traum im Heilsplan Gottes: Deutung und Bedeutung des Traums im Alten Testament*. Freiburg: Herder, 1964.

Richter, W. "Traum und Traumdeutung im AT: ihre Form und Verwendung." *Biblische Zeitschrift* 7, no. 2 (1963): 202–20.

Rimmon-Kenan, S. *The Poetics of Contemporary Fiction*. Tel Aviv: Sifriyat Poalim, 1984 (Hebrew).

Rodin Obersky, T. *From the Oaks of Mamre to Sodom (Genesis 18–19): Structure and Literary Formulation*. Jerusalem: Simor, 1982 (Hebrew).

Rofé, A. *Belief in Angels in the Bible*. Jerusalem: Makor, 1979 (Hebrew).

Roitman, A. "The Structure and Significance of a Jewish Book." Ph.D. diss., The Hebrew University, 1992 (Hebrew).

Rosenson, I. "Exile in Haran and the Exile of Generations: Like Fathers, Like Sons." *Annual of Orot Israel College* 1 (1989): 11–24 (Hebrew).

———. "Tsor'ah-Timnah, Going Up and Going Down: Geographical Descriptions as Commentary in the Samson Stories." *Beit Mikra* 41 (1996): 135–52 (Hebrew).

Rosenberg, J. "Biblical Narrative." Pages 31–82 in *Back to the Sources: Reading the Classic Jewish Texts*. Edited by B. W. Holtz. New York: Simon & Schuster, 1984.

Ross, T. "The *Musar* Movement and the Hermeneutic Problem in the Talmud Torah." *Tarbiz* 59 (1980): 191–214 (Hebrew).

Rouiller, G. "Parabole et Mise en Abyme." Pages 317–33 in *Mélanges Dominique Barthelemy*. Edited by P. Casetti, O. Keel and A. Schenker. Göttingen: Vandenhoeck & Ruprecht, 1981.

Sarna, N. M. *Understanding Genesis*. The Heritage of Biblical Israel 1. New York: Jewish Theological Seminary of America, 1966.

Sasson, J. M. *Ruth*. Baltimore: Johns Hopkins University Press, 1979.

Savran, G. *"He Came Upon the Place": Biblical Theophany Narratives*. Translated by H. Aschheim. Bene Barak: Hakibbutz Hameuhad, 2010 (Hebrew).

Seeligmann, I. L. "Etiological Elements in Biblical Historiography." *Zion* 26 (1961): 141–69 (Hebrew).

———. "Ger." Pages 546–49 in vol. 2 of Cassuto et al., eds., *Encyclopaedia Biblica*.

———. "Jerusalem in the Thought of Hellenistic Judaism." Pages 396–410 in *Studies in Biblical Literature: Isac Arie Seeligmann*. Edited by A. Horowitz, E. Tov and S. Japhet. Jerusalem: Magnes, 1992 (Hebrew).

———. "Man's Heroism and Divine Deliverance: Double Causation in Israelite Historical Thinking." Pages 62–81 in *Studies in Biblical Literature: Isac Arie Seeligmann*. Edited by A. Horowitz, E. Tov and S. Japhet. Jerusalem: Magnes, 1992 (Hebrew).

Shapira, A. "Jacob and Esau: A Reading for Multiple Meanings." *Studies in Bible and Exegesis* 4 (1996): 249–82 (Hebrew).

———. "Jacob and Esau—Two Readings!" Ph.D. diss., The Jewish Theological Seminary, 1988 (Hebrew).

Shifra, Shin, and J. Klein. *In Those Distant Days: Anthology of Mesopotamian Literature*. Tel Aviv: Am Oved, 1996 (Hebrew).

Shinan, A. "The Dream in the Midrash and the Midrash of the Dream." Pages 43–61 in Kerem, ed., *Varied Opinions*.

Simon, U. *Reading Prophetic Narrative*. The Biblical Encyclopaedia Library 15. Jerusalem: Mosad Bialik, 1997 (Hebrew).

———. "Secondary Characters in the Biblical Story." Pages 31–36 in Peli and Shinan, eds., *Proceedings*.

Skinner, J. *Genesis*. International Critical Commentary. Edinburgh: T. & T. Clark, 1930.

Speiser, E. A. *Genesis*. Anchor Bible 1. Garden City, N.Y.: Doubleday, 1964.
Sternberg, M. "A Delicate Balance in the Rape of Dinah." *Hasifrut* 4 (1973): 193–231 (Hebrew).
———. "The Repetition Structure in the Bible Story—Superfluous Information Strategies." *Hasifrut* 25 (1977): 109–50 (Hebrew).
Stone, E. "Ziggurat." Pages 390–91 in vol. 5 of the *Oxford Encyclopedia of Archaeology in the Near East*. Edited by E. M. Meyers. New York: Oxford University Press, 1997.
Talmon, S. *Story Telling in the Bible: According to the Lectures of Shemariahu Talmon*. Edited by G. Gabriel. Jerusalem: The Hebrew University Press, 1965 (Hebrew).
Thompson, T. L. *The Historicity of the Patriarchal Narratives: The Quest for the Historical Abraham*. Berlin: de Gruyter, 1974.
Todorov, T. *Michail Bakhtin: The Dialogical Principle*. Translated by W. Godzich. Theory and History of Literature 13. Minneapolis: University of Minnesota Press, 1984.
———. *The Poetics of Prose*. Translated by R. Howard. Ithaca, N.Y.: Cornell University Press, 1977.
Van Seters, J. *Abraham in History and Tradition*. New Haven, Conn.: Yale University Press, 1975.
———. "Divine Encounter at Bethel (Gen 28:10–22) in Recent Literary-Critical Study of Genesis." *Zeitschrift für die alttestamentliche Wissenschaft* 110 (1998): 503–13.
Weinfeld, M. "The Change in the Perception of Divinity and Ritual in Deuteronomy." *Tarbiz* 31 (1962): 1–17 (Hebrew).
———. *From Joshua to Josiah: Turning Points in the History of Israel from the Conquest of the Land to the Fall of Judah*. Jerusalem: Magnes, 1992 (Hebrew).
———. *Olam Hatanach: Deuteronomy*. Edited by G. Galil. Tel Aviv: Davidson-Atai, 1994 (Hebrew).
———. *Olam Hatanach: Genesis*. Edited by M. Weinfeld. Tel Aviv: Davidson-Atai, 1982 (Hebrew).
———. "Right and Duty: Perception of the Promise in Sources from the First and Second Temple Periods." *Zion* 29 (1984): 115–26 (Hebrew).
Weisman, Z. "The Charismatic Personality in the Bible." Ph.D. diss., The Hebrew University, 1972 (Hebrew).
———. *From Jacob to Israel: The Cycle of Jacob's Stories and its Incorporation within the History of the Patriarchs*. Jerusalem: Magnes, 1986 (Hebrew).
Weiss, M. "Following One Biblical Metaphor." *Tarbiz* 34 (1965): 303–18 (Hebrew).
———. "In the Secret of Biblical Dialogue." Introduction to *The Way of the Bible*, by M. Buber. Jerusalem: Mosad Bialik, 1964 (Hebrew).
———. *Scripture in Its Own Image*. Jerusalem: Mosad Bialik, 1963 (Hebrew).
———. *Scriptures in Their Own Light: Collected Essays*. Jerusalem: Mosda Bialik, 1988 (Hebrew).
Wenham, G. J. *Genesis 1–15*. World Biblical Commentary 1. Waco, Tex.: Word, 1987.
Westermann, C. *Genesis 12–36: A Commentary*. Translated by J. J. Scullion. Minneapolis: Augsburg, 1985.
Wijngaard, J. "hotsi' and he'elah: A Twofold Approach to the Exodus." *Vetus Testamentum* 15 (1965): 91–102.
Yazun, H. "The Formalist School in Research on Folk Literature." *Hasifrut* 3 (1971): 53–84 (Hebrew).

Yehoshua, A. B. *In Praise of Normalcy: Five Essays on Zionism*. Jerusalem: Schocken, 1980 (Hebrew).

Yellin, D. "Educational Theory." Page 62 in *The Writings of David Yellin*, vol. 6. Edited by E. Z. Melamed. Jerusalem: Reuven Mass, 1983 (Hebrew).

Zakovitch, Y. *An Introduction to Inner-Biblical Interpretation*. Even Yehuda: Reches, 1992 (Hebrew).

———. *"And You Shall Tell Your Son": The Concept of the Exodus in the Bible*. Jerusalem: Magnes, 1991 (Hebrew).

———. "The Associative Principle in the Order of the Book of Judges: Its Use in Discerning Stages in the Book's Development." Pages 161–83 in *Isac Leo Seeligmann Volume: Essays on the Bible and the Ancient World*, vol. 1. Edited by A. Rofé and Y. Zakovitch. Jerusalem: Rubinstein, 1983 (Hebrew).

———. "Biblical Traditions Regarding the Beginnings of Jerusalem's Sacred Status." Pages 12–22 in *Jerusalem in the First Temple* Period. Edited by D. Amit and R. Gonen. Jerusalem: Yad Ben-Zvi, 1990 (Hebrew).

———. *"Every High Official Has a Higher One Set Over Him": A Literary Analysis of 2 Kings 5*. Tel Aviv: Am Oved, 1985 (Hebrew).

———. "The Exemplary and the Perfect Character in the Bible." In *Surely There Is Not a Righteous Man on Earth Who Does Good and Never Sins*. Jerusalem: President's Residence, 1997 (Hebrew).

———. "The Exodus from Egypt in Genesis." *Al Haperek* 3 (1987): 25–34 (Hebrew).

———. "The Exodus from Ur of the Chaldeans: A Chapter in Literary Archaeology." Pages 429–39 in *Ki Baruch Hu: Ancient Near Eastern, Biblical, and Judaic Studies in Honor of Baruch A. Levine*. Edited by R. Chazan, W. W. Hallo and L. H. Schiffman. Winona Lake, Ind.: Eisenbrauns, 1999.

———. *"I Will Utter Riddles from Ancient Times": Riddles and Dreams: Riddles in Biblical Narrative*. Tel Aviv: Am Oved, 2005 (Hebrew).

———. "Jabbok, Penuel, Mahanaim, Bethel: Name Midrashim as Reflections of Ideological Struggles." *Ariel* 100–101 (1994): 191–204 (Hebrew).

———. "Jacob's Deception: Genesis 25." Pages 121–44 in *Dr. Baruch Ben Yehuda Volume: Studies in the Bible and in Jewish Thought*. Edited by B. Z. Luria. Tel Aviv: Israel Society for Biblical Research, 1981 (Hebrew).

———. "Juxtaposition in the Abraham Cycle." Pages 509–24 in *Pomegranates and Golden Bells: Studies in Biblical, Jewish, and Near Eastern Ritual, Law, and Literature in Honor of Jacob Milgrom*. Edited by D. P. Wright, D. N. Freedman and A. Hurvitz. Winona Lake, Ind.: Eisenbrauns, 1995.

———. *Life of Samson (Judges 13–16): A Literary-Critical Analysis*. Jerusalem: Mosad Bialik, 1992 (Hebrew).

———. *Olam Hatanach: Joshua*. Edited by G. Galil. Tel Aviv: Davidson-Atai, 1994 (Hebrew).

———. *Olam Hatanach: Twelve Prophets A*. Edited by N. M. Sarna. Tel Aviv: Davidson-Atai, 1994 (Hebrew).

———. "Of the Food Came Forth the Eater: On the Dream and Its Interpretation." Pages 35–43 in Kerem, ed., *Varied Opinions*.

———. "On Recognizing Methods of Hidden Intra Biblical Commentary." Pages 55–67 in *Biblical and Talmudic Studies*. Edited by S. Japhet. Jerusalem: The Hebrew University, 1987 (Hebrew).

———. "'One Thing God Has Spoken; Two Things Have I heard': Ambiguous Expressions in Biblical Literature." Pages 21–68 in *Memorial Gathering for Professor Meir Weiss Thirty Days After His Death.* Edited by S. Japhet, B. Schwartz and Y. Zakovitch. Jerusalem: The Hebrew University Institute for Jewish Studies, 1999 (Hebrew).

———. *The Perception of Miracle*. Tel Aviv: Misrad Habitahon, 1987 (Hebrew).

———. "Reflection Stories: Another Dimension of the Evaluation of Characters in Biblical Narrative." *Tarbiz* 54 (1985): 165–76 (Hebrew).

———. Review of J. P. Fokkelman, *Narrative Art in Genesis: Specimens of Stylistic and Structural Analysis. Shnaton: An Annual for Biblical and Ancient Near Eastern Studies* 14 (1980): 302–8 (Hebrew).

———. "Status of the Synonym and the Synonymous Name in Name Explication." *Shnaton: An Annual for Biblical and Ancient Near Eastern Studies* 2 (1977): 100–115 (Hebrew).

———. "'A Still Small Voice': Form and Content in 1 Kings 19." *Tarbiz* 51 (1982): 329–46. (Hebrew).

———. *Through the Looking Glass: Reflection Stories in the Bible*. Tel Aviv: Hakibbutz Hameuhad, 1995 (Hebrew).

———. "To Abide There, to Place His Name There." *Tarbiz* 41 (1972): 338–40 (Hebrew).

———. *"Who Proclaims Peace, Who Brings Good Tidings": Seven Visions of Jerusalem's Peace*. Haifa: University of Haifa Press, 2004 (Hebrew).

Zakovitch, Y., and A. Shinan. *Abram and Sarai in Egypt: Genesis 12:10–20 in Ancient Translations and in Early Jewish Literature*. Research Projects of the Jewish Studies Institute 2. Jerusalem: The Hebrew University, 1983 (Hebrew).

———. *"And Jacob arrived safely in the city of Shechem": Genesis 33:18–20 in Ancient Translations and in Early Jewish Literature*. Research Projects of the Jewish Studies Institute 5. Jerusalem: The Hebrew University, 1985 (Hebrew).

———. *The Judah and Tamar Story: Genesis 38 in Ancient Translations and in Early Jewish Literature*. Research Projects of the Jewish Studies Institute 15. Jerusalem: The Hebrew University, 1992 (Hebrew).

———. "Midrash on Scripture and Midrash Within Scripture." Pages 259–77 in Japhet, ed., *Studies in Bible*.

———. *That's Not What the Good Book Says*. Tel Aviv: Yediot Aharonot, 2004 (Hebrew).

Indexes

Index of References

Hebrew Bible/		11:28	207			231–33,
Old Testament		11:29	239			243
Genesis		11:30	239	12:11	234, 243	
1:1	246	11:31	203, 204,	12:12–15	208	
1:2	216		210–18,	12:12–13	254	
1:21	134, 164,		221, 222	12:12	222, 234,	
	209	11:32	211, 212		254	
1:28	262	12–50	162	12:13–15	254	
2–12	261	12	74, 234–	12:13	234	
2:7	154		37, 240	12:14	234, 243	
3:3	235	12:1–9	224	12:15–17	254	
3:6	241	12:1–5	203, 217,	12:15	234, 237,	
3:10	80, 81		222		238	
3:16	257	12:1–3	225	12:16	237	
3:19	154, 241,	12:1	204, 210–	12:17	235, 237,	
	257		12, 215,		238, 241,
4:6	209		224, 225,		243
10:12	231		231, 263	12:18–19	234
11	262, 263	12:2	74	12:19–20	243
11:1–9	78, 105,	12:3	61, 74	12:19	238, 239,
	126, 256,	12:4–5	246		242
	258, 259	12:4	212	12:20	242
11:2	261, 263	12:5	210, 212–	13:1	202, 203,
11:3	257, 262		15		228, 242,
11:4–9	90, 260	12:6	128, 132,		243
11:4	85, 257–		237	13:2–13	74
	59, 261	12:7	108, 153,	13:3–4	246
11:5	257, 259		184, 216,	13:9	228
11:6	261, 266		225, 231	13:14–17	216
11:7	257–59,	12:8	246, 265	13:14–16	74
	263	12:10–20	209, 224,	13:14	228, 229
11:8	257, 259,		231, 233,	13:15–17	61, 72
	261–63		237, 246	13:15–16	74
11:9	259, 261–	12:10	109, 116,	13:15	73–75,
	63, 266		138, 200,		108, 153
11:26	212		202, 203,	13:16	74
11:27	163		222–26,		

13:17	108, 153, 231	24:7	153, 218			177, 187–89, 191, 193–99, 201, 202, 251, 259, 262
14	209	24:10	226			
14:15	228	24:62	228			
Genesis (cont.)		24:63	110			
15	15	25–36	187			
15:1	197	25–35	165			
15:7	153, 203, 204, 210, 216–18, 220–22, 232	25	235	28:1–2	177
		25:3–4	153	28:1	177
		25:19–35:22	161	28:2	67, 177, 235
		25:19–27	165		
		25:19	163, 235, 236	28:3–4	153
				28:3	200
15:15	155	25:20	176, 239	28:5	136, 176, 177
15:18	108, 153	25:23	216		
16:2	240	25:34	131	28:6	71
17	69	26	41, 234, 236, 240	28:7	178, 262
17:5	212			28:10–22	1, 3, 22, 24, 41, 44, 49, 50, 53, 59, 62, 95, 97, 102, 121, 127, 143, 145, 159, 160, 162, 165, 176, 187, 194, 196, 199, 246, 248, 249, 254, 255
17:8	153, 223	26:1–14	234		
17:17	236	26:1–2	232		
17:19	68	26:1	232		
18:2	68, 69	26:2	166, 200, 226, 231, 232, 246, 256		
18:13–14	74				
18:22–33	151				
19:9	223				
19:23	227	26:3–4	108		
19:24	210	26:3	73, 224		
19:30	80	26:4–23	13, 16		
20	231, 234–37, 240	26:8	236		
		26:11	235, 236		
20:1–18	234	26:23–24	166		
20:1	228, 231	26:24	166, 197	28:10–19	15, 145
20:2	235, 237, 238	26:29	235	28:10–18	196
		26:34	165	28:10–13	119
20:3–8	13, 16	26:36	165	28:10–12	187
20:3	237	27	177	28:10	22, 43, 47, 50, 52, 54, 69, 131, 136, 137, 161, 163, 176, 177, 183, 188, 193, 226
20:4	235, 239	27:20	189		
20:6	198, 235, 239, 240	27:42	176, 179, 183		
		27:43–45	177		
20:12	235	27:43–44	137		
21:1–2	240	27:43	177, 195		
21:3	235	27:44	263		
21:17	197	27:45	209	28:11–19	54, 58, 59, 61, 144
22:12	81	27:46	177		
23:8	130	28	70, 91, 93, 125, 133, 154, 164,	28:11–15	58
23:18	193			28:11–12	43, 52, 58
24	218				

Index of References

28:11	50, 51, 54–61, 70–72, 87, 95, 127–31, 136, 137, 142, 186, 190, 227	28:13–15	51, 60, 62, 74, 76, 119, 120, 123, 124, 126, 139, 142, 143, 149, 166, 181, 199	28:16–22 28:16–19 28:16–18 28:16–17	202, 249, 251, 255, 259, 263 58 61, 187 60 13, 53, 54, 62, 77–79, 119, 139, 264
28:12–17	78	28:13–14	70, 72, 74–76, 151, 152, 154	28:16	51, 53, 55, 60, 61, 68, 72, 77, 79, 80, 83, 86–88, 122, 123, 127, 129, 136
28:12–16	60				
28:12–15	59, 61, 62, 65, 78				
28:12–13	1–3, 12, 42, 54, 62, 65, 77, 88, 106, 107, 120, 121, 124, 126, 138, 139, 161, 171, 176, 181, 199, 202, 249, 250	28:13	1, 43, 50–52, 60, 62, 66–74, 77, 79, 85, 95, 108, 121, 138, 139, 152, 153, 156, 197, 202, 254		
				28:17–19	58
		28:14–15	43, 52, 72, 262	28:17–18	13, 16, 43, 52
28:12	8, 12, 13, 16, 47, 49, 50, 52, 60–63, 65–67, 69, 70, 72, 76–79, 91, 94, 95, 101, 106, 110–12, 118, 120–22, 130, 136, 138, 139, 142– more–	28:14	50, 70–72, 74, 136, 153, 181	28:17	12, 51–53, 55, 60, 61, 68, 71, 72, 77, 79–81, 87, 91, 104, 108, 119, 121, 123, 136, 140, 141, 188, 258, 259, 262–64, 268
		28:15–16	74		
		28:15	1, 3, 22, 44, 47, 49, 50, 52, 60, 62, 63, 65–68, 70–72, 74, 83, 95, 97, 100, 122, 126, 136, 139, 142, 143, 146, 148, 151–54, 166, 171– more– 176, 178, 180, 189, 191, 192, 194, 197–99, 201,		
28:12	143, 153, 184, 185, 196, 198, 199, 201, 253, 255, 259			28:18–22 28:18–19	59 56, 59, 140
				28:18	51, 54, 57–59, 95, 129, 137
				28:19	43, 51, 52, 54, 55, 59–61, 71, 72, 140, 144, 145, 188, 262
28:13–16	43, 52, 74, 198	28:15			

Index of References

Genesis (cont.)
Reference	Pages
28:20–22	43, 44, 52, 54, 62, 83, 140, 142–45, 151, 156, 157, 194, 201
28:20–21	51, 54, 100, 142, 146, 148, 151
28:20	12, 51, 83, 95, 121, 141, 152, 171, 182, 190, 191, 195, 201, 251, 255, 259
28:21–22	122, 146, 265
28:21	51, 68, 73, 83, 88, 95, 126, 136, 141, 143, 145, 146, 148–52, 154, 155, 180, 181, 193, 194, 201, 251, 259, 262
28:22	51, 52, 54, 87, 91, 141, 148, 150, 156, 260–62
29–31	22, 187
29:1	180, 191
29:5	73
29:15	183
29:26	190
30	180, 182
30:22	97
30:24	181
30:25–43	180
30:25	97, 108, 180, 190
30:37–39	182
30:43	108
31	108, 180–82
31:1–18	180
31:1	181
31:2	181–83
31:3	119, 126, 171, 181, 182, 184, 190–92, 194
31:4	181
31:5	181, 182, 189
31:7	83, 109, 181
31:9	108, 181
31:10–13	8, 13, 16, 22, 122, 165
31:11–13	108, 109
31:11	182, 198
31:12–13	171
31:13	12, 22, 121, 126, 144, 148, 156, 182, 190, 191, 194, 196, 199
31:14	181
31:15	181
31:16	181
31:17–21	179, 182, 183
31:18	176, 181, 190
31:19	181
31:20	182
31:21	182, 190
31:22	109
31:23	109, 183
31:24	13, 16, 182, 198
31:26	183
31:27	182, 183
31:42	83, 189
31:44	183
31:52	183
32	161, 187–89
32:1–3	186
32:1–2	185, 187, 190
32:1	183, 186
32:2–3	77, 126, 184, 185, 192, 253
32:2	63, 105, 126, 130, 176, 184, 186, 188, 189, 191, 194, 199, 253
32:9	189
32:10–13	83
32:10	182, 194, 198
32:14	128
32:23–33	40
32:23–32	145
32:25–33	163
32:25	194
32:26	235
32:33	235
33	155
33:12–17	151
33:13	194
33:17	194
33:18	12, 119, 121, 155, 176, 179, 183, 192–94, 246
33:20	193
34	41
34:21	194
35	161, 164
35:1–15	195
35:1–11	59

35:1–5	194	40:8	4	46:3–4	22, 139,
35:1–4	119	40:9–13	16		153, 176,
35:1	12, 121,	40:9	12, 66		224, 246
	193, 195	40:12	77, 81,	46:3	176, 197,
35:2–3	151		141		199, 226
35:2	193, 195	40:15	195	46:4	112, 176,
35:3	126, 128,	40:16	12, 66		196, 201,
	191, 193–	40:18	81, 141		202, 226
	95	41:1–7	16	46:7	112
35:6–8	195	41:1–3	12, 66	46:8	112, 243
35:6–7	246	41:5–6	12, 66	46:26	112
35:6	193, 194,	41:5	16, 67	46:27	112, 243
	263	41:8	4	46:32	112
35:7	193, 195	41:25	5, 13, 171	47:2	112
35:9–15	59	42:1–2	232	48:3	184
35:9–13	108	42:2–3	226	48:4	153
35:9–12	153	42:2	196	48:5	243
35:9	184	42:7	34, 99	48:16	107, 189
35:14–15	195	42:18	81	49:29–50:13	165
35:15	195	42:29	104	50:4–14	176
35:16	195	42:38	104, 226	50:19–20	195
36	41	43:4–5	226	68:12	69
36:6	215	43:7	226		
37:1	113	43:15	226	*Exodus*	
37:2	163	43:20	226	1:1	237, 243
37:5	113	43:22	226	1:10	258
37:6–8	16	44:21	226	1:12	262
37:7	12, 66	44:23	226	1:13	108
37:9–10	16	44:26	226	1:14	262
37:9	12, 66	45:3	196	2:14	4
37:25	195, 226	45:4–5	219, 220	2:15	183
37:26–27	219	45:9	226	3:2	101, 252
37:27–28	40	45:13	226	3:6–8	108
37:27	219	45:28	196	3:8	226
37:28	219	46	197–201,	3:25	108
37:36	40, 219		246	6:20–25	239
38	2, 113,	46:1–5	13, 16, 22,	6:20	239
	175		105, 154,	7:16	108
38:1	113		165, 166,	9:17	95
38:12	113		195, 196,	10:1	238
38:21	219		198, 199	10:2	238
38:27	67	46:1–4	15, 166,	11:1	238
38:28	219		176	11:9	238
38:36	219	46:1	22, 201	11:10	238
39	113	46:2–5	126, 176,	12:3	238
39:1	195, 219,		196	12:6	108
	226	46:2	232	12:34	127

Exodus (cont.)		12:8	18	Joshua	
12:39	127	14:16	128	6:1	112
14	109	14:17	128	7:7	159
14:5	109, 183	20:15	226	8:29	227
14:8	109	21:2–3	149	10:10	94
14:21	220	21:2	146	10:27	227
15	109	21:33	94	13	229
15:11	81	22:3–8	13, 16	16:7	130
15:12	103	22:8	15	18:6–8	229
15:16	128	22:10–21	16	19:1–40	229
15:17	128	22:19–21	13	19:12–13	229
19:12–13	220	24:25	190	19:13	229
19:12	220	29:17	95	21:38	185
19:13	220	35:5	229	22	87
19:24	220	35:33–34	184	22:19	87
20:2	216			24	202
20:6	218	Deuteronomy		24:2	215
20:12	178	1:19	81	24:4	226
21:2	137	1:22	94	24:16	201
21:3	137	3:1	94	24:17	201, 202
21:5	137	3:27	228		
21:7	137	5:6	216, 218	Judges	
22:25	227	8:15	81	3:16	175
26:18	228	10:17	81	3:19	175
28:10–22	133	10:22	226	3:24	110
32	114	11:11	115	3:25	110
32:1–10	114	11:13–17	223	4:22	110
32:4	114	11:24	228	5:31	227
32:7	114	12:11	86	6:13	151
33:18	151	12:21	86	6:17–18	151
		13:2–6	21	6:22	159
Leviticus		14:23	86	6:36–40	151
9:18	128	14:24	86	7:13–15	16, 89, 102, 120, 121
23:43	127	16:2	86		
25:54	137	16:6	86, 227		
		16:11	86	7:13	12, 34, 66, 121
Numbers		18:15	81		
2:3	229	22:1	223	7:14	121, 123
2:10	229	26:5	86, 226	7:15	16, 122
2:18	229	26:22	86	8:9	155
2:25	229	28:43	112	9:37	228
3:4	207	30:11–14	103	11:30–31	157
5:16	178	32:49–52	207	11:31	40, 155, 157–59
12:4–9	18, 19	33:7	113		
12:6–8	17, 18	34:2	228	11:34	110, 158
12:6	17, 18	34:4–5	207	11:35	158, 159
12:7	18	34:5	207	11:36	158

Index of References

11:37	158	11:10	39	18:1	73
11:39	158	11:11	39	18:3	73
1131	146	12	241	22:20	155
13–15	115	12:9–11	257	25:30	246
14:1	115	12:9–10	241		
14:5	115	15:7–8	146, 150,	*Isaiah*	
14:7	115		155, 156	2:2–4	40
14:19	226	15:7	156	2:2–3	245, 266
15:8	115	15:8	156	2:2	267
15:9	115	15:9	156	2:3–4	266
16:21	115	15:32	110	2:11–12	266
19–21	174	16:1	110	2:15	266
19:29–30	174	17:24	185	3:13	68
19:71	128	17:27	185	6	64, 65,
21:22	239	18:24	110		255
		19:32	185	7:11	103
1 Samuel		20:1–22	190	8:3	239
1	112	20:15	90	9:11	227
1:11	146, 149,	24	265	10:5	222
	157	24:4–8	229	11:16	96
2:6	100, 112			13:10	227
3	9, 13, 15,	*1 Kings*		14:12–15	103
	16, 133	3	15	14:14	228
6:8	94	3:4–15	15	18:2	81
10:5	130	3:5–15	13, 16	18:7	81
10:10	110	3:5	16	21:1	81
13:20	226	3:15	16	21:2	228
15:27–28	174	3:16–28	175	29:22	209
16:1–13	190	5	86	30:1–2	225
22:17	130	7:25	229	35:8	95, 252
23:19	228	8:30	85	40:3	97
24:9–10	67	8:43	85	40:24	228
25	2, 175	13	2, 175,	42:7	244
26:19	87		265	43:5–6	229
26:25	190	18:7	110	45	221, 222
28:5–6	16	19	64	45:1	220
28:6	17, 18	19:20	128	46:10–11	152
		22:17	155	49:1	96
2 Samuel				52:4	226
2:12	185	*2 Kings*		56:5	261
2:29	185	2:1–2	115, 116	57:14	95, 96,
3:25	176	3:8	94		252
4:3	224	3:10	159	62:10	95, 96,
7:9	261	4:31	207		251
8:13	261	5:15–18	87	63:12	261
11	36, 135,	6:5	159	63:14	261
	241	6:15	159	66:1	85, 103
11:1	38, 210	16:2	73		

Index of References

Jeremiah		Hosea		Zephaniah	
1:6	159	4:15	58, 265	3:9	266
4:10	159	5:8	58, 265		
4:15	58	9:3–4	87	Zechariah	
7:16	130	10:5	265	7:10	17
14:13	159			10:2	17, 19
16:14–15	244	Joel		14:4	229
16:15	153, 244	1:15	159	14:8	228
18:15	95	2:2–11	81		
23:25–32	17	2:20	228	Psalms	
23:28	17			2:4	85
23:32	17, 20	Amos		20:2	195
24:10	153	1:1–6	103	23:1	62
25:5	153	1:2	87	34:5	195
25:30	87	2:9	112	37:25	152
26:3	241	2:14	265	62:12	33
27:9	20, 21	4:4	265	68:5	95
29:8	17, 20, 21	5:5	58, 265	81:8	195
30:10	106	6:2	226	89:13	228
31:21	95	7:7	68, 69	91:15	195
32:17	159	7:13	128, 260	103:4	103
34:5	155	7:17	87	103:10–13	103
35:7	224	9:1	68, 69	103:19	85
35:15	153	9:2	103	104:8	112
46:28	106			104:29	154
48:13	265	Obadiah		105:12–15	236
49:36	227	4	106	105:15	235
				107:26	112
Ezekiel		Jonah		108:5	103
1	81	1:1–3	173	115:1	85
1:3–4	64	1:2	116, 118, 173	115:16	84, 103, 117
3:13	64				
4:13	87	1:3	100, 116, 118, 253	120–134	94
4:14	159			139:5	227
5:5	267	1:5	100, 116–18	139:8	103
5:6	267				
5:10	227	2:7	103	Job	
9:8	159	3:4	173, 175	1:6	101, 217
11:13	159			1:9	51, 142
21:5	159	Micah		2:1	101
22	81	4:1–5	40	2:9	34
38:12	228	4:1–2	245	7:9	112
42:16–19	229			10:9	154
48:16–17	229	Habakkuk		11:7–8	103
		3:3	228	11:8	103

Index of References

15:2	227
19:12	95
22:12–14	103
23:8–9	228
23:8	227
23:9	228
28:24	84
30:12	95
34:15	154
42:5–6	184

Proverbs
15:3	84
15:19	95
21:22	112
26:27	103
30:4	103, 112

Ruth
1:2	211
1:4	239
1:5	211
2:10	34
4:11	174
4:13	239

Song of Songs
1:6	134
5:2	13

Ecclesiastes
3:20	154
3:21	112
5:2	17
5:6	17
11:3	228

Daniel
2:31–36	16
2:36	81, 141
4:7–14	16
4:15	81, 141
5:26	81, 141
7:2–12	16
8:16–26	16
10:20	106

Ezra
1:3	244
1:5	244
1:11	244
2:1	244
7:6	244
7:7	244
7:9	244
7:28	244
8:1	244
9:2	239
9:12	239
10:44	239

Nehemiah
3:2	239
7:5	244
7:6	244
7:61	244
9:7	218
9:18	244
12:1	244

1 Chronicles
9:24	229
21:30	265
22:1	264
23:22	239
26:14–16	229
26:17–18	229

2 Chronicles
4:4	229
6:18–21	85
9:11	97
11:21	239
13:21	239
18:16	155
18:26–28	155
19:33	155
20:16	112
24:3	239
34:28	155

NEW TESTAMENT
Acts
7:3–4	203

PSEUDEPIGRAPHA
Jubilees
30:1–2	194

MISHNAH
Pesiqta
88a	108

RABBINIC MIDRASHIM
Genesis Rabbah
69:3	69

Nezikin Avoda Zara
4:4	211

Pirqe de Rabbi Eliezer
35	265, 267

Tanhuma Vayera
23	207

Tanhhuma Vayetse
2	106

Zevahim
54b	244

JOSEPHUS
Antiquities
1:152	208
2:170–176	200

INSCRIPTIONS
Adapa Myth
Part B,
lines 37–38	94

UGARITIC TEXTS
CTA
14, iii I 2–9	92
14, iii I 20–27	92

INDEX OF AUTHORS

Aharoni, Y. 229, 231
Alt, A. 73, 83
Alter, R. 35, 46, 113, 205
Amit, Y. 31, 32, 35, 55, 107, 110, 179, 185, 205, 221, 264, 265
Arpeli, B. 35
Avi-Yonah, M. 230
Avishur, I. 148, 149, 158, 213, 215

Bahar, S. 205
Bal, M. 2, 3, 166-70, 174
Bar, S. 251
Bar-Efrat, S. 58, 61, 69, 110, 146, 170, 171, 180, 183, 190, 207, 211, 223
Barth, J. 109, 168, 169
Baruch, E. 9, 12-14, 66, 84, 88, 122
Barzel, H. 33, 99, 164
Ben-David, A. 239
Bentzen, A. 128
Berlin, A. 110
Berman, J. A. 2, 158, 175
Berton, J. P. 259
Blum, E. 52
Bosworth, D. A. 2, 175
Brauner, R. A. 174
Brecht, B. 134
Brenner, A. 239
Brettler, M. Z. 70
Brin, G. 267
Brogan, W. 33, 99
Brown, C. H. 226-28
Buber, M. 23, 45, 55, 114, 125, 185, 259
Butler, S. A. L. 4-6, 14, 15

Carr, M. D. 24, 74, 143, 145
Cartledge, T. W. 101, 143, 144, 146-49, 151-53, 156, 157
Cassuto, M. D. 43, 44, 162, 209, 213, 233, 237, 242, 256-58
Childs, B. S. 227
Clifford, R. J. 93
Coats, G. W. 185

Cohen, H. R. 77, 89-91, 93, 94, 98, 101-104, 106, 250-52

Dallenbach, L. 2, 3, 171
Dalley, S. 94
Daube, D. 244
De Pury, A. 10, 64, 66, 119, 149, 163
Deurloo, K. A. 70, 74, 215, 222, 225
Diengott, N. 3
Dor, Y. 223
Driver, G. R. 116, 226, 230
Driver, S. R. 43, 52, 79, 143

Efal, I. 227
Ehrlich, L. 6, 9, 11, 14, 19, 66, 69, 122
Eichrodt, W. 84
Elgavish, D. 98, 101, 107, 253
Eliade, M. 4
Elitzur, Y. 256
Elizur, A. 74, 180
Empson, W. 33

Fewell, D. N. 27
Fidler, R. 5, 6, 8-14, 16, 17, 19, 20, 22, 43, 44, 51, 52, 55, 58-62, 64, 66, 70, 73-75, 77, 79, 84, 90, 91, 93, 99, 119, 120, 122-25, 127-33, 140, 142-45, 147-49, 151-53, 165, 166, 172, 173, 178, 179, 182, 185, 187, 195, 197-201, 233, 260
Fish, A. H. 25, 164
Fishbane, M. 26, 46, 94, 108, 141, 161-64, 178, 181, 188
Fisher, L. R. 146-48
Fleishman, J. 239
Fokkelman, J. P. 10, 41, 55, 57-62, 64, 69-72, 75, 77, 78, 101, 119, 120, 130-33, 136, 137, 140, 143, 144, 146-48, 151-53, 155, 156, 162, 165, 176, 177, 179, 181-83, 186, 188, 190, 191, 193-95
Frazer, J. G. 4, 69, 99, 180
Freud, S. 4, 74, 180
Friedman, R. E. 186

Gammie, J. G. 46, 161, 163, 164, 181
Garsiel, M. 115, 164, 228
Gaster, T. H. 15, 127
Geller, S. A. 34
Genette, G. 168
Ginzberg, L. 208
Gitay, Y. 23, 26, 27, 150, 160, 184, 215, 221, 224, 225, 232, 243, 261
Gnuse, R. K. 4-6, 8, 9, 11-13, 15, 17, 19, 21, 53, 57, 89, 91, 93, 99, 119-21, 127, 128, 133
Good, E. M. 128
Gordis, R. 112
Gray, J. 239
Greenberg, M. 33, 34
Greenfield, J. C. 200
Greenspahn, F. E. 90, 95
Greenstein, E. L. 2, 24, 27, 35, 41, 46, 98, 109, 168, 172, 174, 219, 220
Griffiths, J. G. 90, 92, 99
Grossman, J. 30
Gunkel, H. 44, 52, 55, 69, 144, 185, 205, 234
Gunn, D. M. 27

Ha'Efrati, J. 39, 124
Haran, M. 83, 128, 147
Harel, M. 229, 230
Heltzer, M. 96
Hendel, R. S. 164
Henderson, A. 91
Hepner, G. 234
Herbert, A. S. 90
Hezkuni 73
Hoffman, Y. 96, 209, 229
Houtman, C. 57, 68, 89-92, 94, 95, 128-30, 132, 133, 185, 187, 188, 251
Husser, J. M. 16, 18, 52, 54, 74, 97, 120

Iser, W. 36
Izhar, S. 36

Jenks, A. W. 44
Jerfferson, A. 167
Jirku, A. 15
Jung, K. J. 4

Kahana, A. 194
Kaufmann, Y. 11, 12, 87, 178
Keel, Y. 226, 244

Klein, J. 113, 172, 173, 189, 228, 258, 259
Klein-Braslavi, S. 62, 68
Koch, K. 233
Kogut, S. 66, 67, 110
Kselman, J. S. 18
Kutcher, R. 127

Lévi-Strauss, C. 25
Leibowitz, N. 106, 111, 189, 198
Levi, Z. 41
Levin, Y. 4, 5, 74
Lichtenstein, M. 18, 19, 21, 44, 45, 53, 69, 84, 122, 125
Lieberman, S. 241, 267
Lipton, D. 73, 85, 90, 91, 122, 125, 128, 143, 148, 150, 153, 177, 234-36, 244, 246
Loewenstamm, S. E. 223

Machlin, R. 112
Malul, M. 9
Mandelkern, S. 89, 95, 98
Marcus, D. 146, 148, 149, 157
Margalit, B. 99
Mayer, G. 226
McAlpin, T. H. 15, 198
Mendelsohn, I. 11, 12, 127
Millard, A. R. 89, 90, 92, 93, 103
Miscall, P. D. 233, 237
Moriel, Y. 184, 191

Naveh, H. 204
Ne'eman, N. 58, 59
Niditch, S. 174

O'Connor, M. 227, 228
Oppenheim, A. L. 4, 8, 11-13, 15, 17, 22, 118-20, 125, 127, 133, 144, 174
Otto, R. 53, 55, 57, 144
Ottoson, M. 11, 13, 127
Oz, A. 29, 36

Pagolu, A. 59, 83, 148, 149, 151, 154-56
Parker, S. B. 146-49, 154-56
Parrot, A. 256
Peleg, Y. I. 40, 55, 74, 88, 104, 111, 116, 134, 140-42, 153, 173, 175, 200, 203, 205, 208-10, 212, 213, 216, 233, 240, 241, 245, 249, 250, 253, 254, 256, 257, 264, 266
Perry, M. 10, 11, 28, 30, 34-39, 105, 123, 124, 135, 159, 160, 210

Picchioni, S. A. 94
Pines, D. 229
Polak, F. 5, 23, 35, 58, 61, 107, 110, 146, 152, 167, 171, 172, 205, 217
Polzin, R. 233, 239
Procksch, O. 142, 143

Rad, G. von 85, 89-92, 147, 186, 188
Radai, Y. 78, 144
Ravid, D. 31, 35
Reich, R. 229
Rendtorff, R. 43, 52, 54, 55, 57, 58, 60, 77, 79, 80, 91, 132, 140, 144, 149, 153
Resch, A. 6, 15, 132
Richter, W. 12, 62, 120, 122, 123
Rimmon-Kenan, S. 3, 30, 167-70
Ringgren, H. 239
Rodin Obersky, T. 23
Rofé, A. 59, 98, 101, 104, 108, 184, 189, 252
Roitman, A. 23
Rosenberg, J. 32
Rosenson, I. 115-17, 233
Ross, T. 41
Rouiller, G. 3

Sarna, N. M. 10, 55, 57, 64, 101, 119, 120, 144
Sasson, J. M. 239
Savran, G. 53, 69, 132, 140, 142
Seeligmann, I. L. 55, 178, 223, 267
Shapira, A. 25, 30, 31, 33-35, 37, 41, 59, 68, 80, 81, 89, 95, 99, 111, 113, 124, 129, 130, 132, 134, 135, 138, 147, 153, 163, 179, 186, 189, 191, 205, 219
Shifra, S. 173, 258, 259
Shimoni, Y. 227
Shinan, A. 7, 93, 113, 155, 162, 179, 193, 194, 209, 210, 225, 233, 234, 248, 258-60

Simon, U. 206
Skinner, J. 52, 57, 74, 87, 128, 142, 177, 200, 234
Speiser, E. A. 44, 52, 69, 89-92, 97, 132, 180
Sternberg, M. 5, 7, 10, 11, 30, 34-39, 105, 123, 124, 135, 159, 160, 210
Stone, E. 90-92, 260

Talmon, S. 131
Thompson, T. L. 203, 217
Todorov, T. 26, 109, 168, 170, 216

Van Seters, J. 24, 64, 143, 149, 217, 236

Weinfeld, M. 86, 113, 194, 195, 228, 233, 259-61, 267
Weisman, Z. 43-45, 52, 67, 69, 70, 74-76, 83, 121, 130, 148, 162, 164, 175, 192, 198
Weiss, M. 25, 42, 46, 64, 65, 86, 185, 249, 255
Wenham, G. J. 238
Westermann, C. 55, 60, 84, 85, 89, 101, 120, 142, 144, 146, 148, 152, 154, 161, 187, 188, 217
Wijngaard, J. 114

Yazun, H. 45
Yehoshua, A. B. 192, 202, 222, 255
Yellin, D. 30, 35

Zakovitch, Y. 5, 25-27, 33, 34, 41, 42, 46, 54, 58, 64, 67, 69, 85, 89, 102, 103, 108, 109, 113, 115, 117, 118, 130, 155, 158, 162, 163, 165, 177, 179, 180, 182-84, 186, 187, 193, 194, 199, 201, 203, 207-10, 212, 214, 215, 217, 224, 225, 233, 234, 245, 246, 248, 253, 256-61, 263, 265, 266, 268

www.ingramcontent.com/pod-product-compliance
Lightning Source LLC
Chambersburg PA
CBHW072123290426
44111CB00012B/1760